THE BUSINESS OF EMPIRE

The Business of Empire assesses the domestic impact of British imperial expansion by analysing what happened in Britain following the East India Company's acquisition of a vast territorial empire in South Asia. Drawing on a mass of hitherto unused material contained in the Company's administrative and financial records, the book offers a reconstruction of the inner workings of the Company as it made the remarkable transition from business to empire during the late eighteenth century. H. V. Bowen profiles the Company's stockholders and directors, and examines how those in London adapted their methods, working practices, and policies to changing circumstances in India. He also explores the Company's multifarious interactions with the domestic economy and society, and sheds important new light on its substantial contributions to the development of Britain's imperial state, public finances, military strength, trade, and industry. This book will appeal to all those interested in imperial, economic and business history.

H.V. BOWEN is Senior Lecturer in Economic and Social History at the University of Leicester. His previous books include *Elites, Enterprise, and the Making of the British Overseas Empire, 1688–1775* (1996); and *War and British Society, 1688–1815* (1998).

THE BUSINESS OF EMPIRE:
THE EAST INDIA COMPANY
AND IMPERIAL BRITAIN,
1756–1833

H. V. BOWEN

CAMBRIDGE
UNIVERSITY PRESS

CAMBRIDGE UNIVERSITY PRESS
Cambridge, New York, Melbourne, Madrid, Cape Town, Singapore, São Paulo, Delhi

Cambridge University Press
The Edinburgh Building, Cambridge CB2 8RU, UK

Published in the United States of America by Cambridge University Press, New York

www.cambridge.org
Information on this title: www.cambridge.org/9780521844772

First published 2006
Third printing 2007
This digitally printed version 2008

A catalogue record for this publication is available from the British Library

ISBN 978-0-521-84477-2 hardback
ISBN 978-0-521-08982-1 paperback

Contents

Figures

Tables

Preface

During the late eighteenth century the English East India Company, a private trading organisation, established a vast territorial empire on the Indian subcontinent. As the Company extended its power and influence far beyond its coastal trading settlements at Bombay, Calcutta, and Madras, it was transformed into an imperial power, backed by a large army, and it began to exercise administrative control over millions of Indians. The nature and completeness of this extraordinary institutional transformation was such that when the Company lost its last remaining commercial privileges in 1833 it continued to exercise British rule over much of South Asia. Only after the great Indian mutiny of 1857 was it was supplanted on the subcontinent by the representatives of the British Crown.

This book examines how the acquisition and expansion of an empire in India affected the development of the East India Company in Britain. It also looks at how the Company interacted with the world around it and, as such, it focuses on what is sometimes described rather crudely as the domestic 'impact' of empire. The book does not pretend to discuss how the British empire was first established and then developed in India; nor, it has to be said, does it endeavour to cover each and every aspect of the Company's tangled domestic affairs. Instead, through a series of linked thematic studies, it looks inside the Company to see how those in London responded to the unparalleled events that were unfolding in Asia, and it looks beyond the Company to establish the extent to which the influences of the East India trade and Indian empire were felt within Britain's economy and society. It seeks to explore how a trading company underwent a process of metamorphosis that eventually enabled it to persuade a sceptical public that it was a suitable agency for the government of an extended territorial empire.

It is currently fashionable for books to announce the arrival of a 'new imperial history'. This book makes no such claim, and in fact it offers

what might well be considered a somewhat old-fashioned study of institutional change. I offer no apology for this because remarkably little is
known about what went on inside the East India Company as it endeavoured to reinvent itself as an imperial agency, and even less is known
about the material ways in which the Company's acquisition of an Indian
empire affected Britain. In thus undertaking a work of institutional
anatomy many things have been quantified for the first time, and a lot
of basic counting has taken place in an attempt to measure the effects of
change. As a result, although this is not a work narrowly of economic
history, many of the basic building blocks have been provided by numbers
extracted from the Company's voluminous ledgers and account books.
Without them, the book would have no real substance and it would be
impossible to address properly the central question that is to be found
running through each chapter, viz. what happened in Britain when the
East India Company became an imperial power in India?

It has taken me longer to write this book than it did for the East India
Company to establish control over Bengal and, like the Company, I have
accumulated considerable debts and benefited from the assistance of many
collaborators. First and foremost, heartfelt thanks go to my wife and
children who have allowed me to stay 'stuck in the eighteenth century'.
For this and many other reasons the book is dedicated to them. Over the
years, I have benefited enormously from the advice, encouragement, and
example of P. J. Marshall and my former supervisor P. D. G. Thomas.
Peter Marshall has cheerfully fielded many questions and read chapters
when he had better things to do with his time, and I thank him for his
unfailingly courteous and constructive criticism. I am indebted to Bruce
Lenman and the late Philip Lawson for first opening my eyes to the
possibilities offered by the study of the Company's financial records. They
planted a small seed that has taken a very long time to produce any fruit.
K. N. Chaudhuri offered me a piece of crucial advice some twenty years
ago, and since then I have benefited from discussions with historians too
numerous to list. I hope they will forgive me for not naming them here,
but I have endeavoured to acknowledge specific debts at appropriate
points in the book. When the manuscript was at the proposal stage, an
anonymous referee suggested that I advance the study beyond its original
end point of 1813. At the time I did not welcome this intervention because
it meant that datasets had to be extended by twenty years or so, but I now
acknowledge the wisdom of this advice.

Henry Dundas of the government's Board of Control for India once
told Lord Sydney that reading the Company's records was like wading

through a 'load of trash'. This has not been my experience. On the contrary, my work on the Company's records has been entirely pleasurable, and in large part that is because of the expertise, professionalism, and great good humour offered by the past and present keepers of those records. Andrew Cook, Tony Farrington, and Margaret Makepeace of the British Library's India Office Records (now part of the Oriental and India Office Collections) have not only made available their unrivalled knowledge of the records but they have also helped to keep me sane when I have had my head inside ledgers for long periods of time. Margaret Makepeace in particular has offered great assistance by tracking down material, suggesting leads, reading drafts, and saving me from errors. I am very grateful to her. The members of staff who have served at the issue desk also deserve special thanks for the cheerful way in which they have responded to my requisitioning of hundreds of very large ledgers, journals, and minute books. They continue to provide a first-class service and if they ever dreaded my arrival in the Reading Room they were polite enough not to tell me so.

Work of the type undertaken for this book cannot be completed without support from institutions and bodies that provide the time and resources that are necessary for intensive research activity. The University of Leicester has been generous in its provision of study leave, and at departmental and school level my colleagues have offered much-needed support through their advice, assistance, and encouragement. Research on the Company's administrative history was facilitated by a small grant from the British Academy; and on the Company's trade and maritime history by the award of a Caird Senior Research Fellowship from the National Maritime Museum, Greenwich. Crucially, the completion of data collection and final drafting of the book were made possible by the award of a Research Fellowship (RES-000-27-0108) by the Economic and Social Research Council. I am immensely grateful for this essential support, but I am conscious of the fact that I alone am responsible for any errors and shortcomings in the book. Finally, I thank Michael Watson of Cambridge University Press. Without his interest and gentle promptings, the book would probably never have seen the light of day.

Notes on the text

SOURCES AND CITATIONS

Unless otherwise stated, London is the place of publication of all books cited in the footnotes.

Unless otherwise stated, all references to manuscripts and original records are to materials held at the British Library, Oriental and India Office Collections.

THE ACCOUNTING YEAR

Between 1756 and 1813 the Company's accounting year ran from 1 July to 30 June. Hence '1757' refers to the year in which an account was balanced and covers the period 1 July 1756 to 30 June 1757. In 1813/14 only the year ran from 1 July to 30 April. Thereafter the accounting year covered the period 1 May to 30 April. Consequently, '1820' refers to the period 1 May 1819 to 30 April 1820. This must be borne in mind when examining tables and graphs containing financial and commercial information derived from the Company's account ledgers.

DATASETS

During the research undertaken for this book a considerable amount of data was collected on the East India Company's financial and commercial affairs. In most cases, it has been possible to create time-series of figures covering the entire period from 1756 to 1834. Unfortunately, limitations on space mean that it has been impossible to include the datasets in the book, and the figures and graphs that do appear thus represent only the tip of a large statistical iceberg. In due course, however, copies of the datasets will be deposited with the British Library and the UK Data Archive at the University of Essex. It is hoped that these will be of some use to other scholars and students.

Abbreviations and short titles

Add. MS	Additional manuscript
Auber, *Analysis*	Peter Auber, *An analysis of the constitution of the East India Company, and of the laws passed by Parliament for the government of their affairs, at home and abroad* (1826)
B	Minutes of the Courts of Directors and Proprietors of the East India Company
Bentinck correspondence	C. H. Philips (ed.), *The correspondence of Lord William Cavendish Bentinck, Governor-General of India, 1828–1835*, 2 vols. (Oxford, 1977)
BL	British Library
Bowen, *Revenue and reform*	H. V. Bowen, *Revenue and reform: the Indian problem in British politics, 1757–1773* (Cambridge, 1991)
D	Minutes and memoranda of the committees and offices of the East India Company
E	General correspondence of the East India Company
Ec. Hist. Rev.	*Economic History Review*
Eg. MS	Egerton manuscript

FWIHC	*Fort William–India House correspondence and other contemporary papers relating thereto*, 21 vols. (Delhi, 1949–85)
H	Home miscellaneous series
L/AG	Accountant-General's records
L/F	Financial Department records
L/L	Legal Adviser's records
L/MAR	Marine Department's records
L/P&S	Political and Secret Department records
Marshall, *Problems of empire*	P. J. Marshall, *Problems of empire: Britain and India, 1757–1813* (1968)
MSA	Maharashtra State Archives, Mumbai
MS Eur.	European manuscript
NAS	National Archives of Scotland
NLS	National Library of Scotland
NLW	National Library of Wales
NMM	National Maritime Museum
ODNB	H. C. G. Matthew and Brian Harrison (eds.), *Oxford dictionary of national biography: from the earliest times to the year 2000*, 60 vols. (Oxford, 2004)
OHBE	Wm Roger Louis (editor-in-chief), *The Oxford history of the British Empire*, 5 vols. (Oxford, 1998)
PP	*Parliamentary Papers*
Philips, *East India Company*	C. H. Philips, *The East India Company 1784–1834* (Manchester, 1940)
R/10	Canton factory records
Sutherland, *East India Company*	Lucy S. Sutherland, *The East India Company in eighteenth-century politics* (Oxford, 1952)
TNSA	Tamil Nadu State Archives, Chennai
Z	Registers and indexes

CHAPTER I

Introduction

In the half-century after 1756 Britain established a large territorial empire in South Asia, and by the beginning of the nineteenth century many contemporaries considered India to have become the richest jewel in the imperial crown. Yet, remarkably, Britain's Indian empire was not created and expanded as part of any state-sponsored imperial project but through the actions of the East India Company, a private commercial organisation that held a monopoly of British trade conducted east of the Cape of Good Hope. In a few short years the Company ceased to be simply a trading company and it developed into a powerful imperial agency exercising control over territories containing millions of people. No commercial body has ever extended its reach so far or become so fully preoccupied with the business of empire.

The causes, course, and consequences of the East India Company's expansion in South Asia have received considerable attention from successive generations of historians, and this has helped to establish a reasonably clear picture of how and why the Company was able to achieve military and political supremacy, first in Bengal and then elsewhere on the subcontinent.[1] Much is also known about how territorial expansion in Asia had significant political consequences in Britain, where unease about events in India interacted with concerns about recurring financial crisis to cause the reform, regulation, and control of the Company; and much is known about how changing economic outlooks in Britain eventually forced the Company to surrender its India and China trade monopolies in 1813 and 1833 respectively. As a result, the legislative measures implemented

---

1 For two recent studies of British expansion see P. J. Marshall, 'The British in Asia: trade to dominion, 1700–1765', *OHBE*, vol. II: P. J. Marshall (ed.), *The eighteenth century* (Oxford, 1998), pp. 487–507; Rajat Kanta Ray, 'Indian society and the establishment of British supremacy, 1765–1818', ibid., pp. 508–29. For a concise general history of the East India Company see Philip Lawson, *The East India Company: a history* (Harlow, 1993).

by Lord North's Regulating Act of 1773, Pitt the Younger's India Act of 1784, and the Charter Acts of 1793, 1813 and 1833 map out a clear path of political intervention, which resulted in the Company eventually ending its days in 1858 not as an independent private trading company, but as an imperial arm of the British state. Far less well known and understood, however, are the domestic effects that the dramatic and unexpected acquisition of a territorial empire in India had upon the Company itself. Consequently, this book looks inside the Company to explore how it changed in terms of its organisation, personnel, outlooks, and practices; and, because the Company was deeply embedded at the heart of imperial Britain, the book also examines some of the ways in which it interacted with the wider domestic society and economy. In order to establish the general context for discussion of these matters, this introduction first gives brief consideration to the Company's position in India and Britain. An examination of contemporary perceptions of the Company is then undertaken, before attention turns to the ways in which modern historians have approached the Company's domestic history. This enables lines of inquiry to be defined and the thematic scope of the study to be established.

THE SETTING: INDIA AND BRITAIN

In 1709 the formal completion of a long and protracted union of the 'old' and 'new' East India Companies had brought to an end two decades of turmoil among the traders and investors who conducted Britain's trade with Asia. For most of the next half-century the newly consolidated 'United Company of Merchants of England trading to the East Indies' enjoyed a period of internal peace and steady commercial expansion. The Company gained a reputation for financial strength, and this cemented its position at the heart of the City of London and the nation's public finances. Few within the Company harboured any territorial ambitions in India and only a limited presence was maintained at the small coastal trading enclaves that had been established at Bombay, Calcutta, and Madras. Imports to Britain of Indian textiles and Chinese tea shipped from the port of Canton experienced decade-by-decade growth and, because domestic manufactures could not easily be sold in Asian markets, trade imbalances were corrected by the export of treasure, mainly in the form of silver bullion. The Company's internal politics were for the most part unremarkable, and a passive body of stockholders were content to receive their annual dividend payments without being much concerned with the actions of the twenty-four annually elected directors who managed the Company from its headquarters at East India House in Leadenhall Street. As a result, until war with France spilled over into the Indian subcontinent during the mid-1740s, the Company seldom found itself in the public eye, and it did not often capture the full attention of government or Parliament. While too-rosy a picture should not be painted of the Company's development, a range of statistical indicators confirm that the first half of the eighteenth century was usually a time of stability, continuity, and growth.[2] This did not fail to impress contemporaries, and in 1772 the political economist Thomas Mortimer was moved to write that, together with the Bank of England, the East India Company had 'brought the commerce and mercantile credit of Great Britain to such a degree of perfection, as no age or country can equal, and to suppose that this national success could have been accomplished by private merchants, or even by companies not trading on a joint stock, is an absurdity that does not deserve serious consideration'.[3]

Many of the developments celebrated by Mortimer had already been eclipsed by events in India, however, and this led to the emergence of an institution that was very different from that which had existed during the first half of the century. The Company's position in north-eastern India was altered dramatically as military supremacy was established over rival European East India companies and local powers alike. In particular, the catastrophic loss of Calcutta to the Nawab of Bengal, Siraj-ud-daula, in 1756 was followed swiftly by the Company's establishment of absolute control over the province's Indian rulers in the wake of Robert Clive's famous victory at the Battle of Plassey in 1757. Further military success, notably at the Battle of Bhaksar in 1764, culminated in the Treaty of Allahabad of 1765 in which the Mughal Emperor formally acknowledged British dominance in the region by granting the Company the *diwani*, or 'right' to collect the revenues of Bengal, Bihar, and Orissa. The provinces continued to be governed in the name of the Emperor and Nawab of Bengal, but the Company had firmly established itself as the power broker and *de facto* sovereign of the region. The Bengal revenues represented a large financial prize, estimated to generate an annual income of between £2 million and £4 million a year, and they enabled the Company to

2 For the Company's political stability see below, pp. 60–8. For its commercial expansion see K. N. Chaudhuri, *The trading world of Asia and the English East India Company, 1660–1760* (Cambridge, 1978).

3 Thomas Mortimer, *The elements of commerce, politics, and finance in three treatises on those important subjects* (1780, reprinted from the 1772 edition), p. 130.

sustain the growth of its armed forces and strengthen its hold on the territories under its control.

Although those in London were always set resolutely against further territorial acquisition, a series of wars were fought out across the subcontinent against a range of powerful opponents, including the state of Mysore and the Maratha Confederacy, both of which had support from the French. The Company's efforts to achieve supremacy in different parts of India were often fiercely contested, and serious setbacks were experienced from time to time, but war eventually led to the further annexation of territory, especially after the pace of expansion quickened following a decisive victory over Tipu Sultan of Mysore in 1799. A succession of wars were undertaken by Governors-General Richard Wellesley (1798–1805) and Lord Hastings (1813–23) with a view to establishing 'paramountcy' over local states, and the outcome was the final defeat of the Marathas in 1818. This meant that the East India Company had secured direct or indirect control over much of India, and the period ended with the Company consolidating further territorial gains made during the first Burma war of 1824–8 conducted by Governor-General Lord Amherst.[4]

To many in Britain, and not least those within the East India Company, the events that led to the acquisition of a large territorial empire were both remarkable and quite unexpected. As one pamphleteer told the directors and stockholders during the late 1760s, they had been 'suddenly transported from your house in Leadenhall Street and shops abroad to the dominion of the richest Empire in the world and left, as if by dream, in that amazing pitch of exultation'.[5] Clive, it was said by another observer, had 'roused the martial genius of his countrymen, and dragged the cautious, prudent measurer of cloth from behind the counter to the camp'.[6] Consequently, some spoke of a 'revolution' having taken place in Bengal and this is certainly true in a political sense, even though there has been much debate among historians about the extent to which the transfer of power to the British actually prompted any deep economic and social changes in the areas where the Company held sway.[7]

4 For a convenient 'chronology of annexation' between 1757 and 1834 see Michael H. Fisher (ed.), *The politics of the British annexation of India, 1757–1857* (Delhi, 1993), pp. 10–21. See also the table on pp. xv–xvi.

5 *An address to the proprietors of India stock* (1769), pp. 8–9.

6 Captain Joseph Price, *Five letters from a free merchant in Bengal to Warren Hastings esq. . . .* (1777, reprinted 1783), p. 80.

7 For a recent volume containing key contributions to the debate about change within eighteenth-century India society see P. J. Marshall (ed.), *The eighteenth century in Indian history: evolution or*

Whatever the effects of British expansion on Indian society, there is no denying that considerable changes were wrought upon the East India Company, especially in terms of the resources that it had acquired. Endless calculations were made of the people, land, and riches that had been brought under British control, and Clive himself boasted to the House of Commons in 1769 that during the first phase of expansion the Company had taken possession of a 'rich, populous, fruitful country in extent beyond France and Spain united', which brought it the 'labour, industry, and manufactures of twenty millions of subjects'.[8] By 1815 the political economist Patrick Colquhoun thought that the Company had taken possession of over 70 million acres of cultivated land and 'ad infinitum' of uncultivated land. He put the population of British India at just over 40 million and estimated that this represented 65 per cent of all the people living under the protection of the British Empire.[9] Right at the end of the period, in 1833, a detailed calculation indicated that the Company had established control over 500,000 square miles of territory in India, containing 93.7 million 'British subjects' who paid £22,718,794 a year in taxation.[10]

Unsurprisingly, the Company's efforts to defend, govern, and exploit this vast empire brought about a considerable transformation in its own status, standing, and organisation on the subcontinent, and historians have traced the emergence of what is now routinely described as a Company 'state' in India. Underpinned by an extensive revenue-gathering operation and an increasingly sophisticated administrative system, the Company's position was protected by a large Indian army described by Governor-General Sir John Shore in 1794 as a 'mass which forms the bulwark of our power'.[11] This army was used for defence, revenue collection, and pacification or police duties, and by 1797 its importance was such that the director Francis Baring wrote 'the sword once surrendered,

---

revolution? (New Delhi, 2003). Marshall's introduction (pp. 1–49) offers a balanced assessment of the literature, but he nevertheless stresses the importance of long-run economic and social continuities.

8 BL, Eg. MS, 218, ff. 150–1.

9 Patrick Colquhoun, *Treatise on the wealth, power, and resources of the British Empire . . .* (second edition, 1815), pp. 7, 61.

10 Robert Montgomery Martin, *Taxation of the British Empire* (1833), table facing title page.

11 Shore to Dundas, received July 1794, quoted in Holden Furber, *The private record of an Indian governor-generalship. The correspondence of Sir John Shore, Governor-General, with Henry Dundas, President of the Board of Control, 1793–1798* (Cambridge, Mass., 1933), p. 42. For contemporary debate about the proper role of the Company's army see Edward Ingram, 'The role of the Indian army at the end of the eighteenth century', reprinted in Edward Ingram, *In defence of British India: Great Britain in the Middle East, 1775–1842* (1984), pp. 48–66.

there was an end to the Company as sovereigns, and, indeed, of the British Empire in India'.[12] There were some very obvious limitations to British power but, in the words of one recent historian, the Company's post-1818 regime became a 'very military state',[13] and this meant that by 1833 Britain's formal institutional presence in India bore almost no resemblance at all to that of the mid-eighteenth century.

The Indian world of the East India Company was profoundly altered in the decades after 1756, but great changes also affected the domestic world in which the Company was located. This has to be remembered because the external political and economic influences that played upon the Company had a major bearing upon its development as an institution. In particular, general shifts in attitudes towards the empire combined with reform of 'old corruption' to produce much tighter regulation of imperial institutions from the 1780s onwards.[14] At the same time, the advance of the economic ideas of Adam Smith and others saw monopoly practices and principles become increasingly outmoded and unpopular during the last decades of the eighteenth century. On the one hand, therefore, these background movements in metropolitan thought led to closer government control being exerted over the Company, while on the other hand the step-by-step loosening of commercial regulation exposed the Company to ever-greater levels of competition from private British merchants. Stripped of much of its independence and protection, the Company found its domestic status much altered over time, and this process was hastened by the continued growth of Britain's stock market and system of public finance. In 1756 the East India Company was of central importance to the City of London but the development, diversification, and expansion of the financial sector saw its once-prominent position significantly eroded during the first quarter of the nineteenth century. To the end of its days the Company remained an influential institution in the City, but as the financial world moved on apace after 1815 it slipped slowly from the commanding heights it had occupied in earlier times.

12 Quoted in Raymond Callahan, *The East India Company and army reform, 1783–1798* (Cambridge, Mass., 1972), p. 39.

13 D. A. Washbrook, 'India 1818–1860: the two faces of colonialism', in *OHBE*, vol. III: Andrew Porter (ed.), *The nineteenth century* (Oxford, 1998), p. 404. For some of the earlier limitations to the Company's 'military-fiscal juggernaut' see T. R. Travers, '"The real value of the lands": the nawabs, the British, and the land tax in eighteenth century Bengal', *Modern Asian Studies*, 38 (2004), pp. 517–58 (quotation on p. 558).

14 These themes are explored in C. A. Bayly, *Imperial meridian. The British Empire and the world, 1780–1830* (1989), pp. 100–63.

WHAT WAS THE EAST INDIA COMPANY?

It should be abundantly clear from the preceding thumbnail sketch that the East India Company of 1833 was very different from the organisation that had existed seventy years earlier. Territorial expansion in India had transformed the Company into an imperial power and, unsurprisingly, this created considerable uncertainties among contemporaries about what it had become and what role it was to play in Britain and Asia. In turn, these uncertainties shaped both perceptions of the empire in India and the political responses that were made to the Company's many domestic problems.

In the days when the Company had been no more than a maritime trading organisation, few people beyond the world of commerce had been much inclined to express strong opinions about East Indian affairs. This all changed after 1757 as reports of Company corruption and misrule in India began to circulate widely through British society. Consequently, as events unfolded in Asia, East Indian affairs moved to the top of the political agenda, leaving few onlookers neutral in their attitudes towards the Company. Sharply divided opinion was reflected in the variety of ways in which contemporaries chose to describe the Company, and for every positive view there was always to be found a negative.

To some, the East India Company remained what it had always been: a maritime trading company dedicated first and foremost to the pursuit of profit on behalf of its stockholders. Indeed, as will be seen in chapter 7, the Company continued to carry all the hallmarks of a commercial organisation, and its administrative heartbeat in London was still determined by the routines and rhythms associated with the management of long-distance maritime trade. Adherence to familiar routines also imposed an order upon administrative affairs, which meant that meetings and decisions were still scheduled according to timings that altered very little over the years. Such routines provided strong elements of continuity within the Company, and their general importance was summed up by one stockholder who noted in 1813 that 'Regularity and order were the soul of business; and they were the more necessary in an establishment like the East India Company, so multifarious and complex as it was in its arrangements.'[15]

---

15 Alderman Atkins, speech of 1 September 1813, reported in *Debates at the East India, held at various Courts of Proprietors of East India stock, subsequent to the renewal of the East India Company's charter in 1813* (1814), vol. III, p. 78.

The many financial and business transactions needed to ensure the continued smooth running of the East India trade required the support of an elaborate commercial bureaucracy, and this later suggested to John Kaye that the Company had evolved into a 'leviathan mercantile firm'.[16] Accordingly, some were persuaded that the Company's priorities remained commercial rather than territorial or political, and the occupants of East India House indeed often expressed such a view. Thus, although the Company had already established an empire, the Company's Secretary Robert James was emphatic in his declaration to the House of Commons in 1767 that 'We don't want conquest and power; it is commercial interest only we look for',[17] and sentiments of this type were proclaimed mantra-like in the years that followed. They represented part of a sustained drive by those in London to curb any further territorial expansion or offensive warfare in Asia, but they also served as a reaffirmation of what some still believed were the Company's most important core activities.

It was feared that the acquisition of territory would result in the Company losing sight of its long-standing commercial and maritime objectives, and it was believed that this would be unwelcome as well as damaging to the national interest. A pamphleteer put such a case in 1769 when he stated that 'I know nothing we want but a maritime trade; this was the original plan we acted on, and to support the trade properly would bring all the wealth to this nation that could be desired or expected.' Accordingly, he argued that 'It is trade not sovereignty that it is our interest to pursue and the change of our own manufactories for theirs, by which only it can be of advantage.'[18] Similar arguments were later advanced as the Company struggled to secure healthy financial returns from its territorial possessions, and during the late 1770s one harsh critic of the Company argued that it still remained possible for it to 'revert back to first principles'.[19] The virtues of maritime empire and the advantages arising from straightforward commercial exchange were still being proclaimed by some at the very end of the century, long after the Company had extended its territorial possessions well beyond

16 John W. Kaye, *The administration of the East India Company: a history of Indian progress* (1853), p. 134.
17 Quoted in Marshall, *Problems of empire*, p. 17.
18 Anon., *A letter to a late popular director relative to India affairs and the present contests* (1769), pp. 9–10.
19 Price, *Five letters*, p. 80.

Bengal.[20] Indeed, during the late eighteenth century an enormous amount of visual art, and especially paintings of East Indiamen, continued to project a powerful and enduring image of the Company as a maritime trading organisation.[21] Still perceived to be rooted firmly in trade, the Company was described by the political economist David Macpherson in 1813 as 'the most illustrious and most flourishing commercial organisation that ever existed in any age or country'.[22]

Of course, the realities of the political and military situation in India were such that few could deny that a process of profound institutional metamorphosis had begun during the mid-eighteenth century. In 1751, the Company's growing military strength had already suggested to the political economist Malachy Postlethwayt that it 'had commenced a kind of military company instead of a trading one',[23] and events after 1756 served only to confirm that the Company was now able to impose its will and authority upon different parts of India. Thus, to Clive's aide Luke Scrafton the Company was 'No longer considered as mere merchants, they were now thought the umpires of Indostan', and the late Reverend John Entick concluded that through 'many unexpected contingencies' the Company had been converted from 'an incorporated society of private traders into a cabinet of Asiatic princes'.[24] As a result, it could be said by 1772 that the Company had risen 'from very slender beginnings, to a state of the highest importance; their concerns, simple at first, are grown extremely complex, and are immensely extended. They are no longer mere traders, and confined in their privileges; they are sovereigns over fertile and populous territories.'[25] Some well-informed contemporaries

20 W. Playfair, *Strictures on the Asiatic establishments of Great Britain; with a view to an enquiry into the true interests of the East India Company* (1799). Playfair challenged the 'very mistaken and absurd notion that our territorial possessions are of more importance than the trade to India itself' (p. 115).

21 Geoff Quilley, 'Signs of commerce: the East India Company and the patronage of eighteenth-century British art', in H. V. Bowen, Margarette Lincoln, and Nigel Rigby (eds.), *The worlds of the East India Company* (Woodbridge, 2002), pp. 183–99.

22 David Macpherson, *Annals of commerce, manufactures, fisheries, and navigation with brief notices of the arts and sciences connected with them*, 4 vols. (1805). A friend to the directors, Macpherson listed in his dedication the contributions that the Company made to the commercial well-being of the nation.

23 Malachy Postlethwayt, *The universal dictionary of trade and commerce, translated from the French of the celebrated Monsieur Savary . . . with large additions and improvements . . .*, 2 vols. (1751); vol. II, p. xxi.

24 Luke Scrafton, *Reflections on the government of Indostan . . .* (1763, reprinted 1770), p. 120; the late Reverend John Entick et al., *The Present state of the British Empire. . .*, 4 vols. (1774), vol. IV, p. 533.

25 *Monthly Review*, vol. XLVI (1772), p. 236. For views on the transformation of the Company's status in India, as expressed by some of the leading servants in India, see P. J. Marshall, 'Britain and the world in the eighteenth century: III, Britain and India', *Transactions of the Royal Historical Society*, sixth series, vol. X (2000), pp. 13–14.

such as Thomas Macaulay later used the benefit of hindsight to take issue
with the view that the Company experienced a rapid, all-transforming
change in India during the 1750s,[26] but not even he could deny that the
Company's power and influence were greatly enhanced during the middle
decades of the eighteenth century.

People also began to consider the importance of the Company's role as
the *de facto* sovereign power in Bengal. The imperial theorist Thomas
Pownall declared that whatever the 'farce of treaties' and the 'fiction of a
nabob' might suggest, 'the fact is that the government of the country is
dissolved, the sovereignty annihilated', and this drove him to the conclusion that 'The merchant is become the sovereign.'[27] Pownall's phrase
came to be echoed by many commentators, most of whom acknowledged
that the Company had not simply replaced trade with empire but had in
fact taken upon itself the simultaneous management of two interrelated,
but very different, forms of overseas activity. Yet although there could be
no doubt that the Company had acquired full control over Bengal, its
legal standing and status in the region was by no means clear-cut or
accepted by all.

The question of sovereignty in India was long a matter for heated
debate in Britain, and both the Company and the Crown advanced
powerful competing claims for legal possession of the territories that
had been brought under British control.[28] This was not merely an abstract
theoretical debate because the 'right' to possession of the *diwani* revenues
depended upon the outcome. The Company's claims to what it regarded
as its own private property were based upon an interpretation of events
that enabled it to argue that it had secured the *diwani* by way of a grant
from the Mughal Emperor and not simply through an act of conquest.
The settlement embodied in the Treaty of Allahabad thus saw the Company continue to acknowledge Mughal sovereignty, and, in return for the
annual payment of tribute to Delhi, it undertook to collect revenue as the
diwan of Bengal. Successive governments took issue with this claim,
however, by declaring that in reality the Company had secured control
over Bengal (and the Emperor) through military conquest, and since
British subjects could only acquire territory on behalf of the Crown the

---

26 T. C. Hansard, *Parliamentary debates*, third series, vol. XIX, col. 508 (debate of 10 July 1833).
27 Thomas Pownall, *The right, interest, and duty of government, as concerned in the affairs of the East
   Indies* (revised edition, 1781), pp. 3, 26–7.
28 For the political and legal debate surrounding the territorial revenues see H. V. Bowen, 'A
   question of sovereignty? The Bengal land revenue issue, 1765–7', *Journal of Imperial and
   Commonwealth History*, 16 (1988), pp. 155–76.

territorial revenues belonged of right to the state. Much depended upon how the events of 1756 to 1765 were viewed, but matters were further complicated by disputes over whether a declaration of right should be made in Parliament or in a court of law. In 1789 George Dempster MP claimed that in its attempts to settle the claim to the revenues 'The Company had provoked government again and again to decide the question, and had said "go with us into a court of law and let us settle the point, where alone it can be settled".'[29] Four years later Henry Dundas, who had long taken up ministerial responsibility for the supervision of British Indian affairs, was forced to concede that the complexities surrounding rival claims to ownership of the revenues still left 'room for much legal discussion on this subject'.[30] The Company's formal status and position remained a matter for debate and this caused considerable uncertainty about the Company's role in India and its relationship with the British state.

The debate about possession of territories in India did not end until 1813, when the Charter Act formally vested them in the British Crown, but until then it shaped perceptions of what the Company had become. An important ministerial perspective was offered by Lord North in 1773 when he declared that the 'Company could acquire nothing by conquest but for the state', and he went on to argue that by allowing it to continue in its new tax-gathering role in Bengal ministers were placing it in the same position as '[tax] farmers to the publick'.[31] Others agreed, and a quarter of a century later the Company's Chairman Jacob Bosanquet declared to Pitt that the Company had become a 'powerful engine in the hands of government for the purpose of drawing from a distant country the largest revenue it is capable of yielding'.[32] The mathematician William Playfair set the Company within similar terms of reference when he described it as acting as 'stewards to the state', which meant that 'remitting the surplus revenue of India . . . is perhaps the best reason which can be given for the existence of the Company at the present moment'. Playfair was severely critical of the Company's commercial failings, but he took the view that it was best to leave the management of the revenues under its control. The revenues were a 'great accessory

29 William Cobbett, *Parliamentary history of England from . . . 1066 to . . . 1803*, 36 vols. (1806–20), vol. XXVIII, col. 293 (Debate of 1 July 1789).
30 Ibid., vol. XXX, col. 663 (Debate of 23 April 1793).
31 Lord North, speech to the House of Commons, 9 March 1773, as reported in BL, Eg. MS, 244, p. 288.
32 Bosanquet to Pitt, 14 April 1798, H/61, p. 189.

division of the power of Great Britain, not in the immediate hands of the executive government', and he warmly welcomed this arrangement because 'the patronage of India in the possession of an ill-disposed minister would afford means of corruption so extensive as to endanger the pure spirit of the British constitution'.[33] As Playfair's words suggest, fears that the Crown might secure direct access to the riches of the East long acted as a strong counterweight to the arguments of those who believed that the state should step forward and claim the revenue of India as its own. To some, therefore, the Company remained an important bulwark against the unwelcome extension of Crown influence into the wider empire.

The Company's new role in India also attracted considerable attention from those who argued that it did not well serve the people brought under British control. During the 1760s, 1770s, and 1780s critics were preoccupied with the effects of misrule, corruption, and extravagance, all of which were often ascribed to the vigorous pursuit of private interest by Company servants and others who were licensed to operate in India and elsewhere. As a result, it was possible to represent the East India Company as providing shelter and support for powerful private interest groups, in Britain as well as Asia. Thus while the Company was sometimes portrayed as a powerful monolith or 'colossus . . . magnificent in form, and imposing in dimensions',[34] it could also be described as a loose collection of individuals who operated under a flag of convenience and exhibited very little allegiance to any higher form of authority or interest. As one critic put it, the very way in which the Company was organised ensured that 'a preference is given to the interest of individuals, in opposition to that of the corporate body'.[35] Indeed, tensions between corporate interest and private interest were felt even within the trade between Britain and Asia, over which the Company was supposed to hold exclusive rights, and this caused one pamphleteer to question whether the Company could be considered to hold a monopoly at all. Discussing the licensed 'privilege' rights of the Company's maritime officers to trade with Asia on their own account, he claimed that 'at particular seasons the whole mercantile community have been admitted as sharers of the speculation'. The effect of this was such that throughout the Company's history 'the officers of the

33 Playfair, *Strictures*, pp. 65, 66–7. For the notion that the Company was undertaking an 'important stewardship' on behalf of the state see also 'Cossim', *Considerations on the danger and impolicy of laying open the trade with India and China. . .* (1812), p. 10.

34 'Cossim', *Considerations*, p. 218.

35 Anon., *A demonstration of the necessity and advantages of a free trade to the East Indies . . .* (1807), p. 118.

Company's marine, partaking of a commercial character, improved by local knowledge, have been permitted to carry on, if not rival, at least congenial speculations with those of their employers.'[36] One ship owner who closely studied the effects of the Company's long-standing practice of hiring ships from consortia of private investors made the interesting observation that there were in fact two English East India companies in existence: 'one in Leadenhall Street, and the other in shipping'.[37]

The private interest groups that grew up in and around the East India Company were provided with commercial infrastructure, an organisational framework, and protection, and this left them very well placed to exploit the profit-making opportunities that arose from the Company's expansion in Asia. The Company's servants in India joined in with unbridled enthusiasm because, in Captain Joseph Price's words, from 'false notions of economy and glove-like consciences' the Company only paid modest salaries, thus making 'roguery necessary to a subsistence in the service'. The results, he declared, were 'destructive to our national character, for mercantile probity, and common honesty'.[38] Of course, some dutiful servants paid close attention to the Company's interests, but many gave scant regard to their employer's concerns, and it is not difficult to provide examples of occasions when consideration of private interest rather than loyalty to the Company acted as the primary motivation for action.

Scandalous activities caused great bitterness and anger in London, even among the directors of the Company who themselves were well used to advancing their own private interests along with those of the Company. In 1755 the Council at Fort Marlborough (Sumatra) had been warned by the directors that 'if you amuse us with schemes that are not likely to have the desired effect, we shall, in earnest, consider of evaluating a settlement that must be supported at the expense of the Company, for your private emolument only'.[39] When the warning passed unheeded, there were wholesale dismissals of the Company's employees at Fort Marlborough, and similar purges of corrupt officers later occurred in each of the main

36 Anon., *Observations on the territorial rights and commercial privileges of the East India Company, with a view to the renewal of the Company's charter; in a letter to a Member of Parliament* (1813), p. 58.

37 Donald Cameron to Henry Dundas, 23 May 1786, Melville papers, MS 1066, f. 1, NLS.

38 Price, *Five letters*, pp. 181–2. Price was referring specifically to the Company's marine service, but his comments could be applied to other branches of the Company.

39 Directors to Fort Marlborough, 3 December 1755, *Records of Fort St George*, vol. V: *Public despatches from England: 1755–1756* (Madras, 1968), p. 67.

settlements in India as the directors sought to regulate the unfettered pursuit of private interest. Yet the directors themselves were routinely represented as being motivated primarily by personal considerations, and suspicions of powerful groups within East India House often made it difficult for contemporaries to establish where Company and private interests ended and began. As the disaffected ship owner Sir Richard Hotham wrote in 1775, there were

> innumerable instances, that one corruption and abuse introduced another; till they are so interwoven with each other, and so strongly supported by the private interest of such a number of opulent men, deeply intrenched, and locked as it were arm in arm, that it seems to border on folly to offer the clearest truths, or soundest, arguments . . . in defence of the real interest of this very beneficial Company.[40]

Alongside fears that the aggressive pursuit of private ambition was fatally undermining the Company's interests was the belief that it was quite simply wrong for the government of people and territory to be vested in a commercial organisation. Some, such as Arthur Young, took the straightforward view that 'Trade and the sword ought not to be managed by the same people. Barter and exchange is the business of merchants, not fighting of battles and dethroning of princes.'[41] Similarly, Adam Smith argued in *The wealth of nations* that the roles of trader and sovereign were incompatible as long as primacy continued to be given to commercial activity. As part of his wide-ranging criticisms of monopolistic organisations, Smith condemned the Company's apparent inability to act in a manner befitting a sovereign power when he wrote that 'Trade, or buying in order to sell again, they still consider as their principal business, and by a strange absurdity, regard the character of the sovereign as but an appendix to that of the merchant, as something which ought to be made subservient to it.'[42] This strain of criticism endured for decades and, even as the effects of reform of the Company's overseas administration became evident, there was a residual sense of unease about leaving an empire in the hands of traders. Hence when Sir William Pulteney called for a review of British trade with India in 1801 he was returning to a familiar theme when he declared in the Commons that 'The character of

---

40 Sir Richard Hotham, *A candid state of affairs relative to East India shipping* (second edition, 1775), p. 5. Hotham, later MP for Southwark, was a ship owner campaigning for reform of the Company's shipping system.
41 Arthur Young, *Political essays concerning the present state of the British Empire. . .* (1772), p. 518.
42 Adam Smith, *An inquiry into the nature and causes of the wealth of nations* (1776), ed. R. H. Campbell, A. S. Skinner, and W. B. Todd, 2 vols. (Oxford, 1976), vol. II, p. 637.

traders and sovereigns was inconsistent, and their union had never failed to prove ruinous to the mercantile concerns of these counting-house kings, and to make their unhappy subjects suffer under all the evils of oppression and misrule.'[43]

As Pulteney's remark indicates, critics were able to level charges of misrule against the Company, and these carried especially great weight before 1790 as a steady stream of Company servants returned to Britain to be accused of corruption, greed, tyranny, and a host of other crimes thought to besmirch the good name of Britain. As is well known, these 'nabobs' were vilified as ruthless profiteers, and they were satirised in print and on the stage as vulgar *nouveaux riches* who disposed of their ill-gotten gains in an orgy of tasteless spending and accumulation. At the forefront of the condemned men stood Clive, whose actions were subjected to close parliamentary scrutiny, but a large supporting cast of villains was also called to account by politicians and the press.[44] There was a frenzy of wild speculation about the private riches accumulated by Company servants in India, and eager discussion of the despotic 'Asiatic' practices that were held to characterise Company rule in Bengal and elsewhere. Indeed, at times revelations of crimes and corruption captured public attention to the exclusion of all other subjects, as bitter enemies levelled shocking accusations and counter-accusations against one another. Thus in December 1772 the diarist Horace Walpole reported 'new horrors coming out every day against our East India Company and its servants'.[45] And although the strength of public feeling against what Walpole described as a 'crew of monsters'[46] diminished over time, the sharpest critics of the Company continued to represent nabobs as the evil personification of British rule in India. When William Cobbett called for action to be taken against the Company in 1810, he proclaimed that 'It is a duty to God and Man to put the nabobs upon the coals without delay. They have long been cooking and devouring the wretched people of both England and India.'[47]

---

43 Speech of 25 November 1801, Cobbett, *Parliamentary history*, vol. XXXVI, col. 282.
44 For an account of the proceedings against Clive see Mark Bence-Jones, *Clive of India* (1974), pp. 268–90; and for those against Warren Hastings see P. J. Marshall, *The impeachment of Warren Hastings* (Oxford, 1965).
45 Walpole to Sir Horace Mann, 22 December 1772, *The Yale edition of Horace Walpole's correspondence*, ed. W. S. Lewis, 48 vols. (Oxford, 1939–84), vol. XXIII, p. 451.
46 Same to same, 4 November 1772, ibid., vol. XXIII, p. 441.
47 Cobbett to William Creevey, 24 September 1810, *The Creevey papers. A selection from the correspondence and diaries of the late Thomas Creevey, MP*, ed. Sir Herbert Maxwell, 2 vols. (1903), vol. I, p. 134.

If individual acts of greed and corruption enabled Company servants to be characterised as monsters, then so too the Company itself could be described as a monster that was out of control and moving relentlessly forward in search of more profit and territory in India.[48] As one writer put it in 1830 during the course of a vigorous denunciation of the Company's history, politicians and statesmen had 'permitted a gigantic power to exist in opposition to the welfare of the Kingdom, and over which Parliament has but a most *feeble* and *indirect* control'.[49] With good reason, the directors were always sensitive to the charge that an expanding Company could not be restrained from London, and in part this lay behind their attempts to prevent wars of conquest, but critics always argued that the Company was already well past the point of no return on the road to ruin. For, as with the empires of ancient Greece, Persia, and Rome, expansion was thought to bring increasing financial and military burdens as well as the growth of luxury and vice that eroded the empire from within. One pamphleteer gave expression to a widely held belief when he suggested that these were 'the concomitants of wealth, the inevitable consequence of distant empire and extended commerce'. Accordingly, Britain should not 'expect an exemption from those evils which have attended every other ambitious and successful nation, which in its aggrandizement has fostered the seeds of its decline'.[50]

The effects of luxury, vice, and corruption were held to pose a very real threat to the Company's empire and also to the metropolis itself. 'Eastern practices' could damage traditional virtues, while wealth plundered from Asia would serve to unsettle the economic, social, and political balances of Britain.[51] Lord Chatham gave perhaps the most dramatic warning of these dangers when he declared to the House of Lords in 1770 that 'The riches of Asia have been poured in upon us, and have brought with them not only Asiatic luxury, but, I fear, Asiatic principles of government. Without connections, without any natural interest in the soil, the importers of foreign gold have forced their way into Parliament, by such a torrent of private corruption, as no private hereditary fortune could resist.'[52] It was

---

48 See, for example, the former Governor of Bengal, John Zephaniah Holwell, quoted in Bowen, *Revenue and reform*, p. 105.

49 Robert Montgomery Martin, *Remarks on the East India Company's administration over one millions of British subjects* . . . (Dublin, 1830), p. 31.

50 'A Member of Parliament', *Review of the question concerning the government of the British possessions in India.* . . (n.d., ?1783), p. 8.

51 Philip Lawson and Jim Phillips, '"Our execrable banditti": perceptions of nabobs in mid-eighteenth-century Britain', *Albion*, 16 (1984), pp. 225–41.

52 Quoted in ibid., 238.

partly for this reason that Chatham's son, Pitt the Younger, was later able to justify his reform of the Company on the grounds that it offered a defence for a threatened British constitution.[53] And as late as 1825, a writer was moved to remind his readers that the power and influence wielded by the Company was so great that 'Were it not, indeed, that the locality of its wealth is at so remote a distance, the very existence of [such] a body would be so dangerous, not merely to the liberty of the subject, but to the stability of the state.'[54]

These fears offered an acknowledgement that the strength of any threat posed to the metropolis by an overextended empire had been substantially increased by the way that the economic links between Britain and India became far stronger after the acquisition of the *diwani*. As a result, by the early 1770s it was argued that the 'first and immediate' consequence of the loss of India would be 'national bankruptcy',[55] and Thomas Pownall elaborated upon this theme when he declared that because the Bengal revenues had been 'wrought into the very frame and composition of our finances' people 'tremble with horror even at the imagination of the downfall of this India part of our system; knowing that it must necessarily involve with its fall, the ruin of the whole edifice of the British Empire'.[56] Since the Company was one of the main institutions of the City of London, logic dictated to contemporaries that any setback in India could have disastrous consequences for the money markets and the nation's finances,[57] and this spectre was sufficiently frightening to convince several generations of ministers that they should offer extensive support to the Company whenever it ran into financial difficulty.

Concerns about corruption, expansion, and misrule in India were ever-present between 1765 and 1790, but thereafter a number of factors combined to ensure that they no longer dominated discussion about the East India Company. People eventually tired of political campaigns against nabobs, and although the impeachment of former Governor-General Warren Hastings opened amidst great excitement in 1788, the public soon lost interest in proceedings that were to drag on for seven years. At the same time, attitudes towards British India began to change as

---

53 H. V. Bowen, 'British India, 1765–1813: the metropolitan context', in *OHBE*, vol. II: Marshall (ed.), *The eighteenth century*, p. 543.
54 Anon., *The session of Parliament for MDCCCXXV* (1825), p. 42.
55 Anon., *The present state of the British interest in India*, quoted in *Monthly Review*, vol. XLVIII (1773), p. 99.
56 Pownall, *Right, interest, and duty of government*, p. 4.
57 For George Grenville's views see Bowen, *Revenue and reform*, pp. 22–3.

Lord Cornwallis's administrative reforms in Bengal between 1786 and 1793 seemed to improve the standards and behaviour of Company servants. Consequently, when the question of the renewal of the Company's charter came to the fore during the early 1790s the main issue was no longer whether the Company was an appropriate governing agency for Britain's Indian possessions. Instead, attention was focused upon the question of whether the prevailing monopoly trade arrangements represented the best form of economic link between Britain and Asia, and an increasingly concerted assault was made upon the Company's commercial record since the acquisition of the *diwani*.

There had been sporadic attacks on the East India monopoly during the first half of the eighteenth century, but the Company's steady commercial expansion and profitability had ensured that critics made little headway. However, concerns about the Company's performance began to be raised almost from the moment that news of the *diwani* arrived in London. The directors themselves observed in 1768 that without the exercise of financial prudence it would be found that the Company had 'only exchanged a certain profit in commerce for a precarious one in revenue'.[58] As their worst fears began to be realised during the early 1770s, critics began to question whether the acquisition of territorial revenues had in fact generated any financial benefits at all. By the beginning of the 1780s it became commonplace to assert that, in the words of Clive's great enemy George Johnstone, 'the territories we acquired through him had done a greater injury than a benefit to us'.[59]

Optimists continued to believe that in the right circumstances the Company would be able to generate a revenue surplus that could be transferred to Britain, but by the beginning of the nineteenth century there was considerable support for Thomas Creevey's view that since the acquisition of the revenues the Company 'had become a constant burden and grievance to the nation, and even to themselves'.[60] Such arguments only weakened the Company's defences against those seeking to break its monopoly of trade with India, especially the private traders who made increasingly strenuous attempts to demonstrate that the Company's export trade was failing to support British manufacturing industry. The

58 *FWIHC*, vol. V, p. 102.
59 Sir George Colebrooke, *Retrospection: or reminiscences addressed to my son Henry Thomas Colebrooke esq.*, 2 vols. (1898–9), vol. II, p. 18; Johnstone, speech of 9 April 1782, *Parliamentary register*, vol. VII (1782), 37–8.
60 Speech of 6 February 1812, T.C. Hansard, *The Parliamentary debates from the year 1803 to the present time*, vol. XXI, col. 673. See also Bowen, 'British India', pp. 533–4.

Company's commercial privileges were eroded in 1793 and 1802, and by the time of the passage of the Charter Act in 1813 few in Britain believed that the Company was any longer capable of deriving a profit from commercial activities in South Asia.

These various viewpoints reveal great uncertainty about whether the East India Company was a force for good or ill in India and Britain, and this explains why so many descriptive terms were applied to it. And although strong doubts were sometimes expressed about how much those in Britain ever knew or cared about the Indian empire, many in political and public life were nevertheless still inclined to express very strong opinions about the Company. There might not have been a consensus about the Company and what it represented, but contemporaries acknowledged that it was an institution of the first importance located at the very centre of imperial Britain.

HISTORICAL PERSPECTIVES AND LINES OF INQUIRY

As with contemporaries, modern historians have offered a range of different perspectives on the East India Company during the late eighteenth and early nineteenth centuries. Students of domestic politics have been well served by works devoted to the problems of the Indian empire, the development of new administrative relationships between the Company and the British state, and the debates surrounding the major legislative landmarks embodied in the Acts of Parliament passed between 1773 and 1833. P. J. Marshall has offered succinct treatment of all of the major themes in a general study of Britain and India, and over half a century ago forensic examinations of East India politics were undertaken by C. H. Philips and Lucy S. Sutherland.[61] Neither Philips nor Sutherland was motivated, however, by any desire to explore the inner workings or structures of the Company itself. Rather, broadly in keeping with the spirit of Namierite inquiry then prevailing in British eighteenth-century historical studies, they tended to emphasise the importance of the Company as a high political issue of great concern to ministers and Parliament, and they devoted much attention to factional infighting and

61 Marshall, *Problems of empire*; Philips, *East India Company*; Sutherland, *East India Company*. See also V. T. Harlow, *The founding of the second British empire 1763–93*, 2 vols. (1952 and 1964), vol. II, pp. 7–224, and Bowen, *Revenue and reform*. For the Charter Act of 1813 see Anthony Webster, 'The political economy of trade liberalization: the East India Company Charter Act of 1813', *Ec. Hist. Rev.*, 43 (1990), pp. 404–19.

the government's informal 'management' of East India House. Some light was thrown upon the Company's internal history but this was incidental to their main purpose, which was to explore 'East Indian' politics. Thus, although personalities and power struggles are well to the fore in both of these works, other important matters remain hidden in the historiographical shadows, especially the question of how the Company actually worked as an organisation dedicated to the management of long-distance trade and empire. A major aim of this book, therefore, is to recover the Company's internal history from those shadows by creating a moving picture of the institution as it underwent the transformation from trader to sovereign in the decades after 1756.

Of course, in seeking to provide an anatomy of the East India Company in Britain, it is first necessary to consider what type of organisation the Company was before it established a territorial empire during the 1760s. Some economic and business historians have certainly been impressed by the 'modern' attributes of the early eighteenth-century Company, and arguments have been offered to suggest that it possessed many of the organisational and operational characteristics that later became evident in twentieth-century corporations.[62] It has been noted that the separation of management of the Company's affairs from the ownership of share capital had been formalised during the seventeenth century by the creation of an executive board or Court of Directors. This Court was answerable to the Company's stockholders, who elected its members on an annual basis, but the directors had the freedom to supervise the day-to-day running of the Company's affairs in London. In order to achieve this, the Court of Directors was supported by a growing number of subcommittees and associated departments that carried out increasingly specialised tasks. Within this administrative framework, decisions were implemented by salaried managers and officials who routinely processed large amounts of

---

62 See, for example, K. N. Chaudhuri, 'The English East India Company in the 17th and 18th centuries: a pre-modern multinational organization', in L. Blussé and F. Gaastra (eds.), *Companies and trade* (Leiden, 1981), pp. 29–46; K. N. Chaudhuri, 'The "new economic history" and the business records of the East India Company', in P. L. Cottrell and D. H. Aldcroft (eds.), *Shipping and commerce: essays in memory of Ralph Davis* (Leicester, 1981), pp. 45–59; K. N. Chaudhuri, 'The English East India Company and its decision-making', in K. Ballhatchet and J. Harrison (eds.), *East India Company studies: papers presented to Professor Sir Cyril Philips* (Hong Kong, 1986), pp. 97–121; G. M. Anderson, R. E. McCormick, and R. D. Tollison, 'The economic organization of the English East India Company', *Journal of Economic Behavior and Organization*, 4 (1983), pp. 221–38; A. M. Carlos and S. Nicholas, '"Giants of an earlier capitalism": the chartered trading companies as modern multinationals', *Business History Review*, 62 (1988), pp. 398–419.

information and made rational choices about commercial activities conducted by employees at home and abroad. The different well-ordered
functions of the Company are considered to have been integrated effectively by operational arrangements that find expression in a clear and
coherent organisational chart.[63] Consequently, the Company is held to
have been a sophisticated, innovative, and efficient precursor of the
modern multidivisional firm, and it has been proclaimed to have been
the very first 'multinational' company. In view of this, it is perhaps not
surprising to find that the institutional form taken by the East India
Company is sometimes represented as an important staging post between
the early modern and modern worlds of international trade and finance.[64]

There can be no denying that the organisation of the early eighteenth-
century East India Company bears some resemblance to the giant corporations of the twentieth century, but there are two major problems with
analyses that seek slavishly to apply 'modern' attributes to the Company.

First, such analyses tend to downplay or ignore altogether the fact that
in Asia, as well as in the supposedly monopolist trade conducted between
Britain and the East, the directors permitted their employees to pursue
private commercial activities alongside those of the Company. As was
noted in the previous section, the negative effects of this practice were
often acknowledged by contemporaries who were also well aware of the
fact that key areas of Company activity, most notably its shipping operations, were devolved to private interest groups in Britain. The various
overlaps and intersections of Company and private business activity
meant that the institutional boundaries of the Company were never fixed
in the manner of modern firms. These soft edges indeed persuaded a
previous generation of historians that the Company's primary function
was to act as an organisational vehicle for interest groups that were able to
enjoy protected status in the East India trade without having to incur
heavy overhead costs. Hence, to Holden Furber any sharp institutional
definition of the Company disappeared on close inspection of how it
actually worked in practice, and his studies depicted an organisation that
not only pursued its own ends but also served the powerful private interest
groups who were motivated by the making of personal fortunes. Thus, he

---

63 See below, p. 186.
64 For a brief discussion of the place of the East India Company within the long-term development
of British trading companies see Geoffrey Jones, *Merchants to multinationals: British trading
companies in the nineteenth and twentieth centuries* (Oxford, 2000), pp. 2, 20–1. For the role of the
Company in the evolution of company finance see Jonathan Barron Baskin and Paul Miranti
junior, *A history of corporate finance* (Cambridge, 1997), pp. 55–88.

took the view that 'The East India companies, eroded to varying degrees by the private concerns of their "servants", were all to a high degree facades.'[65] As he pointed out, the enthusiasm with which employees pursued their private fortunes during the eighteenth century made the East India companies quite unlike modern firms. C. Northcote Parkinson went even further than Furber and made the somewhat absurd suggestion that by the end of the century 'In a sense, there was no Company; for it had become a mere name to cover the operations of groups and individuals.'[66] This is greatly to exaggerate the position and role of private interests and it entirely overlooks the fact that the Company always retained a strong corporate identity and pursued aims that overrode sectional concerns. Nevertheless, there is clearly a need to strike a balance between interpretations of the Company as an efficient, well-organised firm, and those that view it as little more than a loose collection of private interest groups.

The second problem with depictions of the East India Company as a modern firm is that very little is known about what actually happened to the Company in an organisational sense during its post-1760 imperial phase, especially as far as its metropolitan history is concerned. Almost all modern examinations of the inner workings of the Company concentrate on the years before the Battle of Plassey, and this means that it is still difficult, if not impossible, to offer an assessment of its institutional characteristics when it began to operate as an imperial agency as well as a trading company. Thus, although K. N. Chaudhuri has examined the evolution and working of the Company as a commercial organisation, and P. G. M. Dickson has emphasised the importance of its contribution to Britain's 'financial revolution', the system of public finance, and the emergence of the fiscal-military state,[67] these landmark studies are each located in the century *before* 1760. Hoh-cheung and Lorna H. Mui explore the Company's domestic management of the tea trade after

---

65 Holden Furber, *Rival empires of trade in the Orient, 1600–1800* (1976), p. 227. Furber thought that the word 'façade' was perhaps 'too strong', but he confessed could not think of a better one. He might have chosen the word 'carapace', which is used by Sanjay Subrahmanyam when describing Furber's view of the Company as an institution pursuing its corporate aims while at the same time being 'used by other actors for their own ends'. See his 'Introduction: the Indian Ocean world and Ashin Das Gupta', in Uma Das Gupta (comp.), *The world of the Indian Ocean merchant 1500–1800. Collected essays of Ashin Das Gupta* (Delhi, 2001), p. 17.

66 C. Northcote Parkinson, *Trade in the eastern seas, 1793–1813* (Cambridge, 1937), p. 9.

67 K. N. Chaudhuri, *The English East India Company: the study of an early joint-stock company 1600–1640* (1965); Chaudhuri, *Trading world of Asia*; P. G. M. Dickson, *The financial revolution in England: a study in the development of public credit, 1688–1756* (1967).

1784, Jean Sutton has examined the shipping system, and Martin Moir has outlined the home administration, but for the most part it is still necessary to piece together the internal post-1760 history of the Company from its own records.[68]

Although many aspects of how the Company evolved after 1760 remain unclear, it is nonetheless evident that no single thread of institutional development stretched unbroken from the early seventeenth century to the mid-nineteenth century. To suggest otherwise is to understate or even ignore the importance of the profound changes that occurred in the Company's basic role and outlook after 1756 as it began its long march to political and military ascendancy in India. As Chaudhuri acknowledges, 'The prospect of making money rapidly and on a huge scale, which the control of the public treasury in Bengal made possible, wrought remarkable changes not only among the individual servants of the Company but also in the East India Company itself and even in government.'[69] Although not exploring these changes in any great detail, Chaudhuri observed that the Company's transition from trader to sovereign challenged many of the attitudes, assumptions, and ideas that had long informed contemporary assessments of Company performance and profitability. Indeed, as the Company made the move from commerce to empire, it became affected by a range of powerful new economic and political forces both at the periphery of the empire and in the metropolis. In particular, those running the Company's affairs were obliged to take careful notice of how government and Parliament were developing views about the Company's functions and responsibilities in India, and this caused them to make alterations to internal management, control, and decision-making systems. The Company also had to recast its external administrative, financial, and political relationships. The combined effect of these modifications took the Company some way from the organisational model that has often been invoked by historians, and in a sense therefore this book is all about how the East India Company began to act much less like a modern firm as it began to move along a path of institutional development determined by its responses to events in South Asia.

---

68 Hoh-cheung Mui and Lorna H. Mui, *The management of monopoly. A study of the East India Company's conduct of its tea trade, 1784–1833* (Vancouver, 1984); Jean Sutton, *Lords of the east. The East India Company and its ships (1600–1874)* (second edition, 2000); Martin Moir, *A general guide to the India Office records* (1996), pp. 14–45.
69 Chaudhuri, 'The English East India Company and its decision making', p. 97.

The East India Company's dependence on a host of private interest groups to supply it with commodities, finance, goods, services, and shipping means that there is also a need to look beyond the Company if proper consideration is to be given to some of the wider influences exerted by its Asian trade and empire upon Britain. This is not a matter that has ever concerned historians to any great extent. Few have been inclined to consider in any detail the economic effects that commercial and territorial expansion in Asia exerted upon Britain, and none has placed the East India Company or the East India trade anywhere near the heart of the processes that transformed the British economy during the eighteenth and early nineteenth centuries. Indeed, until quite recently historians have tended to downplay the extent to which Britain's economic growth was driven by external factors before 1850, and many have concurred with the view of Patrick O'Brien, as expressed in 1982, that the 'periphery was peripheral' for the economic growth of early modern Western Europe as a whole, and Britain in particular.[70] Indeed, the view that the principal dynamics of economic growth and development were located within Britain itself has been warmly endorsed in a recent general assessment of trade and the British economy made by C. Knick Harley, even though he concedes that international trade 'unambiguously enhanced' and 'stimulated' industrialisation in many different ways.[71] O'Brien himself now adopts a similar position and, acknowledging the importance of recent revisionist studies, he writes that 'The magnitude of foreign relations may not have been very large, but clearly some factors outside the British Isles influenced the rate and pattern of growth and, conversely, British growth affected all nations and regions.'[72]

These are very important shifts of emphasis, but recent discussions of the contribution of trade and empire to the industrialising economy have been located in analyses framed almost exclusively by the Atlantic economy and the slave trade. Most notably, perhaps, Joseph E. Inikori has made an ambitious attempt to connect British economic development to

70 Patrick O'Brien, 'European economic development: the contribution of the periphery', *Ec. Hist. Rev.*, 35 (1982), pp. 1–18 (quotation on p. 18). For an excellent historiographical survey of British industrialisation, which traces changing attitudes to the importance of overseas trade, see Joseph E. Inikori, *Africans and the Industrial Revolution in England. A study in international trade and economic development* (Cambridge, 2002), ch. 3.

71 C. Knick Harley, 'Trade: discovery, mercantilism, and technology', in Roderick Floud and Paul Johnson (eds.), *The Cambridge economic history of modern Britain*, 3 vols. (Cambridge, 2004), vol. I, *Industrialisation 1700–1860*, pp. 173–203.

72 Stanley L. Engerman and Patrick K. O'Brien, 'The industrial revolution in global perspective', in ibid., p. 459.

international trade by restating the importance of an expanding Atlantic commerce, which he sees as 'the central element which permitted the successful completion of the industrialization process in England [sic]'. By concluding that 'there can be little doubt that the labor of Africans and their descendants was what made possible the growth of Atlantic commerce', he is able to argue that 'Africans made an invaluable contribution to the Industrial Revolution in England.'[73] This has provoked a lively debate, and by no means all historians accept the figures that underpin some aspects of Inikori's study,[74] but by comparison remarkably little attention has been paid to ways in which Britain felt the effect of economic influences emanating from the expansion of trade and empire in Asia. This is perhaps hardly surprising in view of the fact that in statistical terms 'East India' does loom large in historical profiles of British overseas trade,[75] although it has often been acknowledged that an increasing volume of Company and private imports helped to reshape patterns of consumption in Britain, and a recent study has stressed how the importation of Asiatic luxury goods helped to stimulate imitation, innovation, and adaptation in the domestic manufacturing sector.[76] Little support has been given, however, to the notion that direct linkages existed between the processes of domestic industrialisation and commercial or territorial expansion in Asia, and, unlike the case a century or so ago, no one now suggests that the plundering of Bengal sparked a domestic industrial revolution.[77] Similarly, it is not now thought that early British conquests in India were made with a view to capturing markets or supplies of raw materials for the benefit of British manufacturers. There seems little reason to dissent, therefore, from P. J. Marshall's view that 'In the fifty years after the conquest of Bengal spectacular changes took place in the

73 Inikori, *Africans*, p. 486. For a good summary of recent work on the relationship between the Atlantic world and the growth of the British economy see Kenneth Morgan, *Slavery, Atlantic trade and the British economy, 1660–1800* (Cambridge, 2000).

74 See, for example, the round-table discussion and Inikori's response in *International Journal of Maritime History*, 15 (2003), pp. 279–361.

75 For a recent summary of data derived from customs records for the eighteenth century see Jacob M. Price, 'The imperial economy, 1700–1776', in *OHBE*, vol. II: Marshall (ed.), *The eighteenth century*, pp. 78–103 (figures on pp. 100–3).

76 Maxine Berg, 'In pursuit of luxury: global history and British consumer goods in the eighteenth century', *Past and Present*, 182 (2004), pp. 85–142. See also Maxine Berg, 'From imitation to invention: creating commodities in eighteenth-century Britain', *Ec. Hist. Rev.*, 55 (2002), pp. 1–30.

77 For a brief early twentieth-century discussion of the 'vexed question' of 'how far the wealth brought by the Nabobs [to Britain] was responsible for the Industrial Revolution', see James M. Holzman, *The nabobs in England. A study of the returned Anglo-Indian, 1760–1785* (New York, 1926), pp. 88–90.

economy of Great Britain. Possession of an empire in Asia undoubtedly contributed to these changes, but few economic historians would now argue that its contribution had been of major importance.'[78]

Since Marshall wrote these words during the mid-1960s little has happened to suggest that any modification needs to be made to his assessment, and most historians of the British economy still appear to regard the East India Company and trade with Asia as being of only very marginal significance. Yet, as scholarly preoccupations have broadened beyond the dynamics of industrialisation and the share of GDP represented by overseas trade, some historians have begun to suggest new ways in which economic links with Asia were of importance to Britain during the late eighteenth and early nineteenth centuries. In a subtle analysis of the interplay between imperialism and the industrialising economy, for example, J. R. Ward has shown how the creation of an urbanised, wage-earning working class drove the increase in demand for Company tea. This enabled late eighteenth-century growth of the China tea trade to take place, thereby indirectly enhancing the Company's ability to wage war on the Indian subcontinent and sustain territorial expansion beyond 1790.[79] Also exploring the relationship between empire, trade, and war, Javier Cuenca Esteban has argued that transfers of wealth from India made an important contribution to Britain's balance of payments, which helped to offset the great financial pressures imposed by sustained warfare in Europe.[80] In a very different context, Carole Shammas has offered a robust challenge to those whose analyses of economic development have given primacy to domestic demand for European-produced commodities.[81] In doing so, she has emphasised the strength of the relationship that existed between metropolitan demand for tropical goods, including tea and textiles, and the distribution and growth of overseas empires. To each of these historians the effects of what happened in Asia bore heavily upon Britain and their work demonstrates the entangling relationship that was established between trade, empire, and the development of the domestic economy.

---

78 Marshall, *Problems of empire*, p. 92.
79 J. R. Ward, 'The industrial revolution and British imperialism, 1750–1850', *Ec. Hist. Rev.*, 47 (1994), pp. 44–65.
80 Javier Cuenca Esteban, 'The British balance of payments, 1772–1820: India transfers and war finance', *Ec. Hist. Rev.*, 54 (2001), pp. 56–86.
81 Carole Shammas, 'The revolutionary impact of European demand for tropical goods', in John J. McCusker and Kenneth Morgan (eds.), *The early modern Atlantic economy* (Cambridge, 2000), pp. 163–85.

These are all important advances in our understanding of the complex economic relationships that existed between Asia and Britain, but there remains a need to get back to basics in order to establish how, where, and to what extent the domestic economy was affected by the territorial expansion of the East India Company and the growth of its associated private interests at home and abroad. This is a matter of some importance if we are better to understand the development of the financial, industrial, and service sectors. In overall terms, the effects of British activity in Asia were not sufficient to transform the domestic economy, but this is not to say that different sectors and localities remained unaffected. It is certainly possible to identify and quantify ways in which expansion in Asia bore directly and indirectly upon patterns of economic activity in Britain, and this book seeks to establish some of the ways in which East Indian influences were at work. At the same time, historians of Britain's fiscal-military state have examined in great detail how domestic resources were mobilised for war against France and other European powers,[82] but comparatively little attention has been paid to the ways in which the state benefited from the men, materials, and money acquired through overseas expansion. Consequently, this study also attempts to establish the contribution made by the East India Company and its Indian empire to Britain's burgeoning fiscal, military, and naval strength.

Any attempt to explore the linkages that existed between the metropolitan economy and the East India Company's commercial and territorial expansion in Asia must not overlook the fact that a recent major study of British imperialism after 1688 has focused attention upon expansionist impulses emanating from the financial sector in general, and the City of London in particular. By emphasising, or re-emphasising, the importance of the metropolis in the growth of Britain's overseas empire, P. J. Cain and A. G. Hopkins have given primacy to a form of 'gentlemanly capitalism' created by an alliance of land, trade, and finance, which found institutional expression in the City, political expression in government, and socio-cultural expression in an integrated metropolitan elite.[83] They see the East India Company as 'undoubtedly the most impressive overseas manifestation of the alliance between land and finance in the eighteenth century'.[84] In general, it can be argued that for the period before 1850

82 See, most notably, John Brewer, *The sinews of power: war, money, and the English state, 1688–1783* (1989).
83 P. J. Cain and A. G. Hopkins, *British imperialism, 1688–2000* (second edition, 2002), pp. 23–103. The East India Company and British expansion in India before 1857 are discussed on pp. 278–84.
84 Ibid., p. 279.

Cain and Hopkins have given too much weight to metropolitan factors within the dynamics of imperialism, and that they downplay the importance of the British provinces in overseas expansion.[85] It is undeniable, however, that the East India Company played an important part in tying together the City of London, the state, and the empire in a series of entangling relationships that enabled resources to be mobilised at home and abroad, thereby helping to facilitate the emergence of Britain as the greatest financial, imperial, industrial, and military power on the world stage. Various aspects of these multilateral relationships are explored and quantified in the pages that follow as consideration is given to the Company's position at the very heart of imperial Britain.

In order to explore, extend, and modify the perspectives on the East India Company offered by contemporaries and historians, the remainder of the book is organised into linked thematic chapters. Chapters 2 and 3 explore the Company's changing metropolitan relationships with the state, the City of London, and government. Chapters 4 and 5 look at the people who made up the Company in Britain, and attention is focused upon the stockholders and directors, as well as the officials who administered the Company's affairs from East India House. Chapters 6, 7, and 8 examine the methods used by the directors to manage trade and empire at a time when the Company's overseas activities were undergoing a process of immense change and diversification. Finally, chapter 9 establishes how the Company's interactions with the British economy altered as a territorial empire was acquired in South Asia, and it explores how various 'East Indian' influences were felt at local and national level.

---

85 H. V. Bowen, *Elites, enterprise, and the making of the British overseas empire, 1688–1775* (Basingstoke, 1996), pp. 16–21.

CHAPTER 2

Relationships: city, state, and empire

By the beginning of the nineteenth century the East India Company occupied a position of central importance in Britain's trade and empire, and it was considered to have contributed much to the burgeoning strength of the nation at home as well as overseas. Contemporaries sometimes suggested that the Company's resources were fuelling the growth of Britain's armed forces, public finances, and money markets, as well as the wider domestic economy, and consequently this chapter seeks to establish the extent to which the Company's domestic influences were felt within an imperial state that was gradually extending its reach further into the wider world. In particular, because the Company and its overseas possessions were increasingly incorporated into the financial and strategic calculations of ministers and politicians, consideration is given to the contributions made by the Company to the state, especially when its resources were deployed during times of war. At the same time, it is acknowledged that the Company itself could not function without active assistance from the City of London and successive governments, and therefore the chapter also identifies the ways in which the City oiled the Company's financial wheels and ministers offered different forms of support. Taken as a whole, the chapter explores the ways in which the Company forged some of the domestic connections that existed between different elements of Britain's financial, imperial, and military power.

CAPITAL AND CREDIT

By the middle of the eighteenth century the East India Company was firmly established alongside the Bank of England as one of the main pillars of the City of London, and many of its most prominent directors and stockholders were members of the powerful 'monied interest' that dominated metropolitan finance and extended considerable influence into government and politics. The Company had well-established links with the investing community, thereby enabling it to mobilise the funds that were necessary to sustain commercial and imperial activity in Asia, and accordingly there are strong grounds to support the view that the Company was indeed an institutional manifestation of 'gentlemanly capitalism'.

The positioning of the East India Company at the very heart of the metropolitan world of high finance arose from the fact that the Company's domestic development was shaped to a large extent by the demands imposed upon the British state by recurrent warfare with other European powers. In 1698 the extreme financial pressures of the Nine Years War had obliged the 'new' East India Company to make a loan of £2 million to the hard-pressed government of William III in return for the right to trade with the East Indies, and this served to embed the Company within the emerging system of public credit. The position was then strengthened when the new and old East India Companies merged in 1709 to create the United Company. By the middle of the War of Austrian Succession, in 1744, the United Company's advances to the state had risen to £4.2 million, which, together with one-off financial donations, helped smooth the way for the periodic renewal of exclusive commercial privileges.[1] From the Company's perspective, loans to government also provided an essential 'fund of credit', which acted as collateral for its substantial short-term borrowing requirements, and this enabled Lord North to declare in 1773 that 'what makes the credit of the Company the strongest is the debt owing them from the publick'.[2]

Supporters of the Company were thus always able to emphasise the extent to which the Company had provided substantial sums of money that were necessary for the state to meet the challenges posed by extended periods of European warfare and crisis. It was because of this that several commentators likened the Company to a powerful 'engine' driving forward the development of what has become known to historians as the British 'fiscal-military state'. In 1773 the stockholder George Dempster declared that the Company was a 'great money engine of state' whose credit was 'inseparably connected with government and the Bank of England', and a quarter of a century later the Company's Chairman Jacob Bosanquet echoed these sentiments (as well as those of Adam Smith) when he wrote that 'I consider the Bank and the East India Company as

---

1 For these arrangements see W. R. Scott, *The constitution and finance of the English, Scottish, and Irish joint-stock companies to 1720*, 3 vols. (1910–12), vol. II, pp. 128–89.
2 BL, Eg. MS, 246, p. 22.

two of the most powerful engines of the state.'[3] The financial difficulties under which the Company laboured during the late eighteenth century suggest that the great engine was by then spluttering rather badly, but the legacy of a long, entangling financial alliance between the Company and the state ensured that governments always felt strongly obliged to protect the interests of one of the nation's major public creditors. No minister could ever afford to let the East India Company go to the wall.

Although the Company had become firmly established as one of the main financial props of the regime during the first half of the eighteenth century, it was like any other commercial organisation in that it also required regular injections of working capital. Although its overseas activities were funded primarily by local resources – loans, the proceeds of trade, and, from the 1760s, income from revenue collection – the Company's domestic financial system was always heavily dependent upon credit. Commercial transactions in Britain were based upon some re-investment of trading profits, but shortfalls needed to be covered, and consequently the Company could never function properly without the short-term input of funds from metropolitan investors. Stockholders provided the Company's nominal trading capital of £3.2 million and this sum was increased in three stages to £6 million between 1786 and 1793 as the directors sought to tackle acute financial difficulties. These extensions of the share capital were, however, exceptional measures and the Company's routine working-finance requirements always had to be met by a combination of fixed-interest bond issues or short-term borrowing. At all times, therefore, there were three main types of investor underwriting the Company's affairs in different ways, and these stockholders, bond-holders, and lenders tied the Company firmly into the financial world of gentlemanly and gentlewomanly capitalism.

Those who derived most financial benefit from investment in the East India Company were the stockholders or proprietors who bought a 'share' of the joint-stock capital of £3.2 million. By 1756 all of the Company's capital had long been loaned to the state, but trading profits were distributed to the stockholders *pro rata* in the form of dividend payments, which had usually stood at between 7 and 10 per cent.[4] This healthy level

3 George Dempster, *London Evening Post*, 18–20 February 1773; Jacob Bosanquet to William Pitt, 14 April 1798, H/61, p. 185. Smith had referred to the Bank as 'a great engine of state', Adam Smith, *An inquiry into the nature and causes of the wealth of nations* (1776), ed. R. H. Campbell, A. S. Skinner, and W. B. Todd, 2 vols. (Oxford, 1976), vol. I, p. 320.

4 L/AG/18/2, vol. 1, p. 3.

of return was a reflection of a generally profitable commercial performance, but investors also benefited from India stock's reputation as a sober
and respectable investment that was secure at the heart of the system of
public credit. As Dame Lucy Sutherland put it, during the early eighteenth century East India stock was the 'equivalent of a "gilt-edged"
security',[5] and hence it was always much sought-after by investors. In
theory, however, it was still possible for anyone to become a proprietor of
the Company because the charter of 1698 had stated quite unequivocally
that shares could be bought 'by or for any person or persons, natives or
foreigners, bodies politick and corporate (the Governor and Company of
the Bank of England only excepted)'. This lack of any formal restriction
on stock purchasing led rapidly to the creation of a diverse and cosmopolitan proprietary, and the number of foreign investors increased markedly after 1720.[6] A steady turnover of stock ensured that ownership
remained stable, although there was an advance of investors holding
£1,000–£4,999 stock, which meant that by 1748 just over half of the
Company's stock was in the hands of medium-size stockholders. In
contrast to other major companies, however, the East India Company
also retained a considerable number of small proprietors, with 52.7 per
cent of all accounts being of less than £1,000. By mid-century, domestic
ownership of the stock continued to be concentrated in and around
London, with only 0.01 per cent of accounts being registered in the
provinces, but foreign accounts had advanced to around one-fifth of the
total, with most of these being held in the name of Dutch stockholders.
As the Company began to embark on the process of military advance and
territorial acquisition in South Asia, its stock was owned predominantly
by the financial, mercantile, and professional classes, both at home and
abroad, although women held over a fifth of all domestic accounts and
almost a third of foreign holdings.

The Company had long issued bonds in order to raise working capital.
The ease with which it did so depended upon the general state of public
credit, but after 1709 the directors had managed gradually to reduce the
rate of interest from 6 to 3 per cent. Thereafter, the rate of interest was
usually 3 or 4 per cent, although during general credit crises, such as in
1762–3, 5 per cent had to be offered in order to attract funds.[7] The bonds,

5 Sutherland, *East India Company*, p. 42.
6 P. G. M. Dickson, *The financial revolution in England: a study in the development of public credit,
  1688–1756* (1967), p. 312. The remainder of this paragraph is based upon ibid., pp. 287–98, 321–5,
  513–31.
7 For the rate of interest see H/371, p. 383.

usually issued in denominations of £100, were repayable or renewable every March and September, and they were transferable by endorsement. Known within the Company as 'circulating bonds', they were coveted by individuals and companies who required easy access to their funds. As Thomas Mortimer, the leading contemporary expert on the money markets, noted in 1761, 'India bonds are the most convenient and profitable security a person can be possessed of, who has any quantity of cash unemployed, but, which he knows not how soon he may have occasion for.' He concluded that 'There is as little trouble with an India bond as with a Bank note',[8] and consequently they proved to be a particularly popular form of short-term investment for banks and insurance companies.[9]

The value of the bonds in circulation at any one time was always subject to statutory restriction, although the maximum had crept upwards to £6 million during the first half of the eighteenth century and this represented an important contribution to the market for credit. In the three years after 1749, however, the Company's bond debt was sharply reduced from £4,245,723 to £1,848,350 as many bonds were surrendered in return for a share of the East India Annuities that were created as part of Henry Pelham's restructuring of the national debt.[10] Thereafter, the bond debt increased only very slowly, and during the 1760s and early 1770s it fell in a narrow range between £2,881,125 and £2,898,125.[11] Following the Regulating Act of 1773, the size of the debt was subject to tighter parliamentary regulation, and on several occasions it was reduced to

---

8 Thomas Mortimer, *Every man his own broker. Or a guide to Exchange Alley* (first edition, 1761), pp. 147–8. India bonds could be used to purchase goods at Company sales, and it was noted in 1785 that 'the most trifling rate of discount has always been found sufficient to bring bonds instead of cash' (*Report from an open committee of account . . .* (1785), p. 6). For the factors that determined the price of bonds in the market see William Fairman, *The stocks examined and compared; or a guide to purchasers in the public funds* (1795), p. 41.

9 For the extensive purchasing of India bonds by insurance companies and banks see Dickson, *Financial revolution*, pp. 441–2, 446–8; idem., *The Sun Insurance Office 1710–1960: a history of two and a half centuries of British insurance* (1960), pp. 239–40, 243; Barry Supple, *The Royal Exchange Assurance: a history of British insurance 1720–1970* (Cambridge, 1970), pp. 74–5.

10 Dickson, *Financial revolution*, pp. 230–41, 413–4; L. S. Sutherland, 'Samson Gideon and the reduction of interest, 1749–50', *Ec. Hist. Rev.*, 16 (1946), pp. 15–29. The 3 per cent annuities were, in effect, a government security managed by the Company. The annual interest of £126,000 arising from the Company's loan of £4.2 million to the state provided the income for payments to the annuitants, and the government gave the Company £1,687 a year for its management of the annuities. This arrangement lasted until 1793 when the annuities and the residue of the Company loan to the state were placed under the administration of the Bank of England and engrafted on to the 3 per cent Reduced Annuities. The status of the East India Annuities was often misunderstood, but for a good contemporary explanation see F. R. [Francis Russell], *A short history of the East India Company* (1793), pp. 7–8.

11 H/371, p. 379.

£1,500,000, although after a short-term increase to £7,000,000 in 1811 a new limit of £3,000,000 was fixed by the Charter Act of 1813. Throughout this period the interest paid on the bonds was usually 4 or 5 per cent, thus enabling Peter Auber in 1826 to echo Mortimer's words of sixty years earlier by declaring that 'The Company's bonds are a very marketable security, and present an eligible investment for parties or companies who have money to lay out, which they may require at an uncertain period.'[12]

Although bond issues provided much of the Company's working capital requirements, they were never enough to ensure a steady flow of ready cash into the Company's treasury. Consequently, the Company always borrowed money in the form of interest-bearing loans. From its early years, the United Company had routinely used the Bank of England's overdraft facilities but it also borrowed from the Bank on a semi-regular basis, receiving just under £1.5 million between 1710 and 1745.[13] The Bank continued to act in this way, combining large advances with frequent small cash loans, but after mid-century important changes became evident in the general pattern of Company borrowing.

In particular, pressures upon the Bank during the Seven Years War obliged the Company to look to alternative providers of funds, and between 1756 and 1764 other lenders advanced almost half of the Company's loans.[14] Occasionally the Company drew on prominent City institutions such as the Royal Exchange Assurance and the London Assurance Corporation,[15] but most advances were made by wealthy individuals who had close connections with East Indian affairs. During the early 1750s, the financiers Samson Gideon, Gerrard and Joshua Vanneck, and Joseph and Michael Salvador had advanced large sums to the Company,[16] but increasingly to the fore were some of the Company's own directors. Comparatively small-scale 'insider borrowing' involved directors such as Michael Impey and Nathaniel Newnham junior during the mid-1750s,[17] but as the war progressed there was an increase in the scale and frequency of such loans. Especially prominent were George Amyand, Laurence

12 Auber, *Analysis*, p. 294.

13 K. N. Chaudhuri, *The trading world of Asia and the English East India Company 1660–1760* (Cambridge, 1978), p. 439. Bank overdraft repayments amounted to £2,924,251 between 1710 and 1745.

14 The Company borrowed £396,355 from the Bank, and £390,577 from other lenders (L/AG/1/1, vol. 20, p. 115; vol. 21, p. 40).

15 Ibid., vol. 19, p. 284; vol. 20, p. 115; vol. 22, p. 27; L/AG/1/5, vol. 18, pp. 136, 188.

16 L/AG/1/1, vol. 19, pp. 189, 284.   17 L/AG/1/5, vol. 17, pp. 33, 58.

Sulivan, and John Dorrien,[18] and this suggests that the Company was forced back on to the resources of its own directors as it struggled to overcome cash-flow difficulties caused by a poor commercial performance during a period when credit was in short supply.[19] It also suggests that individuals such as Amyand were brought into the Direction because of the resources at their disposal.[20]

Regular financial assistance from directors continued to be made until November 1767, when a group of ten advanced short-term loans totalling £60,650 at 4 per cent interest,[21] and there can be no doubt that this helped the Company survive the financial buffeting it received during and after the Seven Years War. Yet these loans also indicate that the Company's finance was still arranged on a rather small scale during 1750s and 1760s, with inputs from individuals being sufficient to make a difference. As trade and empire expanded, however, such loans could no longer have much effect upon the Company's position, and after 1770 much greater amounts of emergency aid were required, forcing the Company into quite different financial relationships.

The Company's finances were severely dislocated during the transition from trade to empire, and the Company was obliged to borrow far larger sums in London than had hitherto been the case. This became apparent between 1769 and 1772 when there was an urgent need to meet sharply increased levels of payment to government, stockholders, and the holders of large numbers of bills of exchange issued in India. At a time when income from sales of goods was declining, the directors were forced to rely ever more heavily upon the Bank of England from whom they borrowed £5.5 million between 1769 and 1772. However, borrowing on such a great scale could not continue after the City of London was shaken by the severe credit crisis caused by the failure of the Ayr Bank in the summer of 1772. As the director Laurence Sulivan put it, the crisis 'brought the Bank of England (our single resource) to be severely cautious',[22] and it was

---

18 George Amyand advanced £60,000 in October 1760; Laurence Sulivan £65,525 between May 1757 and October 1761; and John Dorrien £171,700 between October 1760 and September 1763 (L/AG/1/1, vol. 20, p. 115; L/AG/1/5, vol. 17, pp. 45, 232, 262, 300). Dorrien was a close follower of Sulivan and served as Deputy-Chairman in 1762 and Chairman in 1763.

19 For details of the Company's financial problems caused by the loss of Fort St David, heavy military expenditure, and damage and delay to returning ships and cargo, see the descriptive note explaining the 'reduction in this year's account' attached to the Stock Computation of June 1760 (L/AG/18/2, vol. 4).

20 When Amyand, a merchant and banker, made his loan he was serving as a director for the first time.

21 L/AG/1/5, vol. 18, p. 255. Most of the loans were of £5,000 or £6,500.

22 Quoted in Bowen, *Revenue and reform*, p. 127. For a full account of the Company's financial difficulties see ibid., pp. 119–32.

neither able nor willing fully to meet the Company's request for further advances. At first the Company sought to stave off impending disaster by postponing the payment of customs duties to the Treasury, and then the stockholders faced up to reality by cutting their annual dividend from 12½ to 6 per cent. Yet these were only palliative measures and, although consideration was given to ways of raising money at home and abroad, the directors were eventually forced to bow to the inevitable and accept an advance of £1.4 million from Lord North's government in return for the reform of the Company. This loan was repaid by the end of 1776,[23] but the government's rescue action of 1773 marked a significant recasting of the debtor–creditor relationship that had existed between the state and the Company since 1698.

It became evident that the Company was now ultimately dependent on the state for financial support even as the directors resumed regular borrowing from the Bank of England. The Company received short-term loans totalling £6.4 million from the Bank between 1776 and 1813,[24] and in October 1823 it borrowed £1.5 million at 3½ per cent.[25] On several occasions, however, the directors were again obliged to seek emergency relief from ministers, notably when wartime financial pressures made it impossible for them to raise funds elsewhere in the metropolis. When the Company teetered on the edge of bankruptcy during the early 1780s it gained relief from payments to the Treasury,[26] and in 1810 and 1812 Parliament authorised loans of £1.5 million and £2.5 million.[27] These actions created a situation that was very different from that which had existed in the days when government had relied upon the Company for substantial levels of financial support, and this was emphasised in 1793 when, in return for extending the Company's exclusive trading privileges for a further twenty years, the state cancelled the loans of £4.2 million made by the Company between 1698 and 1744.[28]

In overall terms, these changes altered greatly the Company's position within the system of public finance. During the 1820s the Chairmen were

23 For details of the repayments and interest see L/AG/18/2, vol. 1, p. 7.
24 Figure totalled from L/AG/1/1, vols. 23–30.
25 L/AG/1/5, vol. 31, p. 631. The Bank also assisted the Company in other ways. When the Company was short of cash in 1803 the Bank agreed to buy £100,000 of silver from it (Sir John Clapham, *The Bank of England*, 2 vols. (Cambridge, 1944), vol. II, p. 37.
26 Sutherland, *East India Company*, pp. 374, 393.
27 *Reports from the select committee on the affairs of the East India Company*, vol. VIII (1831–2), p. 29. The second loan was not discharged until 1822.
28 For a good contemporary account of the history of the Company's stock and its loans to the state see Fairman, *The stocks examined and compared*, pp. 34–8.

authorised to invest almost £1.5 million in government funds,[29] but this took the form of a regular commercial transaction and the Company could no longer be regarded as a major financial partner of the state. Moreover, East India stock had once been London's highest profile security, but it now jostled for position alongside the many new government stocks and annuities that had been created during the great expansion of the national debt after 1793. During the 1750s the prices of only a handful of stocks were quoted in the London press, but by the 1830s details were printed of more than thirty securities, shares, and foreign funds. As a result, investment in the East India Company was of far less significance to those who moved in the London money markets at the end of the period than had been the case sixty years earlier, and this had a considerable effect upon perceptions of the Company and its importance.

COMPANY, STATE, AND EMPIRE

Although the Company became increasingly dependent upon the City and the state for financial support during the late eighteenth century, it was nevertheless believed that the Company's overseas activities generated considerable net gains for its domestic allies, for Britain as a whole, and even for the wider empire. During the 1760s and 1770s few denied the primacy of the Atlantic colonies among Britain's collection of imperial possessions, but commentators were ever more inclined to view scattered overseas possessions as an interconnected global empire in which India occupied an increasingly prominent position.[30] It was already believed by some that an expanding East India trade had contributed much to the economic well-being of the metropolis, and Thomas Mortimer suggested in 1772 that 'our commerce to the East Indies, on its present footing, is one of the chief sources of the power and commercial prosperity of Great Britain'.[31] Others thought that India had even more to offer, and in the same year the troublesome former Company servant William Bolts argued that with good management the Company's Indian possessions could be 'rendered the richest jewel in the British Crown by being an inexhaustible source of extensive commerce, maritime power and

---

29 L/AG/1/1, vol. 31, p. 113.
30 H. V. Bowen, 'British conceptions of global empire, 1756–1783', *Journal of Imperial and Commonwealth History*, 26 (1998), pp. 1–27.
31 Thomas Mortimer, *The elements of commerce, politics, and finance in three treatises on those important subjects* (1780, reprinted from the 1772 edition), p. 130.

national wealth'.[32] Such thoughts prompted some observers to suggest that the future of Company, nation, and empire had become interwoven, and they feared that any dissolution of the bonds between Britain and India would have a devastating effect upon Britain's standing in the world.[33] If such fears were certainly overstated, they nevertheless offered acknowledgement that the Anglo-Indian economic connection was steadily assuming a much greater significance for the metropolis. At the very end of the period under review, one Company stockholder reflected on this long-run process by noting the existence of a 'rope' that had been twisted, 'tying India and England, 14,000 miles apart [*sic*], faster together and which, year after year for upwards of a century, had been increasing in strength and durability'. His conclusion was that 'from the period of the charter of 1698 India had never been the nursed child of England, but a support and source of prosperity to her'.[34]

Defenders of the Company's monopoly and its record in India often sought to give quantitative substance to these claims, and at the beginning of the nineteenth century they were able to assert that, on average, the state had received over £5 million a year from the Company during the past half-century or so.[35] This was an exaggeration, and the state certainly received little by way of direct financial benefit from the Company's acquisition of territorial revenues in India. In 1767 the government of Lord Chatham was granted £400,000 a year as a share of the Company's new riches but, although £2,169,399 was paid into the Treasury, payments were suspended following the Company's financial crisis of 1772 and this brought the state's 'participation' in the Bengal revenues to an abrupt halt. The Company later twice agreed to make annual payments to the state in return for the territorial revenues remaining in its possession, but in both 1781 and 1793 it failed to meet its obligations for more than a year or so. As a result, only a mere £1.4 million was paid into the Treasury.[36]

---

32 Quoted in M. E. Yapp, 'The "brightest jewel": the origins of a phrase' in Kenneth Ballhatchet and John Harrison (eds), *East India Company studies: papers presented to Professor Sir Cyril Philips* (Hong Kong, 1986), pp. 36–7. Bolts, a private adventurer and former Company servant, was a constant thorn in the side of the Company and adopted the view that the nation would only derive benefit from India if the Crown took over the management of British territories.

33 Hugh Baillie to Clive, 6 December 1772, MS Eur. G.37, box 65, f. 59; William Burrell, speech in the Commons, 26 November 1772, BL, Eg. MS, 242, p. 22.

34 Speech of Thomas Fielder of 19 April 1833, reported in *Debates at the General Court of Proprietors of East India stock . . .* (1833), pp. 109, 113.

35 Anon., *Observations on the territorial rights and commercial privileges of the East India Company, with a view to the renewal of the Company's charter; in a letter to a Member of Parliament* (1813), p. 24.

36 £400,000 was paid under the terms of 21 Geo. III, c.65; £1 million under 33 Geo. III, c.52.

This was a deeply disappointing outcome, although optimists continued to believe that surplus territorial revenues in India might yet yield substantial contributions to the public purse in London.[37]

Although the direct returns from the Company's Indian revenues always promised far more than they ever delivered to the British state, substantial benefit was derived from the growth of the East India trade that occurred after 1765. As the Company pumped more Indian funds into the purchase of goods for export to Britain, both directly and via China, so the Company's annual payments of customs duties in London rose sharply, from £430,123 in 1763/4 to £886,922 in 1769/70.[38] There were then fluctuations in the level of payment as trade was disrupted by European war and the Company's finances became dislocated. Indeed, on several occasions the Company failed to meet its obligations to the state.[39] But, as a consequence of the growth of the tea trade, which in part was stimulated by Pitt the Younger's reduction of rates of duty on that commodity, the Company was able to make payments of over £1 million on customs and tea duties in 1786/7.[40] This was more than one-quarter of the government's income from customs revenue, and about 6 per cent of net government income as a whole in that year.[41] Such a level could not be maintained during wartime, and the Company's payments moved erratically from year to year as the effects of wars against France between 1793 and 1815 were felt at sea. However, the return of peace saw payments to

37 See, for example, Patrick Colquhoun, *Treatise on the wealth, power, and resources of the British empire* (second edition, 1815), appendix, p. 49.
38 Figures for the payment of customs and tea duties are derived from L/AG/1/1, vols. 20–31.
39 The first postponement of customs payments was in August 1772, and it occurred regularly during the first decade of the nineteenth century.
40 For the growth of the tea trade, see below, pp. 241–2. Before 1784 tea duty payments were recorded under the general account heading of 'customs'. This reflected the fact that prior to Pitt's reforms, the Company's tea payments to government related to customs duties only. Between 1770 and 1784 buyers of tea for home consumption were responsible for paying an excise duty. After 1784, however, the Company collected both customs and excise duties on tea, and these sums were given a separate heading of, first, 'Customs on tea' and later 'Duties on tea' in the Company's books. For an explanation of this, together with details of changing rates of duty, and the amount of tea duty chargeable on the Company each year, see *PP* 1812–13, vol. VIII, p. 233.
41 B. R. Mitchell with the assistance of Phyllis Deane, *Abstract of British historical statistics* (Cambridge, 1962), p. 388. It should be noted that a substantial proportion of the goods on which the Company paid duty were re-exported following their sale and, as a result, repayments were then made by the Treasury in the form of bounties and drawbacks. However, this did not necessarily lead to a net loss of revenue to the state because those who re-exported East India goods sold them in overseas markets and used the proceeds to procure commodities on which, in turn, import duties were then charged in Britain. For a contemporary discussion of this, together with an account detailing re-export bounties and drawbacks on East India goods see Russell, *Short history*, pp. 30–1, 73–4.

government stabilise at upwards of £3 million a year during the 1820s,
mainly in the form of tea duties. This reflected the fact that tea now
dominated the Company's import trade because it provided the best
means of transferring financial resources from India to Britain, via
Canton. The state benefited from this to a considerable degree and, over
the period as a whole, Company payments contributed between 7 and 10
per cent of the government's total receipts from customs and excise duties.
As many had done before him, a director pointed out in 1833 that the
imminent loss of the Company's China monopoly threatened a trade that
still 'furnishes the most safe and advantageous remittance of the territorial
tribute, and which conducted as it is at present pours into the British
Exchequer an annual revenue of three and a half millions sterling, free of
the charge of collection'.[42] In view of this, it is hardly surprising that some
ministers were deeply anxious about the damaging effect that the ending
of the Company's China trade might have upon government income.[43]

Beyond contributions made to the state's finances, the Company's
growing imperial and commercial presence in Asia also served to generate
wealth and income for a wide range of individuals in Britain. Stockholders, bondholders, suppliers of goods and services, merchants, manufacturers, ship owners, and a whole host of others were tied into the Company
in one way or another, and they all derived benefits from overseas expansion. It is impossible to quantify the sum total of their East Indian wealth
with any degree of accuracy, although in chapter 9 an attempt is made to
measure some of the major flows of funds that found their way from the
Company into different parts of Britain's economy and society. Suffice it
to say at this stage that the many and varied activities of the Company
and its associated private interests were believed by contemporaries
to be increasingly important to the economic health of the nation. The
well-informed director Francis Baring calculated that, on average,
the Company's payments to government, ship owners and suppliers had
'materially benefited' the public to the tune of £2.7 million a year between
1767 and 1781, and he thought that the amount had increased slightly to
£2.8 million between 1781 and 1787.[44] But the 1780s were times of acute
financial difficulty for the Company and by 1812 a very different picture
could be painted. In that year a parliamentary committee estimated that

---

42 Speech of Henry St George Tucker of 15 April 1833, reported in *Debates at the General Court*, p. 2.
43 William J. Ashworth, *Customs and excise: trade, production, and consumption in England, 1640–
    1845* (Oxford, 2003), p. 182.
44 H/338, p. 145. Baring made a detailed calculation but did not include Company payments to
    stockholders and bondholders.

since 1793 almost £11 million a year had been 'diffused in various channels through the whole circulation of the British empire'. 'By this', it concluded, 'its manufactures have been supported, encouraged, and improved; its shipping has been increased; its revenues augmented; its commerce extended; its agriculture promoted; and its power and resources invigorated and upheld.'[45] These were bold claims, and they underlined a strong contemporary belief that the Company had moved steadily towards the centre of Britain's imperial economy since the 1760s.

Faced with such estimates, few contemporaries could deny that the Indian empire and East India trade had the potential to bring great economic benefit to Britain, but doubts were increasingly expressed about whether Britain's interests were best served by the Company's continued survival as a monopolist organisation. These doubts were voiced whenever the Company ran into financial difficulties, and they gave strength to the increasingly vigorous protests mounted by the private merchants who sought unrestricted access to Asian markets. These protests became louder over time as campaigns against the monopoly gathered strength, and the Company's allies were obliged to be ever more forceful in their assertions about the contribution that the Company made to Britain as a whole. Early in the period, general statements were deemed sufficient for this purpose, and thus in 1766 a Company insider declared simply that 'every man almost in these kingdoms finds himself affected by its prosperity'.[46] Ten years later it was suggested with only a little more precision that 'no corporate, or other body of men, in this kingdom, contribute near so largely to the support of the state, or to the general mass of its wealth, in proportion to its income and profits as this Company'.[47] By the early 1780s, Britain's general difficulties at home and abroad prompted one writer to argue that the Company's trade and territories offered hopes of salvation to an ailing domestic economy. 'Certain it is', he wrote, 'that the encrease of duties, and general influx of wealth arising from our connection with India have proved a principal support of this country under the calamities it has of late years experienced, by sustaining the funds, supplying the defective circulation, and preventing such a depreciation of our land as would carry with it both public and private ruin.'[48] This

45 *Fourth report from the select committee on the affairs of the East India Company*, (1812), p. 455.
46 *East India Examiner*, vol. I (1766), p. 1.
47 Anon., *Essay on the rights of the East India Company to the perpetuity of their trade* (1776), pp. 22–3.
48 'A Member of Parliament', *Review of the question concerning the government of the British possessions in India; with the heads of a plan proposed* (n.d.? 1783), p. 8. Internal evidence suggests that this pamphlet was written in 1782 or 1783 (see p. 21).

analysis of economic survival during the War of American Independence was deeply flawed but it nevertheless underlines the extent to which some believed the Company now had a key role to play in calculations of national strength. This role was all the more important in view of the partial disintegration of the Atlantic empire that occurred during the early 1780s, and many pinned their hopes of post-war recovery upon the Company's ability to manage the territory and taxes at its disposal in India.[49]

Different forms of economic connection were seen to be binding India ever more closely to Britain. During the 1780s some commentators could still describe the Company's possessions as being an 'appendage of the British empire', albeit an important one,[50] but others, such as the political economist Thomas Pownall, were able to suggest that a much closer relationship now existed between Britain and India in the form of a 'union of interest' and state of 'co-existence'.[51] This relationship was not of course a union of equals, and it was defined by the desire of the Company (and government) to transfer surplus territorial revenues from Bengal to London. Close observers duly noted that the acquisition of territorial revenues had altered the basic function and purpose of the East India trade because in the words of a former director, Nathaniel Smith, the Company's cargoes were the 'only channel of conveyance' for the revenues.[52] Such thoughts enabled defenders of the Company to argue that any interference with the East India trade would serve only to jeopardise the entire revenue-transfer operation. In the face of such claims, even the most resolute political opponents of the Company backed away from radical solutions to the interrelated problems of trade and empire. Until the beginning of the nineteenth century, most politicians accepted the pragmatic views of Pitt, Dundas, and others that the East India Company's trade continued to offer the best means of transferring revenue from India to Britain.[53] Then, when the India monopoly

49 See, for example, Pitt the Younger's views of the increased importance of India, as expressed in 1784 (William Cobbett, *Parliamentary history of England from . . . 1066 to . . . 1803*, 36 vols. (1806–20), vol. XXIV, col. 1086).

50 'A Member of Parliament', *Review of the question concerning the government of the British possessions in India; with the heads of a plan proposed*, p. 8.

51 Thomas Pownall, *The right, interest, and duty of government, as concerned in the affairs of the East Indies* (revised edition, 1781) p. 4.

52 Nathaniel Smith, *Remarks on the East India Company's balances in England from their trade and revenues . . .* (1781), p. 1.

53 H. V. Bowen, 'British India, 1765–1813: the metropolitan context', in *OHBE*, vol. II: P. J. Marshall (ed.), *The eighteenth century* (Oxford, 1998), pp. 535–6, 544–7.

was lost in 1813, the defenders of the Company fell back on the argument that the remaining China trade was still central to the whole 'Indian system'. As the Company Chairman, Campbell Marjoribanks, put it in 1833, the China trade did much more than simply generate dividends for the stockholders: it also acted as 'a channel of remittance from one treasury to another'.[54]

Growing awareness of the economic importance of the Indian empire caused considerable reassessment to be made of whose interests the Company was now representing in Asia. With the Company's territories and revenues increasingly being regarded as 'national' concerns, the Company was considered to be acting on behalf of the public as well as its own corporate interest. Indeed, the directors held that such an arrangement, or 'union of interests', had to some degree been formalised in 1767 when a 'participation' of the revenues had been agreed with Lord Chatham's government.[55] Consequently, many believed that the Company and the state had been drawn together in an all-embracing partnership of shared or mutual interest, as was noted by Richard Fitzpatrick MP who declared at the opening of Parliament in November 1772 that 'it is needless to say how nearly, how inseparably, the interests of the publick and those of the East India Company are blended and connected together'.[56] A few years later, Captain Joseph Price's proposals for reform of British commercial activity in India were prefaced with the remark that 'It is not the Company's only, but the national interest, which is blended in, and interwoven with, the prosperity of Bengal.'[57] By the 1780s such comments were becoming commonplace and it was routine thereafter for political debates about the Company and India to be punctuated with references to the national or public interest.[58]

WAR AND THE EAST INDIA COMPANY

A gradual strengthening of the union that existed between the state and the East India Company was also reflected in changing British attitudes towards war in South Asia, and it was increasingly recognised that

54 Speech of 22 April 1833 reported in *Debates at the General Court*, p. 147.
55 Directors to Bengal, 30 June 1769, *FWIHC*, vol. V, p. 217. The directors considered that the agreement 'made us in some measure responsible to the public for our conduct'.
56 Speech of 26 November 1772, BL, Eg. MS, 242, p. 14.
57 Captain Joseph Price, *Five letters from a free merchant in Bengal to Warren Hastings esq.* . . . (1777, reprinted 1783), p. 23.
58 For a discussion see Susan Staves, 'The construction of the public interest in the debates over Fox's India Bill', *Prose Studies: History, Theory, Criticism*, 18 (1995), pp. 175–98.

'national' interests were at stake in wars on the subcontinent whether they were fought against Indian states or rival European powers. During the 1770s and 1780s there was widespread unease about expensive Company wars of conquest, but anxiety gave way to patriotic celebrations of triumph following Cornwallis's victory over Tipu Sultan during the Third Mysore War of 1789–92. As late as December 1791 a debate at the Coachmakers' Hall society had led to the 'decision almost unanimous' that the war against Tipu was 'unjust, disgraceful and ruinous',[59] but news of Cornwallis's victory the following year generated an enthusiastic public response which marked something of a shift in popular attitudes towards British military and administrative activity in India.[60] Many in the metropolis were to remain implacably opposed to wars of conquest and annexation on the subcontinent, but whereas India had once been the peripheral domain of a private trading company, it had now became an arena in which power and influence could be exercised in support of important national interests. As such, the defeat of Tipu saw a brief but intense outpouring of metropolitan pride about British success in India.

At the same time, warfare between European powers was becoming ever more global in scope and the British government began to regard India as an important battleground in the broader long-term struggle against France and its allies. Consequently, from the middle of the eighteenth century ever-larger Crown forces were used to bolster the Company's military position on the subcontinent, and they made several timely interventions to preserve its possessions.[61] At the very beginning of the period, for example, naval forces under the command of Vice-Admiral Charles Watson played a key role in Clive's successes in Bengal, while in 1799 a grateful Company awarded £10,000 to Nelson following his victory at the Battle of the Nile which thwarted Napoleon's attempt to use Egypt as a springboard for an invasion of India.[62] The defence of India was thus increasingly to the fore in the minds of ministers, but they also came to regard the Company's own military resources as an important supplement to national strength in the struggles against France, Spain,

---

59 Donna T. Andrew (comp.), *London debating societies, 1776–1799*, London record society publications, vol. XXX (1994), p. 317.
60 P. J. Marshall, '"Cornwallis triumphant": war in India and the British public in the late eighteenth century', in Lawrence Freedman, Paul Hayes, and Robert O'Neill (eds.), *War, strategy, and international politics. Essays in honour of Sir Michael Howard* (Oxford, 1992), pp. 57–74.
61 For the development of the Company–Crown military relationship in India before 1763 see Bruce Lenman, *Britain's colonial wars, 1688–1783* (2001), pp. 83–113.
62 B/129, pp. 55–6.

and the Dutch, and consequently they began to seek the deployment of Company men, ships, and equipment alongside Crown forces in the broader Indian Ocean region.[63]

A mixture of loyalty, self-interest, and political expediency ensured that ministerial appeals for wartime assistance did not fall on deaf ears inside the Company, but preparation for joint military operations was often punctuated by bitter and acrimonious disputes related to the payment of expenses. Nevertheless, although relations between Company officers and royal commanders in the East were usually characterised by ferocious inter-service contests over rank, authority, and the division of spoils,[64] the directors could do little other than declare that they would 'chearfully assist' in executing plans of a 'great national object' such as the conquest and occupation of Manila in the Philippines at the end of the Seven Years War.[65] Hence, during the preliminaries to that ambitious expedition mounted from Madras, they acceded to the King's demands for troops, artillery, transport and hospital ships, engineers, and stores, although their co-operation would undoubtedly have been less forthcoming had they known that it would take them the best part of two decades to recover their expenses.

Even though the Manila expedition of 1762–4 eventually served little strategic purpose and brought no lasting benefit to the Company, it did nevertheless help to establish a blueprint for later military operations combining the use of Crown and Company forces. Hence, after France, Spain, and Holland joined the American war against Britain between 1778 and 1780, ministers and the Company's Secret Committee of directors worked closely together to plan operations in India and further afield. Detailed planning went into proposed expeditions to the 'South Seas' (where the Company hoped to establish a commercial foothold on the islands of Celebes in the Moluccas and Mindanao in the Philippines), the

63 First Lord of the Admiralty Lord Sandwich's concerns about the state of the navy in 1765 prompted him unsuccessfully to advance a plan to increase the Company's marine power in the Indian Ocean by compelling it to use larger heavily armed ships which would 'be a great strength added to the naval force of this Kingdom'. He suggested that his plan would also offer a 'very considerable saving to the publick' because naval squadrons would not have to be sent to the region during future conflicts (Sandwich to George Grenville, 30 April 1765, SAN F/38, no. 1, NMM).

64 For an outline of these disputes see Raymond Callahan, *The East India Company and army reform, 1783–1798* (Cambridge, Mass., 1972), pp. 35–9.

65 Nicholas P. Cushner (ed.), *Documents illustrating the British conquest of Manilla, 1762–3* (1971), p. 15. See also Nicholas Tracy, *Manila ransomed. The British assault on Manila in the Seven Years War* (Exeter, 1995).

Dutch settlements in the Spice Islands, the Atlantic and Pacific coasts of Spanish South America, the Cape, the Seychelles, and Ceylon.[66] The strength of French naval forces in the Indian Ocean region, together with severe setbacks suffered by the Company's armies against the Indian powers of Mysore and the Maratha Confederacy, dictated that these bold plans were only ever partially executed, and indeed some of them never left the drawing board. Nonetheless, discussions of strategic and operational issues became a matter of routine during the last years of the American war, and this reflected awareness amongst ministers and directors that both Company and national interests were under great threat in the East. Serious disputes occurred between the Company and government, especially after 1781 when the Company was obliged to pay for any royal troops despatched to India,[67] but necessity dictated a co-ordinated response to French tactical manoeuvring in Asia. As the 'Chairs' Laurence Sulivan and William James observed in November 1781, 'if the French are suffered to hold possession of the Cape of Good Hope, they will thereby most certainly acquire the means of possessing the territorial revenues in India; and cannot fail to become the controlling European power in that part of the world'.[68] In other words, it was recognised that the lines of defence for British India were now being drawn several thousand miles from the subcontinent itself.

Although peace gradually returned to India, Europe, and the Atlantic world between 1782 and 1784, concerns about the security of the Company's possessions continued to exercise the minds of ministers and directors alike. Indeed, some ministers were now 'taking it for granted that India is the quarter to be first attacked' in any British conflict with a European power,[69] and such fears were heightened when the long struggle

---

66 The detailed planning of these expeditions and attacks on enemy possessions can be traced in detail from the minutes of the Company's Secret Committee, 22 May 1780–26 March 1782, L/P&S/1, vol. 5, passim. For an account of some, but not all, of the operations that did take place see V. T. Harlow, *The founding of the second British empire 1763–93*, 2 vols. (1952 and 1964), vol. I, pp. 104–24. For a recent study providing the general background while also stressing the development of an increasingly integrated commercial, military, and naval strategy in the region see Alan Frost, *The global reach of empire. Britain's maritime expansion in the Indian and Pacific oceans, 1764–1815* (Melbourne, 2003).

67 For details of the serious dispute that occurred in 1787–8 when ministers ordered four regular regiments to India against the Company's wishes see Callahan, *The East India Company and army reform*, pp. 70–103. See also Auber, *Analysis*, pp. 438–47. Thereafter the size of royal forces in India was limited by statute.

68 L/P&S/1/5, book 3, p. 76.

69 Henry Dundas to Lord Sydney, 3 November 1794, quoted in Harlow, *Founding of the second British empire*, vol. II, p. 192.

against Revolutionary and Napoleonic France began in 1793. As a result, considerable attention was devoted to the threats to British India that manifested themselves at the Cape, in Egypt, and elsewhere, and even the faintest hint of enemy shipping movements in the Indian Ocean or eastern Mediterranean served to cause agitated responses in Westminster and Leadenhall Street.

Ministers responded by making considerable use of Company land forces that were larger in size than those of many European states. By 1805 the Company's three Indian armies numbered almost 200,000 men and they were increasingly maintained, via subsidiary alliances, at the expense of Indian rulers such as the Nawab Vizier of Awadh. Although lengthy and determined ministerial attempts to unite this force with the regular army foundered in the face of stiff opposition from the directors and Company officers on the subcontinent,[70] Company troops were used alongside regular army units which themselves eventually numbered around 20,000 soldiers in India. Concerns about cost and uncontrolled expansion ensured that the directors always opposed any 'forward' military policy in India itself, but they were unable to resist ministerial pressure for them to provide support for Crown expeditions elsewhere in the region.[71] As a result, Company troops and ships were sent to Ceylon (1795), Malacca and the Moluccas (1795), the Cape (1795 and 1806), Egypt (1801), Mauritius (1810), and Java (1811). Their contribution to specific campaigns was not always decisive, and the settlement of the costs incurred by the Company during these operations became a fiercely contested political issue.[72] There can be no doubt, however, that the Company's forces played a valuable supporting role in Britain's eventual victory over France, and they certainly enhanced the ability of successive governments to wage war on a worldwide scale.[73]

70 Philips, *East India Company*, pp. 90–1. The highly controversial plans to bring the Company's forces under Crown control brought the Indian army to the verge of mutiny in 1795–6 because officers feared that unification would result in their loss of seniority and special allowances. See Callahan, *The East India Company and army reform*.

71 They were more able to do this after the Company's Indian soldiers were persuaded to volunteer for overseas service, although general confidence in the loyalty of the sepoy army was shaken by the Vellore mutiny of 1806. Cornwallis had first persuaded high-caste sepoy volunteers to overcome their religious reservations about making sea journeys in 1789 when four companies were despatched to serve at Benkulen (Sumatra). For the background to this use of Company sepoys see Seema Alavi, *The sepoys and the Company. Tradition and transition in northern India 1770–1830* (Oxford, 1995), pp. 39–47.

72 For a lengthy parliamentary report which contains full detail of Company claims and expenditure see *PP*, 1805, 197, vol. IV.

73 For an important recent discussion of this subject see Michael Duffy, 'World-wide war and British expansion, 1793–1815', in *OHBE*, vol. II: Marshall (ed.), *The eighteenth century*, pp. 184–207.

At times of war, ministers were also able to draw upon the Company's resources in Britain. As noted earlier, East Indian loan finance had always been important to the state, but it has also been suggested recently that without the accumulated credits arising from transfers of funds from India Britain's attempts to finance war against Napoleonic France would have been significantly weakened. Indeed, it is calculated that without India transfers Britain's foreign borrowing requirement would have grown after 1772 and become unsustainable after 1809.[74] Moreover, the Company also possessed abundant supplies of materials and manpower that were important to any war effort. The Board of Ordnance depended heavily upon the Company's annual imports of saltpetre from Bengal to sustain the production of gunpowder, and the Company's maritime service provided a large reserve force of sailors and officers that could be drawn upon by the navy when it was faced with shortages of men. Indeed, the training and experience of the Company's maritime officers was such that, in the opinion of one commentator, they formed 'a sort of middle link between the Royal Navy and the merchant service'.[75] More obvious to the public, perhaps, was the loyal support offered in 1779 when, following the outbreak of war with France and Spain, the Company provided bounties to men volunteering for sea service, and then paid £95,349 for the construction of three men-of-war.[76] The Company declared self-righteously on this occasion that it was 'a duty on all the subjects of Great Britain but more peculiarly on great commercial societies to make every possible exertion to strengthen this most important and constitutional defence'.[77]

Saltpetre, sailors, and ships were significant additions to the nation's resources, but the state's wartime demands upon the Company in Britain cannot be considered to have been excessive before 1793. There was an

---

74 Javier Cuenca Esteban, 'The balance of payments, 1772–1820: India transfers and war finance', *Ec. Hist. Rev.*, 54 (2001), pp. 58–86.

75 'Cossim', *Considerations on the danger an impolicy of laying open the trade with India and China . . .* (1812), pp. 122–3. For the navy's recruitment of Company seamen see N. A. M. Rodger, *The wooden world. An anatomy of the Georgian navy* (1986), pp. 139–40, 180–1, 269–70. 'Hot presses' of East Indiamen at sea could cause serious problems, about which the Company protested vigorously, and during the American War of Independence violent resistance was offered to naval recruiting parties. (E/1/218, pp. 131–2, 287–8). For the Company's supply of saltpetre to the Board of Ordnance see Jenny West, *Gunpowder, government and war in the mid-eighteenth century* (Woodbridge, 1991), pp. 172, 221.

76 H/338, p. 165.

77 B/95, p. 153 (General Court of 30 June 1779). See also pp. 137–9, 155–7. These measures were first proposed by a group of prominent stockholders headed by General Richard Smith and George Dempster.

abrupt change, however, when war against Revolutionary France combined with domestic political turmoil to impose much greater levels of strain on the home front, and the Company was used to bolster fragile defences during the dark years of the mid-1790s. Fearful of the threat that insurrection posed to its warehouses, the directors formed three regiments of volunteers, and this action was later described by Henry Dundas, the commander-in-chief of these Company forces, as an 'existing monument to the public spirit and beneficial exertions of the East India Company'.[78] By the end of 1796 finance was again the state's greatest need and it is not surprising that ministers turned to the Company for emergency aid. Pitt applied considerable pressure to the directors by pointing out that the Company had much to lose in the 'present important crisis' and he appealed to their commitment to 'the public service'.[79] The directors were in no position to deny the Prime Minister his wish and, although there was some discussion of terms, the Company quickly resolved to make what proved to be by far the single largest contribution to the famous 'Loyalty Loan'. As a result, it pledged £2 million of the £18 million raised through the first direct public subscription undertaken since the end of the seventeenth century.[80]

During these difficult years the resources at the Company's disposal ensured that its contributions to the national war effort extended much further than had been the case in times of earlier European conflict. As far as shipping was concerned, for example, the size of the fleet of East Indiamen enabled one stockholder to suggest that if the Company was to be considered as a naval power, it would have a 'right to rank as the third in Europe',[81] and this thought was no doubt in Dundas's mind in February 1795 as he attempted to combine his role as Minister for War with that of the President of the Board of Control for Indian affairs. He wrote to the directors that 'in the present exigency of affairs, a great and

78 Dundas to Hugh Inglis and David Scott, 17 November 1800, L/P&S/19, box 51.
79 Pitt to the directors, 28 November 1796, B/124, p. 849.
80 John Ehrman, *The younger Pitt: the reluctant transition* (1983), pp. 639–40. Subscribers were given 5 per cent stock offered at £122 10s. for every £100 advanced. The Company had been discussing extending its trading capital by a further £2 million, and thus when Pitt first wrote to the Company about his loan scheme he suggested that such an increase would offer a means of furnishing such a sum to the public (B/262, p. 307). In the event the stockholders only approved the terms of the loan by 214 votes to 211 (ibid., pp. 329–34), and they did not proceed with the extension of capital along the lines suggested. Instead the Company raised a sum of £1,727,122 between 1797 and 1804 in order to meet staged loan payments of £1,835,000 made to government in 1796 and 1797.
81 Speech of Whitshed Keene of 19 January 1813 reported in *Debates at the East India House*, vol. I (1813), p. 70.

immediate addition to the naval strength of the Kingdom is of infinite importance', and he pointed out that 'from their size and construction' East Indiamen 'could be speedily converted into very useful ships of war'.[82] The directors could not ignore this very strong hint and they quickly resolved that the managing owners of their ships be 'exonerated from the engagements they are under to the Company, that they may thereby be enabled to enter into any engagements with Government for public service'.[83] This ensured that ten vessels were made available to the navy and converted into sixty-four-gun warships, and the stockholders then approved Dundas's supplementary suggestion that the Company raise 300 men to serve on board each ship.[84]

Dundas returned to the Company a few months later when the government required a 'very great quantity of tonnage' to be used for a 'special service' in early September. He observed that Indiamen were particularly well suited to the task of transporting troops to the West Indies, and he wished to know whether vessels that had recently returned from Asia could be made available for the operation.[85] The directors responded by identifying fourteen East Indiamen that could be unloaded on the Thames with the 'utmost dispatch' so that the managing owners could agree terms with the government, and this allowed sixteen Company ships of various types to be included in the expeditionary force of 128 vessels that eventually departed for the Leeward Islands in December 1795.[86] Action such as this later enabled the Secretary of the Company, Peter Auber, to write that Company ships were of a 'political as well as a commercial character' which meant that 'on sudden emergencies, both in India and Europe they have been found of the most important aid in promoting the welfare of the state'.[87]

---

82 Dundas to the directors, 8 February 1795, B/120, p. 1044.
83 Ibid., p. 1045. They then moved just as quickly to set out arrangements to prevent them being short of shipping in the coming year (12 February 1795, ibid., p. 1047), but the passage of 35 Geo. III, c.115 was necessary in June 1795 to enable the Company to take up India-built 'proper ships' in order that sufficient tonnage was available for the shipment of cargo from Asia.
84 B/262, pp. 64–9. In October 1794 the General Court had intended to raise 3,000 men to serve in Britain in fencible units during the 'arduous crisis' before using them for 'eventual service in India' (B/262, p. 42). Because of this, Dundas saw 'nothing so natural' that the Company should use these men on the ships given up to the 'service of the state' (B/120, p. 1068).
85 Dundas to the directors, 26 July 1795, discussed at the Court meeting of 29 July, B/121, p. 417.
86 Ibid., pp. 420–1. See Michael Duffy, *Soldiers, sugar, and seapower: the British expeditions to the West Indies and the war against Revolutionary France* (Oxford, 1987), pp. 185–6, 206.
87 Auber, *Analysis*, p. 666. In 1803 the directors chartered 10,000 tons of shipping for six months, at a cost of £67,000, for use by the government (ibid., pp. 665–6). For details of twenty-two ships purchased from the Company between 1795 and 1807 see David Lyon, *The sailing navy list: all the ships of the Royal Navy – built, purchased and captured – 1688–1860* (1993), pp. 239, 241, 270, 274.

Other new and important forms of help for beleaguered Britain were also forthcoming. During acute food shortages that occurred during the summer of 1795 Pitt prevailed upon the Company to arrange for the importation of grain from India.[88] The directors ordered twenty-seven ships to be sent from India with cargoes of grain, and large quantities of rice began to be offered for sale during the second half of 1796.[89] These actions earned the Company warm praise from the City of London's Court of Common Council, which formally thanked the directors 'for the relief afforded to this country'.[90] The Company did not act as a charity, however, and although the directors were always happy to be portrayed as benevolent loyalists, a review of expenditure and income led them to resolve in 1797 that the balance 'must be placed to the debit of the public on whose account the purchase and importation of grain was made'.[91] This type of hardheaded attitude persuaded ministers to be much more robust when they next required the Company to supply grain to Britain during a food crisis. In 1800 Dundas told the Chairmen that the Company's contributions to the war effort weighed 'but as a feather in the scale of public service' compared to the emergency supply of rice to the people of Britain. But, because he felt that the Company was not exerting itself fully, he told the directors that in return for the grant of its monopoly 'the public have a right to expect that on such an occasion as the present the powers and resources which that monopoly have procured to the Company should be brought into exertion with the utmost vigor and promptitude'.[92] Yet although this was a stern reminder that the Company now acted first and foremost in the national interest, the directors continued to look after their own financial concerns.[93] Strong commercial instincts

---

88 See Chairman (Stephen Lushington) to Pitt, 25 June 1795 (L/P&S/1, vol. 9, ff. 190v–1). Lushington himself drafted orders to the Company's Presidencies between 4 and 8 July, but he was very anxious about a 'subject highly delicate and important in its nature' and greatly concerned that it be known in the Company and elsewhere that the idea had originated with ministers (Memorandum of 30 September 1795, ibid., f. 193).

89 On 25 May 1796 it was resolved that 350 tons of rice be sold, and 17,000 bags were put up for sale on 6 July. 20,000 bags were put up on 29 September, and a further 20,000 on 22 December (B/123, pp. 236, 337, 589; B/124, p. 886).

90 B/123, p. 380 (6 July 1796).

91 B/124, p. 1354 (5 April 1797).

92 Dundas to Inglis and Scott, 17 November 1800, L/P&S/19, box 51.

93 The same point can be made about the Company's supply of armaments to the government, and the 162,900 small arms that found their way from the Company to the Board of Ordnance between 1793 and 1815 should be represented as purchases and not requisitions. This is stressed by D. F. Harding, *Small arms of the East India Company 1600–1856*, 4 vols. (1997), vol. I: *Procurement and design*, p. 31. The small arms were mainly muskets. For full discussion and details of Company arms sales to Government see ibid., vol. I. pp. 30–3, 372–3.

ensured that they kept an eye on the balance sheet and they sought financial compensation for most of the Company's contributions to the national war effort. As a result, one of the defining features of the relationship that existed between government and the East India Company during the wars of 1793 to 1815 was the large amount of money that the state eventually paid for armaments, goods, and stores supplied by the Company.[94]

Before 1756 the East India Company had been of considerable importance to the British state because of the role it played in the creation of the national debt, stock market, and system of credit. The overseas activities of the Company had, however, borne quite lightly upon the metropolis and, beyond the routine regulation of trade, ministers had never much concerned themselves with East Indian affairs. This all changed after 1756 as the effects of war and expansion were felt in Britain, and the importance of the Company to the state was greatly enhanced as it was realised that it had taken possession of large wealth in India. The Company was cast in the role of guardian of an important national concern, and India and the East India trade increasingly featured in the strategic calculations of ministers and politicians. And although little wealth derived from India was ever translated directly into a flow of cash into the national Treasury in London, ministers could still utilise the Company's considerably increased resources at home and abroad. The British state was thus able indirectly to draw on the wealth of India to sustain itself during its long struggle with European powers, and contemporaries acknowledged the extent to which this contributed to Britain's long-term success. As Sir John Malcolm reminded the Company's stockholders at the very end of the period, there was no doubt that 'England was in a considerable degree enabled to maintain her present exalted situation amongst the nations of the earth, by possessing that great, that extraordinary [Indian] empire. England . . . had been benefited, assisted, and defended by that empire.'[95]

---

94 The settling of wartime accounts between the Crown and the Company was a complex and lengthy business that was only completed in 1822 (Auber, *Analysis*, pp. 643–4).
95 Speech of 15 April 1833, as reported in *Debates at the General Court*, p. 12.

CHAPTER 3

Relationships: government and the Company

The previous chapter showed how the late eighteenth-century acquisition of an empire in India greatly enhanced the East India Company's importance to the British state and nation. It was widely acknowledged, however, that if Britain was ever fully to benefit from territorial expansion in Asia it was absolutely imperative that the Company be strong, stable, and, above all, well managed. Such institutional qualities had often been evident in the development of the Company in the half-century after 1709, but during the 1760s the initial adjustment to empire proved to be difficult and uncomfortable for those charged with the management of East Indian affairs in Britain. The Company was almost fatally weakened by a series of internal political crises, and this brought sharply into focus the question of whether an independent trading organisation was an appropriate body to administer a valuable territorial empire in India.

This chapter begins by examining institutional failings that were so serious that sustained government attention had to be focused on the Company in Britain as well as India. From 1767 onwards, successive ministerial interventions in Company affairs saw remedies applied to a whole host of domestic ills. These interventions were at first haphazard, and not all of them were successful, but, as is established in the second part of the chapter, they stabilised and regulated the Company, and paved the way for all non-commercial British activities in India to be brought under the supervision of government. This process, which culminated in the creation of a Board of Control in 1784, served to mark out a general path of domestic institutional development for the East India Company as an administrative arm of the imperial state, and it brought into being an entirely new system of home government for British India, the workings of which are set out in the final part of the chapter.

DOMESTIC INSTABILITIES

Historians have long recognised that the acquisition of a territorial empire in India administered a powerful external shock to the East India Company in Britain. The prospect of financial windfalls attracted droves of speculators to East India stock, and a fierce battle for political control of the Company was fought out, firstly by Robert Clive and Laurence Sulivan, and then more broadly by representatives of the ministry and parliamentary opposition who recognised the importance of establishing their own influence at East India House.[1] These factors combined to effect a marked and very rapid change in the defining institutional characteristics of the Company during the 1760s, and this is no better illustrated than by the movements that occurred in the price and turnover of East India stock.

In the years between the South Sea Bubble of 1720 and 1760, a steady commercial performance saw speculators expressing only a limited interest in the Company, and consequently East India stock was quite stable. This is illustrated by figure 3.1, which shows that the price of £100 stock fell in a range between 120 and 200, and by figure 3.2, which indicates that the number of transfers each year usually stood below 1,500. Major movements in the stock prices were determined primarily by general market conditions in London, and Company stock prices moved broadly in line with those of Bank of England stock, as was the case in 1754–5, for example, when the threat of war with France badly dented investor confidence.[2] The arrival of good or bad news from India exercised surprisingly little effect upon prices or rates of stock transfer,[3] but things

---

1 Dame Lucy Sutherland provided the definitive account of the origins and course of the Clive–Sulivan power struggle (Sutherland, *East India Company*, chs. 4 and 5). See also B. Lenman and P. Lawson, 'Clive, the "Black jagir" and British politics', *Historical Journal*, 26 (1983), pp. 801–29. For an excellent analysis of all aspects of the Company's crisis see Thompson Shearer, 'Crisis and change in the development of the East India Company's affairs, 1760–1773', unpublished DPhil thesis, University of Oxford (1976).

2 For movements of East India Company, Bank of England, and South Sea Company stock prices, and analysis of the factors that influenced them, see Larry Neal, *The rise of financial capitalism. International capital markets in the Age of Reason* (Cambridge, 1990), pp. 118–40, 231–57, and P. E. Mirowski, 'The rise (and retreat) of a market: English joint-stock shares in the eighteenth century', *Journal of Economic History*, 41 (1981), pp. 559–77.

3 The loss and subsequent recapture of Calcutta in 1756 and 1757 caused little movement in or out of Company stock, and the price was barely affected. In part, this was because when news of the loss of Calcutta arrived in London on 4 June 1757 the price of India stock was already very low (143½) and investor confidence had been bruised by the war in Europe, which was then going badly for Britain. As a result the price did not slip below 130 during the rest of June (L/AG/14/7,

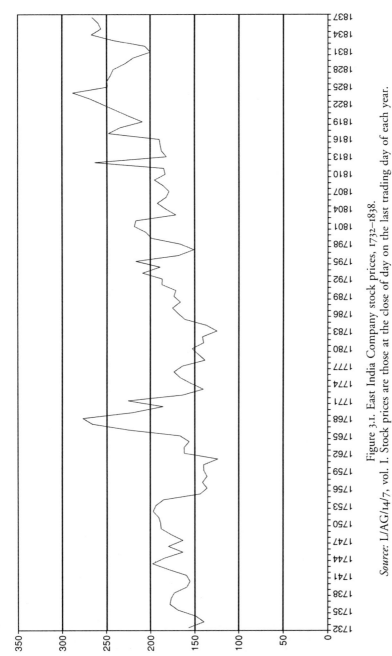

Figure 3.1. East India Company stock prices, 1732–1838.

Source: L/AG/14/7, vol. I. Stock prices are those at the close of day on the last trading day of each year.

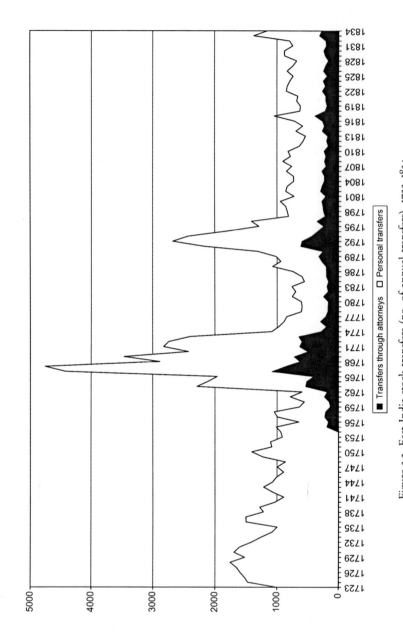

Figure 3.2. East India stock transfers (no. of annual transfers), 1723–1834.

Source: Dickson, *Financial revolution*, pp. 530–1 (for 1723–54); L/AG/14/5, vols. 77–153 (transfer ledgers), and L/AG/14/5, vols. 184–235 (transfer through attorney ledgers) for 1755–1834.

Note: Dickson did not distinguish between personal transfers and transfers through attorneys.

■ Transfers through attorneys □ Personal transfers

were very different after 1760 when the Company's territorial advances had a positive effect upon investor confidence and the financial markets as a whole. As the political economist Thomas Mortimer put it in during the early 1770s, 'The return of great wealth, derived from our Asiatic commerce and territorial jurisdiction . . . [is one of] the chief events which may make the funds rise above five per cent from the concourse of purchasers, who will find no other channels open for employing their money to equal advantage.'[4]

The Company's military successes of the 1760s fuelled the widespread belief among speculators that East India stockholders would be rewarded with increased dividends, and one pamphleteer later recalled that 'When the first news arrived of our acquisitions in Bengal, so sudden an encrease [*sic*] of wealth naturally drew the attention of every enterprizing man, who, having little to lose, thought his entanglements could not possibly be too large in a stock where there appeared a certainty of gaining much.'[5] Those with an ear close to the ground were aware that Clive (who had greatly exaggerated the size of the Company's financial windfall in India) had told his friends in Britain that an investment in Company stock was well advised, and they knew that Clive's attorneys had already begun to scour the London money market for funds with which to purchase stock on his behalf.[6] One of the attorneys, John Walsh, later told a committee of the House of Commons that 'he did not make any secret of the opinion he entertained at that time of India stock, but spoke of it to many persons as a very beneficial thing, some of whom, as he understood, bought in consequence'.[7] As a result, there was a marked increase in the trading of India stock, and prices rose sharply from 165 in January 1766 to 214 in July, prompting an early report that 'More money was made on the buying and selling of India stock following the late good news from Lord Clive than at any time during

vol. I). The general state of the war also perhaps explains why the remarkably low-key announcement that Clive had driven Siraj-ud-daula from Calcutta caused only a partial recovery in the price to 141 by the end of September.

4 Thomas Mortimer, *The elements of commerce, politics, and finance in three treatises on those important subjects* (1780, reprinted from the 1772 edition), p. 409.

5 Anon., *A letter to the proprietors of East India stock, containing a brief relation of the negotiations with government from the year 1767 to the present time respecting the Company's acquisitions in India* (1769), p. 1.

6 For a detailed study of Clive's extensive speculative activities (which he later denied in the House of Commons) see H. V. Bowen, 'Lord Clive and speculation in East India Company stock, 1766', *Historical Journal*, 30 (1987), pp. 905–20.

7 *Third report of the select committee* (1773), *Reports from committees of the House of Commons, 1715–1801*, 15 vols. (1803), vol. III, p. 314.

the late war.'[8] The total nominal value of the stock traded in 1766 was over £4 million, almost three times the amount the previous year (see figure 3.3).

This frenetic activity suggested to some onlookers that the market might be heading towards 'another South Sea Year',[9] but in the short term these fears proved to be unfounded and East India stock continued to hold the attention of speculators. When a crash did eventually occur in 1769, following the circulation of rumours about the Company's loss of Madras to the army of Haidar Ali, many overextended investors had their fingers badly burned as the price of stock fell from 274 at the end of April to 230 a month later. An observer noted that 'the late fall of stock may have introduced a pause amidst the delirium of prosperity',[10] but in fact there was more than a pause and it was many years before confidence in the Company was fully restored. Indeed, although speculators beat a hasty retreat from East India stock, the damage had been done. The payment of unjustifiably high dividends, which rose to 12½ per cent at Christmas 1770, contributed to the financial storm that broke over the Company in 1772, and this caused further downward pressure on the price of stock and pushed it below 150 in April 1773.

Speculative activity was partly responsible for the sharp increase in the number of stock transfers that is evident in figure 3.2, but the use of stock for political purposes also contributed to higher levels of trading. The factions led by Clive, Sulivan, and others left no stone unturned in their search for support among the stockholders, and, in addition to well-organised canvassing campaigns, they vigorously encouraged their friends and associates outside the Company to purchase the £500 stock that was necessary to qualify for a vote at the General Court. Rather more unscrupulously, they also used short-term stock transfers to divide existing large holdings into multiple votes for distribution to their supporters,[11] and they bought up stock to be 'split' into £500 voting units. After these votes were cast at ballots or the annual election of directors held every April, stock was then sold or returned to the original owner. As a result, 'splitting' became an important word in the East Indian lexicon, and a large number of individuals were drawn into the elaborate vote-creation

---

8 *Lloyd's Evening Post*, 28 April 1766. The short-term effect upon other prices was limited, and Bank stock hovered around 135 before moving upwards at the beginning of 1767.

9 Scrafton to Clive, 6 May 1766, Clive MSS, 52, p. 157, NLW.

10 Anon., *An address to the proprietors of India stock* (1769), p. 9.

11 For Laurence Sulivan's description of the way such transactions were conducted between individuals see Sutherland, *East India Company*, p. 103.

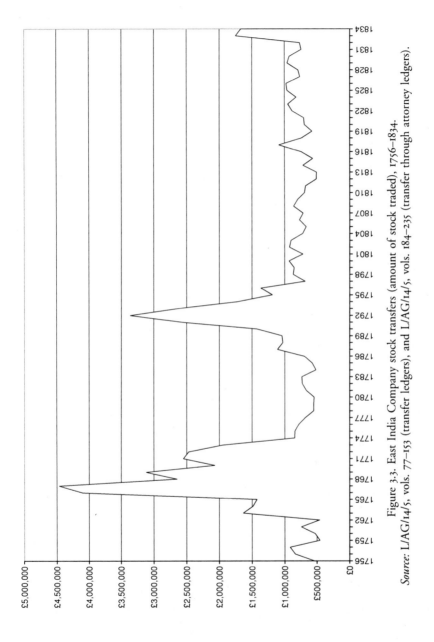

Figure 3.3. East India Company stock transfers (amount of stock traded), 1756–1834.
Source: L/AG/14/5, vols. 77–153 (transfer ledgers), and L/AG/14/5, vols. 184–235 (transfer through attorney ledgers).

process as the providers, distributors, or receivers of votes. There is evidence that 'splitting' had occurred on a small scale during the first half of the century,[12] but the practice became widespread and routine during the 1760s, despite the fact that a Company by-law of 1709 had outlawed the procuring of votes by 'indirect means' such as 'menaces, threats, promises, or the collusive transfer of stock'. Indeed, the rapid mobilisation of voting strength became so efficient during the 1760s that one veteran stockholder later recalled that 'by the system of transferring stock, 250 persons could be brought into that Court at a few hours notice, ready to support any measures that their friends proposed'.[13]

As figure 3.2 indicates, stock-splitting campaigns caused East India stock transfer activity to increase sharply at the beginning of the 1760s – well before the Company acquired control over the Bengal revenues – with 2,287 transfers being recorded in 1763 and 2,116 the following year. Thus although the attraction of profit-hungry speculators to East India stock undoubtedly fuelled the considerable transfer activity that was evident in 1766, 1767, and 1769, there can be no doubt that 'splitting' played a very important part in causing substantial movements of investors in and out of stock. In 1763, for example, almost half of the year's transfers occurred in the months of February and March as stock was split prior to the April election (see figure 3.4), and 859 (82 per cent) of these 1,048 transactions involved transfers of the minimum voting qualification of £500.[14]

The volatile mixture of factional politics and financial speculation had a considerable effect upon stockholder participation in Company affairs during the 1760s. The change was most obvious on the day of the annual election when large numbers of stockholders trooped into East India House to cast votes for their favoured candidates. On the whole, Company elections before 1760 had generated little interest from stockholders and during the ballots of the 1740s and 1750s only a couple of hundred proprietors had ever cast votes.[15] This changed dramatically, however, during the early 1760s (see figure 3.5).

---

12 Ibid., pp. 34–5.
13 Whitshed Keene, speech reported in *Debate at the East India House . . . 25 February 1814* (1814), p. 86.
14 Trading of stock was less heavy after the election but, even so, 646 transfers were made during April and May, and 499 of these involved £500 as stock was sold or returned to its original owner.
15 For the challenges offered to the incumbent directors during the early and mid-1730s and in 1749–50 see Sutherland, *East India Company*, pp. 39–41.

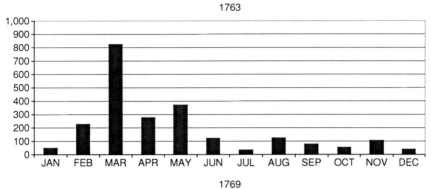

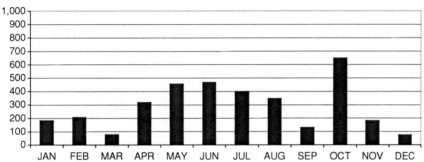

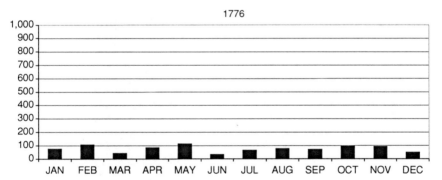

Figure 3.4. East India Company stock transfers 1763, 1769, and 1776.
Source: L/AG/14/5 vols. 81–3, 94–5, 103–4, 106, 186–7, 194–5, 199–200.

In 1762 a mere 176 votes were returned for the leading candidate, but the following year there was a spectacular seven-fold increase to 1,239, a figure that comfortably surpassed the record of 1,071 votes that had stood since 1711. In 1764 and 1765 1,174 and 1,253 votes were recorded as the

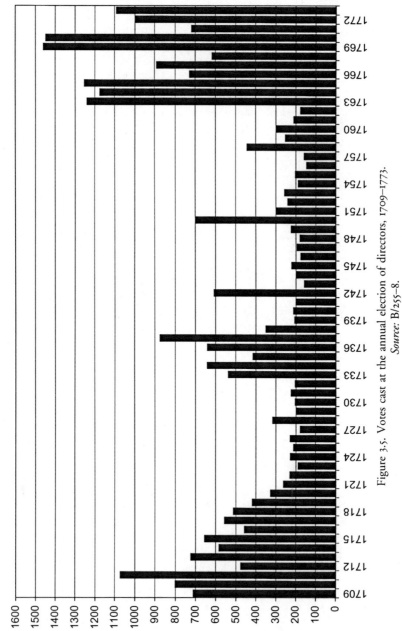

Figure 3.5. Votes cast at the annual election of directors, 1709–1773.

Source: B/255–8.

Note: The figures refer to the number of votes for the leading candidate, which is not necessarily the same as the total number of electors, although this was the case in uncontested elections.

mass mobilisation of stockholders continued and, although there was then a decline in numbers, a new peak was reached in 1769 when a particularly fierce election campaign resulted in 1,459 votes being cast for the leading candidate. Voting on this scale meant that a far greater proportion of the stockholding community was actively engaging in the electoral process and, although it is not possible to offer a figure for each year, it can be calculated that while only around 16 per cent of eligible stockholders cast a vote in the annual election in 1760, the proportion increased to 45 per cent in 1773.[16] During the hotly contested elections that took place in the intervening years the percentage figure must have been even higher.

Beyond the fierce electioneering and splitting that stimulated voting activity, there are several other indicators suggesting that the nature of Company politics changed during the 1760s. The number of General Courts rose sharply as stockholders more frequently exercised their right to convene meetings devoted to 'special affairs'.[17] Before 1760, the General Court rarely met on more than the statutory minimum of five occasions a year (as represented by four Quarterly Courts and the annual election), and when stockholders did gather they seldom bothered to hold the directors to account or subject them to searching scrutiny. Satisfied with the Company's commercial performance, which was reflected in a steady rate of dividend, the few who did attend the routine quarterly meetings did so only briefly and then only to observe a few formalities. At the Court of 28 September 1749, for example, the Chairman told the Court that the annual account had been prepared and 'the [cash] balance was ready to be laid before them if called for', but with 'the same not being required' the Court was promptly adjourned.[18] During the 1760s, however, stockholders often attended meetings in their several hundreds and the severe overcrowding of the Court Room at East India House was such that almost half of the Courts held during the mid- and

---

16 The calculations are based upon the votes cast for the leading candidates (298 in 1760 and 1,089 in 1773) and details of eligible voters recorded in printed lists of stockholders produced shortly before the election (1,849 in 1760 and 2,437 in 1773) (*A list of the names of the members of the United Company of Merchants of England, trading to the East Indies, the 26th of March 1760* (1760); *A list of the names of all the proprietors of East India stock . . .* (1773). The second list was compiled on 9 March 1773.

17 A Court of 'special affairs' could be requested by nine stockholders giving notice to that effect. For a study of the organisation and procedure of the General Court see H. V. Bowen, 'The "little parliament": the General Court of the East India Company, 1750–1784', *Historical Journal*, 34 (1991), pp. 857–72.

18 B/70, p. 119.

late 1760s were moved to the nearby Merchant Taylors' Hall where large gatherings could be accommodated in a greater degree of comfort.[19] Moreover, the stockholders met much more frequently (see figure 3.6), as the political climate changed in East India House and the Company then became engulfed by crisis during the early 1770s. Not even during later crises, such as in 1783–4 or 1812–13, did meetings of the General Court occur as regularly as in 1773. In that year the stockholders gathered on forty-six occasions, mainly because they were trying to frustrate Lord North's attempts to impose a regulatory settlement upon the Company.

A greater level of stockholder involvement in Company politics was also reflected in the frequency of ballots held at the General Court and in the substantial number of stockholders who cast a vote on those occasions. Formal ballots had been very few and far between during the first half of the century, with decisions usually being ratified by the stockholders on a show of hands or division of the Court. However, the rancour and discord of the 1760s caused disaffected stockholders to force decisions to a formal vote on a regular basis. This allowed them time to mobilise support before ballots which, according to Company practice, took place a few days after the motion was first made. Thus, while only seven ballots had taken place in the General Court in the fifty years before 1766, there were forty-five such occasions during the following seven years. At the same time, important ballots created high levels of involvement from within the stockholding community and great interest was taken in those likely to embarrass the directors, overturn Company policy, or reinstate disgraced servants who had been dismissed from the overseas service. An average of 277 stockholders participated in the 45 ballots held between 1766 and 1773, but the highest figure recorded was 893 in April 1767 when the Court was asked to decide between alternative proposals for a settlement with government that had been put forward by the directors and Laurence Sulivan. Horace Walpole commented on the importance of these ballots in 1769 when he wrote from the West End of London that 'People trudge to the

---

19 Between March 1764 and the end of 1769, thirty-nine of the eighty-six Courts met at Merchant Taylors' Hall, with the venue last being used for the election of April 1770. It is not possible to be precise about attendance levels at the Court because no register was kept, and the minutes often only refer vaguely to a 'large appearance of the generalty'. It seems reasonable to assume, however, that, as with the period 1784–1834, 200–300 stockholders attended routine Courts, with double that number or more present on important occasions (Philips, *East India Company*, p. 3).

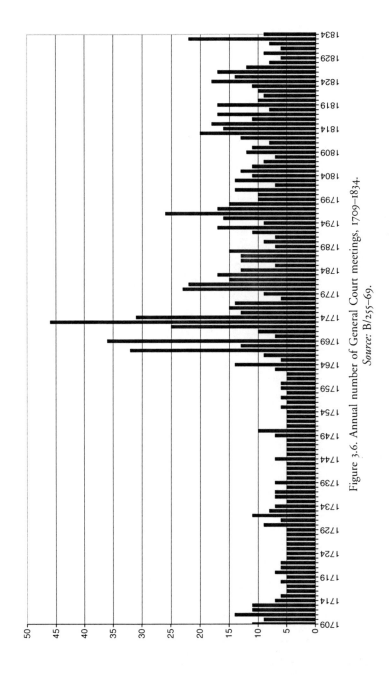

Figure 3.6. Annual number of General Court meetings, 1709–1834.
Source: B/255–69.

other end of town to vote who shall govern empires at the other end of [the] world.'[20] In the forty years after 1773, however, the average annual number of ballots at the General Court fell to only 2.5, thereby reflecting a general reduction in the political temperature at East India House.[21]

Finally, the fiercely contested nature of Company politics after 1760 ensured that General Court meetings sometimes became tumultuous, and debates became greatly extended by procedural wrangling and the sharp practice of those who had honed their techniques and tactics in the House of Commons and elsewhere.[22] Although the standard of debate was often high, there was sometimes a volatile atmosphere in the Court. Great tension could swiftly be translated into considerable uproar and confusion as factions heckled and abused their opponents, as was the case in 1767 when one first-time visitor to East India House came away with the impression that the Court was the 'most riotous assembly I ever saw'.[23] There were also plenty of would-be orators who liked the sound of their own voices, and their lengthy rambling speeches meant that debates sometimes lasted well into the night and then had to be adjourned. Indeed, on some occasions the proceedings were extended over several days, thereby greatly slowing down the decision-making process. For many, this was tiresome and deeply frustrating, not least because the Company itself seemed to lack the will necessary to put its own legislative chamber in order. Laurence Sulivan was not alone when in 1767 he placed the blame for many of the Company's growing troubles fairly and squarely upon the stockholders' assembly, remarking that 'General Courts as they have been, and may be, are the springs of all our mischiefs.'[24] As the Secretary to the Treasury John Robinson put it a decade later, *after* initial attempts had been made to reform the General Court, 'nothing can be more absurd and preposterous than the present system: the government of several Asiatic provinces at six thousand miles distance is ultimately in the hands of the Court of Proprietors; the most democratic body that ever existed; who not only make laws for

---

20 Walpole to Sir Horace Mann, 19 July 1769, W. S. Lewis (ed.), *The Yale edition of Horace Walpole's Correspondence*, 48 vols. (Oxford, 1939–84), vol. XXIII, p. 133.
21 Ballots were held on 101 occasions between 1774 and 1813, with 39 votes being related to overseas appointments.
22 Bowen 'The "little parliament"', pp. 868–9.
23 B. Cozens-Hardy (ed.), *The diary of Sylas Neville, 1767–1788* (1950), p. 7.
24 Quoted in Bowen 'The "little parliament"', p. 868.

the government of them, but interpose in the execution of these laws whenever they think proper'.[25]

The political standpoints and perspectives of Sulivan and Robinson were quite different, but both men identified 'democracy' or stockholder participation in decision-making as being the Achilles' heel of the Company in Britain and, as many other observers noted, one consequence of this was that the directors' authority and control of the Company were far weaker than had hitherto been the case. In earlier years, the grip of the directors on Company affairs had been so firm and unyielding that they had enjoyed almost complete freedom of action in the realm of decision-making,[26] but as a consequence of the struggle for control of East India House, a long and debilitating war of attrition was fought out between the stockholders and the directors. The remaking of alliances and fluctuating electoral fortunes meant that the personnel on each side often changed from year to year, but throughout the 1760s and early 1770s there was often open conflict between the 'ins' and the 'outs'. Thus in 1773, when the *Annual Register* reflected on the events of the last few years, it remarked that 'The directors and a strong body of proprietors were in a continual state of hostility'; and by the time Adam Smith came to write *Wealth of nations* he was able to state that the stockholders were gaining the upper hand, with the directors now 'necessarily more or less under the influence of the proprietors'.[27]

The principal managerial consequence of the fiercely competitive nature of East India politics during the 1760s was that substantial changes of personnel occurred each year within the Court of Directors. In earlier decades the incumbent directors had simply presented a 'House list' of candidates to the stockholders for approval. Most elections had been uncontested, and this had established great continuity of personnel within the Directorate, with changes usually occurring only when directors died or, as a Company by-law of 1734 dictated, they were obliged to stand down for twelve months after four successive years in office. Even then, a new practice known as 'going out by rotation' had ensured that those

25 John Robinson, 'Considerations on East India affairs' (1778), reprinted in P. J. Marshall, *Problems of empire*, p. 118.

26 K. N. Chaudhuri, 'The English East India Company and its decision-making', in K. Ballhatchet and J. Harrison (eds.), *East India Company studies: papers presented to Professor Sir Cyril Philips* (Hong Kong, 1986), p. 100.

27 *Annual Register* (1773), p. 66*; Adam Smith, *An inquiry into the nature and causes of the wealth of nations* (1776), ed. R. H. Campbell, A. S. Skinner, and W. B. Todd, 2 vols. (Oxford, 1976), vol. II, p. 752.

standing down from the Court of Directors were readmitted after only a year's absence. This enabled directors to concentrate their undivided attention on the routine management of trade and shipping, and they were able carry forward strategies and policies from year to year.

During the 1760s, however, the violent ebb and flow of political fortunes within the Company was such that the outcomes of the election often meant that significant numbers of directors were voted out of office each year. Indeed, after particularly hard-fought elections, the casualty rates were high, and sometimes only around half of the twenty-four new directors had been in office the previous year. This was damaging in a number of different ways, but in particular it caused disruption to the membership of the subcommittees that formulated policy for different aspects of the Company's affairs. In 1754 half of the twenty-four directors had sat in the Court for more than a decade in total, but by 1765 only three directors had served for such a period of time and this meant that the fund of experience and knowledge was greatly diminished at a crucial time in the Company's history.[28] One writer lamented that the Company was now 'inhabited by momentary proprietors and governors, divided by different interests opposed to each other',[29] and some suggested that by the end of the 1760s an all-consuming preoccupation with the annual election was threatening to become fatal. Clive, who was frustrated by his inability to impose his will upon the directors, had become deeply critical of the management of the Company and went as far as to suggest that 'The East Indies also I think cannot remain long to us if our present constitution be not altered. A direction for a year only and that time entirely taken up in securing directors for the year to come cannot long maintain that authority which is requisite for the managing such extensive, populous, rich and powerful kingdoms as the East India Company are possessed of.'[30] Ministers could not afford to run such a risk, and consequently they were drawn into the ever-closer regulation of the Company's domestic affairs. Indeed, as Charles Grant, who was to become an influential Chairman, later remarked, it was only when 'internal dissensions' occurred within the Company that the government was given the 'first handle' to intervene in East Indian affairs.[31]

28 J. G. Parker, 'The directors of the East India Company, 1754–1790', unpublished PhD thesis, University of Edinburgh (1977), p. 333.
29 *London Magazine*, vol. XLI (1772), p. 275.
30 Clive to Claud Russell, 10 February 1769, Clive MSS, 61 (no foliation), NLW.
31 Charles Grant, writing in 1795, quoted in Ainslie Thomas Embree, *Charles Grant and British rule in India* (1962), p. 134.

GOVERNANCE, REFORM, AND CONTROL

Whatever ministers might think about the legal right to possession of territory in India, practical realities determined that before the 1820s no government ever wished the Crown to assume direct responsibility for the administration of British India. Ministers were, however, impelled to adopt an increasingly interventionist stance towards the Company because they could not afford to ignore the potentially disastrous combination of misconduct abroad and institutional instability at home. Thus although attempts were made to improve the administration of British India, an equal if not greater amount of attention was devoted to tackling the Company's domestic problems. Between 1767 and 1784 successive political interventions resulted in reform, followed by regulation, and then finally the establishment of metropolitan control over the Company.[32] In part, this creeping process represented part of a broader move towards a tighter regulation of the empire during the late eighteenth century, but it was also a specific acknowledgement that the future of the Company, and therefore an important British interest, was threatened by mismanagement at home as well as abroad. Much closer routine supervision over East Indian affairs was required, and ministers recognised that legislative action was necessary in order to bring the full weight of the law and parliamentary authority to bear upon the Company in Britain.

It is possible to discern several lines of ministerial intervention in the Company's domestic affairs, which came together in 1784 to effect a substantial recasting of way in which the Company operated as an organisation. During the 1760s, the urgent priority of ministers was to stabilise the Company by correcting the very obvious weaknesses that were evident within the internal electoral and decision-making machinery. Only six of the original thirty-one by-laws of the United Company related to the General Court or the Company's own regulatory framework. In 1765 and 1766 the directors failed narrowly in attempts to secure a statutory prohibition of stock-splitting, and it was not until the

---

32 For detailed accounts of the first parliamentary inquiry of 1767 see Bowen, *Revenue and reform*, pp. 48–66; Philip Lawson, 'Parliament and the first East India inquiry, 1767', *Parliamentary history*, vol. I (1982), pp. 99–114; Sutherland, *East India Company*, pp. 138–76. The genesis and passage of the Regulating Act of 1773 is discussed in Bowen, *Revenue and reform*, pp. 133–86 and Sutherland, *East India Company*, pp. 213–90. For the India Act of 1784 see Sutherland, *East India Company*, pp. 365–414. Subsequent modifications to Pitt's Act are described in Philips, *East India Company*.

following year that legislation (7 Geo. III, c.49) was enacted to regulate the proceedings of the General Court and the conduct of ballots. At the same time, another Act (7 Geo. III, c.48) regulated voting qualifications in all joint-stock companies in an effort to prevent the collusive transfer of stock for electoral purposes. It was stipulated that stockholders now had to be in possession of £500 stock for six months before they were deemed qualified to vote in ballots or elections. In practice, however, this measure proved to be ineffective because the well-organised factions were well able to 'split' holdings six months before the annual election in April, and, as can been seen in figure 3.4, considerable movements of stock now occurred every September and October as votes were distributed to allies. Consequently, the Act did not serve much to diminish the number of votes artificially created before each election although, as was evident in 1769, it did serve to increase the risks involved for those who borrowed heavily to fund large-scale splitting operations.[33]

It was clear that more systematic and far-reaching reform was required, and this followed in 1773 when Lord North used the opportunity presented by the passage of the Regulating Act to reform the Company's flawed electoral system. To ensure greater levels of continuity within the executive, the annual election of all twenty-four directors was replaced by a new system in which only a quarter of the directorate was replaced each year, and further changes were made to the voting qualifications of stockholders in a final attempt to eliminate 'splitting'. A proportional voting system was introduced to replace the existing arrangement, and from October 1773 onwards only proprietors who had owned £1,000 stock for twelve months were deemed eligible for a single vote. In addition, however, possession of £3,000 stock gave the owner two votes; £6,000 stock brought three votes; and £10,000 stock carried four votes. Amidst much controversy, the disenfranchisement of the £500 proprietors served to strengthen the political position of the larger stockholders by removing any influence that could be exerted by ordinary small investors or temporary 'split' voters. In March 1773 owners of £500 stock held 1,350 or 55.4 per cent of the votes that could be cast at the General Court,[34] but a year later they were not entitled to cast any votes at all. More power and influence were concentrated in fewer hands and thus, while 2,437 stockholders were entitled to vote at the General Court in

---

33 Sutherland, *East India Company*, pp. 188–93.
34 Calculated from *A list of the names . . .* (1773).

March 1773, the number had fallen to 1,810 by April 1795, although under the proportional qualification system they were able to cast 2,434 votes.[35] This important change removed the threat to political stability posed by the artificial creation of large numbers of temporary stockholders and, as figure 3.4 illustrates for 1776, stock-splitting immediately became a thing of a past. At the same time, North's reforms shook members of the Company out of their near-obsessive preoccupation with the annual election, even though important business could still occasionally be suspended because the directors were heavily engaged in electioneering activity. This was the case in 1808, for example, when the President of the Board of Control, Robert Dundas, failed to get the directors to consider his plans for the reform of recruitment to the Company's army.[36]

A second line of ministerial intervention was gradually established after the mid-1760s as ministers took advantage of the opportunities presented by parliamentary inquiries and negotiations with the directors to regulate the Company's domestic financial and commercial affairs. With the Indian empire increasingly acknowledged to be an important economic asset, ministers could ill-afford to allow the Company's new riches to be squandered. Thus, statutory restrictions were imposed upon the amount of dividend payable to stockholders in order to prevent speculators combining in the General Court to force through increases, as had been the case in 1766.[37] More broadly, the directors were required to pass detailed accounts to Parliament and the Treasury on a regular basis, and steps were taken to regulate the development of the Company's trade. Any interference from outside East India House always provoked an outcry from stockholders who were extremely sensitive to encroachment on their chartered rights, but in the wake of successive financial crises the Company was forced to submit to statutory regulation of its export trade, shipping, and bond debt.[38] Day-to-day management of the Company's business affairs remained in the hands of the directors, but they found their performance was increasingly scrutinised by ministers and

---

35 In April 1795 the distribution of stockholders across the different categories of qualification was as follows: one vote (1,379), two votes (293), three votes (83), four votes (55). See *A list of the names of the members of the United Company of Merchants of England, trading to the East Indies, who appear qualified to vote at their General Courts . . .* (1795).

36 Robert Dundas to Lord Minto, 30 April 1808, MS 1063, f. 16, NLS.

37 For dividends see 7 Geo. III, c.49; 8 Geo. III, c.11; for shipping see 12 Geo. III, c.54.

38 The Regulating Act of 1773 stated, for example, that the Company should annually export manufactured goods to the value of £287,000.

Parliament. From 1773 half-yearly Company financial statements were submitted to the Treasury, and from 1788 an annual 'East India' budget was presented to the House of Commons. Moreover, by the 1780s the Board of Trade was exerting a much greater influence than ever before upon the making of commercial policy for Asia, and it was paying particular attention to ways in which exports of British manufactures might be increased.[39]

A third and rather different line of intervention in the Company's domestic affairs was established as ministers began closely to monitor the Company's conduct of its external relations in India. The involvement of Crown and Company troops in mid-century wars against French forces in South Asia had established a need for ministers to keep an eye on the region and this ensured that the military and diplomatic affairs of the Company were increasingly brought before the Secretary of State for the South. When the Seven Years War ended in 1763, ministers continued to keep a vigilant watch on any signs of French attempts to recover their greatly weakened position in Bengal, and they were swift to intervene when alerted about possible dangers. In the light of events since 1756, they also began to address the problem of whether a private trading company should still be permitted to wage war and make peace with sovereign powers in India. This was a matter of some importance because ministers feared that Crown forces might be dragged into un-welcome and expensive future conflicts in support of the Company, and also because in the treaty that accompanied the Peace of Paris of 1763 George III formally acknowledged the title and authority of several Indian rulers. In such circumstances, it was held that the Company could not now be granted an entirely free hand to conduct British foreign relations in Asia, and thus, in an important and highly controversial development, a Crown Plenipotentiary was appointed in 1769 to act as the diplomatic 'voice' of the ministry in the Indian Ocean region.[40]

By the end of the 1760s British political and diplomatic affairs in Asia were still considered to be marginal in the broader scheme of things, but they were being afforded a much greater degree of ministerial attention than had hitherto been the case. As a result, ministers and officials in London required access to information about Company affairs in India

---

39 For the actions of the Board of Trade during the 1780s and 1790s see V. T. Harlow, *The founding of the second British empire 1763–93*, 2 vols. (1952 and 1964), vol. II, pp. 497–527. See also below, pp. 228–31.

40 Bowen, *Revenue and reform*, pp. 67–83.

on a regular basis, and attempts were made to increase the flow of intelligence between East India House and Whitehall. Such a flow had occurred somewhat haphazardly during the Seven Years War,[41] but arrangements were codified by parliamentary statute and, in theory if not always in practice, the government was drawn into the formal monitoring of the Company's overseas affairs. The Regulating Act stipulated that incoming despatches from India were to be scrutinised by ministers and, although an Act of 1781 stipulated that only outgoing Company instructions about relations with Indian states should be sent to ministers for scrutiny, clauses related to financial matters soon began to be submitted to the Treasury for approval.[42] As was the way with eighteenth-century government, however, logic only very slowly dictated that dedicated bureaucratic apparatus be established for the monitoring of the Company in London. It was not until 1784 that such apparatus came into being when Pitt's India Act saw the establishment of a Board of Commissioners granted power 'from time to time, to superintend, direct, and controul, all acts, operations, and concerns, which in any wise relate to the civil or military government or revenues of the British territorial possessions in the East Indies'.[43] The establishment of the Board should not be seen therefore as representing a sharp break with the recent past; rather it marked the culmination of a long-run process by which ministers had endeavoured to extend gradually the reach of the state over the Company.

By the mid-1780s, successive ministries had intervened to regulate the Company and restore stability to its domestic political affairs. Some contemporaries were scathing in their criticisms of Lord North's reforms,[44] but in the long run the measures embodied in the Regulating Act did largely achieve their objectives as far as the Company's internal affairs were concerned. In particular, they brought an end to stock-splitting and because it was now impossible to manipulate short-term stock ownership for political purposes there were far fewer violent movements of investors into and out of the Company. The overall effect of this is not entirely clear from figures 3.2 and 3.3 because additions to the

---

41 See below, pp. 163–4.   42 See, for example, B/97, p. 314.
43 24 Geo.III, c.25, vi. By the Charter Act of 1793, this clause was amended to give the Board 'full power and authority' (33 Geo. III, c.52, ix).
44 See the famous comments of Edmund Burke, author of the *Ninth Report from the Select Committee, appointed to take into consideration the state of the administration of justice in the provinces of Bengal, Bihar, and Orissa* (1783), reprinted in *The writings and speeches of Edmund Burke*, vol. V; P. J. Marshall (ed.), *India: Madras and Bengal* (Oxford, 1981), pp. 198–220.

Company's capital between 1786 and 1793 serve to cloud the picture, but the annual turnover of stock had certainly decreased significantly by the early years of the nineteenth century. This reflected the fact that India stock was no longer being traded for political reasons, and consequently a much greater degree of stability returned to the community of East India stockholders. The annual transfers of stock fell below 600 for the first time ever in 1812 and thereafter, although a burst of trading activity accompanied the loss of the Company's last commercial privileges in 1833–4, the number was usually between 600 and 900, and the amount of stock traded was less than £1 million. This was a far cry from the high-volume trading years of the 1760s and early 1770s.

North was also successful in his attempt to re-establish continuity to the leadership of the Company. Although no government was ever able fully to manipulate the Company's electoral process to its own advantage in the way that North had hoped, the reforms of 1773 did reduce greatly the severe disruption to the Court of Directors that had bedevilled the Company during the early 1760s and 1770s.[45] With only six directors now standing down each year, the Directorate again became something of a closed body and, backed by the ministry, the incumbent directors were usually able to secure the return of their 'House list' of candidates. In practice, the vacancies within the Court only occurred when a director died in office or was disqualified, and it thus became almost impossible for outsiders or independent stockholders to force their way into the Court of Directors. To all intents and purposes the Directorate became a 'permanent body',[46] and reference was often made to there being thirty members of the Court: the twenty-four incumbent directors and the six men who were out 'by rotation' at any one time. Directors once more enjoyed long periods of service broken only by the need to step down every four years, and the Court was able to draw upon its members' accumulated wealth of experience of the Company's affairs. As was noted of the key Committee of Correspondence in 1814, 'The present junior member has been eleven years in the Direction.'[47] Of course, the length of service of the directors did not by itself mean that East Indian affairs were necessarily being well managed, but the ending of wholesale annual

45 For the organisational effort undertaken by the ministry to 'manage' the Company during the 1770s see Sutherland, *East India Company*, pp. 270–80.
46 *Alexander's East India Magazine*, vol. VII (1834), p. 395.
47 *Proceedings of the Select Committee appointed by the General Court of Proprietors on the 6th October 1813* . . . (1814), p. 22.

changes of personnel within the Direction at least restored a sense of permanence to the highest positions within the Company.

Although the political temperature inside East India House was much reduced by North's reforms, there was not, however, a full return to the passive stockholder behaviour that had been evident during the first half of the century. During the 1760s a tradition of stockholder participation in Company politics had become firmly established and a significant number of proprietors continued to take part in debates, ballots, and elections. As a result, the reformed General Court could still be a painful thorn in the side of directors and ministers alike. In 1773–4, for example, its debates about the future government of Bengal were so fierce and protracted that the directors were unable to formulate instructions for the new Governor-General and his Council as soon as they would have wished.[48] And in May 1776 the stockholders referred back to the Court of Directors a decision to recall Warren Hastings and Richard Barwell from Bengal.[49]

Emboldened by these and other successes, the General Court sought to act as guardian of the Company's interests, and a committee of stockholders was established to 'watch over the rights of the Company and maintain their privileges', which meant that the directors and ministers were kept under close scrutiny during times of political crisis.[50] The Court was swift to condemn any actions believed to be damaging to the Company, most notably in 1783 when Henry Fletcher was forced to resign as Chairman and director because of his close association with Charles James Fox, whose East India bills proposed to transfer responsibility for the administration of India to seven government commissioners.[51] The eventual defeat of Fox's proposals was the cause of much celebration and self-congratulation within the General Court, and the collective sigh of relief was such that when the reforms that were later to be embodied in Pitt's India Act were put before the stockholders in January 1784 a large majority agreed 'chearfully to acquiesce' in them in return for financial assistance being granted to the Company.[52]

The choice of the lesser of two evils did, however, have very important long-term consequences for the stockholders because Pitt's Act of 1784 removed the power of the General Court to overturn any decision of the

48 Directors to Bengal, 2 February 1774, *FWIHC*, vol. VII, p. 46.
49 B/259, pp. 182–4. For this episode see Sutherland, *East India Company*, pp. 301–10.
50 B/260, pp. 223–6.
51 Philips, *East India Company*, p. 24.   52 B/260, pp. 302–19.

directors that had been endorsed by the newly established Board of Control. As a result, the stockholders were no longer able to influence the Company's civil, military, or revenue policy, although they did continue to alert the directors whenever they felt that the interests of the Company and British India as a whole were being threatened by unwelcome government initiatives. In May 1797, for example, the stockholders urged the directors to resist the powers the ministry was proposing to grant to Marquis Cornwallis if he returned to Bengal as Governor-General because they tended to 'establish a system which can terminate only in the destruction of all the rights and privileges of the East India Company and be dangerous in the extreme to the British interests in India', and very similar sentiments were expressed later the same month when the Board of Control ordered the Company to advance £1.2 million towards the payment of the Nawab of Arcot's debts.[53] To all intents and purposes, however, the late eighteenth-century stockholders could only wield real influence in the Company's internal affairs and they could still make life extremely uncomfortable for a director such as David Scott whose private business interests were deemed to threaten the well-being of the Company.[54] They also continued to issue challenges to the authority of the directors by voting to restore overseas servants who had been dismissed from their posts.

Occasional shows of strength and independence enabled stockholders to cling to the belief that they still had an important role to play in British Indian affairs, and in 1814 one of their number suggested that 'Those who belonged to the Constituent Body were invested with a situation of high national trust. They were appointed to watch over the Executive Body.'[55] This was indeed the case and no one could ever afford to ignore the stockholders, least of all the directors, but the position and influence of the General Court within the Company after 1784 was a far cry from what it had been during the 1760s when it had often held the centre of the national political stage and caused endless difficulties for directors and ministers. By the 1820s the formal business of the

---

53 B/263, pp. 9, 21–7, 35–8. In the event, Cornwallis decided not to take up his appointment because the directors refused to increase the size of the Company's army (Philips, *East India Company*, p. 93).

54 In 1798 a majority of the stockholders balloted in favour of Scott being 'disengaged from every interest in a House of Agency' because it compromised his position as a director (B/263, pp. 86–93, 97–9). See also below, p. 123.

55 Humphrey Howarth, speech reported in *Debate at the East India House . . . 18th March 1814* (1814), pp. 21–2.

Court seldom extended beyond votes of thanks, the approval of grants of money, and the routine amendment of by-laws.[56] Of course, the situation in India was discussed from time to time, and during the late 1820s lengthy debates took place on the subjects of flogging, the education of doctors, the practice of *sati*, idolatry, and the role of the press in India.[57] But these deliberations were similar to those of a debating club and they did not influence directly the implementation of policy on the ground in India. Hence, when the Company's Secretary, Peter Auber, was asked by a Committee of the House of Commons in 1832 whether it was correct that the stockholders were now 'virtually precluded from all substantial interference in the affairs of the Company', his emphatic response of 'Yes, certainly' indicated that the discussions and votes of the General Court now bore only very lightly on the development of British India.[58]

The effects of late eighteenth-century reform upon the Court of Directors were no less profound. The authority of the Court of Directors within the Company was gradually re-established after 1773 and, as the potency of the stockholder 'democracy' was diluted, the directors were able to restore some degree of control over the General Court.[59] This produced a welcome return to managerial stability after the squalls of the 1760s, but the manner in which the directors exerted influence over overseas policy was fundamentally altered by the establishment of the Board of Control. After 1784 the directors were constrained by the need to secure formal approval from ministers for instructions and decisions relating to the implementation of military, political, and revenue policy in India. Naturally this had the potential to cause difficulties, and relations between the directors and ministers became strained, especially when there were early disputes over patronage, appointments, and the contents of despatches destined for India.[60]

Over time, however, the preparation of despatches became far less of a battleground for supremacy between directors and ministers. This was primarily because the potential for conflict was much reduced by the use of 'previous communication', a system through which the content of draft

---

56 B/267–9, passim.   57 *Debates at East India House*, vol. II: 1825–30 (n.d.), passim.
58 *PP* (1831–2), 735–1, vol. XI, p. 6.
59 For a study of the long-run erosion of 'democracy' within the Company between 1783 and 1858 see Timothy L. Alborn, *Conceiving companies: joint-stock politics in Victorian England* (2000), pp. 21–52.
60 For examples of early disputes over the content of despatches, see the letters from the directors to the Board, 8 December 1784, 30 March, 2 July 1785, E/2, vol. I, pp. 51–3, 81–9, 120–1. For a detailed contemporary account of the various disputes that occurred between the Court and the Board between 1784 and 1791 see H/342, pp. 1–684.

despatches was discussed and agreed informally prior to the exchange of official versions between the Company and the Board.[61] The routine passing of draft despatches back and forth from East India House to Westminster did nothing to advance the conduct of Indian business at any great pace, and the remorselessly increasing volume of correspondence eventually prompted a thorough overhaul of the system by the President of the Board Lord Ellenborough during the late 1820s.[62] Nevertheless, the use of previous communication did have the great virtue of ensuring that differences of opinion were usually resolved in such a way as to avoid open and full-blooded confrontation between directors and ministers.

IMPERIAL PARTNERS

Although the system of home government for India established in 1784 eventually began to work smoothly, there was no disguising the fact that the Board of Control was very much the senior partner in its relationship with the Company, and this position strengthened markedly during the late 1820s. The Board was able to insist on a particular line of policy being adopted by the Company and it could always make an alteration or amendment to a despatch. The Board's wishes were often made known through personal communication from the President to the Chairman of the Company, and this enabled Thomas Courtenay, Secretary to the Board between 1812 and 1829, to claim that the influence of ministers on the content of despatches was 'to a very great extent in matters involving great principles as well as in matters of detail'.[63] He pointed to many detailed examples of decisive government intervention in the making of Indian policy and declared that on occasions the Board had overcome considerable opposition from the Court of Directors. Moreover, on matters of highest political policy, the Board had been empowered by the Act of 1784 to communicate directly with India via a three-man Secret Committee of Directors whose members were

---

61 The use of previous communications was developed as a means of overcoming the problems associated with the need for the Board to comply with the terms of the India Act of 1784 by returning drafts of official despatches to the Company within fourteen days. For more detail see Philips, *East India Company*, pp. 20–1 and Martin Moir, *A general guide to the India Office Records* (1996), pp. 42–4.

62 For details see Philips, *East India Company*, pp. 264–8.

63 Evidence to the House of Commons, as reprinted in *Alexander's East India Magazine*, vol. III (1832), pp. 445–6.

required to swear on oath that they would not discuss the content of secret despatches with the full Court of Directors. It has been shown that the Secret Committee managed to exercise some degree of influence on the formulation of these despatches,[64] but the Board's use of this means of communication with India did preclude the majority of the Company's directors from participation in the making of policy relating to war and relations with independent states. The effect of this was to restrict most directors to only a partial knowledge and understanding of the Company's external affairs, and in 1832 Courtenay was able to claim that 'Certain very important discussions which took place in the Council of Fort William [Calcutta] in 1814 are still kept secret from the Court of Directors.'[65] Finally, a President of the Board of Control could always seek to circumvent the directors entirely by establishing private lines of communication with senior figures in India. This enabled a direct working relationship to be developed with men on the spot, and private letters could also be used as a means of passing on information without bringing it to the attention of the directors. All Presidents of the Board took the opportunity to do this from time to time, although they usually respected the need for them to use the proper channels of communication with India that were routed through East India House.

Pitt's Act thus greatly strengthened the hand of ministers in the exercise of direct control over the government of British India, but it would be wrong to suggest that the directors were left without any influence at all on matters beyond trade. For example, the directors stubbornly resisted several senior Indian appointments proposed by ministers, and during the late 1820s they were successful in their opposition to the Board's plan to disband six regiments in India as part of a cost-cutting exercise.[66] These actions demonstrated that ministers could never simply impose their wishes upon the Company, and there were in fact always limits to the Board's influence on the making of policy for India. Indeed, the Board

---

64 Philips, *East India Company*, pp. 11, 301. The Secret Committee comprised the Chairman, Deputy Chairman, and a senior director. Philips notes (p. 301, n. 1) that the Committee discussed and amended drafts of secret despatches and occasionally passed them to the full Court of Directors.

65 *Alexander's East India Magazine*, vol. III (1832), p. 444.

66 See, for example, the contest over the appointment of a successor to Warren Hastings as Governor General (Philips, *East India Company*, pp. 41–3). For problems over later appointments see Holden Furber, *Henry Dundas, First Viscount Melville, 1742–1811: political manager of Scotland, statesman, administrator of British India* (1931), pp. 126–34. For the directors' resistance to the Board over the six regiments see J. G. Ravenshaw to Bentinck, 3 September 1829, *Bentinck correspondence*, vol. I, pp. 279–80.

was often prevented from taking a firm lead in East Indian affairs by the nature of its supervisory role, which dictated that many of its interventions were responses to previous Company actions or decisions. As the outgoing and well-regarded President, George Canning, lamented in December 1820, the functions of the Board were of a 'somewhat invidious character' because they were 'simply corrective, coercive, and depressive'. The Board, he complained, exercised 'a power which may reduce or abolish establishments but cannot create or extend them; may negative appointments but cannot nominate to them; may check or stint the flow of beneficience, but cannot originate or suggest a single act of grace and favour'.[67]

As Canning's rather aggrieved comments suggest, by no means all of the directors' power and influence had been ceded to ministers, and they were able to retain the initiative in the preparation of the vast majority of ordinary despatches destined for India. Indeed, between 1813 and 1830 only forty-nine of more than 8,000 despatches were prepared on the express instructions of the Board of Control.[68] Detailed instructions for Company servants in India were usually formulated first by the Company's directors and officials at East India House, and only later were they revised in accordance with ministerial wishes, usually without any great controversy. As a result, in 1832 Company Secretary Peter Auber could recall that although there had 'frequently' been differences of opinion between the Board and the Company over the content of despatches, there had been only one occasion, in 1815, when a 'mandamus' had been issued by ministers in order to compel the directors to make an alteration to a despatch.[69] In part, as Auber conceded, this reflected the fact that the Board was always able, if necessary, to assert its 'absolute control' over the content of despatches, but it also suggested that directors and ministers were usually able to settle matters by negotiation and compromise. In such a scheme of things, the views of the Company very often formed the basis of policy for India and the vast bulk of the day-to-day business of empire was conducted at East India House, not in the offices of the Board of Control.

67 Canning to the Chairman and Deputy Chairman, 25 December 1820, MS Eur. F142/20.
68 Douglas M. Peers, *Between Mars and Mammon: colonial armies and the garrison state in India, 1819–1835* (1995), p. 21.
69 *PP* (1831–2), 735–1, vol. IX, p. 9. The Board's order was issued to compel the directors to pay Major Hart £10,000 for rice he had sold to the army under suspicious circumstances in 1799. For details of this episode see Philips, *East India Company*, pp. 204–6. In 1832 the Board did also have to resort to legal action in order to force through a despatch relating to the settlement of debts between agency houses and the Nizam of Hyderabad (see ibid., pp. 281–2).

From time to time, frustrated Presidents of the Board of Control contemplated extending the powers of the Board in order to establish direct ministerial control over all British affairs in India but they were always persuaded otherwise by contemplation of the considerable practical implications involved in any such transfer of responsibility. They also had to acknowledge that, whatever misgivings they might harbour, the system of dual governance established by Pitt's Act and refined during Henry Dundas's long tenure of office as President of the Board between 1784 and 1801 worked tolerably well. As early as 1792 Dundas was able to declare that the home government of India was reasonably effective, and this persuaded him, against his instincts, to state in both private and public that it was now better 'to adhere to what has had the test of experience than to give way to the theories of speculative men'.[70] Many of his successors came to share this pragmatic view and it was largely because of this that Company–state relations continued to be founded on more or less the same basis until the end of the Company's days in 1858. Indeed, assessments of the relationship between the Board and the Company increasingly emphasised the fact that routine co-operation had gradually broken down institutional boundaries to create an ever-more unified system of home government. Thus to the Assistant Secretary of the Board, John Meheux, in 1804 'the good understanding which, with few interruptions, has for many years subsisted between the Board and the Court, in proportion as it has facilitated the transaction of Business, has obviated the necessity of calling forth the exertions of the Board's officers'.[71] In 1800 Dundas was himself moved to suggest, somewhat disingenuously, to the Chairman of the Company that the close relationship between the directors and the Board was such that 'the existence of that institution [the Board] is now interwoven with the affairs and property of the East India Company'.[72]

This is not to suggest the system always operated without any difficulty because much depended on the leading personalities to be found at any

---

70 Letter to Sir Charles Oakley, 20 Sept. 1792 quoted in Furber, *Henry Dundas*, p. 131. For similar sentiments expressed in the Commons during a debate on the renewal of the Company's charter in 1793, see William Cobbett, *Parliamentary history of England from . . . 1066 to . . . 1803*, 36 vols. (1806–20), vol. XXX, col. 666.

71 Memo of 7 September, H/341, p. 552.

72 Dundas to Hugh Inglis, 12 August 1800, ibid., pp. 429–30. In order to secure better office accommodation for the Board, Dundas hoped that the Company would purchase two houses in Downing Street. Since he already lived in Downing Street this would have been of great convenience to him, and it no doubt inclined him to flatter the Company rather more than might otherwise have been the case.

one time at the Board of Control and the Court of Directors. When a majority of the directors were favourably disposed towards a capable minister, routine business could be conducted on the basis of mutual trust and respect. This was evidently the case in 1818 when the Deputy Chairman Campbell Marjoribanks sketched a picture of easy relations between the Company's senior officers and the President of the Board of Control, George Canning, based upon his experience of a weekly meeting 'at which they make their respective reports and amicably arrange matters for future proceedings'.[73] Relations were far less harmonious, however, when the directors were confronted by a hostile President of the Board, as was the case with the Earl of Buckinghamshire, an embittered former Governor of Madras, between 1812 and 1816, and with the high-handed and abrasive Earl of Ellenborough who often treated the Company's Chairmen with thinly veiled contempt between 1828 and 1830.[74] Equally, those at East India House found it difficult to work with the talented but indolent Charles Grant junior, who was described as being 'sadly inert' during a critical time in the Company's history.[75] The underlying strength of system established in 1784 was such, however, that it never collapsed or broke down completely even when one director reported a state of 'open war' between the Board and the directors in 1813 over proposed reforms to the revenue system in Madras.[76] As a result, almost twenty years later Thomas Courtenay reflected that the system of 1784 had functioned effectively because co-operation between the Board and the Court had allowed for a division of responsibilities and the emergence of a form of mutually reinforcing administrative partnership. He declared that 'Neither body, as at present constituted and assisted, would have well administered the functions imposed upon the two, if either had been without the assistance of the other.'[77]

Diehards within the Company long bemoaned the erosion of the Company's authority and the loss of independence, but realists accepted

---

73 *The diary of Joseph Farington*, vol. XV, *January 1818–December 1819*, ed. Kathryn Cave (New Haven, 1984), p. 5282.

74 On Ellenborough's frosty relations with the directors see Lord Colchester (ed.), *A political diary 1828–1830 by Edward Law, Lord Ellenborough*, 2 vols. (1881), passim. Amidst much controversy, the abrasive Buckinghamshire, formerly Lord Hobart, had been recalled from Madras in 1797 when he was in line to succeed Sir John Shore as Governor-General.

75 Peter Auber to William Bentinck, 14 November 1831, *Bentinck correspondence*, vol. I, p. 718.

76 Sweny Toone, as quoted in T. H. Beaglehole, *Thomas Munro and the development of administrative policy in Madras 1792–1818. The origins of the 'Munro system'* (Cambridge, 1966), p. 100.

77 *Alexander's East India Magazine*, vol. III (1832), p. 446.

that ministers and directors each now played a part within a system of imperial administration that was by no means perfect but nevertheless offered a much improved method of managing British territories and interests in India. As the Company's Secretary, Peter Auber, put it in 1828, 'The present is a system of checks – it has effectually led to more of probity and honour in conducting the affairs than formerly existed. It may stand in need of alteration, but it will demand great caution in introducing any change which shall put to hazard the immense empire which has been brought under British rule.'[78] By the end of the period, most Company directors, members of the Board of Control, and senior administrators at East India House and Cannon Row saw themselves as acting together in support of British interests, and, as if to symbolise their unity of purpose and growing sense of collegiality, they met together at what were described as 'family dinners' in order to socialise and celebrate their collective achievements.[79]

After 1767 statutory regulation and control redefined the East India Company's relationships with the British government, and this placed the Company in a domestic position very different from that which had existed during the first half of the eighteenth century. No longer a free-standing and independent trading company, the Company had to all intents and purposes been incorporated within the Hanoverian state machinery of empire, and this caused two leading lawyers to suggest that by the end of the eighteenth century it had become a 'limb of the government of the country'.[80] This represented a process of considerable institutional metamorphosis and it renders almost entirely inappropriate the model of the modern firm that has been applied by historians to the Company for the earlier part of its existence. As will be seen in later chapters, there was certainly great continuity of internal practices, procedures, and methods through and beyond the 1760s, but the Company was increasingly refashioned as an agency of imperial government that was obliged to serve national interests as well as its own narrower corporate concerns. This process served to interconnect the Company's twin roles as trader and sovereign, and set it on a path of development that was quite unlike that followed by any other institution, either before or since.

---

78 Peter Auber to Lord William Bentinck, 11 April 1829, *Bentinck correspondence*, vol. I, p. 187.
79 See, for example, the circular invitation to a dinner held at the Albion Tavern on 6 August 1828, E/1/264, no. 1985.
80 Lord Chief Justice Lord Kenyon and Mr Justice Lawrence, quoted in Auber, *Analysis*, p. vii.

CHAPTER 4

People: investors in empire

The financial speculation and political infighting at the heart of the deep internal crisis that shook the East India Company during the 1760s ensured that the collective characteristics of the several thousand proprietors who 'owned' the Company changed dramatically in a very short space of time. Further alterations then followed as late eighteenth-century additions were made to the Company's joint-stock capital and greater numbers of Britons began to invest in stocks and shares. As a result, the geographical, social, and structural profiles of the East India stockholding community of the 1830s were very different from those that had been evident seventy years earlier. Analysing these changes is a matter of some importance in order to establish the collective identity of the men and women who constituted the East India Company in Britain. The stockholders derived financial reward from the Company's overseas activities and, although they were far removed from active involvement in the process of overseas expansion, they participated in the decision-making processes that shaped the political development of East Indian affairs in London. Accordingly, this chapter seeks to examine the Company's stockholders with a view to establishing who they were, why they held stock, how they acted, and how their group composition altered over time.

PROFIT, POWER, AND PUBLIC SERVICE

No restrictions were placed upon the purchase of East India stock, and consequently the General Court was often represented as a popular assembly in which the rich and powerful rubbed shoulders with small investors. The stockholders were indeed diverse in their origin and background because, as Peter Auber correctly noted in 1826, 'The books of the Company are open at all times for the admission of British subjects and foreigners: no distinction exists as to religion, profession, or sex.'¹ This had always been the case, and thus among the 3,000 or so individuals who owned a whole or part share of the 2,826 East India stock accounts that existed in March 1773 were a great variety of individuals, ranging from Ann Wright, spinster, who was recorded as having owned 8s. 10d. since February 1713 and Elijah Pereira Davidsz who had held £46,000 for less than a month.² The distribution of these accounts is represented according to their size in table 4.1.

The reasons why most investors owned East India stock can never be established with any degree of certainty, and it is difficult to explain, for example, why Robert Armstrong held £600 stock for only a single day in October 1806. Clearly, though, many were motivated by a simple desire to find a safe and profitable home for their savings. As a proprietor of forty years put it in 1833, he had invested in the Company principally because it offered him 'good security for his money', although he noted rather pragmatically that the Company also 'possessed warehouses to which he might send his children'.³ The investment decisions of some stockholders were, however, based upon rather more than financial considerations. For, as was observed at the very end of the period, 'Exclusive of the profitable investment of capital which India stock has hitherto afforded, individuals have become proprietors, from connection with that country [India], and previous residence there, from a desire to take part in discussion of India affairs at the general courts, to promote the election of their friends, and participate in the patronage.'⁴ This observation noted that alongside those who sought long-term or short-term returns on their investment there were always to be found stockholders who wanted play an active part in the Company's affairs. Indeed, by the end of the period there were some proprietors such as David Salomon who openly acknowledged that the duties and obligations of the proprietors extended beyond 'pecuniary objects' to the 'much higher purposes

1 Auber, *Analysis*, p. 349.
2 It can be calculated that in March 1773 3,084 individuals owned East India stock in 2,826 separate holdings. Some accounts were joint accounts; others were in the name of partnerships or corporations. See *A list of the names of all the proprietors of East India stock . . .* ([9 March] 1773). Details of Pereira Davidsz and Wright are on pp. 44 and 62. It is known that some individuals accumulated more stock than Pereira Davidsz but then screened it from public view by holding it in the name of others. Thus Clive's private records indicate that in 1766 he owned £74,500 stock but only a fraction of that amount was registered in his own name (H. V. Bowen, 'Lord Clive and speculation in East India Company stock, 1766', *Historical Journal*, 30, (1987), p. 912).
3 'Mr Goldsmid', speech of 19 April 1833 reported in *Debates at the General Court of Proprietors . . .* (1833), p. 108. At this time there were several Mr Goldsmids who owned stock.
4 *Alexander's East India Magazine*, vol. IV (1832), p. 571.

Table 4.1. *Ownership of East India stock, 9 March 1773*

Size of holding (£s)	No. of accounts	%	Amount of stock	%
<500	389	13.8	78,478	2.5
500	1,350	47.8	675,000	21.2
501–999	123	4.4	84,941	2.7
1,000	295	10.4	295,000	9.2
1,000–5,000	600	21.2	1,385,086	43.4
5,001–10,000	55	1.9	402,557	12.6
10,0001–20,000	11	0.4	142,700	4.5
20,000>	3	0.1	124,266	3.9
Total	2,826	100	3,188,028	100

Note: Average holding; £1,128. Although the total amount of the Company's nominal stock was £3,194,080, only £3,188,028 is accounted for on the list on 9 March.
Source: see note 2, p. 85.

of what had been called an Indian public'.[5] He stated that although he was not indifferent towards his dividends, 'he was not ignorant that he had also an important trust to perform as a proprietor of India stock'. Salomon was perhaps unusually high-minded, but his comments demonstrate that East India stockholders were often interested in more than personal profit. Some sought power and influence within the Company; while others undertook what they thought to be a public duty to assist in the making of British India. The distribution between these broad categories of investor was never equal or constant, and it altered over time as the Company's commercial, imperial, and political fortunes fluctuated. Throughout, however, there was always a rich mixture of people and personalities within the stockholding community.

Investors committed resources to the Company for varying periods of time. Some within the merchant community moved in and out of East India stock as they adjusted the balance of broadly diversified investment portfolios, and they put their surplus cash to work for short periods of time.[6] As had long been the case, however, other investors regarded East

---

5 Speech of 18 April 1833, reported in *Debates at the General Court*, pp. 82–3.
6 For detailed analysis of investment in the East India Company and other funds by a small group of merchants see David Hancock, *Citizens of the world: London merchants and the integration of the British Atlantic community, 1735–1785* (Cambridge, 1985), pp. 260–72, and David Hancock, '"Domestic bubbling": eighteenth-century London merchants and individual investment in the Funds', *Ec. Hist. Rev.*, 47 (1994), pp. 679–702. As Hancock stresses, merchants also used investments as a means of exercising influence in the monied companies.

India stock as a permanent safe haven for their savings. After the Company's financial turmoil of the early 1770s, stockholders were able to enjoy annual payments that recovered to 8 per cent in 1777 and then were fixed at 10½ per cent from 1793 onwards.[7] This compared very favourably with Bank of England stock, which, with a brief exception in 1806, always paid out a lower rate of dividend,[8] and, as a result, a significant number of investments were left untouched for long periods of time. This was often the case with female investors, who generally owned less stock and were far less active as traders than their male counterparts, and East India stock remained popular with widows and spinsters. Other long-term investors were corporate and charitable bodies,[9] and a considerable amount of stock remained in the name of deceased stockholders whose dividends were paid to trusts or beneficiaries. Investors of this general type were content to accumulate half-yearly dividend payments, and thus even during periods of great volatility within the stockholding community there was always a solid core of investors at the very heart of the Company. In March 1773, for example, just fewer than 14 per cent of the 2,826 stock accounts holders had remained unaltered for a decade or more.[10] Many of the stockholders who owned these accounts were 'passive' in the sense that they maintained their holding without ever adding to or subtracting from their initial stake in the Company, but they were also passive in the sense that they could not play, or did not wish to play, a great part in proceedings at East India House. According to the ship owner John Fiott, they were investors who 'love their ease and tranquillity, or who are placed at a distance from the scene of the action, [and] rarely take part in the controul of the Company's affairs'.[11]

Beyond the solid core of long-term investors were those whose actions ensured that the composition and characteristics of the stockholding

7 For details of the legislative arrangements that determined the rate of dividend paid by the Company see Auber, *Analysis*, pp. 299–308.
8 See Sir John Clapham, *The Bank of England*, 2 vols. (Cambridge, 1944), vol. I, p. 292; vol. II, p. 428.
9 According to the printed list compiled on 9 March 1773 there were nine such bodies: The Parnassims of the Portuguese Nation (£10,200), The Fellows of Trinity College Cambridge and 'Lois Andrews, spinster' (£1,000), The London Company of Weavers (£800), The President and directors of the 'Noble family of Whatteville' (£200), the Fellowship of Insurance, Discounting, and Lending of Rotterdam (£7,900), and the Chambers of Orphans of Amsterdam (£12,000), Delft (£5,000), Utrecht (£1,000), and The Hague (£625).
10 Calculated from the printed list of 9 March 1773.
11 John Fiott, *An address to the proprietors of East India stock and to the public, containing a narrative of the cases of the ships Tartar and Hartwell, late in the Company's service* (1791), p. 61.

community altered quite rapidly during the mid-1760s, when rising
prices brought in profit-seekers in much greater numbers than ever before.
Speculators fell into one of four categories, although only three of them
included individuals who actually took possession of any stock. Those
capable of deploying considerable resources in the market attempted to
engross stock in the hope of later selling it at a substantial profit, and
this group included prominent figures such as William Burke and the
former Paymaster-General Lord Holland.[12] A second group included
more active professional traders who seldom owned a large amount of
stock at any one time, but instead accumulated small profits on a large
number of transactions. Leading the way between February 1764 and
the end of 1766 was John Berrow whose 250 transactions involved stock
of a nominal value of almost £200,000, and he was followed by those
such as Sir Francis Gosling of the banking firm Gosling, Gosling & Clive,
and two London-based Dutchmen, Charles van Notten junior and Pieter
Clifford. The third type of speculator perhaps contributed most to the
high rate of turnover of India stock when news of the Company's
acquisition of the *diwani* was reported in 1766. These were investors
whose transactions were conducted on a limited scale, but they bought
into the Company, accumulated stock, and then sold out with their
accounts seldom holding more than £5,000 at the time of closure. Finally,
there were those whose transactions required no transfers at all because
their speculative activity took the form of time bargains standing between actual buyers and sellers of stock. This type of activity conducted
by brokers and agents who made the market was a form of private betting
based on the margins arising from rises and falls in price. Its extent was
thought to be considerable,[13] and although it had no direct impact on the
Company it certainly helped to fuel the widespread contemporary belief
that East India stock had been transformed into a gaming stock.

Speculative activity occurred on a considerable scale again in 1768–9
and 1772–3 and this later caused Thomas Mortimer to recall that even
during the mid-1770s East India stock had been the 'most dangerous of

---

12 L. S. Sutherland and J. Binney, 'Henry Fox as paymaster-general of the forces', *English Historical
Review*, 70 (1955), pp. 229–57; L. S. Sutherland and J. A. Woods, 'The East India speculations of
William Burke', *Proceedings of the Leeds Philosophical and Literary Society*, 11 (1964), pp. 183–216;
For Clive see Bowen, 'Lord Clive'. For speculative activity see also J. M. N. Maclean, *Reward is
secondary: the life of a political adventurer and an inquiry into the mystery of 'Junius'* (1963), pp. 178–
84, 219–35.

13 See, for example, the comment in *Middlesex Journal*, 3–5 June 1769, which suggested that only
one-fiftieth of the deals involving East India stock were actually recorded in the Company's
ledgers.

any fund, on account of its extreme variations'.[14] Thereafter, there were occasional reports of jobbing operations designed to force prices up or down,[15] but on the whole there was a retreat of speculators from the Company. At the end of the century, only a few individuals such as Mark Sprot and Christopher Terry were still dealing extensively in stock,[16] and by the 1820s and 1830s the only really active accounts belonged to a handful of traders, most of whom were based at the Stock Exchange.[17] Their activities primarily involved broking transactions rather than extensive speculative operations of the type seen during the 1760s, and the overall reduction in the number of active accounts is reflected in the changes to the annual number of stock transfers that were noted in the previous chapter.[18] Generally speaking, therefore, many of those holding East India stock after the mid-1770s did so because they valued it as a long-term financial investment, and they probably would have concurred with the assertion made by *The Times* in 1786 that once more India stock 'may justly be considered as secure and permanent as any of the other funds'.[19]

Other investors were motivated by a desire to exercise influence within the Company. To John Fiott's mind, the more active investors cared little for dividend payments or even the common good of the Company, and he argued that they were driven by a need to secure access to contracts, wealth, and patronage.[20] He had his sights fixed firmly upon commercial groups, and in particular on members of the 'shipping interest', who used the Company to advance the position of themselves, their family, and their associates. These types of groups were the subject of detailed examination by C. H. Philips and, although his division of the Company into coherent and permanently organised interests was

---

14 Thomas Mortimer, *The nefarious practice of stock-jobbing unveiled* (1810), p. 60.

15 See, for example, the draft of a pamphlet by Francis Russell entitled 'A serious and seasonable address to the proprietors of India stock' (internal evidence, 1790), H/371, pp. 333–64. Russell condemned those stockjobbers as 'the chief instruments' who would 'stop at nothing however vile and base' (p. 334), and were playing upon fears of Company bankruptcy by spreading false rumour about recent poor sales of goods.

16 During the 1790s Sprot, of King's Road and the Stock Exchange, conducted hundreds of transactions, on a near-daily basis (See L/AG/14/5, vol. 31, pp. 148–61). Between 1796 and 1803, Terry, of the Stock Exchange or Kingston, Surrey, Gent., was responsible for almost 1,200 transactions, mainly in a range between £100 and £1,000 (ibid., pp. 190–213).

17 L/AG/14/5, vol. 36, pp. 53, 95, 96–103 (Samuel Bayley); ibid., vol. 37, pp. 175–7, 187*–89* (William Hammond junior); ibid., pp. 38, pp. 39–55 (Moses Levy of Great Alice Street, Goodman's Fields); ibid., pp. 39–53 (Luke Leake); ibid., pp. 170–81 (Andrew Amedee Mieville).

18 See above, pp. 73–4.

19 *The Times*, 8 August 1786.   20 Fiott, *Address to the proprietors*, p. 62.

subsequently questioned by P. J. Marshall, it seems clear that some directors and stockholders did always put their own concerns before the Company as a whole.[21] The shipping interest certainly remained powerful well into the 1790s, and ship owners and builders were always strongly represented in the General Court. In July 1796 twenty-eight managing owners of East Indiamen possessed £82,210 stock, and it has been estimated that they could mobilise the votes of around 200 friends and associates.[22] These men retained a firm grip on the management of maritime affairs until reform of the system for hiring ships helped to create new shipping interest groups during the late 1790s. But, as Marshall suggests, it would be quite wrong to suggest that this or any other group was able to exert influence on each and every aspect of Company policy.

Also to be included within the category of 'active' investors were those who used their stock to achieve political ends. As Adam Smith wrote in *The wealth of nations* (after the General Court voting qualification had risen to £1,000):

Frequently a man of great, sometimes even a man of small fortunes, is willing to purchase a thousand pound share in India stock, merely for the influence which he expects to acquire by a vote in the Court of Proprietors. It gives him a share, though not in the plunder, yet in the appointment of the plunderers of India; the Court of Directors though they make that appointment, being necessarily more or less under the influence of the proprietors, who not only elect those directors, but sometimes over-rule the appointment of their servants in India.[23]

Among this category were considerable numbers of stockholders whose interest in the Company arose from their political connections and associations beyond East India House.

Investors who believed East India stock represented a form of political as well as financial capital used their stock in a variety of different ways. Some individuals were able to take advantage of the voting and speaking rights associated with the stock in order to establish a political career at East India House. They were able to voice opinions in the General Court, and their views were then placed before the wider public through the detailed reports of meetings that always appeared in the London press after the 1760s. If these men were fortunate, a reputation gained at

---

21 Philips, *East India Company*, passim. For Marshall's criticism see *Problems of empire*, p. 46.
22 Figure calculated from L/AG/14/5, vols. 24–7; Philips, *East India Company*, p. 81.
23 Adam Smith, *An inquiry into the nature and causes of the wealth of nations* (1776), ed. R. H. Campbell, A. S. Skinner, and W. B. Todd, 2 vols. (Oxford, 1976), vol. II, p. 752.

the General Court enabled them to climb the political ladder. This was the case, for example, with 'Orator' William Crichton, a West India merchant. He was one of the most frequent speakers of the 1770s, and he ultimately gained widespread respect for his dedication and commitment to the Company. His prominent role in the General Court helped him to become Alderman of Cheap ward in the Court of Common Council, before he then served as Sheriff of the City of London during the Gordon Riots of 1780, and he would undoubtedly have stood for election to the House of Commons had he not met with an untimely death in 1782.[24] East India stockholding provided him with an opportunity to establish a political reputation, thereby illustrating how the General Court could serve as what C. H. Philips described as a 'training ground' for men launching their careers.[25] Among the notable figures that used the Court in this way were George Tierney and the former Bengal medical officer Joseph Hume who both made their marks as radical Members of Parliament.[26]

Stockholders such as Crichton, Tierney, and the censorious Hume held the directors to account and subjected their actions and decisions to close scrutiny. Indeed, at the time of Hume's death in 1855 it was recalled that he had become dedicated to the 'constant exposure of Indian abuses in each periodical meeting of the proprietary'.[27] By acting as a check on the executive, Hume and others were often aided and abetted by a small 'awkward squad' of proprietors who routinely harassed the directors. The Chairman George Abercrombie Robinson observed rather bitterly in the mid-1820s that a handful of stockholders were 'barkers on all subjects' in the General Court,[28] and although this group were never more than a tiny minority they were often successful in making life difficult for the directors.

Rather less effective were lone individuals whose interventions were ill-focused or irrelevant to the subject under discussion, and the proprietors often had to endure long and rambling speeches from would-be orators who liked the sound of their own voices. Poor or inexperienced speakers might be excused, but when individuals repeatedly tested the

24 H. V. Bowen, 'Crichton, William', *ODNB.*   25 Philips, *East India Company*, p. 3.
26 Hume has been the subject of two modern biographies although they do not pay much attention to his long career in the General Court. See Valerie Chancellor, *The political life of Joseph Hume 1777–1855* (1986) and Ronald K. Huch and Paul R. Ziegler, *Joseph Hume: the people's MP* (Philadelphia, 1985).
27 *The Times*, 22 February 1855.
28 Robinson to Lord Amherst, 20 November 1826, MS Eur. F.142/28.

patience of their fellow stockholders they were subjected to loud heckling and calls to order. In 1772 a group of stockholders 'kept up such a continuous clapping' that Allan Ramsey had to abandon his attempt to read out an entire parliamentary bill, while Sir Joseph Mawbey was heavily criticised for presenting 'a very large and cloying mess of porridge'.[29] After 1810 William Lowndes regularly infuriated his listeners with tedious and often pointless speeches,[30] and during the early 1830s Captain William Gowan often spoke at length on trifling matters. It was probably Gowan, a former officer in the Bengal army, who was in the mind of Dr John Gilchrist when he told the Court that he was 'often surprised that a certain number of orators were allowed to get up in that court, and to talk as often and as discursively as they pleased'.[31] Gowan went further than this, however, by tabling motions on a large number of subjects, and on several occasions he was accused of smearing or 'libelling' the directors by making wild allegations about them.[32] Angrily shouted down on several occasions by his fellow stockholders, Gowan was a maverick who must have appeared to the directors as a loose but not very dangerous cannon. His erratic behaviour ensured that he gained no support whatsoever for any of his motions, including one interesting proposal that 'They [the Company] should have the Indian public represented in Parliament and in that Court in order to protect Indian interests.'[33]

On most occasions the directors could afford to ignore Gowan and his ilk, but they always had to take notice of well-organised groups of individuals who purchased stock with a view to stirring up trouble on single issues. Former servants who had an axe to grind against the Company often led these groups, and their actions could both cause and greatly extend controversies. In particular, and much to the chagrin and embarrassment of the directors, it was possible for malcontents to marshal votes in the General Court in order to stop disciplinary action being taken against rogue Company servants. This began to happen on a regular basis during the late 1760s when a powerful coalition was

29 *London Evening Post*, 25–7 August 1772; *Public Advertiser*, 26 November 1772.
30 Philips, *East India Company*, pp. 3–4. Philips suggests that Lowndes was nearing the end of his career as an East India orator in 1822 but in fact he was still speaking in debates a decade later.
31 Speech of 10 June 1833 reported in *Debates at the General Court*, p. 233.
32 See, for example, his speeches of 28 September 1831 and 22 March 1832 reported in *Debates at the East India House*, vol. III, pp. 66, 89–93; and those of 18 and 22 April 1833 reported in *Debates at the General Court*, pp. 67–9, 156.
33 *Debates at the General Court*, p. 69.

assembled to throw out the directors' plan to instigate legal action against John Johnstone and other disgraced servants who had been rooted out of the Bengal administration by Clive.

It was with a view to tackling this sort of problem, which was exacerbated by the temporary splitting of stock, that Lord North was moved in 1773 to alter the Company's minimum voting qualification to £1,000. As North himself put it, 'many of the voters who now take a part in the East India Company embark from trifling fortunes of £500'.[34] Events were to prove that North's legislative action was not entirely successful, however, because although the Regulating Act did prevent the creation of temporary votes before ballots and elections, disaffected former servants were still able to rally considerable support to their cause. Moreover, troublesome individuals were permitted to attend and speak at the General Court, no matter how little stock they owned. Laurence Sulivan complained bitterly about this in 1778 when he wrote that 'at present every person buying even five pounds stock has this privilege. Mr [William] Bolts did this, and many brokers and others from £10–£20 each.'[35] Sulivan proposed restricting participation in debates to the owners of £1,000 stock or more, but the stockholders did not share his view and instead in December 1779 they resolved unanimously to allow attendance at the General Court to all of those who owned at least £500 stock.[36] As a result, for the rest of the period £500 stockholders were permitted to attend the Court, where they could speak but not vote on Company affairs.[37]

At the other end of the political spectrum were men whose wealth and connections enabled them to build up a loyal band of personal followers within the stockholding community, and this made them very valuable indeed to any faction endeavouring to exert control over Company affairs. Pre-eminent during the 1760s and 1770s was Lord Sandwich, the First Lord of the Admiralty, who built up considerable voting strength at East India House. He displayed only a passing interest in the affairs of British India, and was instead motivated by a desire to exert influence within an important sphere of domestic patronage. He backed candidates for the Direction and those who were elected to the Court, such as William James, Robert Jones, John Stephenson, and George Wombwell,

---

34 Speech of 5 May 1773, reported in BL, Eg. MS 246, p. 39.
35 Sulivan to Samuel Wilks, 9 October 1778, H/208, p. 8.
36 B/259, p. 309.
37 Evidence of Peter Auber, 14 February 1832, *PP* (1831–2), pp. 735–1, vol. IX, p. 5.

repaid their debt to their 'protector' by securing posts for his friends and acquaintances in different branches of the Company's service. Most notably, perhaps, Sandwich played an important part in securing the governorship of Madras for Thomas Rumbold in 1777, but at a more humble level his influence was used to obtain employment and promotion for a good number of others. Contemporaries often overstated Sandwich's influence on Company politics, but no one seeking to control the Company could afford to ignore him and thus, in view of his political leanings towards the North administration during the 1770s, he liaised closely with the Prime Minister's inner circle on Company affairs, and then passed on agreed voting instructions to his band of stockholding supporters in the Navy Office and elsewhere.[38]

As the North ministry's dealings with Lord Sandwich indicate, those who sought control over the Company's affairs made by far the most extensive and well-organised use of East India stock. This arose from the entry of the ministry and the opposition into the fray in support of Clive and Sulivan during the early 1760s, which brought a new sharp edge and degree of sophistication to Company politics. Parliamentary politicians became important power brokers in the struggle to control the Company, and thereafter governments and their opponents always sought to ensure that their supporters were strongly represented among the stockholding community. Throughout the period, therefore, many experienced political operators were to be found exerting influence in and around East India House. The extent of their interest in the Company is reflected in the number of MPs and peers who thought it prudent to purchase East India stock in order to qualify for a vote at the General Court.[39]

During the 1760s and 1770s senior political figures such as Richard Rigby held a voting qualification without ever much bothering themselves with the Company's internal affairs,[40] but others participated more actively in a number of different ways. Sir Lawrence Dundas and Lord Verney, for example, committed enormous sums of money to the government's vote-creation campaign of 1769, and they paid a heavy price

---

38 For Sandwich's canvassing activities and his ability to secure Company appointments for associates see SAN/F/38–40, NMM. For the development of his 'unique' position see Sutherland, *East India Company*, pp. 124–5, 277–9.
39 For a detailed study and identification of such figures see H. V. Bowen, '"Dipped in the traffic": East India stockholders in the House of Commons 1768–1774', *Parliamentary History*, 5 (1986), pp. 39–53.
40 See his comments of May 1773 reported in BL, Eg. MS 250, p. 7.

when the market collapsed; while prominent men such as Charles James Fox, Sir Fletcher Norton, and the Duke of Grafton purchased stock for a short period of time in order to lend their weight to the factional struggles at East India House.[41] Some, of course, regarded the stock as an attractive financial investment,[42] but others were motivated by a desire to play a prominent and continuing part in East Indian affairs. As a result, the number of stockholding MPs increased sharply during the mid-1760s, and Horace Walpole suggested in 1767 that at least one-third of the House of Commons was 'dipped in this traffic' of East India stock.[43] This was probably not too far wide of the mark in view of the heated political and speculative activity that took place in that year, and it can be calculated that, on average, 118 (or just over one-fifth) of MPs held stock at any one time during the Parliament of 1768 to 1774. Very revealing of their motives for ownership is the fact that around a half of them owned just the minimum amount of stock necessary to qualify for a vote. Indeed, following the passage of the Regulating Act the number of MPs owning £500 stock fell sharply from 61 to 20 as individuals sought to increase their stockholding in order to meet the new voting qualifications. As a consequence of this, the amount of stock held by sitting MPs rose to a new high of £235,576 (or 7.4 per cent of the total), although their 133 votes were held in only 94 pairs of hands.

With a tradition of ownership established during the 1760s, large numbers of MPs continued to hold stock throughout the rest of the period. This is clear from C. H. Philips's analysis of each Parliament between 1780 and 1834, although his placement of stockholding MPs and others into one of two different East Indian 'interests' in the House of Commons exaggerated the coherence and permanency of any such groups. There can be no doubt that loose groups of stockholding MPs did coalesce from time to time in order to defend or attack the Company, but to suggest the permanent existence of East Indian interests or even a single Company interest in the Commons runs the risk of constructing patterns of political association that would have been

---

41 Grafton held stock during some of the time he was First Lord of the Treasury.
42 Like Clive, not all MPs were open in their dealings in Company stock. In 1767 the Chancellor of the Exchequer, Charles Townshend, went to some lengths to conceal the fact that he was speculating in East India stock to a considerable extent (Sir Lewis Namier and John Brooke, *Charles Townshend* (1964), pp. 159–60, 167).
43 Walpole to Sir Horace Mann, 19 March 1767, *The Yale edition of Horace Walpole's correspondence*, ed. W. S. Lewis, 48 vols. (Oxford, 1939–84), vol. XXII, p. 498.

unknown to contemporary observers of the parliamentary scene. As the historian John Brooke quite properly remarked of the period 1754–90, 'so many men with so many different purposes makes it impossible to talk of an East India interest as if it were a pressure group with a clearly defined aim'.[44] The overall number of stockholding MPs did nevertheless remain high, and up to 100 were to be found in each of the Parliaments that sat between 1790 and 1820.[45] Some probably took no more than a passing interest in East Indian affairs, but when former Company servants and military or naval personnel who had served in the East are added to this number it becomes clear that there was a substantial body of men within the House of Commons who had some form of connection with either the East India Company or its Indian empire.[46]

THE STOCKHOLDING COMMUNITY: CONTINUITIES AND CHANGE

As noted in chapter 2, the collective profile of the East India Company's stockholders in 1750 very much reflected the metropolitan commercial and financial world in which the Company was located. The Company's stockholders were then notably cosmopolitan, and in particular they included many Dutch investors and members of Anglo-Dutch business communities. It is going much too far to suggest that the East India Company of the 1780s might more properly be called the 'Anglo-Dutch East India Company',[47] but it is legitimate to represent

44 John Brooke, *The history of Parliament. The House of Commons 1754–1790*, 3 vols. (1964), vol. I, p. 221. Philips conceded (*East India Company*, p. 299) that 'the East India members in Parliament were not in the habit of organising themselves into one or more clearly defined parties, and they seldom co-operated, except when India affairs were at issue', but he nevertheless proceeded to classify MPs according to membership of an 'Indian interest' or 'Company (City and Shipping) interest' (ibid., pp. 307–35). For Marshall's rejection of this schema see *Problems of empire*, pp. 37–8.
45 R. G. Thorne, *The History of Parliament. The House of Commons 1790–1820*, 5 vols. (1986), vol. I, p. 322. Their number included Henry Dundas, President of the Board of Control, who opened an account on 23 August 1791 and by April 1796 owned £3,138 stock (L/AG/14/5, vol. 24, p. 253).
46 Philips estimates that at any one time there were around 60–100 MPs whose only connection with the Company was the fact that they owned stock (Philips, *East India Company*, p. 307). Thorne suggests that the MPs who sat in the Commons between 1790 and 1820 included just over 100 civilians who had lived in India, thirty military or naval personnel who had served there, and twenty-five merchants who traded between Britain and India (*House of Commons, 1790–1820*, vol. I, p. 325). Since a good proportion of these were probably stockholders, it might be reasonable to suggest that at any one time around 120 sitting MPs had some sort of connection with the Company or India.
47 Holden Furber, 'The United Company of Merchants of England trading to the East Indies, 1783–1796', *Ec. Hist. Rev.*, 10 (1940), p. 139.

the mid-eighteenth-century Company in Britain as exhibiting some of the supranational characteristics that historians have occasionally applied to its presence in Asia.[48]

The violent short-term speculative and political movements of investors in and out of the Company that occurred during the 1760s served greatly to alter this profile of the stockholding community. Then other factors also promoted changes to the structure and geographical distribution of stock ownership, with increases to the joint-stock capital during the 1780s and 1790 opening the Company's doors to new investors. Conventional wisdom had long suggested that at any one time there was only ever a very limited amount of stock available to potential purchasers in the London market, but in 1786 the Company was permitted to add £800,000 to its existing joint-stock capital of £3.2 million in order to alleviate its burden of domestic debt.[49] Stock was offered *pro rata* to existing proprietors, and many of those who took up the option to subscribe then chose to dispose of their 'scrip' to new investors in the hope of realising a small profit. Further increases in the joint-stock capital followed when £1 million was subscribed in both 1789 and 1793, enabling the Company to pay off loans and reduce its bond debt.[50] As a result, the Company entered the nineteenth century with a nominal trading capital of £6 million, and this served to increase the number of account holders, so that by the 1830s its stock was distributed across more than 3,500 accounts.[51]

At the very time that the East India Company was opening its doors to a greater number of investors, it was also influenced by broad changes that were affecting the ownership of all British stocks and securities.[52] As

48 As suggested, but not examined in any detail, in Holden Furber, 'The history of the East India Companies: general problems', in Holden Furber, *Private fortunes and Company profits in the India trade in the 18th century*, ed. Rosane Rocher (Aldershot, 1997), item XIV, p. 416.

49 26 Geo. III, c.62. The Act allowed existing proprietors to add stock up to 50 per cent of their existing holding. However, if the stock issue was oversubscribed a proportionate deduction was to be made from each subscription. In the event, the issue was greatly oversubscribed when 2,929 individuals came forward with £2,229,780. As a result, the Company's issue of £800,000 new stock eventually raised £1,240,000 through subscriptions at 155 per cent. For details of the subscribers see the subscription ledgers, L/AG/14/5, vols. 246–7.

50 Following the practice established in 1786, preference was given to existing stockholders by 29 Geo. III, c.65 and 33 Geo. III, c.47. The stock issue of 1789 was sold at 170; that of 1793 at 200. For details see William Fairman, *The stocks examined and compared; or a guide to purchasers in the public funds* (1795), p. 37. Unfortunately the subscription ledgers of 1789 and 1793 do not appear to have survived.

51 On 4 March 1836 there were 3,590 stock accounts, as calculated from a manuscript list of stockholders in L/AG/14/5, vol. 248.

52 By this time the South Sea Company had long since ceased to function as an active trading company, and it now only managed annuity funds.

has recently been demonstrated in some detail, foreign investment in British stocks continued to rise during the third quarter of the century, so that a holding of over £20 million (or some 16 per cent of the total) was maintained after 1760, but during the late 1780s this began sharply to diminish.[53] When the national debt began to expand in size once more after the outbreak of war against France in 1793, these two trends ensured that the percentage of British securities held in overseas accounts fell to under 3 per cent in 1815. This general outline pattern of foreign investment can be applied to East India stockholding, although an appreciably higher proportion of Company stock – over a third of all accounts – was in overseas hands during the early 1760s, and withdrawal was not subsequently quite as complete as it was for other securities. As already noted, by the middle of the eighteenth century Dutch investment was of particular importance to the Company, and thus the withdrawal of Dutch investors after 1775 was the primary reason why foreign investment in East India stock represented only 7.5 per cent of the total in 1810. This quite clearly had a considerable effect upon the overall structure and distribution of stockholding, but what remains unclear is who filled the 'gap' left by the departure of the Dutch from the Company (and indeed from British funds in general). Was Dutch-owned stock simply redistributed within the existing narrow circle of metropolitan investors, or did it pass into the hands of new types of investor?

This question can be addressed by an examination of the long-term changes that are evident in stock ownership during the period. First, as far as the structure of the stock is concerned, there was an increase in the proportion of medium-sized accounts of between £1,000 and £4,999 (see table 4.2).[54] These rose from 42 per cent of the total in 1756 to 73.4 per cent in 1830, with a sharp increase occurring between 1769 and

---

53 J. F. Wright, 'The contribution of overseas savings to the funded national debt of Great Britain, 1750–1815', *Ec. Hist. Rev.*, 50 (1997), pp. 657–74.

54 Unless otherwise stated, the following analysis is based upon 10 per cent systematic samples of stock accounts covering alternate ledger periods between 1756 and 1830: L/AG/14/5, vol. 12, 5 April 1756–5 April 1761 (364 accounts); ibid., vols. 14–15, 5 Jan. 1764–5 Jan. 1767 (511 accounts); ibid., vols. 18–19, 5 July 1769–5 Jan. 1774 (542 accounts); ibid., vols. 22–3, 5 July 1783–5 July 1791 (491 accounts); ibid., vols. 28–31, 5 April 1796–5 April 1807 (663 accounts); ibid., vols. 36–9, 5 April 1818–5 April 1830 (698 accounts). This allows the structure, composition, and distribution to be analysed for every date on which accounts were balanced at the closing or opening of a ledger. Some of this data was originally analysed in H. V. Bowen, 'Investment and empire in the later eighteenth century: East India stockholding, 1756–1791', *Ec. Hist. Rev.*, 42 (1989), pp. 186–206. Since then, the analysis has been extended and some details slightly refined, notably because it has been possible more precisely to categorise some stockholders and/or their addresses.

Table 4.2. *The structure of East India stockholding, 1756–1830 (% no. of accounts)*

Size of holding in £s	1756	1761	1764	1767	1769	1774	1783	1791	1796	1807	1818	1830
<99	2.5	3.0	1.2	0.5	1.3	2.5	3.3	1.7	2.1	2.6	1.8	1.8
100–499	24.4	22.0	21.4	14.6	13.9	16.1	14.6	12.7	15.1	13.5	13.3	8.4
500	22.3	28.0	26.2	35.4	46.2	21.7	11.3	5.4	3.6	3.8	3.5	3.9
501–999	6.7	5.5	9.3	6.6	3.8	2.8	4.6	7.0	5.4	8.2	6.0	7.1
1,000	12.2	13.6	12.1	12.3	12.6	30.2	44.6	39.8	31.4	40.7	44.9	47.5
1,001–4,999	29.8	26.7	24.2	24.5	17.6	22.1	19.6	27.1	34.4	25.6	25.9	25.9
5,000–9,999	1.7	0.4	2.8	4.2	3.4	3.9	1.2	4.3	5.1	3.8	2.3	2.9
10,000>	0.4	0.8	2.8	1.9	1.3	0.7	0.8	2.0	2.7	1.8	2.3	2.4
	100	100	100	100	100.1	100	100	100	99.8	100	100	99.9

Source: see note 54, p. 98.

1774 which reflects the impact of the changes to voting qualifications introduced by North's Regulating Act of 1773. At the same time, the increase of the minimum voting qualification led to a long-term reduction in the number of accounts of £500 or less. Such accounts stood at 49.2 per cent of the total in 1756, but they increased to 61.4 per cent in 1769 (when almost half of all accounts belonged to £500 stockholders), before falling to 40.3 per cent in 1774. Thereafter, the most common stock transfers involved £1,000 rather than £500, and the ongoing decline in the number of small stockholders was such that by 1830 only 14.1 per cent of the accounts were in the hands of investors of £500 or less.

The number of large investors remained small, with accounts of £5,000 or more never representing more than 7.8 per cent of the total (as was the case in 1796), but the amount of stock owned collectively by these proprietors was at times very considerable. In 1764 and 1767, for example, over 40 per cent of the stock was engrossed by less than 6 per cent of the stockholding community (see table 4.3), most of whom were passive long-term investors who did not adjust the size of their holding during periods of even the most feverish speculation. Thereafter, as the price declined, the overall amount of stock in holdings of £5,000 or more was reduced to a low of 14 per cent in 1783. There was then a recovery, partly because the subscriptions of 1786–93 allowed existing medium-sized accounts to be increased beyond the threshold figure of £5,000, and for the remainder of the period large holdings always accounted for between 25 and 37 per cent of the Company's stock.[55] Because, with the exception of the mid- to late 1760s, the stock held in medium-sized accounts was always above 56 per cent of the total, the increase of stock in large holdings meant that a considerable squeeze was exerted on the proportion of stock in the hands of small investors. The political importance of the £500 voting qualification had served to ensure that over a fifth of the Company's stock was owned by small stockholders in July 1769, but the effect of the Regulating Act was greatly to diminish the overall amount of stock held in units of £500 or less. By 1830, a mere 2.6 per cent of the Company's stock was owned by small investors. In overall terms, therefore, changes to the structure of East India stock served to

---

55 In view of later discussion it is noteworthy that none of the large investors in the sample for 1818 was Dutch. The largest amount in the sample was £22,000 owned by John Hodson, esq. of Plymouth. Hodson was noted in the ledger as being deceased, but it is unclear when his death had occurred.

Table 4.3. *The structure of East India stockholding, 1756–1830 (% stock)*

Size of holding in £s	1756	1761	1764	1767	1769	1774	1783	1791	1796	1807	1818	1830
<99	0.1	0.1	0	0	0	0.1	0.1	0	0	0.1	0	0.1
100–499	5.8	4.7	3.3	2.4	2.5	2.7	3.0	1.7	2.0	2.2	2.2	1.3
500	9.8	12.2	8.4	10.9	19.1	8.3	4.8	1.5	1.0	1.2	1.1	1.2
501–999	3.8	3.2	4.1	2.7	2.0	1.5	2.5	2.8	1.9	3.5	2.7	3.0
1,000	10.7	11.9	7.7	7.6	10.4	23.1	37.6	22.4	16.8	25.6	28.7	28.1
1,001–4,999	57.3	51.1	35.0	33.9	34.7	37.2	37.9	34.7	41.3	38.8	39.3	38.4
5,000–9,999	8.0	2.0	12.6	18.6	17.8	18.5	7.0	16.7	17.3	15.2	8.2	9.9
10000>	4.6	14.7	28.9	23.9	13.5	8.5	7.0	20.2	19.7	13.5	17.8	18.0
	100.1	99.9	100	100	100	99.9	99.9	100	100	100.1	100	100

Source: see note 54, p. 98.

strengthen the position of the larger investors within the Company, and as a reflection of this, the average size of a nominal holding rose, with some fluctuations, from £1,135 in 1756 to £1,688 in 1830.[56]

As is to be expected, the underlying shifts in the structure of the Company's stock were accompanied by changes to the socio-occupational profile of the stockholding community. This becomes clear from analysis of the personal information recorded in each stock account under the broad descriptive heading of title or 'style' (see table 4.4). This information is far from complete before the early 1770s,[57] but although the noting of personal details by the ledger clerks cannot be regarded as ever having been an exact science, it was recorded far more systematically after the mid-1760s.[58] As a result, the collective profile of the stockholders becomes much sharper over time and this provides evidence to support a view that the social composition of the Company during the early nineteenth century was in many ways quite different from that of fifty years earlier.

Most notable among male stockholders was a substantial advance in the proportion that can be classified by formal title or use of the style 'esq.' or 'gent.'. As with the City at large, members of the landed class or aristocracy were not strongly represented within the East India stockholding community, and few committed substantial amounts of finance to the Company for any length of time.[59] Members of the aristocracy were, however, always to be found in the categories of small or short-term investor, having been driven there by the imperatives of portfolio management, speculation, or politics. Some individuals made astute use

---

56 For the strengthened political position of the large investors see above, pp. 70–1.

57 In 1756 only 57 per cent of the stockholders were identified by title or occupation in the stock ledgers, but the proportion rose to 85 per cent by 1774. By the 1790s descriptive information was noted on around 90 per cent of accounts, and in 1830 the percentage figure had risen to over 94 per cent. Of course, what was recorded depended upon what stockholders told the clerks, and thus the details upon which any socio-occupational analysis of the stockholders is based represent the self-perceptions of individuals rather than any objective classification.

58 The Transfer Office was much busier after 1760, and stock-splitting activity meant that the volume of business conducted by the eight staff was at times considerable. Whereas accounts had been recorded in only one ledger in 1756, they were distributed across four ledgers by 1796. It was particularly important that the ledger clerks be able to identify individuals presenting themselves at the Transfer Office so as to prevent deception of the type that occurred in 1771 when Robert Powell was charged with 'personating Taylor Barrow and thereby fraudulently transferring £400 East India Stock' (*Annual Register* (1771), pp. 208–11). For a case involving a forged transfer of stock in 1770 see L/L/6, vol. 1, no. 147, p. 201. Changes to the general working practices of the Stock Transfer Office are set out in L/AG/9/3, vol. 1, nos. 23, 26, 26a.

59 For the limited amounted of aristocratic investment in the City see J. V. Beckett, *The aristocracy in England, 1660–1914* (Oxford, 1986), pp. 84–6.

Table 4.4. *The social composition of East India stockholders, 1756–1830 (% no. of accounts)*

	1756	1761	1764	1767	1769	1774	1783	1791	1796	1807	1818	1830
Male												
Titled	5.0	4.7	6.4	5.7	5.9	5.3	8.3	7.3	6.7	5.6	8.1	5.5
Esq.	14.7	15.2	20.6	24.1	26.5	29.8	31.3	31.4	36.3	40.9	39.8	43.0
Gent.	0	2.1	4.0	6.6	6.3	9.5	9.2	11.4	8.8	8.9	5.8	5.5
Merchant	0.8	4.7	3.7	9.4	8.0	8.8	7.5	6.4	3.6	3.8	4.0	2.9
Finance	0.8	0.4	0.8	0.9	2.1	1.7	3.3	4.4	1.2	1.5	1.4	1.3
Profession	2.1	3.8	3.7	4.7	5.0	7.0	5.0	5.0	7.2	5.9	5.7	8.7
Army, navy, Company armed and marine service	1.7	2.1	2.0	2.4	3.8	3.2	5.0	4.7	3.6	5.1	8.4	7.4
Trade, retail, manufacture	2.5	4.7	5.2	6.1	3.8	7.7	2.1	6.4	4.2	4.4	3.5	3.2
Agriculture	0	0	0	0	0	0	0	0	0.3	0.8	0.3	0.5
Unclassified	39.1	31.8	27.0	20.7	24.4	13.7	12.1	8.4	10.9	7.8	6.0	5.3
Female												
Titled	2.5	2.1	1.2	1.4	1.7	1.7	0.8	0.7	1.2	1.3	0.3	0.8
Wife	0.8	0.8	1.6	2.8	1.7	0.7	2.1	1.7	1.5	1.0	1.4	0.8
Widow	12.6	11.0	11.3	6.1	4.6	5.9	7.1	4.7	5.4	4.4	6.3	6.3
Spinster	12.6	12.3	8.9	6.6	4.2	3.2	4.6	7.0	7.5	7.2	8.6	8.4
Unclassified	3.4	3.0	3.2	2.4	1.9	1.4	1.2	0.3	0.9	1.0	0.3	0.5
Corporations	1.3	1.3	0.4	0	0	0.4	0.4	0.3	0.6	0.5	0	0

Note: For the definition of categories see note 64, p. 105.
Source: see note 54, p. 98.

of the funds to diversify their investments and advance their family fortunes,[60] and it was Lord Holland who led the headlong rush of speculators into the Company in 1766. The lure of East India politics was also a powerful one and a number of peers took out a voting qualification at the General Court. As a result, thirty-four peers held East India stock at one time or another between 1764 and 1774, with a high point of twenty being reached in July 1769.[61]

In spite of this, the imprint of the aristocracy and the landowning classes upon the Company remained a faint one, unlike that of London's gentlemanly élite. In the sample of stockholders for 1756, fewer than 20 per cent of all the proprietors were denoted by a male title or 'esq.', and none was described as 'gent.',[62] but by 1807 these categories together accounted for over a half of all stockholders. Of course, not too much should be read into this because there was a large number of unclassified accounts in 1756 and the terms 'esq.' and 'gent.' are notoriously slippery and imprecise. Throughout society as a whole, the self-application of these marks of status and social standing extended greatly during the second half of the eighteenth century,[63] and some of the stockholders who bestowed gentlemanly status upon themselves could equally be described in occupational terms as merchants, financiers, or tradesmen. It is clear that for reasons of self-esteem a good proportion of the male stockholders wished to distance themselves from the world of work and thus, legitimately or otherwise, they identified themselves with the leisured élite or *rentier* class. They might therefore be considered to have been archetypal 'gentlemanly capitalists'.

There was a marked long-term increase in the proportion of male stockholders described in the ledgers by occupation, from 7.9 per cent of the overall total in 1756 to 24 per cent in 1830. In part this again simply reflects the fact that, over time, information was recorded more systematically by the transfer clerks. And, reinforcing a point made above, although the categories of 'merchant' and 'financier' never between them

---

60 See, for example, J. V. Beckett, *The rise and fall of the Grenvilles, Dukes of Buckingham and Chandos, 1710–1921* (Manchester, 1994), pp. 38, 50–1.

61 H. V. Bowen, 'British politics and the East India Company, 1766–1773', unpublished PhD thesis, University of Wales (1986), pp. 99–101. For most of the decade, the average size of the holdings owned by peers stood between £942 and £1,600, although between 1767 and 1771 the figure was substantially inflated by the presence of Lord Holland's account, which stood at £39,000 by the latter date.

62 In the case of joint accounts the description applied to the first-named partner has been used.

63 For a discussion of this and other related matters see P. J. Corfield, 'Class by name and number in eighteenth-century Britain', *History*, 72 (1987), pp. 38–61.

contained much above 10 per cent of all stockholders,[64] many of the individuals denoted as 'gent.' or 'esq.' were in fact active participants in the worlds of trade and business. Therefore these figures do not properly represent the strength of the connection between the Company, the City, and the world of business. Nevertheless, it is still possible to discern some other noteworthy trends within the male stockholding community. In the gradually expanding professional category, for example, there was a significant advance of clergymen, and by the end of the eighteenth century clerical stockholders were to be found in many of the southern, midland, and eastern counties of England. There was also a sustained long-term increase in the number of stockholders who were officers in the army, navy, or the Company's armed forces, so that in 1818 stock was owned by men such as General Sir Robert Baird of the 54th Regiment of Foot (£1,000), Admiral Ross Donnelly (£3,000), and Major-General Thomas Dallas of the Company's army (£2,500). Indeed, in 1818 over 8 per cent of the Company's entire stock was owned by such men, many of whom were on overseas tours of duty. The proportion of stockholders describing themselves as engaged in domestic trade or manufacture never rose beyond 8 per cent of the total, but this category contained some substantial investors as well as those of a more humble standing, and thus in 1807 it included James Maddocks, a timber merchant of Rosemary Lane (£6,000) and Alexander Adams, a cooper of Whitechapel (£1,000), as well as Henry Morrell, a stationer of Fleet Street (£100).

In broad terms, the most obvious long-term change to the social composition of East India stockholders was a marked reduction in the presence of women. The full extent of this change was perhaps concealed from contemporaries by the fact that a considerable number of women participated in the Company's political process by voting at ballots and elections.[65] Some of them played an even more active role by acting as lobbyists for candidates for election to the Court of Directors, as was the

---

64 'Finance' embraces descriptions such as banker, broker, and 'GS' or goldsmith. 'Merchant' includes all those who were not specifically engaged in domestic retail trade.

65 During the 1760s women routinely received 'split' stock and used their votes accordingly. There is no evidence that any woman ever spoke at a General Court debate, although some, such as Mary Barwell, the sister of Richard Barwell, were prominent as political agents at East India House. In March 1773 women held 245 (10 per cent) of the 2,437 votes that could be cast at the unreformed General Court, while in April 1795 199 women possessed 230 (9.5 per cent) of the 2,434 votes that existed under the terms of the proportional qualification system. For 1773 see the printed list of 9 March (note 1); for 1795 see *A list of the members of the United Company . . . 8 April 1795 . . .* (1795). For a general discussion of female investors see Susan Staves, 'Investments, votes and "bribes": women as shareholders in the chartered companies', in Hilda Smith (ed.), *Women and the early modern British political tradition* (Cambridge, 1998), pp. 259–78.

case in 1798 when the aspiring director Colonel Sweny Toone found that 'Mrs. Morgan, Mrs. Metcalfe, Mrs. Floyer and all the beauty of Portland Place are canvassing against me. Hard upon a man who loves the sex so well!'[66] Even so, while the general characteristics of male and female stockholding had always been dissimilar, the differences were sharpened after 1760. Most notably, women always held a smaller average amount of stock than men. The size of difference was especially marked during the late eighteenth century, although it steadily diminished thereafter (see table 4.5). The overall proportion of female stockholders was also reduced over time, especially between 1756 and 1774 (table 4.6).

In 1756 women owned almost one-third of East India stock accounts, and over a quarter of the stock itself, but during the turbulence of the 1760s many took flight from the Company, motivated either by a desire to cash in on the rise in prices or, alternatively, by fear that their hitherto secure investment was being jeopardised by the actions of speculators. In 1761 almost 70 per cent of the women who had owned stock in 1756 still did so, but this type of medium-term stockholding subsequently declined as speculators and politicians engrossed East India stock. Thus in 1767 only half of the women who had been stockholders in 1764 remained as owners of stock. The considerable increase in the size of their average account suggests that it was the smaller female stockholders who were selling their stock, and this is confirmed by the sharp reduction in accounts of £500 or less that were owned by women. At the same time, the rise in the size of the average holding was driven by a marked increase in the proportion of the female-owned accounts held by Dutch investors – from 19.4 per cent in 1756 to 56.1 per cent in 1767 – and this would suggest that these women were more inclined than their British counterparts to accumulate stock in the hope of realising a short-term profit. Such a view can be supported by a calculation which suggests that after the speculative bubble burst in the early summer of 1769, the Dutch holdings of female-owned stock fell to only 24.2 per cent, and this caused the size of the average female holding to slump back to just over £1,000.

After the upheaval of the 1760s had subsided, women were left in a position in which they held a much smaller share of the accounts than had previously been the case. In 1769 women owned only 13.9 per cent of accounts but, although the proportion slipped further by 1774, there was then a slight recovery so that for the rest of the period between 14 and 17

---

66 Quoted in Philips, *East India Company*, p. 6.

Table 4.5. *Average size of stockholdings in £s, 1756–1830*

	1756	1761	1764	1767	1769	1774	1783	1791	1796	1807	1818	1830
Male stock holders	1,150	1,160	1,673	1,641	1,246	1,367	1,239	1,913	1,954	1,630	1,610	1,703
Female stock holders	974	951	1,254	1,530	1,013	779	911	1,015	1,346	1,161	1,341	1,615

Source: see note 54, p. 98.

Table 4.6. *Female stockholders, 1756–1830*

	1756	1761	1764	1767	1769	1774	1783	1791	1796	1807	1818	1830
Accounts (%)	32.3	29.7	25.4	19.3	13.9	12.6	16.2	14.7	16.3	14.1	17.0	16.9
Stock (%)	27.7	24.7	20.3	18.3	11.6	7.5	12.5	8.4	11.7	10.3	14.6	16.1

Source: see note 54, p. 98.

per cent of the accounts were owned by female investors. The proportion of Company stock they owned, however, was less than this and at times during the mid-1770s and the early 1790s the amount of stock in female hands fell to less than 10 per cent of the total. There was something of a re-emergence of foreign investors among the female stockholders during the 1780s and early 1790s, but this was not sufficient to arrest the reduction in the stock and accounts owned by women. The proportion of stock held by women did increase again during the 1810s and 1820s, but it can be calculated that in 1836 only 11.9 per cent (£715,516) of the Company's total stock was held by women in single-owner accounts. By that time, women owned 17.3 per cent of all accounts, and this meant that they were less visible in the Company than they had been three-quarters of a century earlier when widows and spinsters had between them accounted for over a quarter of all stockholdings. It also meant that the broad distribution of investment in the Company was somewhat different from that which existed across the full range of government securities. By 1840 almost one-half of Britain's public creditors were female, thus giving rise to a distinctive form of 'gentlewomanly capitalism',[67] but this was not mirrored in the East India Company where male investors continued to represent a substantial majority.

It is clear that changes to the overall position of women within the stockholding community were determined in part by the ebb and flow of investment in the Company by foreigners, and the broad issue of foreign investment was a matter of considerable interest to observers who feared that the Company might be undermined from within by combinations of hostile foreign investors acting in concert in the General Court.[68] If such anxieties were misplaced, the issue of foreign investment remains important because it is central to any discussion of the Company's collective identity and the distribution of profits arising from British commercial and imperial expansion in India and other parts of Asia.

As with other aspects of East India stockholding, significant changes were evident in the geographical distribution of investors after 1760. This becomes quite clear from analysis of the addresses of account holders

---

67 David R. Green and Alastair Owens, 'Gentlewomanly capitalism? Spinsters, widows, and wealth holding in England and Wales, c.1800–1860', *Ec. Hist. Rev.*, 56 (2003), pp. 510–36.
68 See, for example, *London Evening Post*, 6–8 May 1773. Since votes by proxy were not permitted in the General Court, it is unlikely that this ever happened, although it was claimed that Dutch stockholders had once chartered a vessel in order to travel to London to cast their votes at an important ballot (Governor George Johnstone, speech in the Commons, 8 June 1773, as reported in BL, Eg. MS 250, p. 5).

recorded in the stock ledgers. Again, however, this evidence needs to be handled with a degree of caution. First, as with social descriptions, some account details did not contain any information about a stockholder's address or place of residence, and in the early part of the period this affected around one-fifth to one-quarter of all accounts. As recording procedures were tightened, however, the proportion of accounts unclassified by address fell to about 10 per cent of the total; and by the beginning of the nineteenth century it was only a very small number. The second problem is that addresses were given by account holders primarily for identification purposes and therefore they do not always represent an accurate record of place of residence. Thus, some stockholders named their place of work, as was the case with some of those who were employed at East India House or those who frequented the Stock Exchange. Others gave town house addresses rather than details of any home in the provinces, and some who belonged to the mobile foreign merchant community gave temporary London addresses rather than details of any more permanent home in Amsterdam or elsewhere. Table 4.7 would seem to suggest, for example, that there were no Scottish stockholders before 1783, and only a small number thereafter, but this was clearly not the case and simply reflects the fact that those prominent London Scots who did own stock provided the ledger clerks with an address in the capital, rather than one in Scotland or 'North Britain'. Even so, while any analysis of address information must necessarily be prefaced by these caveats, several trends can be identified which point to significant long-term changes to the geographical redistribution of the Company's stock.

After 1769, when the vast majority of accounts contained address information, the number of accounts registered in London and the Home Counties always represented between 55 and 65 per cent of the total. Moreover, it can be calculated that after 1790 the amount of stock owned by investors with addresses in London and the Home Counties had risen to over 60 per cent of the total. This ensured that the Company retained the major defining characteristic it had possessed since its creation: a close association with the merchant, financial, professional, titled, and gentlemanly classes who lived in and around the metropolis. At the same time, however, the remainder of the stock underwent some profound changes in terms of its ownership and geographical distribution.

Without doubt, the major cause of change to the geographical profile of the stockholders was the withdrawal of Dutch finance from the

Table 4-7. *The geographical distribution of East India stockholders, 1756–1830 (% no. of accounts)*

	1756	1761	1764	1767	1769	1774	1783	1791	1796	1807	1818	1830
London	34.0	30.9	37.5	50.5	57.6	49.1	52.1	50.5	51.4	46.8	47.3	45.9
Home Counties	5.9	8.0	5.2	4.7	8.8	8.4	7.9	9.7	10.9	10.0	14.7	15.0
Southern counties	2.9	2.5	2.0	2.8	3.8	3.2	5.0	4.0	7.5	8.9	6.3	7.6
West Country	2.1	2.1	0.4	0.5	1.3	2.1	1.7	3.0	1.5	3.1	4.0	4.2
Midlands	2.5	1.7	2.0	1.4	0.8	1.0	2.5	2.7	3.0	2.3	2.6	2.6
South West	0	0	1.6	0.9	0	0.7	0.8	1.0	3.0	1.5	0.9	1.0
East Anglia	1.7	1.7	1.6	0.9	0.8	2.8	1.7	2.3	2.4	2.0	3.5	3.2
North	0	0	0.4	0.5	0.4	0	0	1.7	1.9	1.3	0.9	1.8
North West	0.4	0.4	0	0	0	0.4	0	0	0	0	0	0
North East	0	0	0.4	0.5	0	0	1.7	1.3	0.3	0.8	0.6	0
Scotland	0	0	0	0	0	0	0.4	1.0	1.2	3.1	2.3	3.9
Wales	0	0	0	0	0	0.7	0	0.3	0.3	0.2	0.3	0.3
Ireland and Islands	0	0	0.4	0	0	0.4	0.4	0.7	1.9	1.0	0.6	1.3
Holland	21.0	28.0	30.2	22.6	14.7	20.3	12.9	13.0	8.4	10.0	7.2	4.5
Rest of Europe	3.4	3.0	4.0	3.3	2.1	3.9	7.1	5.0	3.0	3.1	2.6	1.6
Beyond Europe	0	0	0	0	0	0	1.2	0.3	0.6	2.6	2.6	5.5
Crown/Company service	0.8	0.4	0	0	0	0	0.4	0.7	0.6	1.3	2.3	0.8
Unclassified	25.2	21.2	14.1	11.3	9.7	7.0	4.2	2.7	2.1	2.0	1.4	0.8

Note: So as to enable comparisons to be made with Dickson's findings for the mid-eighteenth century, the Home Counties have been defined as Middlesex, Surrey, Essex and Herts. The other English regions have been defined in the following way. London: City and suburbs (without county specified in address). Southern counties: Kent, Hants, Sussex, Berks., Bucks., Oxon, Dorset, Isle of Wight. West Country: Gloucs., Somerset, Wilts., Worcs., Herefordshire. Midlands: Warwicks., Northants., Beds., Leics., Notts., Derbys., Lincs., Salop., Staffs. South West: Devon and Cornwall. East Anglia: Norfolk, Suffolk, Cambs. North: Lancs., Yorks., Cheshire. North West: Cumberland and Westmoreland. North East: Durham and Northumberland. Wales includes Monmouthshire. Ireland and Islands includes the Isle of Man and the Channel Islands. 'Crown/Company service' includes all those who are denoted as being in the forces or Company service but whose location is unspecified.

Source: see note 54, p. 98.

Company. At twin peaks in 1764 and 1774 Dutch investors held over 30 per cent of East India stock, although in terms of the number of accounts the percentage figure was usually rather lower. Thus in January 1774 the amount of stock held in accounts with Dutch addresses stood at 33.6 per cent of the total, and the number of accounts at 20.3 per cent. As this suggests, average Dutch holdings were considerably larger than those of stockholders as a whole, and indeed they were over twice as large during the late 1760s and early 1770s. However, the high-profile position of the Dutch within the Company was lost during and immediately after the War of American Independence when the ending of Dutch neutrality and a loss of confidence in British credit were followed by large numbers of investors taking up French loans and American securities.[69] This led to the amount of Dutch-owned stock falling quite sharply to 14.2 per cent of the total in 1791 and 6.8 per cent in 1796, by which time the number of Dutch accounts represented only 8.4 per cent of the total. There was then a small recovery in the Dutch position so that by 1807 the amount of stock held in Dutch hands was 9.9 per cent of the total and the number of accounts stood at 10.0 per cent, but this was still a far cry from the heavy investment of the 1760s and 1770s.[70] By 1836 a mere 3.2 per cent of accounts were held by stockholders in Holland, and only 1.2 per cent (£74,990) of the Company's stock was owned by Dutch investors (see table 4.8).

In terms of other foreign or overseas investment in the Company, the evidence suggests little overall change during the period as a whole. Accounts held in parts of Europe other than the United Provinces fluctuated between 2.1 and 7.1 per cent of the total, with small pockets of investors always to be found in Antwerp, Brussels, Geneva, and Leghorn. There were, however, signs of a slight advance in investment from individuals in the wider world, although only very rarely were these foreign investors. In 1806 there was a small handful of investors in the United States, including three members of the Church family of New

---

69 The reasons for the Dutch withdrawal from British funds and companies are outlined in C. H. Wilson, *Anglo-Dutch commerce and finance in the eighteenth century* (Cambridge, 1941), pp. 189–96.

70 Estimates for the proportionate amount of stock held in Dutch hands in 1791, and indeed in the overseas accounts as a whole, are somewhat lower than those offered by J. F. Wright, who fails to take into account the second (£1 million) stock increase of 1789 thus leading to an overstatement of the East India stock still held in foreign hands (Wright, 'The contribution of overseas savings', p. 669). An adjustment of Wright's figures to take into account the £1 million subscription of 1789 reduces the amount of stock held in foreign hands from his estimate of 20.6 per cent of the total to 16.5 per cent.

Table 4.8. *East India stock ownership, 4 March 1836*

Location of stockholder	No. of accounts	% accounts	Amount of stock in £s	% stock
London	1,687	47.0	3,201,676.2	53.4
Home Counties	422	11.7	617,907.4	10.3
Southern counties	308	8.6	482,741.6	8.0
West Country	209	5.8	299,569.8	5.0
Midlands	98	2.7	135,749.2	2.3
South West	76	2.1	93,950.1	1.6
East Anglia	76	2.1	110,844.5	1.8
North	58	1.6	101,799.7	1.7
North West	6	0.2	4,879.3	0.1
North East	13	0.4	11,799.6	0.2
Scotland	153	4.3	240,944.6	4.0
Wales	39	1.1	79,633.4	1.3
Ireland and Islands	39	1.1	44,649.0	0.7
Holland	115	3.2	74,990.4	1.2
Rest of Europe	28	0.8	27,794.0	0.5
Beyond Europe	155	4.3	282,407.4	4.7
Crown/Company service	90	2.5	148,532.0	2.5
Unclassified	18	0.5	39,727.3	0.7
Total	3,590	100	5,999,595.5	100

Note: Definition of geographical categories as in table 4.7.
Source: L/AG/14/5/248.

York, and in 1830 Susanna Stephens, spinster, of Boston owned £400 stock, but their presence amounted to little more than the occasional colonial American investor who can be identified in the period before 1760.[71] Instead, investors in the wider world were usually Britons serving or living overseas, and thus in 1807, for example, accounts belonged to James Laing, esq. of Dominica (£1,000) and John Spencer Smith esq. of Constantinople (£1,000). Most notably, and not surprisingly, small concentrations of investors were to be found in the Company's major overseas settlements. From 1790 onwards, the ledgers reveal increasing numbers of stockholders in Bombay, Calcutta, and Madras, and in March 1836 155 account holders (4.3 per cent of the total) had places of residence

---

71 P. G. M. Dickson, *The financial revolution in England: a study in the development of public credit, 1688–1756* (1967), p. 317, n. 3. For the short-term investment of the Church family and Catherine Cruger, wife of Philip Cruger of New York, who owned stock for a similarly brief period of time see L/AG/14/5, vol. 28, p. 305.

beyond Europe, with a further 90 (2.5 per cent) being military or Company personnel whose location was unspecified. It is also known that some individuals serving overseas transferred stock accounts to attorneys for management during extended periods of absence so too much should not be read into these figures, but it is noteworthy that some heading to India were now leaving a part of their fortune at home. This is quite a contrast with earlier times when Company servants endeavoured to utilise every possible financial resource in order to engage as fully as possible in private trade.

With the proportion of accounts in London and the Home Counties fairly stable, and the Dutch presence diminishing after 1780, there was a steady growth in the presence of provincial British investors in the Company. In the middle of the eighteenth century, the number of accounts registered to stockholders with addresses beyond the Home Counties was around 10 per cent, and it stayed that way until the 1770s when a steady advance was accompanied by an increase in the size of provincial holdings. The proportion of accounts belonging to those in the mainland provinces rose to just over 13 per cent in 1783 and to 17.3 per cent in 1791, before it broke through the 20 per cent barrier in 1796 where it remained thereafter.

The geographical broadening of the investment base within the Company's stock occurred partly because a number of developments were helping to create a more integrated financial market in late eighteenth-century Britain.[72] Potential investors were increasingly better informed about investment opportunities, and they were able to follow news about Britain's fluctuating overseas fortunes via the intelligence, speculation, and rumour that featured prominently in provincial newspapers as well as the London press. They were also able to take advantage of a growing network of brokers, agents, and attorneys, which helped more effectively to channel provincial resources from most regions towards London.

Even so, there was no dramatic increase in the use of agents and attorneys for the purchase and sale of East India stock, and the great majority of transactions were made by individuals who conducted business on their own behalf at the Transfer Office in Leadenhall Street.[73] The

---

72 On this theme see M. Buchinsky and B. Polak, 'The emergence of a national capital market in England, 1710–1800', *Journal of Economic History*, 53 (1993), pp. 1–24.

73 Between 1751 and 1816 letters of attorney executed in the country had to be witnessed by a minister and churchwarden of the parish where the stockholder lived. If the letter was executed 'in town', it had to be witnessed by 'persons well known'. See L/AG/9/3, vol. 1, no. 24a.

proportion of transfers made by attorneys remained quite stable, usually in the range between 20 and 34 per cent, with only a very slight upward trend discernible between 1756 and 1834. Beneath the surface, however, there were changes to the type of stockholder who used an attorney. Necessity had long obliged foreign investors to use a well-established network of specialist agents to conduct transactions and collect dividend payments, but as their position in the Company diminished so provincial British investors came to the fore among those using intermediaries to make transfers of stock. These factors, together with the continuing expansion of the war-driven national debt, helped to establish an investment culture in Britain which promoted an expansion in the number of public creditors from around 60,000 in the mid-eighteenth century to somewhere in the region of 500,000 at the end of the Napoleonic War.[74] This served to reduce the prominence of East India stock alongside the vast amount of government stock that was available, but it also meant that by the early decades of the nineteenth century there was a much wider circle of domestic investors who had the means, knowledge, and opportunity to secure their own financial stake in the overseas empire.

Investors were always to be were found in the southern counties of England where the Company's military and maritime tentacles were extended in a number of different ways, and thus there was a sustained and growing stockholder presence in Kent, Sussex, and Hampshire.[75] But by the beginning of the nineteenth century stockholders were also to be found in clusters in the west and south-west (especially in Bath, Exeter, and Plymouth), and in East Anglia (scattered across Suffolk and Norfolk), the Midlands, Yorkshire, and Scotland. By March 1836, 728 stockholders (20.3 per cent of the total) lived in the mainland provinces (153 of them in Scotland), and between them they owned £1,079,170 (18 per cent) of the Company's capital stock.

The only parts of Britain where there were scarcely any investors were the north-west and the north-east of England, and it is noteworthy that East India stockholders were conspicuous by their near-absence from the western ports – Bristol, Glasgow, and Liverpool – where there continued to be plenty of alternative maritime, commercial, and industrial investment opportunities in the Atlantic world, despite the loss of America in

---

74 Dickson, *Financial revolution*, pp. 285–6, n. 1.
75 For Company stockholders in the southern counties during the late eighteenth and early nineteenth centuries see James H. Thomas, 'The East India Company and the Isle of Wight, 1700–1840', *The Local Historian*, 30 (2000), pp. 16–19.

1783. Equally, the evidence does not suggest that many of the provincial merchants and manufacturers who were agitating for access to Indian markets bought East India stock with the intention of undermining the Company and its monopoly from within.

What is discernible, however, is that the new provincial investors drawn into the Company were in some ways quite different from their metropolitan counterparts. During the early 1800s the gender balance was approximately the same, with between 12 and 14 per cent being female, but the provincial accounts were rather smaller and less 'active' in terms of the amount of buying and selling that went on. The provincial investors contained a far higher proportion of men who styled themselves 'gent.', and there was a noticeable absence of the merchants, bankers, and tradesmen who were prominent in the ranks of London's East India investors. These were clearly not investors seeking immediate gains, for they purchased their stock long after the great waves of speculative activity had subsided and as the Company returned to its pre-1760 associations with stability, security, and guaranteed annual returns.

Throughout the period, around two-thirds of East India stock was held in the hands of investors located in London and south-east of England, and thus it could be argued that the Company was held firmly in the hands of an emerging gentlemanly capitalist elite. Yet, beyond its solid core of City investors, the Company's financial foundations were far from unchanging. The gradual replacement of foreign investors by those drawn from the provinces reduced the Company's cosmopolitanism and helped to ensure that after 1800 the fruits of trade and empire were distributed almost exclusively to investors resident in Britain. The upheavals within the stockholding community caused by politics and speculation, changes to investor behaviour on the Continent, and the maturing of Britain's own financial markets, combined to ensure that the Company ceased to offer a home for large amounts of Dutch capital and instead it presented opportunities to investors drawn from across the British provinces. As a result, ownership of the Company became much more firmly rooted in Britain, and this served to sharpen the Company's profile as an institution incorporating the whole nation, and not just the City of London.

Of course, the Company's stockholders were unable to exert much, if any, influence upon the process of expansion in India. The general problem of how any metropolitan control could be established over actions and events in South Asia is discussed in later chapters, but here it is sufficient to say that the structures of the Company's finances and decision-making systems were such that the stockholders' resources and votes were not brought directly to bear upon British activity in Asia. Nevertheless, the stockholders did elect the directors of the Company, and in doing so they bestowed upon their representatives the responsibility of managing the Company's affairs at home and abroad. Consequently, the next chapter turns to consideration of those in London who were charged by the stockholders with directing, managing, and administering the business of empire.

CHAPTER 5

People: Company men

Several thousand stockholders provided the human fabric of the East India Company in Britain, but a much smaller body of men managed the Company and made the policies and decisions that defined its corporate values. Twenty-four directors and a supporting cast of officers and clerks worked at East India House to supervise, regulate, and control the Company's affairs. They processed vast amounts of information, formulated strategy, agreed decisions, and composed lengthy despatches that were sent to India, China, and elsewhere in the hope that the overseas servants would then act responsibly and in the best interests of the Company. Much depended, therefore, upon the skills, knowledge, and application of the men in London who acted as the guardians of the Company's interests and formed what became known as the 'home government' of India.

The profitable conduct of long-distance trade had always offered formidable challenges to the directors and their London servants, and the problems of distance and the slow speed of communication made it similarly difficult for them to govern a vast territorial empire. Those in the metropolis could do little to influence the course of expansion or the actions of Company servants, yet many critics of British activity in India were swift to point the finger of blame at the occupants of East India House. As reports of misrule and corruption began to filter back to Britain from India during the 1760s and 1770s, commentators argued that the roots of these problems lay in the mismanagement of the Company's affairs at home. The Company's senior figures were certainly not without individual or collective failings, but much of the abuse aimed at them came from disaffected or politically motivated men who often bore the bitterest of grudges against the Company in general and the directors in particular. Getting beyond harsh contemporary criticism in order to make a fair assessment of those who occupied high Company office in Britain is thus no easy task, but it must be undertaken if a better understanding is to be gained of how the Company evolved in the way that it did, and how it responded to the problems of trade and empire. Consequently, this chapter considers the background, qualities, and characteristics of the men who worked at East India House, and it examines how assiduous and effective they were in fulfilling their obligations to the Company and, increasingly, the nation at large.

THE DIRECTORS

By the beginning of the nineteenth century the directors of the East India Company had long ceased simply to be the managers of a commercial organisation, and Joseph Hume described them as 'the ministers of a state, or as the monarchs of an empire, greater in extent and population, if he excepted China, than any other in the world'.[1] The mid-Victorian historian John W. Kaye thought along similar lines and wrote that any man who wished to be a director of the East India Company during the early part of the nineteenth century 'aspired to be nothing less than the twenty-fourth part of a king – of one of the greatest sovereigns in the world'.[2] These were bold claims, but although the influence and control exerted by these 'sovereigns' upon events in Asia were always strictly limited, the actions, attitudes, and ideas of the directors did nevertheless serve to shape the general development of the Company's trade and empire. As the former Chairman Charles Grant put it, the conduct of the Company's affairs 'depended essentially upon the character and conduct of the gentlemen composing the Direction'.[3]

Occupying what Hume described as an 'arduous but most respectable office',[4] some public-spirited men endeavoured to contribute to the exertion of British power and influence in Asia. At the same time, however, many were attracted by the rewards and opportunities associated with being a director and in 1814 one stockholder declared that 'There was no officer under the Crown, except the first Lord of the Treasury, who possessed such advantages as the directors of the East India Company;

---

1 *The speech of Mr Joseph Hume at the East India House on the 6th October 1813* . . . (1813), p. 10. Any study of the Company's directors is heavily indebted to the detailed work in J. G. Parker, 'The directors of the East India Company, 1754–1790', unpublished PhD thesis, University of Edinburgh (1977). This chapter is no exception and I am especially grateful to Dr Parker for providing me with a copy of his thesis.
2 John William Kaye, *The life and correspondence of Henry St George Tucker, late Accountant-General of Bengal and Chairman of the East India Company* (1854), p. 325.
3 *Adjourned debate at the East India House* . . . *6th October 1813* (1813), p. 140.
4 *Speech of Mr Joseph Hume*, p. 14.

and, he believed, no gentleman could deserve them better.'[5] Directors received little by way of direct financial return for fulfilling their duties and obligations, and their annual allowance was fixed at £150 until it was doubled in 1793. This enabled one stockholder to declare in 1831 that the stipend was 'barely sufficient to defray coach hire',[6] but the fringe benefits enjoyed by the directors were substantial, not least perhaps because they were able to enjoy regular hospitality at the Company's expense. Meetings of the Court of Directors were preceded by breakfast and followed by a good dinner, and in 1784 the bill for such gatherings amounted to the unprecedented sum of £3,311.[7] The directors were also able to offer lavish entertainment to guests and dignitaries, and when one former employee later recalled the heyday of the Company's banquets, he wrote that 'the City had not seen the like of them before or since' because they combined the 'the splendour of regal festivity with the comfort and sociality of a private Company'.[8] This assessment is certainly borne out by descriptions of the 'grand entertainments' hosted by the directors at the Albion Tavern in 1828 and 1829.[9] As a result, when the directors' expenditure on entertainment was scrutinised at the beginning of the 1830s, the Chairman, Robert Campbell, had to acknowledge that the public perception of his colleagues was that they 'assembled chiefly to eat and drink, and make merry', before he went on to argue that in fact 'hardly any set of men could be found, in any situation of life, who were more abstemious'.[10] The following year Campbell returned to the subject with the emphatic declaration that there was no substance at all to the charge that the directors were 'guttling and gormandising at the expense of the Company'.[11]

Of course, the rewards on offer to Company directors were known to be far greater than the ability to enjoy entertainment in a princely style. A few ambitious men sought to use the Court of Directors as a stepping-stone to high office in India, but the attention of most contemporaries was fixed primarily upon the value of the patronage that lay at the disposal of each director. This was because every year members of the Court were

5　Whitshed Keene, *Debate at the East India House . . . 25 February 1814* (1814), p. 88.

6　Mr Rigby, *Debates at the East India House*, vol. III, p. 68 (8 September 1831).

7　H/362, p. 73. This amount was thought to be unusually high because there had been a large number of Court meetings during the course of the year.

8　*Cornhill Magazine* (1860), p. 119.

9　*The Times*, 14 November 1828 and 25 June 1829.

10　*Debates at the East India House*, vol. III, p. 67 (28 September 1831).

11　Ibid., p. 91 (22 March 1832).

permitted to nominate, according to seniority, a certain number of applicants to positions as writers, cadets, surgeons, chaplains, home officers, and warehouse labourers in the Company's service. As such, the Company was, in the words of one historian, a 'major source of aristocratic patronage'.[12] In addition, the directors also licensed free merchants, granted passage to those wishing to travel to the East, and allocated voyages to the commanders of the privately owned East Indiamen.

In effect, the directors exercised control over the flow of people to Asia, and, as a result, fanciful calculations were undertaken to establish how much this was worth to them in monetary terms. During the first decade of the nineteenth century, in particular, there was fevered speculation about the profits generated from the buying and selling of places and appointments, and this prompted detailed Company and parliamentary inquiries into the matter. It was eventually concluded that there was no systematic abuse of the East India patronage system, although the actions of some individual directors were called into question. The President of the Board of Control, Robert Dundas, noted this in 1809 when he wrote that George Thelluson had been 'most unjustly' forced out of the Direction 'from the mere effect of popular clamour', while the veteran director John Manship had thought it prudent to resign 'on account of some circumstances transpiring in regard to the disposal of his patronage which he did not wish brought before the House of Commons'.[13] Other instances of abuse were few and far between, however, and C. H. Philips was able to suggest that, although some irregularities had occurred when patronage was used to support parliamentary interests, Company posts were for the most part distributed 'honestly and well'.[14] This view has been endorsed by a recent historian of patronage

---

12 J. M. Bourne, *Patronage and society in nineteenth-century England* (1986), p. 55. For a more detailed study of the Company's system of patronage see idem, 'The civil and military patronage of the East India Company, 1784–1858', unpublished PhD thesis, University of Leicester (1977). For a good contemporary description of how the appointments of writers and clerks were made by the directors see James Coggan, junior to David Scott, 12 March 1800, MS Eur. D1087 (loose letter). This volume was Scott's patronage book, and it details the numerous applications made to him.

13 Dundas to Lord Minto, 24 April 1809, Melville papers, MS 1063, f. 44, NLS.

14 Philips, *East India Company*, p. 15. On this matter see also Ainslie Thomas Embree, *Charles Grant and British rule in India* (1962), pp. 178–85, and Suresh Chandra Ghosh, *The British in Bengal. A study of the British society and life in the late eighteenth century* (1970, republished 1998), pp. 10–32. John Woodhouse had been obliged to resign in 1791 when he was implicated in the sale of a ship's command. Ghosh (ibid., p. 21) indicates that Edward Cruttenden had earlier also resigned after an inquiry into the sale of a nomination but this was not the case and in fact Cruttenden died in 1771 while still in office.

who concludes that although some abuses were evident during the early nineteenth century they were 'relatively few and often arose from incompetence, inattention, and naivety on the part of the directors rather than from corruption'.[15] On the basis of the available evidence, this seems to be a fair assessment, although it is one that suspicious contemporary critics of the Company would probably have been unwilling to accept. Indeed, it was revealed in 1832 that the last-known sale of a director's patronage had occurred only five years earlier.[16]

Although the directors might not have been trading in places for direct pecuniary profit, the real value of the patronage system lay in the opportunities it presented them with to provide for their families, friends, and associates. This was thought to be a legitimate perquisite of office, and even one of their sternest critics was prepared to concede that 'There is a degree of patronage (and that far from inconsiderable) to which Directors, under the present constitution of the Company, are honourably entitled, to compensate for their attention to our affairs.'[17] As a result, networks of East India patronage were established by directors who created links between the Company and different parts of the country where they had family, business, and political connections. Historians have long acknowledged that this was notably the case with Scottish directors whose actions over time ensured that their kinsmen became disproportionately well-represented in all branches of the Company's service.[18] Typical of them was Sir James Cockburn, of whom it was said: 'To give him his due, he has been always very friendly disposed to his country men, and has provided for many of them.'[19]

As with Cockburn, few directors failed to take advantage of their position, and the growth of Bosanquet influence within the Company during the late eighteenth century serves as a good example of the way in which a tradition of family service could be developed through use of the patronage system. It began in a small way when the Huguenot Jacob Bosanquet, a Hamburg merchant, was elected to the Directorate for a single term in 1759; then grew through his son, the notorious rake and bankrupt Richard, who served as a director between 1768 and 1773; and culminated during the time of Jacob (II) who was a director and

---

15 Bourne, *Patronage and society*, p. 62.   16 *PP* (1831–2), 735–1, vol. IX, p. 11.

17 John Fiott, *A second address to the proprietors of East-India stock, and to the public . . .* (1792), p. 125.

18 See below pp. 272–5.

19 Thomas Tod to Lord Tweedale, 1 November 1780, Yester papers, MS 14439, f. 79, NLS.

Chairman between 1782 and 1827. At every stage, the influence of the Bosanquets was extended further into the Company's affairs through dextrous use of the patronage system, and by the 1820s family members and associates were in different branches of the Company's civil, commercial, and maritime service.[20] Many similar examples could be cited, although perhaps none would be quite so remarkable as the networks established by the Braund, Branfill, and Harrison families whose business links were reinforced and extended by marriage and friendship. Had it been possible to arrange a gathering of these families under one roof in 1760, past, present, and future directors of the Company would have rubbed shoulders with senior officials and suppliers, as well as with the owners, managers, and commanders of East Indiamen. Forty years later, many of their male offspring were to be found serving the Company in Madras and Canton.[21]

Beyond patronage, further benefits could also be enjoyed by directors who were not unduly scrupulous about observing any rules, by-laws, or unwritten codes of behaviour intended to prevent them entering into conflicts of interest with the Company's own commercial affairs. In 1782, for example, John Townson was accused of using inside information to compete against the Company in order to secure a contract from the Board of Ordnance for the importation of 400 tons of saltpetre.[22] Directors were also known to have conducted illicit private trade with Asia, and David Scott was dogged by accusations that his position was fatally compromised by his involvement in illegal private ventures. Scott was eventually cleared of the most serious charges against him, but there can be no doubt that he was always closely engaged in private trade with Asia.[23] Others managed to keep their activities hidden from scrutiny, but in October 1811 the diarist Joseph Farington was told that when the Company had prohibited the private export of particular types of cloth to China, the director Francis Baring responded smartly by procuring consignments and shipping them to Canton through an American partner.[24] There were plenty of opportunities for

20 Grace Lawless Lee, *The story of the Bosanquets* (1960).
21 See the family trees in L. S. Sutherland, *A London merchant, 1695–1774* (1933), pp. 10–12. For family connections see also Parker, 'Directors', pp. 473–81.
22 B/260, pp. 177–84. Townson eventually managed to escape censure by securing an adjournment of the General Court, *sine die*.
23 For details see Philips, *East India Company*, pp. 82–5, 97–100.
24 *The diary of Joseph Farington*, vol. XI, Kathryn Cave (ed.), *January 1811–June 1812* (New Haven, 1983), p. 4009.

men to advance their own interests from inside the Court of Directors, and it would be naïve to think that they were not tempted to take advantage of their situation in order to do so. It did not take great ingenuity to bend the rules of tender that were supposed to stop directors supplying goods to the Company, and some ignored the by-law prohibiting their involvement in part-ownership of Company ships.[25] Others used their Company influence to further their business interests, and thus Henry Crabb Boulton was supposed to have established a monopoly on the supply of rope to the firms that fitted out the ships used by the Company.[26]

Operating openly or behind associates and front men, it was clearly possible for directors to engage in different forms of private East Indian business, and many undoubtedly acted as the representatives of outside interest groups who had much to gain from the expansion of the Company's affairs in Asia. However, the overall effects of their actions tended to be greatly exaggerated by suspicious contemporaries, especially those who had an axe to grind over the award of Company orders or contracts. In particular, the supposedly all-pervasive influence of shipping interests in the Court of Directors attracted much hostile comment, causing one critic to declare that the directors had become 'blended and knit together' with the owners and commanders of East Indiamen.[27] Such views invariably reinforced the widespread belief that the general well-being of the Company was sacrificed by directors whose actions were motivated by the pursuit of private interest. This was perhaps understandable in view of the long existence of an unreformed shipping system which brought great financial rewards to a small coterie of ship owners, but it is going much too far to represent all of the actions of the Court of Directors as having been determined by considerations of a personal nature. It is more appropriate to suggest that, as with many contemporary public servants, the directors always combined a sense of duty with the pursuit of private interest.

---

25 See, for example, the well-documented case of William Braund in Sutherland, *London merchant*, pp. 81–125, 150–7.

26 Parker, 'Directors', pp. 411–12.

27 Captain Joseph Price, *Five letters from a free merchant in Bengal to Warren Hastings esq. . . .* (1777, reprinted 1783), p. 186. In all, twenty-three former commanders became directors between 1754 and 1790, and the number sitting at any one time reached nine in 1773 and 1779 (Parker, 'Directors', pp. 413–23). For the origins, development, and workings of the shipping interest see Sutherland, *London merchant*, pp. 81–110.

Even so, motivations and outlooks were not unchanging, and the directors of the 1820s and 1830s were far less inclined than their predecessors to exploit their position for personal gain, and most of them appear to have been content to enjoy the legitimate rewards of office. There were a number of reasons for this. At a practical level, reform gradually reduced the scope for illicit activities and made the Company more open to public and parliamentary scrutiny, while, more generally, attitudes to public service and officeholding underwent something of a sea change. Commentators were increasingly inclined to emphasise the honour, dignity, and status that public-spirited men secured from serving the Company as directors. Some indeed feared that the payment of enhanced allowances would attract the wrong type of man into the Direction, and would thereby erode its collective qualities and characteristics. The office of director, argued Joseph Hume, ought to be regarded 'in no other light than as a post of honour', and he declared that if a directorship of the Bank of England was considered 'as a sort of COMMERCIAL PEERAGE in the City' then 'why should not a Director of the East-India Company be viewed as a personage worthy of the highest respect, as belonging to a class of men eminent for their prudence, ability, and integrity?'[28] In such a scheme of things, service as an East India director represented one of the highest stations to which an individual could aspire, and it was suggested in 1814 that 'there was not a gentleman in the Direction whose importance would be so great if he were removed from it'.[29] Considerations such as these now entered into calculations of private gain to a much greater degree than they had fifty years earlier and, as with politicians and officers of the state, directors' concerns for their reputations led them increasingly to consider their position as a public or shareholder trust rather than as a means of advancing their personal fortune.[30] As a result, they cultivated an image of probity, and sought to distance themselves from charges of greed, extravagance, and the pursuit of self-interest.

Acutely mindful of the considerable benefits and status bestowed upon directors, men devoted considerable energy and resources to securing election to the Court of Directors. This was especially the case when vacancies to the Direction became few and far between after the electoral

28 *Speech of Mr Joseph Hume* . . . (1813), p. 46.
29 Keene, *Debate at the East India House . . . 25 February 1814*, p. 89.
30 For identical attitudes among politicians and public servants, see Philip Harling, *The waning of 'old corruption': the politics of economical reform in Britain, 1779–1846* (Oxford, 1996), pp. 154–9.

reforms of 1773. Candidates had to ensure that they were deemed suitable by ministers as well as a majority of the incumbent directors, and they had no prospect of success if they could not gain the backing of the major factions or interest groups within the Company. Moreover, securing the approval of the ordinary stockholders was a long and painful process, and candidates accepted that they would usually have to prepare the ground carefully by campaigning for several years before they stood a reasonable chance of securing election. Any man aspiring to become a director thus had to dedicate himself to an extended canvass for support among the stockholders. This required a considerable organisational effort and, as had become the case during the 1760s, much work was undertaken by committees of friends and associates. The committees published public appeals for support in the newspapers; sent out solicitations for votes, election addresses, reminders and letters of thanks to stockholders; and organised dinners and balls. By the early nineteenth century, an election campaign could cost £1,000, but such an outlay was deemed to have been wasted if a candidate failed to make personal contact with as many voters as possible. This was a difficult task in view of the fact that 'the constituency was scattered all over the British islands' and it was considered risky to rely upon 'epistolary solicitation'.[31] Because of this, Henry St George Tucker worked hard during the early 1820s to gain the support of the main business houses in the City, and he also set out dutifully to visit Bath, Cheltenham, Clifton, Malvern, and other places where he could meet significant numbers of stockholders at particular times of the year. Either in person 'or through the agency of a zealous friend', he 'beat up the quarters of the voters'. He left no stone unturned in the search for votes, causing his biographer to comment that the task demanded 'no common amount of energy and perseverance' as well as time and money.[32]

Once elected, men clung tenaciously to their hard-won prize and more often than not they were only removed from office by death or extreme infirmity. Their position was reinforced by the closed nature of the electoral system, which made it difficult for outsiders to break into the inner Company circle, and consequently some individuals served as directors over many decades. John Manship, for example, was first elected as a director in 1755 and he was still in office in 1809, with his service

---

31 Kaye, *Life of Tucker*, p. 334.
32 Ibid., p. 333. Tucker's lengthy campaign is described on pp. 325–37. For details of electioneering activity see also Philips, *East India Company*, pp. 5–7.

usually having been interrupted only by the need to 'go out by rotation' every four years. William Thornton (later Astell) was one of the youngest men ever to enter the Court of Directors at the age of twenty-six in 1800, and he continued in office for forty-six years, acting as Chairman on four occasions. There were plenty of others who served as directors for twenty years or more, and this provided a strong thread of continuity within the Court of Directors. Whether such long service was ultimately of any great benefit to the Company is a moot point, however, and there certainly came a time when elderly or infirm directors were unable to make any meaningful contribution to East Indian affairs. It was said that the blind and deaf John Bebb continued in office for as long as possible solely to protect his patronage,[33] and when the influential James Pattison and George Robinson were both 'attacked with paralysis' in 1828, J. G. Ravenshaw feared that 'neither of them will ever be efficient again'. He suggested that 'some of our *young old men* therefore must soon come into play' in the Direction.[34]

In terms of birth and early background, directors were drawn from all parts of the British Isles, and it is notable that a number of those from the provinces were able to rise to positions of considerable influence at East India House. Many of the directors were originally from London and the Home Counties, but at various times the Company in Britain came to be dominated by men such as Laurence Sulivan, who was born in County Cork, and Charles Grant who was born at Glen Urquhart in Inverness-shire. Other Chairmen born in the provinces included Francis Baring (Exeter), Henry Fletcher (Cumberland), Robert Gregory (Galway), Hugh Inglis (Edinburgh), William James (possibly from Pembrokeshire), John Michie (Aberdeenshire), David Scott (Forfarshire), and George Wombwell (Yorkshire). Few of these men were of humble origins, but their success reveals much about the ways in which careers in the Company and the City provided stepping-stones for personal advancement into the London world of business, politics, and society. At the same time, their presence indicates that the Court of Directors was a melting pot containing a rich mixture of personalities representing diverse backgrounds, experiences, outlooks, and traditions.

Before 1760 most directors had pursued earlier careers in finance, trade, or shipping, and this continued to be the case for several decades. The

---

33 *Alexander's East India Magazine*, vol. VII (1834), p. 398. Bebb was eventually obliged to step down in 1830 under pressure from his fellow directors (Philips, *East India Company*, p. 5).
34 Ravenshaw to Bentinck, 14 April 1828, *Bentinck correspondence*, vol. I, p. 25.

number of former commanders of East Indiamen in the Direction peaked during the 1770s and did not begin to diminish until the end of the century, and merchants and monied men continued to be well-represented among the directors. Some of these men were government contractors, and a sizeable number were prominent in the major insurance companies.[35] Others served on the boards or courts of major trading companies such as the Levant Company or the Russia Company. No individual was permitted to serve simultaneously as a director of the Company and the Bank of England, but John Harrison, Henry Plant, and William Snell each held office at India House before they made the short move to Threadneedle Street where they were to serve the Bank for many years. All of these individual ties reinforced the more formal institutional alliances that had been established by the Company over the years.

Men such as these were well able to move easily in the world of high finance and business, but they were often ill-equipped to deal with the problems of empire. Some of those in office early in the period had briefly visited India as the commanders of East Indiamen, and a handful had served in the navy in the Indian Ocean, but far fewer had been employed in the senior ranks of the Company's military or civil service in Asia. Even then, those who had been Governors of Indian Presidencies tended to have occupied those positions well before the Company acquired its territorial empire, and thus when the transition from trade to empire was being made detailed first-hand knowledge was in short supply in the Court of Directors.[36] As a result, strong doubts were often raised about whether those managing Company affairs in London could rise to the considerable new challenges confronting them. Clive led the way by condemning the inferior qualities of even those directors who were his own supporters. He thought that Thomas Rous, elected Chairman in 1764, was incapable of acting effectively in 'the management of so great a machine of government as that of the East India Company in its present state of political and commercial importance', and he castigated Rous's successor, Henry Crabb Boulton, as a man 'whose knowledge of

---

35 Norman Baker, *Government and contractors: the British Treasury and war supplies, 1775–1783* (1971), pp. 227–8; P. G. M. Dickson, *The Sun Insurance Office 1710–1960: a history of two and a half centuries of British insurance* (1960), p. 278; Barry Supple, *The Royal Exchange Assurance: a history of British insurance 1720–1970* (Cambridge, 1970), p. 76.

36 Directors during the 1750s, 1760s, and early 1770s who had served in the most senior positions in India included William Barwell (Governor of Bengal, 1748–9), Stephen Law (Governor of Bombay, 1739–42), and Thomas Saunders (Governor of Madras, 1750–5).

the Company's affairs abroad is very slight'.[37] He also accused his arch-rival Laurence Sulivan, who had served in Bombay, of wishing to protect his own pre-eminent position in the Company by preventing anyone becoming a director who had 'experience, capacity or general knowledge'.[38] Clive was often prone to malicious exaggeration but there was more than a grain of truth in his assertions that the leaders of the Company in London were not well-suited to the task of managing a territorial empire.

This unsatisfactory state of affairs was very slow to change, and the number of 'East Indians' serving as directors remained small for several decades. Talented men of experience were often unable to break into the faction-ridden Direction and although the number of former servants acting as directors rose from five in 1761 to seven in 1765, the number fluctuated thereafter and only three were serving during the crisis year of 1773 when a working knowledge of India was most needed by those directing the Company's affairs. The situation was then not helped by a clause in the Regulating Act, which decreed that returning civil or military servants had to reside in Britain for two years before they were deemed eligible to stand for election to the Court of Directors.

An able former servant, Hugh Inglis, eventually secured election as a director during the 1780s but he was one of only a few members of the Court who had any real knowledge or understanding of India. Yet, even then, Inglis would have been unable to apply his experience properly to the Company's affairs for some years because of a long-standing tradition, which saw the appointments of directors to key committees made on the basis of seniority rather than any special talent or skills. Thus in 1785 it was noted that the Committees of Correspondence and Treasury 'are generally composed of those Gentlemen who have been longest in the Direction, and such as have filled either of the Chairs'.[39] Although it was suggested that the Committees of Buying, Shipping, and Warehouse did usually contain 'Gentlemen of professional knowledge', the overall effect of the system was that those who had served most recently in India did not have an early opportunity to apply their knowledge and skills in the areas where they were most needed. It could be a decade or more before a director with experience of India found himself in a position where he could exert any influence at all upon the making of overseas

37 Clive to George Dudley, 29 September 1765, Clive MS 236, p. 1, NLW.
38 Quoted in M. Bence-Jones, *Clive of India* (1974), p. 202.
39 Thomas Morton to Charles Boughton Rouse, 28 April 1785, H/362, p. 6.

policy, and until that time he might find himself engaged in entirely different forms of Company business. Onlookers, some of whom suggested that senior directors would never release their grip on power and patronage, condemned this mismatch of skills and duties within the Directorate.[40] Similar complaints were still being voiced in the early 1830s when one critic wrote that a director was often employed 'in duties quite of an opposite nature to those which have formed the great business part of his life, viz. warehouse affairs, and in all that minuteness and littleness of detail and petty transactions so repugnant to every man of an enlarged mind and cultivated standing'.[41]

It was not until the 1790s that the traditionally constructed Directorate began to be replaced by a broadly based executive that was more representative of the Company's interests as a whole.[42] This was because ministers began to support candidates who were better able to understand the complexities of Indian government, and even the directors themselves acknowledged the need for specialists within their own ranks. As a result, more individuals with experience of India began to put themselves forward as candidates for election and they increasingly drew public attention to the fact that they had gained considerable first-hand knowledge of the Company's affairs in India.[43] At their forefront in terms of ambition, conviction, and personality was Charles Grant who had served the Company in Bengal for over twenty years before returning to Britain in 1790. He was elected as a director four years later with such strong backing from Dundas and Pitt that his canvassing campaign proved to be one of the shortest on record, and he went on to serve as a very influential director who was Deputy Chairman or Chairman of the Company on six occasions between 1804 and 1815.[44] Grant was followed into the Direction by other former civil or military servants such as Alexander Allan, John Baillie, Robert Clerk, Samuel Davis, Neil Edmonstone, John Hudlestone, George Millet, Edward Parry, Richard Plowden, J. G. Ravenshaw, George Abercrombie Robinson, Sweny Toone, and Henry St George Tucker, all of whom had gained substantial experience in India and

40 See, for example, H/399, p. 36.
41 *Alexander's East India Magazine*, vol. I (1831), p. 460.
42 For this process see Parker, 'Directors', pp. 344–51, 362–93, 399–425, 450–9.
43 See, for example, the election addresses of Alexander Allan, Hugh Baillie, Robert Clerk, and Henry St George Tucker in Airth papers, MS 10922, NLS. These candidates set out their Indian careers in varying degrees of detail and published testimonials extracted from the Company records.
44 For a detailed study of his career see Embree, *Charles Grant.*

thus in theory were well-prepared for engagement with the Company's affairs in London.

The presence of these men served considerably to increase the overall number of 'East Indians' in the Court of Directors. One calculation suggests that over half of the 110 different directors who sat in the Court between 1784 and 1834 had been at one time resident in India,[45] and it is instructive to compare the situation in 1790 with that which existed forty years later. In the former year, two-thirds of the directors still had strong personal connections with the City or the Company's maritime affairs, and only six of the twenty-four had actually served in India in a civil, commercial, or military capacity.[46] By 1830, however, things were very different, underlining the extent to which the Company had changed as an organisation. Members of the City's commercial and financial classes still heavily populated the Court, but it was now estimated that two-thirds of the directors had acquired 'practical knowledge' of India.[47] Nine of them had been in the Company's civil service, and four had served in the armed forces. Of course, service in India did not by itself offer any guarantee at all of suitability for important executive office, or even of an up-to-date understanding of the local administrative difficulties confronting the Company, and at the end of the period there were still plenty of outspoken critics who were of the opinion that the directors held 'defective qualifications' for the government of people and territory.[48] In general terms, however, there can be no doubt that the directors of 1830 were rather better equipped to tackle the problems of empire than their predecessors of seventy years earlier.

Whether their career background lay in India or Britain, most of the Company's directors were men whose personal development had been shaped by practical learning acquired in the fields of administrative, commercial, maritime, or military endeavour. Very few of them brought any philosophical or theoretical ideas to their daily work and, on the whole, the Court of Directors tended to take a narrow view of Company affairs. It was partly because of this that the directors were routinely

---

45 Philips, *East India Company*, p. 8. For an attempt to identify the 'interest' which each director 'represented' between 1784 and 1833 see ibid., pp. 335–7.
46 This calculation is based upon analysis of the biographies of individual directors in Parker, 'Directors'.
47 Evidence of Peter Auber, *PP* (1831–2), 735–I, vol. IX, p. 6.
48 *Alexander's East India Magazine*, I (1831), p. 456. Unsurprisingly, the director Henry St George Tucker took an altogether more positive view of the qualities exhibited by the Court of Directors of the early 1830s (*Debates at the General Court of Proprietors on 15th, 16th, 18th, 19th, 22nd, 23rd, 25th April 1833* . . . (1833), p. 9).

condemned by their critics for possessing the minds of 'shopkeepers' or 'cheesemongers' who considered nothing other than the bottom line of the Company balance sheet. This was unfair, but responses to the problems of trade and empire were usually governed by considerations of pragmatism, precedent, and expediency, and there is little evidence to suggest that any more than a few directors ever possessed a far-sighted vision of the development of the Company's affairs. Indeed, those who endeavoured to apply moral or religious ideas to their Company work often encountered deep hostility and suspicion from colleagues whose conservative instincts ensured that they were always wary of any form of innovation. Accordingly, during the early nineteenth century, evangelical Christians such as Charles Grant and Edward Parry, who were founder members of the Clapham Sect, ran into stiff resistance when they sought to promote greater levels of missionary work as a means of anglicising, civilising, and improving Indian society. Many directors always feared that an unrestricted flow of missionaries to the subcontinent would have a profoundly destabilising effect upon the Company's territorial possessions, and they fiercely resisted those within their ranks who called for a stronger degree of Christian influence to be exerted in India.[49] Consequently in 1808 'much warmth' was caused by 'theological discussions' within the Court of Directors, and even though Grant and Parry were often able to dominate the proceedings of the Court, they were on this occasion left in a small minority and forced to abandon the issue.[50] The matter was put to one side and Grant and Parry only achieved their aim in 1813 when, following the exertion of considerable pressure in Parliament by William Wilberforce and others, the Charter Act of 1813 established an Indian Bishopric and opened up the Company's territories to a greater number of missionaries.

Thereafter, as utilitarian and evangelical ideas of reform began to circulate more widely in metropolitan society, directors such as the long-serving William Astell became more inclined to the view that the Company should intervene to alter the moral and religious characteristics

---

49 It has been argued, quite correctly, that the Company was not hostile to all missionary activity before 1813. See Penelope Carson, 'Missionaries, bureaucrats, and the people of India, 1793–1833', in Nancy Gardner Cassels (ed.), *Orientalism, evangelicalism, and the military cantonment in early nineteenth-century India: a historiographical overview* (Lampeter, 1991), pp. 126–30.

50 Robert Dundas to Lord Minto, 27 December 1808, Melville papers, MS 1063, ff. 32–3, NLS. For the background to this dispute see Philips, *East India Company*, pp. 158–65. On the missionary question in general see Andrew Porter, *Religion versus empire? British Protestant missionaries and overseas expansion, 1700–1914* (Manchester, 2004), pp. 68–75, 99–103.

of British India, but many of his colleagues still stubbornly refused to apply any form of doctrinaire ideas to their management of the Company's affairs. The general attitude of the pragmatists was perhaps best summed up by Henry St George Tucker, who was asked by a group of stockholders during the 1820s if he would promote their religious cause within the Court of Directors. He responded with the emphatic declaration that he would never commit himself 'to any abstract proposition whatever'.[51] Tucker did not wish to tie himself to any special interest group, but he also knew only too well that to adopt such an approach to the Company's affairs would place him firmly out of favour with many of his fellow directors. The Court of Directors was a forum in which men were always expected to exercise straightforward common sense, and they were not encouraged to use their office to conduct reformist experiments or serve interests wider than those of the Company itself.

If a majority of the directors were reluctant to move beyond very narrow terms of reference when they gave consideration to the Company, the ever-changing situation in Asia meant that from the 1760s onwards they needed to consider more than trading accounts if they were to understand an increasingly wide range of subjects related to administrative, military, and political affairs in India. The veteran stockholder Whitshed Keene made this point in 1814 when he identified the areas with which the modern director should be familiar:

To be properly calculated for holding such an office required a great variety of information: he who aspired to it should be perfectly conversant with the history of India; he ought to be minutely versed in the history of the Company, from its origin to the present day; he should be acquainted with the leading features of the Indian population, subdivided, as it is into so many different parts; he should study attentively the reports of the Secret Committees; in short, he should read every authentic work on the subject of Indian affairs. Such a man would find that his whole time was not too much for the acquirement of information on these various topics.[52]

These were unreasonable expectations, but there was no denying the strength of Keene's underlying message that directors needed to gain a full understanding of the Company's affairs if they were to stand any chance of making an effective contribution to the work of the Court of Directors. In fact, the directors were already working much harder in their

---

51 Kaye, *Life of Tucker*, p. 346.
52 Keene, *Debate at the East India House . . . 25 February 1814* (1814), p. 87.

pursuit of that understanding than they had in earlier times, and candidates for the Direction acknowledged this in their election addresses.
When George Abercrombie Robinson sought election for the first time
in 1802 he drew the attention of stockholders to his record of long
Company service in India and also pledged that he would devote his time
'unremittingly' to the conduct of business and study of Company affairs.[53]
Such a public commitment to duty had become necessary because, as
Assistant Secretary James Cobb remarked a decade later, the expansion of
the Company's empire had 'most unquestionably' resulted in a great
increase in the amount of business brought before the directors.[54] The
basic task of reading documentary material generated in India and elsewhere was immensely time-consuming. More information had to be
processed and understood, discussions became longer, and a greater
number of decisions had to be taken on a wider range of subjects. All of
this obliged directors to devote more time to Company affairs.

Directors who served the Company during the transition from trade to
empire found that part-time involvement with the Company was no
longer adequate or acceptable. Charles Grant observed in 1813 that while
the office of director had once been 'so far an easy situation as to be very
compatible with other serious avocations', this had ceased to be the case
after 1793. Since then, he noted, 'the business transacted at home was
become far more laborious and harassing' and this meant that 'no director
could properly perform the duty of his office without devoting a considerable portion of his time and attention to it, without a sacrifice of other
objects, or injury such as he could not abandon'.[55] Stephen Lushington
took the view that 'the labours of the Directors had been at least doubled'
between 1793 and 1813.[56] As a result, directors were required to devote long
hours to Company affairs, and this imposed considerable demands upon
conscientious individuals, many of whom occupied positions in other
companies, traded on their own account, or served as Members of
Parliament. It was observed in 1814, for example, that seventeen of the
twenty-four directors were 'either Chairmen, or Deputy Chairmen, or
Directors of some other joint-stock companies, or merchants on their
own account; and in some instances all of these'.[57] In 1825, six Company

53 See the printed copies of Robinson's election address of 1802, MS Eur F.142/16.
54 *Proceedings of the Select Committee appointed by the General Court of Proprietors on the 6th October
   1813. . .* (1814), p. 32.
55 *Adjourned debate at the East India House . . . 6th October 1813* (1813), p. 132.
56 Ibid., p. 89.
57 Humphrey Howorth in *Debate at the East India House . . . 18th March 1814* (1814), p. 17.

directors were listed as being directors of three or more other major companies or societies.[58] Yet, although there were occasional calls for the directors to abandon these types of interest beyond East India House, most stockholders appear to have been satisfied with the commitment shown to the Company by their representatives, and whatever other criticisms were levelled at the directors they were seldom accused of failing to attend to their duties. They were generally assiduous in their application to Company business, and their conscientious work ethic was similar to that being adopted by many in the public service.[59]

As far as ordinary directors were concerned, a great deal of time was spent in full Court meetings, usually up to three times a week, although at times of crisis an even higher level of attendance was required. The Courts began in mid-morning and continued until six or seven in the evening, although it was not unknown for them to be extended until ten o'clock. The length of these proceedings was determined in part by the reading of despatches 'in which many hours have been occupied', and in part by the afternoon adjournments that were necessary so that subcommittees could meet.[60] All of the twenty-four directors were expected to be present in full Court, but on the rare occasions when there was not a quorum of thirteen those present devoted themselves to 'reading unimportant letters and despatches, and swearing [in] mates [of East Indiamen]'. For the most part, however, attendance at the Court of Directors was very good and, on average, nineteen directors were present at each meeting held between 1773 and 1812.[61] Moreover, directors were also obliged to attend committee meetings held on days when the full Court was not in session, and it was noted by James Cobb in 1813 that 'hardly a day passes without a committee meeting'.[62] In addition, the directors were required to be present whenever the stockholders met in the General Court, and junior directors were also expected to be in attendance at the Company's sales of goods. Sale duty could represent a considerable commitment in view of the fact that between 1793 and 1812 there were, on average, 161 sale days every year.[63]

---

58 *The Times*, 7 February 1825. I am indebted to Philip Cottrell for this reference.
59 Harling, *Waning of 'old corruption'*, pp. 159–62.
60 Unless otherwise stated, details and quotations in the following paragraph are taken from *Proceedings of the Select Committee*, pp. 22–6. By 1803 a Company official served as 'reader to the Court' (*East India register and directory* (1803), p. xii).
61 *Proceedings of the Select Committee*, pp. 95–6, 164–5.
62 Ibid., p. 27.
63 Details of the type and number of sales are to be found at ibid., p. 119. At the beginning of the period, attendance at sales was arranged according to a rota. See, for example, B/70, p. 304 for

As is to be expected, the heaviest burdens fell upon the Chairman and his deputy who spent much of their time at East India House attending to a broad range of business. Matters of all types required their personal attention and, as a reflection of this, Sir George Colebrooke wrote that in his time of office during early 1770s the 'number of letters I received . . . was equal to that of a Prime Minister'.[64] The Chairs also acted as the official 'voice' of the Company in meetings with government ministers, and they were required to speak regularly in the House of Commons on East Indian affairs. All of these official duties were arduous and James Cobb acknowledged this in 1813 when he declared that

It seldom or ever occurs that a day passes without the Chairman and Deputy Chairman attending the House during the whole morning. Indeed, they are both frequently here from an early to a late hour; and their constant attention is indispensible [*sic*], from the frequent communication with ministers and the government offices. Nor is their attendance upon the Company's business exclusively confined to the India House: the above-mentioned communication renders their presence at the west end of town indispensible [*sic*] very frequently.[65]

Such personal commitment to the Company could be demanding, especially at times of crisis, as was reflected in the comment of the Chairman Edward Parry who complained in November 1807 that 'My present arduous situation is close confinement so that I have not had a day's country recreation all the Summer.'[66] Deputy Chairman David Scott thought that 'From early in the morning in the India House until late, two o'clock almost every morning at the House of Commons is very severe indeed.'[67] Francis Baring was exhausted by his periods in office, and his private business affairs suffered accordingly; while stress, anxiety, and sustained hard work pushed the highly strung Jacob Bosanquet very close to a nervous breakdown.[68]

Of course, sheer hard work alone did not create effective and powerful Chairmen. Good leadership always required a mixture of administrative

1749, and according to Robert Wissett this was still the case early in the nineteenth century (*Proceedings of the Select Committee*, p. 38).

64 Sir George Colebrooke, *Retrospection: or reminiscences addressed to my son Henry Thomas Colebrooke*, 2 vols. (1898–9), vol. I, p. 196.

65 *Proceedings of the Select Committee*, p. 21.

66 Parry to Anthony Hamond, 13 November 1807, HMN 4/343, Norfolk Record Office.

67 C. H. Philips (ed.), *The correspondence of David Scott director and Chairman of the East India Company relating to Indian affairs 1787–1805*, vol. I: *1787–1799, Camden*, third series, vol. LXXV (1951), p. 48.

68 John Orbell, 'Baring, Sir Francis', *ODNB*. For Bosanquet see Philips, *East India Company*, p. 95.

and political skills, together with a strong personality, but those who were single-minded enough could establish a considerable degree of personal control over the Company. Accordingly, in 1772 Laurence Sulivan's all-pervasive influence marked him out to one opponent as 'the dictator of Leadenhall Street'.[69] In part, he was able to achieve this position because only the Chairman and his deputy were able to develop a full overview of Company affairs. They were shown all the information entering East India House, and as members of every committee they engaged in all areas of discussion and had access to every set of minutes.[70] At the same time, it was the Chairman who dictated when business was brought before the full Court of Directors, and this enabled him to determine the agenda and timing of any discussions. As Pitt was told in 1784, 'The chairman brings forward what he pleases, when he pleases', and this gave him a great advantage over any opponents in the Court.[71]

Moreover, as influential figures became firmly established within the system, they were able to retain the lead in Company affairs even when they no longer actually occupied the office of Chairman. Thus, in 1781 Lord Macartney suggested that the veteran Laurence Sulivan's 'abilities, experience, secrecy, discretion and long habits of business, certainly point him out as the first man in the Direction', even though he then only held the position of Deputy Chairman.[72] Twenty-five years later, Charles Grant was able to take the lead in Company affairs by acting as the dominant figure in a partnership with his close friend Edward Parry who was then Chairman.[73] Grant was also thought to exercise considerable influence over William Astell, a man described by the former Chairman Stephen Lushington as a 'vain empty blockhead totally unequal to the situation where he has to sit alone and when he has time to consult, wholly in the hands of Charles Grant'.[74] By no means all Chairmen were able or willing to act in the manner of Grant, but it was certainly possible for ambitious and resourceful men to impose themselves on East India House, and Sir James Stephen was justified in his later suggestion that Grant's stranglehold on the Directorate was

69 Bowen, *Revenue and reform*, p. 99.
70 Their position was strengthened further by the fact that minutes of two of the most important committees – Treasury and Secrecy – were not accessible to those directors who did not serve on them.
71 Quoted in Philips, *East India Company*, p. 13.
72 Macartney to Lord Sandwich, 13 January 1781, SAN, F/39 no. 36, NMM.
73 Embree, *Charles Grant*, pp. 205–6.
74 Quoted in R. G. Thorne (ed.), *The History of Parliament. The House of Commons 1790–1820*, 5 vols. (1986), vol. V, p. 380.

so firm that he could be regarded as having been 'the real ruler of the rulers of the East, the Director of the Directors'.[75]

Although Chairmen were sometimes condemned as tyrants or despots, it would nevertheless be wrong to suggest that strong-minded individuals such as Colebrooke, Sulivan, or Grant were ever able to act with complete freedom within the Company. Decisions of all types had to be formally ratified by a vote in the Court of Directors, with contentious issues being decided by the use of a secret ballot, and this helped to define clear limits beyond which no Chairman could step. The sentiments of ordinary directors could not simply be ignored or brushed aside, as was demonstrated when Sir Henry Fletcher was obliged to resign as Chairman in 1783 when his support for Fox's India Bill was vigorously opposed by the General Court and a majority of his colleagues.[76]

Warring factions were often to be found in the Court, and conflicts were sometimes lengthy and bitter, but, generally speaking, the directors held a strong belief that they exercised collective responsibility for the Company's affairs. As a result, although the number of dissents entered on the Court's minutes always increased during periods of factionalism or crisis,[77] most directors frowned upon those who consistently followed an independent line. Individuals who broke ranks could pay a heavy price, as was shown in 1768 when John Manship was dropped from the directors' list of candidates for the forthcoming election, and several stockholders publicly supported this decision by observing that he had for years 'adopted and pursued schemes diametrically opposed to the opinion of the whole direction'.[78] In fact, Manship went on to recover his seat in the Direction and he entered more dissents on the minutes than anybody else,[79] but most of his colleagues were far more circumspect and tended to accept the decisions of the majority. Over time, there was a gradual increase in the number of dissents entered on the minutes each year, but resignations on points of principle were few and far between.[80]

75 Quoted in William Foster, *The East India House: its history and associations* (1924), p. 234.
76 For this episode see Sutherland, *East India Company*, p. 407; Philips, *East India Company*, p. 24.
77 See Z/B/97, Index to dissents 1764–1857.
78 *Gazetteer*, 13 April 1768.
79 Manship recorded twenty-eight dissents between 1764 and 1792, protesting against the election of the Deputy Chairmen in 1775 and 1776, and the election of the Chairman in 1784. Sir Francis Baring was also a frequent dissenter, with twenty-six protests between 1781 and 1810. Many of his dissents related to the Company's conduct of its commercial business.
80 It was reported that George Dempster resigned in February 1773 in protest at the directors' handling of financial affairs. This was an action greeted with 'universal applause' by the

This reflected the fact that, apart from the tumultuous years of the 1760s and early 1780s, the Court of Directors was usually well-disciplined, and it presented a reasonably united front to the stockholders and the outside world.

MANAGERS, CLERKS, AND THE WORLD OF COMPANY WORK

Over the years, directors came and went, and, even though some held office across several decades, their periods of service were often interrupted by swings of electoral fortune or the need to step down every four years. As a result, some of the strongest elements of continuity and leadership within East India House were provided by the Company's senior managers, who were often to be found performing a role similar to that of a modern-day chief executive officer. This certainly seems to have been the case with the experienced Accountant-General Charles Cartwright who in the summer of 1804 was said to have taken a 'great lead with the management of the Company, and is highly respected'.[81] Beneath men like Cartwright were other 'regular officers' of East India House who performed the routine tasks that kept the administrative machinery ticking over. In total, the numbers on the permanent home clerical establishment rose from 159 in 1785 to 241 in 1813, and they were supplemented by part-time 'extra officers' at busy times of the year, but it was often said that a vast and expanding empire was being administered from London by a bureaucracy that was small in comparison with some of the offices of state.[82] As former Chairman Charles Grant noted in 1819,

such has been the progressive increase, such was especially now the prodigious extent of the Company's dominions, producing proportionate details of military, political, revenue, judicial and miscellaneous correspondence from hence, that persons who were at all acquainted with the subject must confess they were conducted by fewer instruments than those employed by any other government on the face of the earth of equal importance.[83]

stockholders (*London Evening Post*, 25–27 February 1773). In 1786 Samuel Smith junior resigned because he felt that the Court of Directors had been reduced to a 'mere cypher' by the creation of the Board of Control (*The Times*, 8 July 1786).

81 James Arthur to Edmund Larken, 24 August 1804, Mon/25/6 no. 12, Lincolnshire Record Office.

82 For the size of the clerical establishment see H/362, pp. 9–77 (for 1785); and *Proceedings of the Select Committee*, p. 119 (for 1813).

83 *Asiatic Journal and Monthly Register*, vol. VII (1819), p. 512.

Clearly the skills, knowledge, and personal qualities of these 'instruments' were of considerable importance to the Company, and much depended upon how well they responded to the administrative challenges posed by the transition from trade to empire.

The earnings of the Company's established clerks were comparable to those of men who occupied similar positions in the offices of state. Between the 1780s and 1820s the average real income of a clerk of 21–25 years' service rose from £200 to £600 a year and this placed the Company's administrative staff among the highest-paid category of clerical workers in the country.[84] A sense of responsibility for the Company's servants ensured that the directors also authorised pension, compensation, and hardship payments to former employees and their dependants, and the Company had long held a reputation for looking after its own.[85] There were always plenty of people who considered the directors to be parsimonious and penny-pinching, but pensions or fixed-term annuities were increasingly granted to worthy and deserving individuals among the clerical staff. In 1789 payments amounting to over £13,000 were made to sixty-four individuals, and the recipients included former senior figures at East India House such as Samuel Wilks and John Hoole who received £400 and £300 respectively.[86] By 1809 regular pension and annuity payments had reached almost £40,000 before the deduction of income tax, and they were distributed amongst 166 recipients. As part of broader moves towards the retrenchment and rationalisation of the Company's financial affairs, these somewhat arbitrary pension arrangements were tidied up by the Charter Act of 1813 in the hope that the number of payments could be limited by regulations defining remuneration according to age, state of health, and length of service.[87] In fact, the Company continued to make a large number of discretionary awards to the dependants of deceased Company servants. Thus in May 1817 345 pensions amounted to £58,510, ranging from the £30 distributed to the three children of the deceased porter Jeremiah Hill through to the £1,020 paid to the former Clerk to the Committee of

---

84 For a study of the salaries earned by the Company's clerical staff, and details of reforms made to the system of remuneration, see H. M. Boot, 'Real incomes of the British middle class, 1760–1850: the experience of clerks at the East India Company', *Ec. Hist. Rev.*, 52 (1999), pp. 638–68.

85 See, for example, Clement Downing (1718) quoted in Jean Sutton, *Lords of the east. The East India Company and its ships (1600–1874)* (second edition, 2000), p. 81.

86 L/AG/9/4, vol. 1 (Pension warrants, December 1788–December 1809).

87 T. C. Hansard, *The parliamentary debates from the year 1803 to the present time*, vol. XXVI (1813), cols. 561–2. For details of the new scheme see 53 Geo. III, c.155, xciii.

Warehouse, Robert Wissett. Ten years later, the annual pension bill had risen to £101,923, with 520 separate payments made to former Company servants and their dependants.[88]

Generous financial rewards, security, and pension provision made the Company's home service an attractive proposition for many who sought professional employment for themselves or their sons. Unsurprisingly, therefore, there was fierce competition for places at East India House and, as with all other branches of the Company's service, success was ultimately dependent upon connection and influence rather than the possession of any skills and aptitude for the post. Candidates for clerical positions within the Company were often only fifteen or sixteen years of age but they needed to be well-connected in order to gain the favour of the Chairman, his deputy, and the members of the Committee of Correspondence who nominated most of the candidates for vacant clerical posts within East India House.[89] Even then, strong backing from influential public figures offered no guarantee of success.

Following acceptance into the Company, which was formalised by the submission of a bond for good behaviour, the placement of an individual within a department or office was often determined by a family connection. James Coggan, James Annis, and William Ramsay junior were all appointed to posts in offices run by their fathers while in an extreme case the small Examiner's Office became a family fiefdom when four members of the Wilks family served there during the late 1770s. After a three-year period of unsalaried probation, men usually remained in the office to which they were originally appointed and transfers between departments were very few and far between.[90] Most clerical staff thus ended their working lives where they began, and this meant that although some men became very familiar with a particular branch of Company affairs, very few could ever have gained a full understanding of increasingly complex overseas activities. Equally, the speed of promotion within any department was to a large degree determined by rates of death and departure among senior colleagues further up the local

---

88 *PP*, 1831, vol. V, 320A, pp. 690–701. These figures include payments made to former home and overseas servants.

89 H/67, p. 71.

90 An exception to this rule was provided by John Hoole. He began his career in the Auditor's Office, where he served as Deputy Auditor before eventually becoming the head of the department in 1771. He later moved to the key post of Compiler of the India Correspondence, and when this position was abolished in 1781 he became Clerk to the newly established Committee for Government Troops and Stores (H/362, p. 31).

hierarchy. As a result, those who eventually came to occupy positions as heads of departments or offices always had many years of Company service to their name. William Sibley, the Treasurer, had been employed by the Company for sixty-two years when he died in office in 1807; while William Ramsay joined the Company in August 1763 and then served as Secretary from 1792 until the time of his death in 1814. Most notable of all, perhaps, Samuel Johnson, the influential Examiner of Indian Correspondence, served the Company from 1764 until he too died in office in 1817.[91] He entered the Company just as it was embarking on the process of territorial expansion in India, and like many others he served throughout the tumultuous period of transformation from trader to sovereign.

The promotion system also ensured that long service was a characteristic of many those lodged in the middle and lower ranks of the Company's administrative service. In 1801 well over a quarter of the established officials on the Company's payroll had been employed for more than two decades, and the average length of service stood at almost sixteen years.[92] The directors were concerned that the Company in London was being served by an ageing workforce, and the extent of the problem was brought out in an analysis which revealed that while forty employees died in service and seventy retired between 1800 and 1817, only twenty resigned and three were posted abroad.[93] This confirmed that a large number of employees were working for thirty or forty years through to retirement or death in service, and there were particular concentrations of long-serving staff in the largest offices. One important consequence was that any career ambitions harboured by junior employees were often thwarted by the fact that there were always departmental colleagues ahead of them who had far longer terms of service to their name. T. S. Clarke and J. J. Thompson provide good, if extreme, examples of what could happen in large departments. They entered the Accountant's Department in August and December 1764 respectively, but neither of them had made much progress up the pecking order before they both died in service forty years later. Many clerks had little real prospect of any advancement and as a result they stayed in position performing the same repetitive tasks, year after year.

91 L/AG/30/3, vol. 24, p. 143.
92 H/67, pp. 161–5. For administrative careers in the offices of central government see John Brewer, *The sinews of power: war, money and the English state, 1688–1783* (1989), pp. 80–1.
93 L/AG/30/3, vol. 24, pp. 143–51.

Unchanging entry procedures and a rigid organisational structure meant that members of the clerical staff were brought up in the Company's service from a young age. There were some benefits to be derived from such a system, as was acknowledged in March 1819 by Charles Grant when he told the General Court that until the last decade

the functionaries in the various offices of the house then appropriated to the home affairs and to the foreign were generally introduced into the service at very early age, and initiated and carried on in their respective offices, in which they usually rose by the rule of seniority. This had been a long established practice, recommended by reason and experience, as the best mode of forming a stock of official knowledge, and providing for the due conduct of all business of routine.[94]

There were also considerable drawbacks, however, because few of the home staff had experienced any form of working life beyond the Company and, with the notable exception of some of the men appointed to senior positions in the Examiner's Office after 1809,[95] hardly any of them had first-hand experience of India. Few of the London administrators had served in other branches of the Company's service, and it was simply not possible for mature and well-travelled men to secure direct entry into the middle ranks of the hierarchy. This represented a serious problem and, although the Company's managers were able to glean information about India from the paper that crossed their desks or from wider private reading, their understanding of the Company's affairs was always limited by the fact that they had not themselves ventured overseas. The Company itself did nothing in a formal sense to help them come to terms with distant or unfamiliar worlds, and only at the very end of the period was it suggested that the home officers would benefit from being sent out to visit India.[96] Moreover, no formal training or preparation was ever given to those entering the home service, and practical skills and a working knowledge of the Company's internal affairs were developed through a form of apprenticeship based upon a rudimentary process of instruction and observation during a clerk's probationary period. This type of instruction was invariably limited to the technical tasks performed within an individual's own office or department, and thus few clerks could ever have gained any real understanding of how their daily duties related to the Company's activities in the wider world.

94 *Asiatic Journal and Monthly Register*, vol. VII (1819), pp. 510–11.
95 See below, p. 192.
96 Peter Auber to Bentinck, 12 November 1833, *Bentinck correspondence*, vol. II, p. 1135.

The way in which the Company organised its domestic affairs offered plenty of ammunition to its critics, and contemporary assessments of the skills and abilities of the Company's servants were sometimes very harsh indeed. In 1819 one of the assistant examiners was told that it long been a 'matter of surprise' how the 'multiplicity of business' handled by the directors was 'ever managed at all by the feeble instruments they employed'.[97] The Company certainly had its fair share of useless time-serving drones, and Thomas Love Peacock ruthlessly mocked their un-challenging daily routine in verse when he began work in the Examiner's Office in 1819:

> From ten to eleven, ate breakfast for seven,
> From eleven to noon, to begin was too soon;
> From twelve to one, asked, 'What's to be done?'
> From one to two, found nothing to do;
> From two to three, began to foresee
> That from three to four would be a damned bore.[98]

But among the staff at East India House were to be found men who offered more than simply the ability to eat large breakfasts and occasion-ally copy out accounts. There is plenty of evidence to suggest that the Company employed some men of real talent and intellectual ability, and many of the managers and clerks worked very hard indeed.

Over the course of long careers a number of senior servants accumu-lated considerable knowledge of East Indian affairs, which they translated into a variety of books and practical guides for readers within the Com-pany and beyond. During the 1780s, for example, Charles Cartwright published collections of documents relating to import duties and smug-gling intended for circulation to Company employees.[99] Robert Wissett, Clerk to the Committee of Warehouse, spent a great deal of time gather-ing commercial statistics during the 1790s, and this endeavour laid the foundations for his important studies of the Company and the East India trade.[100] Three decades later Peter Auber drew on his long experience in

97 Colonel A. Walker to William McCulloch, 6 June 1819, quoted in Nancy Gardner Cassels, 'An historiographical challenge: correspondence between an Indophile and an Indophobe', in Cassels (ed.), *Orientalism*, p. 61.
98 Quoted in Felix Felton, *Thomas Love Peacock* (1973), p. 161.
99 Charles Cartwright, *A list of the duties payable to the King on all goods imported after 25th July 1782 from the East Indies* (1782); *An abstract of the orders and regulations of the honourable Court of Directors, and of other orders relating to the pains and penalties the commanders and officers of ships are liable to, for breach of orders, illicit trade etc.* (1788).
100 R. Wissett, *A view of the rise, progress, and present state of the tea trade in Europe* (1801); idem., *A compendium of East India affairs, political and commercial, for the use of the Court of Directors*, 2

order to produce a detailed study of the Company, which remains an invaluable guide to its inner workings, and he then went on to write a general history of British India.[101]

These types of publications were spin-offs from the official duties of these men, but other servants possessed the intellectual curiosity and energy necessary for private endeavours that were unconnected to their day-to-day working activities. Even before such luminaries as Peacock and the historian James Mill were recruited into specialist posts from outside East India House during the early nineteenth century, several Company employees had already established respectable literary reputations. If the most prominent of these men was the essayist Charles Lamb who worked for thirty-three years as a clerk in the Accountant's Office,[102] the most productive was probably James Cobb who joined the Secretary's Office in 1771 and rose through the ranks to become Assistant Secretary in 1792 and Secretary in 1814. Cobb, who long served as the Company's translator of French, was well known to the public as a dramatist who produced an endless stream of plays, operas and musical dramas. Other literary figures were John Hoole the translator of Tasso, Walter Wilson of the Accountant's Office who was an ecclesiastical historian and author of a life of Defoe, and Thomas Rundall who worked in the Secretary's Office before promotion to assistant examiner in 1814 and later produced historical works related to discovery and the Japanese empire.[103]

Of course, it was one thing for Company servants to possess able and active minds, but quite another for those minds to be stimulated and applied appropriately to the work undertaken at East India House. Much clearly depended upon the office in which an individual was situated,

---

vols. (1802). For examples of the data gathered by Wissett see 'Selection of papers exhibiting a view of the East India Company's commercial concerns', H/449. He also published a work of a rather more practical nature: *On the cultivation and preparation of hemp; as also of an article called sunn . . . as a substitute for . . . hemp etc.* (1804).

101 Auber, *Analysis; Supplement to an analysis of the constitution of the East India Company . . .* (1828); *The rise and progress of the British power in India*, 2 vols. (1837).

102 For biographical details of Charles Lamb's colleagues at East India House see Claude A. Prance, *A companion to Charles Lamb: a guide to people and places 1760–1847* (1983). See also Samuel McKechnie 'Charles Lamb of the India House', *Notes and Queries*, 191 (1946), 178–80, 204–6, 225–30, 252–6, 277–80; 192 (1947), 9–13, 25–9, 53–6, 72–3, 103–6. This multi-part article sheds considerable light on office life at East India House during the early part of the nineteenth century. For working practices see also Foster, *East India House*, passim.

103 For Hoole and other literary figures at East India House see Foster, *East India House*, pp. 155–64, 238–9. Thomas Rundall produced *Narratives of voyages towards the north west, in search of a passage to Cathay and India, 1496–1631 . . .* (1849) and *Memorials of the Empire of Japan in the XVI and XVII centuries* (1850).

and the extent to which he was prepared to rise to the challenges before him. Certainly within the Examiner's Office, where much of the Company's overseas policy was formulated, officials such as James Mill and Thomas Love Peacock found that their daily work was intellectually demanding. Mill was all too aware of the great extent of his responsibilities which he saw as 'the very essence of the internal government of 60 millions of people', and although he thought that his Company work was 'laborious enough' he reported that it 'is to me highly interesting'.[104] Peacock was similarly enthused about his early experience of work as an assistant examiner and he wrote that 'It is not in the common routine of office, but is an employment of a very interesting and intellectual kind, connected with finance and legislation, in which it is possible to be of great service, not only to the Company, but to the millions under her dominion.'[105] On the other hand, a routine diet of monotonous administrative tasks took a heavy toll on the energy and enthusiasm of a third assistant examiner, Nathaniel Brassey Halhed. The noted Oriental scholar complained in 1811 that 'four or five hours of official apathy and solitude' combined with a daily eight-mile walk to and from his place of work to produce 'a fund and bank of tamogunism that obstructs and absorbs all the powers of attention, and superinduces an intellectual torpor bordering on the dull serenity of a monk'.[106]

It is unlikely that day-to-day duties ever offered any intellectual challenge to the vast majority of ordinary officers who worked outside the Examiner's Office, and the effects of the Company's commercial and imperial expansion in India were often very keenly and painfully felt by those who were charged with preparing and copying a never-ending stream of accounts, despatches, letters, memoranda, and minutes. In spite of a rise in the number of clerical staff and minor revisions of working practices, it was still difficult to control the rising tide of paper.[107] As a

---

104 Quoted in Eric Stokes, *The English Utilitarians and India* (Oxford, 1959), p. 48.
105 Quoted in Felton, *Thomas Love Peacock*, p. 161. John Stuart Mill later commented that his office duties were 'sufficiently intellectual not to be a distasteful drudgery, without being such as to cause any strain upon the mental powers of a person used to abstract thought, or to the labour of careful literary composition' (quoted in R. J. Moore, 'John Stuart Mill at East India House', *Historical Studies*, 20 (1983), p. 497).
106 Quoted in Rosane Rocher, *Orientalism, poetry and the millennium: the checkered life of Nathaniel Brassey Halhead, 1751–1830* (Delhi, 1983), p. 214.
107 In total, 191 new clerks were appointed between 1785 and 1801 (*Proceedings of the Select Committee*), p. 155. In December 1813 the Accountant-General Charles Cartwright declared that the amount of business conducted in his department had not 'materially increased', but he qualified his statement by reporting that 'the new mode which has been introduced, relative to

result, some individuals had to labour under considerable burdens, and in 1819 it was said that the workload of the Military Secretary, James Salmond, was so heavy that it might 'stagger Hercules himself'.[108] Clerks and copyists had to perform dull repetitive tasks of the type described by Charles Lamb when he told a friend that 'I am just now engaged in the addition of 900 pages, continent [*sic*] of twenty sums apiece.'[109] This work required sustained concentration and attention to detail, and thus a visitor to East India House in the winter of 1804 described a scene in one office where 'six quill-driving gentlemen . . . [were] too profoundly immersed in their oriental studies to have any sense of my presence'.[110]

Such endeavour could bring additional pay when the workload was increased, but at times the working day was long and exhausting. The strains of office life were indeed such that during the 1780s William Cabell of the Examiner's Office was said to have suffered 'a fit of illness brought on you entirely from excess of fatigue, of duty, and sitting up on nights'.[111] Then in 1800 East India House experienced a 'most melancholy catastrophe' when John Burford, the Clerk to the Committee of Buying, in a 'fit of insanity threw himself from the window of his office and was dashed to pieces'.[112] It is not clear whether this tragic event was caused by work-related strain or some other cause, but it is surely no coincidence that this dramatic end to Burford's life occurred in the place where he had worked for over thirty-six years.

The writings of Charles Lamb provide the best insight into the world of work that existed at East India House and they demonstrate the existence of a disciplined and hard-working regime. Most of Lamb's colleagues appear to have displayed a satisfactory level of commitment to their

---

the journals and ledgers, facilitates the performance of such increased business without a proportionate increase of clerks' (ibid., p. 66).

108 Joseph Hume in *Asiatic Journal and Monthly Register*, vol. VII (1819), p. 508.

109 Quoted in McKechnie, 'Charles Lamb', *Notes and Queries*, 191 (1946), p. 226. In a later autobiographical note, Lamb played down the importance of his literary publications, describing them as his 'Recreations', and he suggested that his 'true works may be found on the shelves of Leaden Hall Street, filling several hundred folios'. Note written to William Upcott in 1827, George Woodcock (ed.), *The letters of Charles Lamb* (1950), p. 12.

110 Quoted in Foster, *East India House*, pp. 182–3.

111 Maria Jane Johnson to Cabell, 28 August 1786. The wife of Samuel Johnson was intervening in office politics by reminding Cabell how he had once professed an 'everlasting attachment' to her husband because of his 'mild, liberal, and gentlemanly treatment' of his staff (E/1/78, f. 435).

112 B. Charlewood to Henry Dundas, 7 May 1800, Melville papers, MS 1074, f. 165, NLS. Charlewood reported this tragic event to Dundas on the day it occurred in the hope that he might fill the vacancy created by Burford's death. His wishes were not fulfilled.

duties, and they were generally professional and serious-minded in their approach to work. From time to time an easy-going camaraderie was translated into boisterous office horseplay,[113] but it was well understood that any breach of unwritten codes of behaviour could result in disciplinary action, and persistent absenteeism, poor work, or inappropriate behaviour would lead to offenders being dismissed or placed on probation.[114] Thus when the unfortunate Tommy Bye arrived in the Accountant's Office one morning still very much the worse for drink he was dismissed after thirty-six years of 'tolerably good' service.[115] His annual salary of £600 was reduced to a pension of £100, although after an appeal it was later restored to £300. Such disciplinary actions were rare, however, and between 1800 and 1817 only four clerical employees were dismissed from service at East India House.[116]

During his early years in the Accountant's Office, Lamb often worked hard and late, to the point that he arrived home every night 'o'erwearied [and] quite faint'.[117] He found the strain unbearable at times, and he suffered from what today would be regarded as work-related stress. His working life did not improve in later years, and in 1815 he was driven to complain to his close friend William Wordsworth about his general conditions:

On Friday I was at office from 10 in the morning (two hours dinner except) to 11 at night—last night till 9; my business, and office business in general, has increased so. I don't mean that I am there every night; but I must expect a great deal of it. I never leave till 4, and I do not keep a holyday now once in ten times, where I used to keep all red-letter days, and some fine days besides.[118]

Hard work had once more taken its toll on Lamb and he declared that 'the head-ache I have is part late hours at work the 2 preceding nights'. Such was his level of dissatisfaction with the length of the working day and the treatment meted out to clerks by the Company's managers that in 1815 he declared to a friend that God should 'curse the India House & fire it to the ground'.[119]

---

113 For examples see Foster, *East India House*, pp. 185–7, 236–8.
114 For examples see McKechnie, 'Charles Lamb', *Notes and Queries*, 191 (1946), p. 178.
115 Charles Lamb to Thomas Manning, 28 May 1819, Woodcock (ed.), *Letters of Lamb*, pp. 132–3.
116 L/AG/30/3, vol. 24, pp. 143–51.
117 Quoted in Foster, *East India House*, p. 181.
118 Lamb to Wordsworth, 7 April 1815, Woodcock (ed.), *Letters of Lamb*, p. 115. For the reduction of holidays which led to a general change in the pattern of working activity in London see Hans-Joachim Voth, *Time and work in England, 1750–1830* (Oxford, 2000), pp. 119–20.
119 Lamb to Matilda Betham, undated, 1815, Woodcock (ed.), *Letters of Lamb*, p. 122.

Lamb's anger had not abated three years later when he denounced the Accountant and Deputy-Accountant as 'true liberty-haters' and 'tyrants', a ferocious outburst caused by alterations made to the general conditions of service of employees at East India House in 1816–17.[120] As part of a campaign of retrenchment designed to cut costs and improve efficiency, working practices were reviewed, and several significant restrictions were imposed upon clerical staff. A holiday allowance of £10 a year was no longer paid to new members of staff; Saturday became a full working day rather than a half-day; holidays on Saints' Days were no longer permitted; the long-standing annual dinner or 'yearly turtle feast' was abolished; and Company employees were no longer permitted to send postage-free private letters from East India House. Worst of all, perhaps, those who had been used to some freedom in the workplace were now obliged to sign their name in a book every time they entered or left their office.[121] These changes were bitterly resented by Lamb and others, and their reaction seems to suggest that previously there had been little monitoring or supervision of those who worked at East India House. Lamb himself eventually moderated his views to the point that he laughed off his complaints against the Company as 'Lovers' quarrels',[122] but he still later likened his retirement in 1825 to emancipation from slavery.[123]

As Charles Lamb's experience would seem to suggest, the Company's clerks worked harder and their activities were subjected to greater levels of regulation and control. Conditions of service, career paths, salaries and pensions all became standardised; working conditions became regular and uniform; practices and attitudes became more professional. In part, these important changes occurred as a necessary response to the increasing volume and complexity of the business that needed to be conducted by the East India Company, but they also mirrored the emergence of a permanent civil service within the British state. As a result, Lamb had hundreds of counterparts in offices across London who performed the same tasks for similar rewards, and in that sense he was entirely typical of a new breed of full-time, salaried administrator. What was different

120 Lamb to Dorothy Wordsworth, 18 February 1818, ibid., p. 132.
121 Foster, *East India House*, pp. 92, 180, 183, 184; McKechnie, 'Charles Lamb', *Notes and Queries*, 192 (1947), pp. 73, 105. It seems that Lamb was often able to write and despatch private letters while at work.
122 Lamb to Bernard Barton, 9 January 1823, Woodcock (ed.), *Letters of Lamb*, p. 147.
123 Lamb to William Wordsworth, 6 April 1825, ibid., p. 160.

about all Company men, however, was the fact that their minds and skills were being applied to the government of a vast new territorial empire as well as to the continuing management of an expanding trade. How the directors and Company officials in Britain sought to come to terms with this unprecedented set of circumstances, and how they responded to a unique set of administrative problems, is explored in the next three chapters.

CHAPTER 6

Methods: an empire in writing

The fact that the directors, officials, and clerks of the East India Company spent much of their time reading, preparing, or copying lengthy documents underlines the central importance of written communication to the domestic management of the Company's overseas affairs.[1] The significance of this cannot be overstated because exchanges of despatches between Britain and Asia formed the basis of long-distance working relationships between men who sometimes had never set eyes on one another.[2] Despatches contained instructions and orders but, just as importantly, they provided a means by which those in Britain could form a view of events and developments in the East. Yet, of course, the realities of distance and the speed of communication meant that those at East India House could never be in possession of up-to-date news about their overseas territories and settlements. The problem of asymmetric information, or a situation in which the directors always knew considerably less about the prevailing state of overseas affairs than did their employees in Asia, was ever-present during this period and offered a considerable obstacle to the effective management of the Company. But, having accepted that their view of the East would always be at least several months out of date, the Company's directors and senior managers nevertheless dedicated themselves to the establishment of a full and accurate picture of events in Asia.

The occupants of East India House also increasingly sought better knowledge of the societies, cultures, and economies being brought under

---

1 Anyone studying the Company's written communication is deeply indebted to Martin Moir's detailed studies of practice and procedure. As far as this chapter is concerned, see especially '*Kaghazi Raj*: notes on the documentary basis of Company rule, 1773–1858', *Indo-British Review*, 21 (1993), pp. 185–93.

2 The career movements of individuals meant that the paths of some important figures never crossed. Thus in 1796 the Chairman of the Company David Scott, who had spent many years in Bombay, claimed that he had never met Governor-General John Shore, whose career had been based in Bengal (Ainslie Thomas Embree, *Charles Grant and British rule in India* (1962), p. 137).

Company control in India. Although the extent to which the British ever properly knew anything at all about India has been a matter for great scholarly debate in recent years,[3] there can be no denying that the Company attempted in an increasingly systematic fashion to arm itself with a better understanding of its empire, and consequently those in London developed a near-obsessive desire to collect each and every snippet of information emanating from Asia. Motivation was provided by the firmly held belief that the possession of information represented the key to effective administration, enlightened government, and the close supervision of overseas servants. The directors thus gathered political and military intelligence to inform their decision-making, and they organised and arranged material in an attempt to impose some degree of administrative order and coherence upon the Company's affairs. As a result, East India House became an enormous archival repository for information about India's economy and society as well as the Company's own affairs.

Of course, the accumulation of vast amounts of written information can be represented simply as an administrative response from men who were suddenly confronted with complex problems rooted in an unfamiliar world that was located thousands of miles from their own. Indeed, from the very beginning of its days, the Company had exhibited a deep commitment to information gathering and the keeping of detailed commercial and maritime records. Since experience dictated that reasonably effective management of long-distance trading activity was based upon the possession of intelligence, it was entirely natural for those in London to believe that close supervision of territorial possessions could similarly be achieved through the establishment of command over all forms of information about India. As has recently been demonstrated, the British accumulation of knowledge about India became more far more extensive, proactive, and sophisticated after 1785 and this has been ascribed to the action of the men who served under Governors-General Cornwallis and Wellesley.[4] This might well be so, but the initial creation and development of the Company's 'empire of information' in India arose in no small measure from the sustained encouragement given to all forms of information gathering by those in London who cultivated a corporate culture in which every piece of useful intelligence was recorded and stored at East India House for possible future use in the Company's decision-making processes.

3 For a summary discussion see C. A. Bayly, *Empire and information. Intelligence gathering and social communication in India, 1780–1870* (Cambridge, 1999), pp. 6–9.
4 Ibid., pp. 56–96.

The Company did not act in isolation, however, and the intellectual climate of the age helped to foster a close and sustained metropolitan interest in the wider world in general, and in Asia in particular.[5] Moreover, the Company was carried along on the strong tide of late eighteenth-century institutions, societies, offices of state, and departments of government that became dedicated to the pursuit of better information, knowledge, and understanding about their different spheres of endeavour. Across the wider British state and empire, there was a movement towards the creation of ever more complex systems of information gathering, handling, and classification,[6] and a vigorous search for useful knowledge underpinned the reformist actions of government agencies both at home and abroad. These influences helped to shape the Company's response to the establishment of its empire in India, and this was markedly so after 1783 when the loss of the American colonies prompted considerable anxiety in Britain about the future strength and well-being of the nation and empire. Strongly represented in particular among the responses to the general imperial crisis of confidence of the 1780s was the belief that it was in the national interest to ensure that colonies were managed more effectively, in terms of both their administration and economic development. As with many of the agencies and departments of the late eighteenth-century imperial state, the East India Company therefore became committed to 'improving' its overseas territories.[7] This offered the prospect of better government and the more efficient exploitation of resources, but it also enabled the Company to lay great stress upon its broad contribution to British intellectual life. The development of Company interests in agriculture, botany, literature, linguistics, science and surveying were all in themselves useful tools for the better administration of an expanding empire, but in the propaganda wars surrounding the periodic renewals of charters they enabled the Company's friends in Britain to proclaim a virtuous and enlightened commitment to the advancement of the nation's knowledge and learning.

5 P. J. Marshall, 'Asia: growing awareness and changing perspectives in the eighteenth century', in P. J. Marshall and Glyndwr Williams, *The great map of mankind. British perceptions of the world in the age of enlightenment* (1982), pp. 67–97.

6 Daniel R. Headrick, *When information came of age. Technologies of knowledge in the age of reason and revolution, 1700–1850* (Oxford, 2000).

7 For the Company's attachment to the cause of improvement see Richard Drayton, *Nature's government: science, imperial Britain, and the 'improvement' of the world* (New Haven, Conn., 2000), pp. 115–20. See also Richard Drayton, 'Knowledge and empire', *OHBE*, vol. II: P. J.

LINES OF COMMUNICATION

The first priority of the directors in London was always to ensure early receipt of news of events in Asia so that appropriate instructions could be formulated for despatch back to the Company's overseas servants. Yet, because most of the written communications exchanged between Britain and Asia had to be carried on board the East Indiamen that plied the Company's major trade routes, flows of information and instruction were not always regular or reliable. In particular, patterns of information exchange between Britain and Asia were determined by the fact that cargo-carrying Indiamen could not simply commence their voyages at any time of the year.[8] Instead, they were obliged to set forth during an annual sailing 'season' determined by favourable prevailing winds and the monsoon, and the established practice was for most voyages to Asia to begin between December and April, with return legs commencing during the autumn and early winter. If all went well, routine letters from London might arrive in India during the summer, and replies would be sent home several months later in the hope that they would be delivered to East India House in the early summer of the following year. A late eighteenth-century exchange of despatches between the directors and their servants might therefore take around eighteen months, and inevitably this meant that there were long periods of time when the directors were starved of news. As they complained in December 1782, the last letter they had received from Calcutta was dated 4 April and consequently they were 'unable to judge of the situation of our affairs'.[9] Accordingly, whenever news from overseas did arrive at East India House it was hungrily consumed by the directors, and all other Company business ground to a halt for several days.[10]

Marshall (ed.), *The eighteenth century* (Oxford, 1998), pp. 231–52. For the links between science and empire established by the formal and informal institutions of the late eighteenth century see John Gascoigne, *Science in the service of empire. Joseph Banks and the uses of science in the age of revolution* (Cambridge, 1998), pp. 111–46. The contribution of the Company to this process, as prompted by Sir Joseph Banks, is discussed in detail on pp. 135–45.

8 For discussion of voyages between Britain and Asia see Sir Evan Cotton, *East Indiamen. The East India Company's maritime service*, Sir Charles Fawcett (ed.), (1949), pp. 108–40 and Jean Sutton, *Lords of the east. The East India Company and its ships (1600–1874)* (second edition, 2000), pp. 94–115.

9 *FWIHC*, vol. IX, p. 84.

10 See, for example, John Wordsworth to Captain John Wordsworth, 12 December 1804, Carl H. Ketcham (ed.), *The letters of John Wordsworth* (Ithaca, NY, 1969), p. 149. The ill-fated Wordsworth waited for two days at East India House before being sworn in as a ship's commander because the directors first had to read despatches that had recently arrived from Bengal.

By the late 1780s, it was possible for *William Pitt*, a regular Company vessel of 800 tons, to sail to Bengal and back in just under a year.[11] This was an exceptional performance, but it offered an indication of shortening voyage times between Britain and India. Thereafter, there was a steady reduction in average sailing times,[12] and this can be attributed to two main causal factors. First, as a result of energetic interventions by Gabriel Snodgrass, the Company's long-serving Surveyor of Shipping, significant improvements, including the coppering of hulls, were made to the construction of Indiamen during the last quarter of the eighteenth century and these enhanced speed and handling.[13] Second, the tragic loss of *Colebrooke* in 1778 acted as a spur to navigational advances. These were largely based upon the work of Alexander Dalrymple who began to process and analyse the vast amount of maritime information held at East India House. He prepared a selection of printed charts and plans for distribution to the commanders of Indiamen with a view to making voyages safer, faster, and more predictable, and this work was continued by James Horsburgh during the early nineteenth century.[14] These improvements to navigation offered the directors some prospect of more frequent and faster exchanges of information between London and Asia, but even then the process of communication remained very slow and was subjected to all manner of disruptions, including the loss of ships to fire, storm, and enemy action in wartime.[15] Various unfortunate circumstances led to the loss or capture of nineteen ships between 1779 and 1783; and a further eighteen were lost in 1808 and 1809.[16]

11 On 25 April 1789 *The Times* reported that the *William Pitt* had made the return journey in a record time of eleven months and sixteen days, an achievement that is confirmed by the vessel's log and journal.
12 This can been seen in the details of voyage times presented for each Company vessel in Anthony Farrington (comp.), *Catalogue of East India Company ships' journals and logs 1600–1834* (1999).
13 For details of the design and construction improvements inspired by Snodgrass and others see Sutton, *Lords of the east*, pp. 41–3.
14 Andrew S. Cook, 'Establishing the sea routes to India and China: stages in the development of hydrological knowledge', in H. V. Bowen, Margarette Lincoln, and Nigel Rigby (eds.), *The worlds of the East India Company* (Woodbridge, 2002), pp. 119–36. The background to Dalrymple's appointment is outlined in Howard T. Fry, *Alexander Dalrymple (1737–1808) and the expansion of British trade* (1970), pp. 222–31. Details of his application are on pp. 229–30.
15 For a case study of the problems that could be encountered see James H. Thomas, 'The voyage of the Eagle, 1773', *Mariner's Mirror*, 82 (1996), pp. 165–74. The *Eagle*, a packet boat destined for Madras, took seven months to sail from Deptford to Plymouth.
16 The Company calculated that it lost 51 of the 1,038 ships that sailed for Asia between 1760 and 1796 (L/AG/10/2, vol. 4, p. 19). The blackest day was 9 August 1780 when the *Gatton, Godfrey, Hillsborough, Mountstuart*, and *Royal George* were all lost to a combined Franco-Spanish fleet.

Acknowledging that they could do little or nothing to prevent the hazards of sea and war, the directors nevertheless endeavoured to ensure that news was sent to them as swiftly and securely as possible. Their hopes for early intelligence of events in India rested with those in the Company's Presidencies and much depended upon the speed with which vessels were prepared for return voyages to Britain. This was often a matter of concern for the directors, and during the early part of the period their letters to India were liberally sprinkled with complaints about the late arrival of news, which prevented them from sending up-to-date instructions to India on the next season's ships. Thereafter, those in India were reminded on a regular basis that one of their primary responsibilities was to establish an 'exact punctuality' in the Company's correspondence.[17]

Overseas servants were also routinely reminded that, in order to avoid a complete breakdown in communication, despatches were always to be consigned to more than one carrier. Normal practice was for copies of a despatch to be sent on three or four different ships, and, when circumstances demanded, an additional copy was carried by messengers who travelled over land, along the so-called 'direct' route through the Persian Gulf or, alternatively, along the rather more hazardous Red Sea route.[18] This required laborious and time-consuming preparation of documentation in India, and the Bengal Council complained in 1783 that a 'multiplicity of copies must retard our dispatches', even though they undertook to 'lessen the time and inconvenience of it as much as possible'.[19] Routine letters, accounts, and papers were consigned to the 'general packets' on board regular Company vessels, while important news was sent in 'special packets', either on Indiamen sailing early in the season or on hired schooners that were capable of making good time regardless of the weather conditions. In wartime, important encrypted instructions from London were often carried on naval vessels taking up station in the Indian Ocean, while the Company itself took up special 'express' packet boats or 'advice vessels' in the hope of avoiding French cruisers that were on the lookout for heavily laden East Indiamen. The performance of the special packet boat *Surprise* demonstrated in 1785 that, given good conditions, it was not unreasonable to expect an 'express' to complete a voyage from Bengal in around four months.[20]

17 Directors to Bengal, 27 March 1787, *FWIHC,* vol. X, p. 168.
18 For details see Holden Furber, 'The overland routes to India in the seventeenth and eighteenth centuries', *Journal of Indian History,* 29 (1951), pp. 105–33.
19 *FWIHC,* vol. IX, p. 375.
20 The *Surprise* left the Bengal pilot on 16 December 1784 and made Limerick on 9 April 1785. An officer then carried despatches to London, via Holyhead, and a packet containing a letter dated 10 December 1784 was delivered to East India House on 17 April 1785 (*FWIHC,* vol. IX, p. 237).

Yet, although the directors always professed to welcome the early arrival of news they were never inclined to support the establishment of a regular packet system based upon the use of special vessels sailing out of season. As a result, Governor-General Cornwallis found that his detailed plan for the despatch of packets every August was ignored by a Court of Directors whose desire for information was overridden by concerns about the cost of hiring additional vessels.[21] The directors clearly placed strict limits on the price they were prepared to pay for news from India, and they baulked at the idea of freeing the flow of information from the considerable constraints imposed by the use of ships sailing in season. As a result, the Company's lines of communication continued to be embedded in the broader commercial system, and this meant that most despatches moved at the same speed as passengers and cargo carried on board East Indiamen. Towards the end of the period the Company did begin to consign some despatches to private vessels, but a regular steam packet service between Britain and India was only introduced after the Company lost its last commercial privileges in 1833.

ATTENTION TO DETAIL

It was not enough for the directors to hope that news and information would be received from Asia as early as possible. They also needed good-quality intelligence to enable them to assess the actions and performance of their servants. In order to obtain this, the directors laid down increasingly well-defined guidelines to ensure that servants in India and elsewhere sent back to East India House the information that was necessary for them to establish a full and detailed picture of the Company's affairs. Yet, it was one thing to lay down guidelines, and it was quite another to secure compliance from servants whose self-interest, incompetence, neglect of duty, or downright disobedience meant that they often failed to provide the information required by the directors. Individuals might seek to put themselves and their actions in the best possible light, and thus Henry Dundas noted rather pointedly to Sir Archibald Campbell, the new Governor of Madras, in 1787, that 'It is a fault of all the despatches of former governors of India to be mixt with an insufferable quantity of egotism.'[22] More seriously, the directors occasionally expressed the belief

---

21 For Cornwallis's plan of 1788 see *FWIHC*, vol. X, pp. 627–8.
22 Dundas to Campbell, 26 July 1787, quoted in Holden Furber, *Henry Dundas, First Viscount Melville, 1742–1811: political manager of Scotland, statesman, administrator of British India* (London, 1931), p. 57.

that information was being deliberately withheld from them by senior figures in India,[23] and their attempts to secure what they wanted sometimes developed into an ongoing and at times bitter war of attrition between East India House and the Presidencies.

When the Company acquired an empire, the directors did not neglect the collection of commercial intelligence but after 1756 new types of information had to be reported from India. As a result, much more space in despatches had to be devoted to government, diplomacy, military affairs, revenue collection, and a whole host of other subjects related to the Company's position as an imperial power. The directors required that actions be explained in greater detail, and close attention was paid to the functioning of Company administration. In particular, the directors continued to insist that the records of the Councils and various boards established in the different Presidencies be sent to London, and an enormous collection of 'proceedings' and 'consultations' found its way to East India House. Scrutiny of these copious documents enabled the directors to conduct a retrospective review of the day-to-day workings of their overseas government, and it enabled them to assess the extent to which their orders and instructions were being followed. As a result, senior officials were often told 'to mention every matter of importance in your letters with marginal references to your consultations',[24] and in 1821 the Bengal Council was reminded by the India Board and the Chairmen that 'It is principally with a view so to inform us that the system of copious and full reports from all subordinate functionaries and detailed minutes from the members of the government has from early times been adopted.'[25]

The insatiable metropolitan demands for information helped to cultivate an attitude of mind within the Company which placed a very high premium upon full and accurate record keeping. Some in India responded positively to the need to commit every transaction to paper, and one such enthusiast was Cornwallis who during the 1780s wrote to the directors of his 'earnest desire to give you the most compleat information in my power, of every transaction of this Government, and of the general state of your affairs in this country'.[26] Not all were as assiduous as

---

23 Charles Grant levelled this charge at Governor-General Lord Wellesley in 1805 (Embree, *Charles Grant*, p. 212). It was said in 1829 this had been a 'thing not uncommon' in earlier years. See J. G. Ravenshaw to Bentinck, 19 November 1829, *Bentinck correspondence*, vol. I, p. 355.
24 Directors to Bengal, 28 August 1782, *FWIHC*, vol. IX, p. 71.
25 L/P&S/5, vol. 571, p. 144.
26 Cornwallis to Directors, 3 November 1788, *FWIHC*, vol. X, p. 628.

Cornwallis in their pursuit of 'compleat information', however, and on numerous occasions the directors had cause to rebuke their overseas servants for poor standards of record keeping. Indeed, in 1782 the Bengal Council was severely admonished for its failure to send home any of its consultations for the year 1780, and the directors noted their 'great astonishment and surprise' as well as their 'displeasure for such great neglect'.[27] Time after time, the directors pointed out the gaps in records which caused them to 'labor under the utmost inconvenience',[28] and they began to define very precisely what records should be sent home and when. This undoubtedly led to improvements, but the servants in India found it difficult to keep up with the demand for an uninterrupted flow of information, and breakdowns in the system generated over 100 complaints from the directors between 1810 and 1830.[29] Consequently, the directors remained in the dark about some important matters, and it was noted with some despair in 1819 that they had learned more about the ending of the Maratha war from a speech of Governor-General Hastings reported in the *Calcutta Gazette,* and then reprinted in London, than they had from the sketchy details set out in official despatches.[30]

Although much time and attention were devoted to reading despatches, proceedings, and consultations, the directors' most urgent need was for financial information. In particular, the formulation of up-to-date statements of the Company's position in India after 1756 could only be achieved through the submission of accurate accounts detailing income and expenditure relating to the armed forces, civil administration, and revenue collection as well as traditional forms of commercial activity. The number of factors or variables determining overall levels of profitability was much increased, and this was reflected in the handling of greater amounts information as well as in the need to construct more complex balance sheets and financial projections. The auditing, ordering, and analysis of financial information in London assumed an even higher level of importance than before, and considerable emphasis was placed upon the submission of regular, detailed, and accurate accounts from overseas. As a result, the directors and officials at East India House led a sustained drive to establish a much greater degree of rigour and sophistication within the Company's accounting system.

27 *FWIHC,* vol. IX, p. 48.
28 Ibid., vol. IX, p. 173; vol. X, p. 279. For the response of those in Bengal to earlier complaints about 'several blanks' in these consultations see ibid., vol. X, pp. 509–10.
29 Moir, '*Kaghazi Raj*', p. 187.
30 Board of Control to Lord Hastings, 30 January 1819, L/P&S/5, vol. 571, p. 47.

The directors had always been preoccupied with the quality of the financial information they received from their servants in Asia. At the beginning of the period, they had much to complain about and their despatches drew attention to accounts and books riddled with errors, inconsistencies, and omissions. They noted in early 1754, for example, that the books sent from Bengal had been 'very badly copyed', while some papers and accounts had not been sent at all.[31] As a result, none of the information could be considered reliable. The directors pointed out that, although certain people were to blame for this state of affairs, senior figures in Calcutta were ultimately responsible for bringing order to the Company's accounts in India. Their displeasure was made known in the form of a sharp reprimand to the Bengal Council who were told that they were 'most culpable as it is evident you have left every servant to his own liberty to work or play without controul or giving yourselves the least trouble to concern to look into the conduct of your servants in their several employments and offices'.[32] On this occasion, improvement was to be achieved by reordering books and creating new sets of journals.

Following the acquisition of the *diwani*, the directors made it clear that they now required full details of all of the funds flowing into the Company's treasury. A scrutiny of the early revenue accounts sent from Bengal revealed considerable shortcomings, and this led to the formulation of precise instructions on the future collection of data.[33] The Bengal Council were then told how to compile revenue accounts, and adjustments were subsequently made to these instructions so that the directors could receive a 'distinct statement' of every form of Company income.[34] Having established what financial information was required from India, much time and effort were then spent ensuring that accounts were prepared and delivered according to good practice. As a result, some praise began to be directed towards those in India who were responsible for an increasingly high standard of book-keeping.[35]

In addition to obtaining accurate and comprehensive financial information, it was also essential that those in London were able to offer early

---

31 Directors to Bengal, 23 January 1754, *FWIHC*, vol. I, p. 31.
32 Ibid., vol. I, p. 32.
33 Directors to Bengal, 21 November 1766, ibid., vol. IV, pp. 220–1.
34 Directors to Bengal, 20 November 1767, ibid., vol. V, pp. 48–51, and to Bengal, 16 March 1768, ibid., vol. XIV, p. 24.
35 See William Wright's comments on improvements in Bengal, H/208, pp. 91–2. By the late 1780s despatches from India routinely ended with a 'State of this Treasury this day', which detailed the cash and bills held at each Presidency.

comparisons between previous estimates and actual outcomes, because only then could precise statements be made about the prevailing state of the Company's affairs. This matter became especially important after 1787 when the directors were required to submit a full statement of the Company's finances to the Board of Control, prior to the presentation of an annual East India 'budget' to the House of Commons. Hitherto, only Bengal had been submitting 'estimated and actual accounts' to London, but the directors now required that all of the overseas settlements despatch 'uniform accounts made up to the same period, and exactly corresponding with the estimates of receipts and disbursements'.[36] This was easier said than done in view of the fact that in 1787 Bombay had still not returned final accounts for 1783 and 1784, but a determined campaign waged by the Auditor of Indian Accounts, William Wright, seems to have had the desired effect. During the late 1780s he sent to each Indian Presidency a detailed five-year review pointing out mistakes, errors, and missing information, and he served reminders about the basic rules governing general procedure.[37] The effects were such that in August 1791 the directors reported that for the first time ever they had been able offer Parliament 'regular accounts' for all three Presidencies up to the end of the preceding financial year.[38] Moreover, the quality of information was held to be much improved. Dundas declared that the budget of 1791 had been based upon accounts 'more perfect' than ever before, and he reported that the estimates of recent years had proven to be 'accurate to a degree almost incredible'.[39] Two years later he took the view that the introduction of an annual East India budget had been 'productive of all those salutary effects, which must ever attend publicity in matters of account and revenue'.[40] Consequently, it can be held that during the 1780s a much greater degree of order was brought to the Company's finances in India. The accounts were by no means perfect, and during the 1820s the directors still had occasion to complain about shortcomings in India,[41] but by the end of the period the financial information at the

36 Directors to Bengal, 31 July 1787, *FWIHC*, vol. X, pp. 292–3.
37 See and compare the drafts of the lengthy reports sent to Bengal, Bombay, and Madras in 1787, H/208, pp. 91–54. The amended report sent to Bengal is in *FWIHC*, vol. X, pp. 241–52. For Wright's fifty-paragraph report sent to Bengal in 1790 see ibid., vol. XI, pp. 109–20.
38 Directors to Supreme Council, 4 Aug. 1791, ibid., vol. XI, p. 176.
39 William Cobbett, *Parliamentary history of England from . . . 1066 to . . . 1803*, 36 vols. (1806–20), vol. XXIX, cols. 603, 611.
40 Ibid., cols. 496–7.
41 See, for example, Directors to Bengal, 3 January and 5 March 1823, E/4/708, pp. 65, 287.

disposal of those in London was certainly of a much better quality than had been the case seventy years earlier.

As well as struggling long and hard to ensure that they received a regular flow of good quality intelligence from Asia, the directors also had to try to ensure that they maintained control over news and information when it arrived in Britain. Commercial secrecy had always been important to the directors, but the management of information from India now became of paramount importance as the fortunes of war and politics in India began to bear increasingly heavily upon the Company's credit. As a result, the directors became acutely aware of the need to protect the Company against the potentially fatal effects of rumour-mongering conducted for the purposes of financial speculation. At the same time, the increased importance of India to the economic and strategic thinking of ministers meant that the Company had to share news and information with government. During the 1760s, therefore, careful thought had to be devoted to news management and the directors were obliged to come to terms with the unwelcome fact that much of the Company's business was henceforth to be conducted under intense political and public scrutiny.

First and foremost, the directors always endeavoured to prevent any new information about the Company's affairs reaching the public domain before they had themselves had the opportunity to digest it. The need to ensure that the directors were the first to receive information from Asia was self-evident at a time when speculators were hungry for any snippet of information that might affect the buying or selling of Company stock. But the directors were aware of the need to conceal military information from foreign rivals, and they were also becoming sensitive to the fact that rumours and half-truths were important factors in shaping popular attitudes towards the Company and its servants. Thus in 1757 the directors announced new regulations intended to 'prevent the messengers delivering any private letters whatsoever, until their arrival at the East India House, and to conceal all intelligence until the packets are delivered'.[42] This proved to be ineffective and thirty years later the directors were still complaining that private letters were being delivered to India House from

---

42 Directors to Bengal, 11 November 1757, *FWIHC*, vol. II, p. 48.

Company ships quicker than the official correspondence, and they again felt obliged to issue a new set of regulations to prevent this happening.[43]

Unable to regulate the delivery of private letters, the directors attempted in 1766 to impose an outright ban on servants in India communicating any information at all about the Company to private individuals in Britain.[44] They were prompted into this utterly futile gesture by the actions of Clive who in September 1765 had written from India to friends and acquaintances in Britain informing them of the acquisition of the *diwani*.[45] The response of the directors was of course doomed to failure because nothing short of the censorship of private letters could ever prevent news about the Company finding its way to individuals and then into the newspapers. That they were ultimately fighting a losing battle on this front was made clear during the mid-1780s when they felt compelled yet again to issue instructions to prohibit discussion of Company affairs in private letters, and they also endeavoured to restrict access to the Company's records, accounts and papers in India.[46]

The failure of the directors to close private channels of information between India and Britain was matched by their inability to keep news and intelligence within the confines of their meeting rooms at East India House. Before the 1750s they had seldom been required to share information with stockholders, ministers, or the wider public, although shipping and commercial news had routinely been posted up at the Royal Exchange and afforded a small amount of space in the press. But casual public indifference towards the Company's affairs did not long survive the beginning of the Seven Years War. The directors found themselves assailed from all quarters by requests for information.

Most significantly, practical necessity dictated that news be shared with ministers who were directing the war effort against France and thus in June and July 1759, for example, full extracts of despatches from India were prepared and sent to William Pitt and Lord Anson.[47] This was, however, a slow and cumbersome method of passing on information, and the Chairman began to write letters to ministers containing short

---

43 Directors to Bengal, 20 August 1788, ibid., vol. X, p. 360.
44 Ibid., vol. IV, p. 161.
45 H. V. Bowen, 'Lord Clive and speculation in East India Company stock, 1766', *Historical Journal*, 30 (1987), pp. 909–11.
46 Directors to Bengal, 21 September 1785, *FWIHC*, vol. IX, pp. 263–4. For full details of successive attempts to prohibit overseas servants discussing Company affairs in private letters sent to important people in Britain between 1732 and 1782, see H/78, pp. 649–61.
47 D/22, ff. 83, 84, 88, 92.

summaries of recently received despatches.[48] This practice continued after
the end of the war when ministers became preoccupied with the possibility of a French resurgence in India, and the directors now routinely passed
on intelligence relating to shipping movements, troop deployments, and
diplomatic initiatives.[49] Although there were occasionally tensions between the directors and ministers, notably when Lord Weymouth made
a clumsy intervention in Company politics in 1769, a close working
relationship developed between the Company and the Southern Department as the latter began to take a more active interest in matters that were
now deemed to be of national concern in the Indian Ocean region.[50]
From this position, it was only a short step to the more regular flows of
information from Company to government established by the Regulating
Act and Pitt's India Act.

From the late 1760s, the Company was also obliged to share information with Parliament. It did so by presenting half-yearly financial
statements and by supplying documentation to the committees established to examine various aspects of the Company's affairs. Critics believed that the directors were often selective with the material they
released, and Clive saw this as an attempt to deflect blame for the
Company's failings away from East India House and on to the overseas
servants.[51] Others were later uneasy about the government relying upon
the accuracy of accounts prepared by Company servants.[52] There is no
evidence to suggest, however, that the directors sought systematically to
conceal information from ministers or Parliament, and orders for papers
were usually expedited by the employment of extra clerks to copy out
the small mountains of documents that were requested. Indeed, *The
Times* remarked in 1786 that 'one good effect' of Parliament calling for
written evidence was that it generated 'considerable extra perquisites' for
Company clerks who were obliged to work overtime.[53]

Successive parliamentary inquiries into the Company's affairs resulted
in a considerable amount of information finding its way from Leadenhall
Street to Westminster. Many ministers and politicians freely confessed

48 On 2 April 1764 the Chairman, John Dorrien, wrote to the Earls of Egmont and Halifax with
    news received from Bengal the previous day (D/23, f. 114).
49 For numerous examples of such information see H/101–14, passim.
50 Bowen, *Revenue and reform*, pp. 73–83.
51 Speech of 24 March 1773, BL, Eg. MS, 245, pp. 133–4.
52 See, for example, Anon., *A letter to the proprietors of East India stock, respecting the present
    situation of the Company's affairs both abroad and at home* . . . (1802), p. 5; Anon., *A demonstration
    of the necessity and advantages of a free trade to the East Indies* . . . (1807), p. 98.
53 *The Times*, 23 March 1786.

their deep ignorance of Indian affairs, and thus common sense dictated that any reform of the Company had to be preceded by an examination of its recent history. As John Burgoyne remarked in 1772 when he called for an inquiry into the Company's affairs, Parliament could not be expected 'to apply a remedy without any information of the disease'.[54] Consequently, all manner of letters, accounts, estimates, and minutes were published in late eighteenth-century parliamentary papers and committee reports, and these became invaluable storehouses of information about the Company's affairs. There were occasional grumbling protests that the Company's secrets were being revealed to the French, but this could not prevent a great deal of this material finding its way into the public domain as publishers and newspaper editors took it upon themselves to reprint extensive selections of minutes and reports generated by the parliamentary committees.[55]

Over time, the processes by which information about the Company was disseminated to the public via Parliament became more regular. Extracts from lengthy parliamentary committee reports continued to find their way into newspapers, books, and pamphlets, as well as into periodicals such as the *Asiatic Journal* and *Alexander's East India Magazine* that later were dedicated to the close scrutiny of the Company's affairs. At the same time, the directors acknowledged that they could do nothing to stem the flow of information from East India House to Westminster, and they adopted the practice of arranging their own publication of reprints of parliamentary accounts, papers, and reports. They did this in the hope that officially endorsed works would carry a greater weight of authority than items produced by enemies of the Company who might well be selective about printing information placed before Parliament. This practice appears to have developed during the 1790s, and by 1813 the directors were routinely sanctioning the publication of volumes such as *Minutes of evidence taken before the Select Committee of the Honourable House of Commons*, which carried the declaration that it was 'Printed by order of the Court of Directors for the information of the proprietors'.

The directors were powerless to prevent the outward flow of information to government and Parliament, but they were at least able to exert some degree of control over the release of news to the stockholders. Ever mindful of stock prices and the Company's credit, the directors often endeavoured to portray events in India in as favourable a light as possible,

54 *Parliamentary History*, vol. XVII, col. 455 (13 April 1772).
55 See, for examples, the advertisements in the *Public Advertiser*, 19 and 23 Nov. 1772.

and they carefully selected the parts of despatches they deemed suitable
for release to the stockholders and the wider public. In April 1764, for
example, close attention was devoted to the question of which paragraphs
relating to the reinstatement of Mir Jafar as Nawab of Bengal should be
extracted from the despatches and then published above the Secretary's
name in the newspapers.[56] The attribution of articles in this way was seen
by the Company as being an important means of offering readers a way of
discriminating between fact and fiction, and thus in May 1764 when
William Say, the printer of the *Gazetteer*, asked whether the Secretary
would acknowledge that he was the author of an article about Bengal
published three months earlier he was told that the item had been
submitted by order of the directors.[57] This was clearly a matter of some
importance to Say who feared being prosecuted by the Company for
publishing inaccurate information about East Indian affairs. That his fears
were well grounded became evident in 1767 when he begged the directors
not to press charges against him by claiming that an article in the
Gazetteer 'stating that the Company's forces in India had been defeated
by the Marathas was inserted without his knowledge by someone desirous
of reducing the value of East India stock'.[58] Say does not appear to have
been prosecuted but this episode reveals the extent to which the public
dissemination of accurate news and information about East Indian affairs
had become a highly sensitive matter.

The responsiveness of the stock market to news from India was no
better illustrated than in May 1769 when rumours of Company setbacks
at the hands of Haidar Ali caused swift and violent fluctuations of prices.
Newspapers commented upon on the speed with which stories circulated
around the City after the arrival of despatches carried by *Lord Mansfield*,
and they also reported the widely held belief that the directors were
deliberately concealing information from the public.[59] As a result, the
directors were urged by the General Court to place a notice in the press,
'tending to quiet the minds of the Proprietors without doors', and it was
agreed that this action had the desired calming effect.[60] The outcome
seems to have persuaded the directors that it was in their interests
routinely to publish summaries of all despatches 'in order to prevent the
public from being imposed upon by the spurious accounts inserted into

56 D/23, f. 114.   57 Ibid., f. 118v.
58 D/148, ff. 227–8.
59 *Middlesex Journal*, 27–30 May, 30 May–1 June 1769; *London Chronicle*, 25–27, 27–30 May 1769.
60 *London Chronicle*, 1–3 June 1769.

the papers by interested men to serve their own ends', and one newspaper commented that 'It is a matter of astonishment that so obvious a method of preventing scandalous impositions has not been before put in practice.'[61] Thereafter, official Company news from India usually appeared in the press under headings such as 'East India intelligence', although unscrupulous publishers still found plenty of room for items of gossip, rumour, and speculation prefaced with remarks such as 'It is said' or 'We hear'. Thus during the late 1780s *The Times* still found it necessary to point out the difference between official information and the false stories published in other newspapers 'with an intent to commit plunder in the Alley'.[62] Thereafter, it published statements about news of East Indian affairs which carried the signed endorsement of senior officials and directors at East India House.

The directors also gave much thought to the information they reported verbally in the General Court, knowing that whatever they announced to the stockholders would be reported in the press within a day or two. In June 1766, when they were motivated by a desire to dampen public expectations about the value of the riches secured for the Company by Clive, they discussed the matter on three occasions before agreeing a selection of material to be read out to the proprietors.[63] But, of course, not all stockholders were prepared uncritically to accept news and information placed before them and the directors were sometimes forced into revealing more details than they would otherwise have wished. It was reported in December 1768, for example, that the proprietors had detected an accounting 'manoeuvre' that had enabled the directors 'to conceal the present brilliant state of the Company's affairs'. This action, described as a 'pious fraud', was represented as an attempt to hide £1.2 million and prevent the Company being squeezed dry by the government.[64] Three years later, several proprietors declared that they could not accept the Chairman's 'bare assertion' that the Company was in a better situation than the previous year, and this began a sequence of events that led eventually to the revelation of a stock-jobbing operation orchestrated by a group of leading directors in order to maintain the Company's credit.[65] No doubt learning a lesson from this unhappy episode, the directors became more prepared to release information to the stockholders,

61 Ibid., 27–30 May 1769.
62 *The Times*, 15 August 1789.
63 D/24, 17 June 1766. See also 12 and 13 June.
64 *Gazetteer*, 23 December 1768.
65 *London Evening Post*, 24–26 September 1772. See Bowen, *Revenue and reform*, pp. 125–30.

and the minutes of late eighteenth-century General Court meetings usually record the formal reading of accounts and papers. On occasions, the stockholders still had to press hard to secure full information about the Company's affairs,[66] but by the beginning of the nineteenth century there were signs that some stockholders were being fatigued by the number of accounts, papers, and despatches being placed before them. As a result, in 1801 forty-three proprietors signed a letter asking whether more information was required from the directors in order to 'form an intelligent, just and final conclusion' on the state of trade between Europe and India, but their proposal was rejected in the General Court by 135 votes to 80 on the grounds that such action was unnecessary and time-consuming.[67]

In spite of the fact that the Company's affairs were increasingly open to scrutiny during the second half of the eighteenth century, many people harboured the deep suspicion that the directors still concealed a considerable amount of information from external scrutiny. Late in the period, hostile critics continued to represent the directors as a cabal who deliberately sought to prevent the public gaze penetrating too far into the dark corners of East India House. As one complained in 1835, 'any heretic can get more information concerning the interior of the Holy offices of the Inquisition, even in Goa, than Parliament can of the India House in London'.[68] Such colourful accusations are perhaps hardly surprising in view of the existence of a number of secret committees within the Company, and there were certainly occasions, especially in wartime, when the Chairmen developed policy initiatives without the knowledge of their fellow directors, let alone the stockholders.[69] On the whole, however, Company affairs undoubtedly became more open and transparent after 1773, and by the 1820s and 1830s any interested stockholder, politician, or member of the general public had access to a great array of information about the Company, its trade, and its Indian empire. Indeed, they were likely to be overwhelmed by the great tide of written material that had flowed out of East India House during the previous half century, and making sense of it all posed a challenge that defeated all but the most determined of them.

66　See, for example, the case in 1783 when the stockholders demanded, and eventually received, more financial information than the directors had originally been prepared to release (Vahé Baladouni, 'East India Company's 1783 balance of accounts', *Abacus*, 22 (1986), pp. 59–64).

67　B/263, pp. 276–88.

68　*Alexander's East India Magazine*, vol. IX (1835), 414.

69　See, for example, L/P&S/19, box 3.

ORDERING THE PAPER EMPIRE

Making sense of a great accumulating mass of written material also posed a considerable challenge to the directors and officials of the Company. As was said of Military Secretary James Salmond in 1819, an 'infinitude of paper' passed through their hands,[70] and ways had to be devised of organising and ordering the documents so that they could be used to good effect. This was particularly the case with information coming into East India House from India because there was a relentless rise in the number and length of the despatches that passed between London and the Indian Presidencies. Early in the period general letters usually contained only thirty or forty paragraphs, but it was later commonplace for despatches to be of 100 paragraphs or more. As a result, between 1793 and 1812 despatches from India filled 9,094 leather-bound folio volumes at East India House, but 12,414 such volumes were created between 1814 and 1829.[71]

The increase in the number and length of despatches was caused by the fact that the transformation of the Company's affairs in India required great changes to be made to the type of information contained in despatches. Company letters had always contained much more than commercial instructions, details of appointments, and shipping information, but after 1756 administrative necessity dictated that greater space had to be devoted to matters of government, diplomacy, military affairs, revenue collection, and a whole host of other subjects. Over time, this diversity of content obliged the directors to consider how the presentation and structure of despatches could best be arranged, and more generally they began to address the question of how the information at their disposal could be utilised for the more effective management of the Company's affairs. As a result, they imposed a much greater degree of order upon the Company's written material, and this gave rise to the creation of ever more sophisticated systems of information handling and retrieval.

Despatches had always been arranged into numbered paragraphs so as to facilitate ease of location and cross-reference, and it became standard practice for each page to be divided into two columns so that replies could be placed directly alongside the subjects to which they related. Before the 1780s, however, only rudimentary attempts had been made to group

70 This comment was made in the General Court by Randle Jackson and reported in *Asiatic Journal*, vol. VII (1819), p. 513.
71 *PP* (1831–2), IX, p. 16.

paragraphs under subject headings or place them in any order of importance, and matters related to trade and shipping continued to be placed
before items devoted to military, political, or revenue affairs. In part, this
occurred because of the way that despatches were written, with individual
comments or instructions being entered as and when decisions were taken
over an extended period of time, but it also reflected an adherence to
long-established practice. As a result, many despatches were assembled
with little sense of organisational logic or coherence. In 1782, for example,
a very important statement of Company policy towards India was contained in the sixty-fourth paragraph of a seventy-nine-paragraph letter,
tucked away between details of routine appointments and promotions.[72]
This was clearly an unsatisfactory state of affairs and, following the India
Act of 1784 which laid down statutory guidelines for the conduct of secret
correspondence between Britain and India, a much greater sense of order
and uniformity was imposed on the Company's despatches.

In 1785 the directors formalised the organisation of despatches along
lines of subject division designed to correspond with new administrative
boards, which, at the prompting of Laurence Sulivan, had been established in each of the Indian Presidencies.[73] Five 'departments' of correspondence were created, with the overall aim of ensuring that 'by a
subdivision of the detail of our business, the whole will be conducted
with regularity, dispatch, and economy'.[74] As had long been the case,
general or important material was to be contained in the public or secret
letters that passed to and from the Presidency Councils, but routine
business was now to be conducted in separate commercial, military, and
revenue letters. It took a few years for this system to be become properly
established, and on several occasions the directors had to remind their
servants about the need carefully to place subjects under the proper
heading and to ensure that separate letters were written for each department.[75] By 1789, however, the directors were able to report that they
'daily' felt 'much convenience in the dispatch of business by the arrangement we have made in the conduct of our correspondence with you'.
Accordingly they defined a sixth 'political' department, 'by which we
mean all correspondence with or relative to other parts of India, whether
native or European'.[76] This new arrangement became operational the

72 *FWIHC,* vol. IX, p. 62.
73 Philips, *East India Company,* p. 45.
74 Directors to Bengal, 21 September 1785, *FWIHC,* vol. IX, p. 263.
75 Directors to Bengal, 31 July 1787, 28 Mar. 1788, ibid., vol. X, pp. 264, 271, 319.
76 Directors to Bengal, 8 April 1789, ibid., vol. XI, p. 53.

following year, and further additions were made so that by the 1820s there were also 'customs house', 'ecclesiastical', and 'territorial finance' departments.

The steady accumulation of miscellaneous information by the Company in its despatches and other documents was accompanied by attempts to establish some degree of order upon the papers and materials that found their way to East India House. The beginning of this process can be traced to the late 1760s and early 1770s when several new appointments began to reflect a more sophisticated approach to administrative activity and record keeping. These appointments can be seen as part of a broader movement towards the cultivation of experts, which saw individuals with a proven experience and understanding of the Company's affairs established in a variety of specialist positions. In London, where the Company had already accumulated a vast store of information about its commercial and maritime activities, some began to appreciate the practical uses and benefits that could be derived from the ordering and systematic study of such material. As James Rennell observed during the mid-1770s when he made an application to undertake a scheme of research and publication on maritime subjects, 'it is well known that there are deposited in the India House a variety of maps, charts, views of lands, sea journals, and other geographical and hydrographical information of various kinds; all (or most) of which, according to the present system, appear to be laid by to perish'. He argued that this 'vast collection of materials' contained much 'useful matter', but as things stood in the 'present confused (I might say chaotic) state, the good and bad are blended together and the whole rendered useless either for want of criteria to distinguish their value, or of arrangement to convey an idea of connection'.[77] The directors did not endorse Rennell's particular scheme of research, although the value of his services to the Company was acknowledged when he was granted a pension and an advance of £150 for the production of a new set of maps of Bengal.

Others were more successful in the competition for the directors' favour, however, and support was forthcoming for Alexander Dalrymple and Robert Orme who were both eventually added to the home establishment. Dalrymple, whose research had been advanced by access to Company records, published collections of nautical charts and plans before he

---

77 Quoted in Andrew S. Cook, 'Major James Rennell and A Bengal Atlas (1780 and 1781)', *India Office Library and Records. Report for the year 1976* (1978), p. 15.

was placed on the Company's payroll in 1779.[78] Orme, who had recently published the first volume of his *Military transactions of the British nation in Indostan*, was officially charged in 1769 with conducting research into the Company's history, and from 1772 he was paid an annual annuity of £400, before he was appointed, together with John Bruce, as Historiographer to the Company in 1793.[79]

Dalrymple and Orme were at the forefront of those in London who sought to exploit the information collected by the Company's administrative, maritime, and military personnel. As senior officials in the home administration set about compiling the accounts, reports, and briefing papers that were necessary for an informed understanding of the Company's position, they increasingly spent much of their time poring over material sent home by overseas servants. Moreover, as directors grappled with the problems of empire, they often required that information be set in context, and reports and accounts prepared for their use routinely took the form of 'narratives' carrying lengthy preambles outlining historical developments. A great deal of the work of officials was thus retrospective in nature, and a strong sense of the past underpinned efforts to order and organise the Company's affairs. The vast bulk of their briefing documents remained unpublished, but common sense dictated that some practical information be disseminated more widely within the Company and beyond, and thus growing naturally out of internal documents were semi-official digests, books, and tracts published on the authority of the directors.[80]

The Company's directors and servants in London sought increasingly to exploit the rich information resources they had at their disposal, but before the 1770s any individual who endeavoured to make use of the Company's growing archive was hindered by the fact that many records had long suffered from neglect. As early as 1720 attempts had been made to store and classify materials in a 'book office',[81] but by the early 1770s

---

78 In 1762 Dalrymple had been assisted by Rennell on the voyage of the *London* to China and the Philippines. Like Rennell, Dalrymple arrived back in Britain in 1777 following overseas service and thus the former colleagues were in competition with one another for the right to bring order to the Company's hydrographical affairs.

79 For the post of Historiographer, the reasons for the joint appointment, and the fruits of Bruce's labours see Sir William Foster, *John Company* (1926), pp. 233–45.

80 For examples see above, pp. 144–5.

81 William Foster, *A guide to the India Office Records 1600–1858* (1919), pp. i–ii. In June 1750 the Senior Clerk Obadiah Anbury had been appointed to register the Indian books and keep them in good order. He was told that 'if the books were not kept in such manner that any might be immediately delivered, to which it should be necessary to have recourse, the Court would certainly resent the same . . .' (B/71, p. 94).

any rudimentary system that might have been established appears to have been overwhelmed by the sheer volume of paper being received from Asia. In March 1771 the directors noted with concern 'the present confused and disorderly state of the repository for books, records and accounts from several Presidencies and factories in the East Indies consisting of many thousands of volumes, which are annually increasing'. This situation was causing 'inconvenience and difficulties, and loss of time', and they deemed it necessary that 'a capable and experienced officer be appointed to have the care and custody of the said books, records and papers, to arrange, number, and register them in proper catalogues, also to keep an account of the deliveries thereof to any person or persons so that the same may be preserved from being lost or injured'.[82] Accordingly, William Barnett became Register and Keeper of India Records, and, because much labour was involved in 'ranging, disposing, and keeping clean' the Indian books, Matthew Walls was appointed to assist him.

The functions of these officers remained the same until the mid-1780s when, as a result of a proposal made by Thomas Wilks, the directors eventually sanctioned an enhanced role for the senior official. In May 1786 Wilks, who was seeking to escape from the bitter intrigues and infighting of the Examiner's Office, proposed a scheme of organisation and programme of research into the Company's historical affairs on the grounds that 'A regular and systematical investigation of the Company's records, as well ancient as modern, must be considered, by every intelligent person, as an object of the highest importance.' He argued that 'an universal ignorance prevails' as far as the records before 1765 were concerned, not least because 'the modes hitherto adopted for the investigation of these, have been as totally removed from regularity and system (occasioned by the great variety, and magnitude of the subjects contained therein) as harmony are from discord and confusion'. He thus suggested that the Register, whose role was to be separated from that of the Keeper, take on responsibility for organising the 'books of entry' for each Presidency in a manner 'best calculated for the purposes of general reference and utility', collecting information from returned servants, and investigating the Company's land grants and other subjects.[83] The directors approved the substance of Wilks's proposal in March 1787 although they waited a year before they separated the roles of Register and Keeper and

82 D/26, pp. 343–4, 345 (26 March 1771).
83 For Wilks's plan see E/1/78, ff. 416–21. This is enclosed with his memorial to the directors outlining his reasons for asking for a transfer from the Examiner's Office (ibid., ff. 412–14).

appointed Wilks to the former position. His brother William, who succeeded him in 1791, assisted Wilks and together they oversaw the listing, abstracting, indexing, and transcribing of materials, and the fruits of their labours are to be found today in the Oriental and India Office Collections.[84] In a practical sense, these appointments were important for the storage, organisation, and swift retrieval of archive information, but they also allowed the Company to refresh its corporate memory, thereby better enabling it to understand its own past and bring historical precedent to bear upon the making of policy.

THE KNOWLEDGE OF EMPIRE

The work of Dalrymple, Orme, the Wilks brothers, and others revealed that much useful information could be gleaned from the despatches, accounts, and papers that were routinely sent to East India House by the Company's overseas servants. But this process had its limitations, and the directors also began to encourage more extensive searches for information in India so that a better knowledge and understanding could be gained of the territories, peoples, and societies that had been brought under the Company's control. The directors were sometimes painfully slow to develop ideas suggested to them by scholars or practical men, and during the early part of the period they were often very reluctant to sanction expenditure on non-relevant scholarly activity.[85] Later, however, they could point to an increased level of financial support for learning at home and abroad, and during a few months in 1770 and 1771, for example, they responded positively to John Ferguson's offer to compile a 'Dictionary of the Hindostan Language', and they advanced £525 to George Nicol and Archibald Hamilton who, under the guidance of Master of the Temple Gregory Sharpe, were producing a 'new Oriental dictionary and grammar principally compiled from the latest lexicographers of the East'. They then subscribed to the 'improved edition of Meninski's dictionary of the Persian, Arabic, and Turkish Languages' being prepared 'under the patronage of the Universities of Oxford and Cambridge as revised by William Jones with a supplement by Dr Uri',

---

84 See, for example, MSS Eur. K122-32 (Wilks Collection).
85 In 1756, for example, they partially acceded to a request from Madras by sending out a parcel of the 'most useful' books and a pair of globes, but they warned those at Fort St George that the Company's precarious financial and military position was such that 'this is not time for forming a Library'. Directors to Madras, 19 December 1755, *Public despatches from England*, vol. LIX: *1755-6* (Madras, 1968), p. 30.

and bought 100 copies of the Persian grammar recently published by Jones.[86] During the late 1780s similar encouragement was offered to those in India such as Joseph Champion, Francis Gladwin, and William Kirkpatrick who, among other scholarly endeavours, were engaged in translation work and lexicography.[87] In all of these cases the directors were motivated primarily by a desire to improve the linguistic skills of their overseas servants and the efficiency of their written communication, but they also believed that they were making an important contribution to the development of a better understanding of Asia. A grateful Kirkpatrick was moved to declare that the directors were 'always ready to encourage even the humblest attempts to contribute to the stock of useful knowledge on every subject connected with India'.[88]

The directors had indeed always encouraged their servants to collect useful information, but the practical demands of revenue collection, military-policing operations, and political administration drew the Company into new spheres of inquiry in India. At the most basic level, those in London needed to know about the territory and resources that had been secured, and this could only be achieved through extensive fieldwork of the type that began in earnest during the late 1750s and early 1760s when Hugh Cameron and James Rennell were charged with surveying new lands brought under Company control. This action had been prompted by senior figures in Bengal, but in 1765 the directors felt it necessary to remind their Calcutta servants of the importance of maximising the advantages gained from the recently acquired province of Chittagong. In doing so, they underlined that the first necessary stage in this process was the undertaking of a formal survey 'that we may know what is cultivated, what waste, what pays taxes, what free, and how the whole is disposed of'.[89] Even so, knowledge and understanding of the geography and topography of India remained patchy, often being limited to basic route surveys, and it was only after 1780 that the directors began to make systematic efforts to ensure that they received the information that was essential for the establishment of a full picture of the territory and wealth under their control. Thus, in an attempt to enable James Rennell to create one 'general' map of India in London, the different Presidencies were

---

86 D/26, pp. 223–4, 294, 353.
87 *FWIHC*, vol. X, p. 182. In the event Kirkpatrick, author of *An account of the Kingdom of Nepaul*, was unable to complete his proposed Hindustani Grammar and Dictionary (ibid., vol. X, p. 569).
88 Quoted in the introduction to ibid., vol. X, p. 44.
89 Directors to Bengal, 24 December 1765, *FWIHC*, vol. IV, p. 124.

encouraged to act swiftly to provide the directors with outline maps and surveys of their lands and adjacent territories.[90] During the late 1780s the directors urged those in Bengal to send them newly drawn maps and charts 'by the first conveyance', and instruments and oil paper were sent to India to ensure that work was carried out accurately and then copied before being sent to Britain.[91]

Practical assistance helped to promote scientific fieldwork as a key component of enlightened imperial governance, and sustained backing from London led eventually to the great trigonometrical surveys of the subcontinent undertaken by William Lambton, George Everest, and others during the early decades of the nineteenth century. This, it has been argued, enabled the Company to conceptualise and legitimise its empire, as well as to believe that it had acquired complete knowledge of India.[92] A combination of pressure and encouragement from London thus helped to ensure that, alongside efforts to promote the scholarly study of indigenous cultures and languages, strategies were developed in India for the gathering of geographical and navigational measurements, agricultural data, and economic statistics from territories under the Company's control and beyond. Indeed, the strength of the Company's commitment to information-gathering as a tool for facilitating control, exploitation, improvement, and progress meant that it led the way for others engaged in administration in Britain and across the wider empire.[93]

By the end of the eighteenth century the Company was able to boast of an extensive patronage of scholarly pursuits and practical experiments. In 1792 the directors declared that they had 'never been deterred by the want of a spirit of enterprise, and still less from a false principle of economy, from using every endeavour to extend the trade, and to cultivate knowledge of science in every way that might prove beneficial to the British Empire'. A spirit of inquiry and exploration was held to be present in all branches of the Company's overseas affairs, embracing the 'literature and science of the ancient and modern inhabitants of the East but likewise

---

90 In Bengal the Company army engineer John Call had been endeavouring to complete a general map of India, but he died while carrying the partially finished work to London. The directors made it clear that Rennell's expertise equipped him as the best man for the task.

91 See, for example, *FWIHC*, vol. X, pp. 145, 362–3.

92 For two recent studies that lay different interpretative emphasis on the Company's surveying and mapping operations after 1765 see Matthew H. Edney, *Mapping and empire: the geographical construction of British India, 1765–1843* (Chicago, 1997), esp. pp. 9–16, 121–64, and Ian J. Barrow, *Making history, drawing territory. British mapping in India, c.1756–1905* (New Delhi, 2003), pp. 35–89.

93 C. A. Bayly, *Imperial meridian: The British Empire and the world, 1780–1830* (1989), pp. 121–6.

their arts, manufactures and commerce'. Aiming a careful blow at the anti-monopolist claims of the free trade lobby in Britain, it was suggested that wide-ranging intellectual interests 'distinguishes the system of an exclusive company',[94] and friends of the Company were able to proclaim to the world that the directors' 'noble encouragement of literature and science have raised the mercantile character to the highest degree of exultation and dignity'.[95] Company servants certainly played their part in feeding a public appetite hungry for information about the wider world, and after 1757 an increasing number of scientific articles about Asia were published in the *Philosophical Transactions* of the Royal Society. Many of these articles were subsequently summarised in the *Gentleman's Magazine*, and late in the century volumes of *Asiatick Researches* began to be reprinted in London, having first been published in Calcutta.[96] None of this scholarly activity did any harm to the Company's public image at a time when it was attempting to navigate difficult political waters.

In order to give tangible expression to the Company's virtuous commitment to learning and the accumulation of useful knowledge, the directors proposed in 1798 to open 'a public repository in this country for Oriental writings', and shortly thereafter it was reported that the Company was seeking to establish a Museum at East India House.[97] This initiative was described by Warren Hastings as a 'new scheme for ingrafting the knowledge of India on the commercial pursuits of the Company', and it was advanced by the persistent advocacy of Charles Wilkins, a former Company servant who was a well-connected Sanskrit scholar and founder member of the Asiatic Society of Calcutta. He offered to 'take charge of the Museum, and give up my whole attention towards rendering it a monument of the taste, as well as of the munificence of its founders', and his unashamed flattery of the directors was rewarded when he was appointed as Librarian to the Oriental Repository in 1801.

The scope of Wilkins's vision had been ambitious and he proposed that the Repository should house a wide range of natural history collections, as

---

94 'Third report of the Select Committee [of directors] appointed to take into consideration the export trade from Great Britain to the East Indies' (1792), manuscript version, H/400, pp. 317, 320, 321.

95 Dedication to the directors in David Macpherson, *Annals of commerce, manufactures, fisheries, and navigation, with brief notices of the arts and sciences connected with them*, 4 vols. (1805).

96 J. R. Osborn, 'India, Parliament and the press under George III: a study of English attitudes towards the East India Company and empire in the late eighteenth and early nineteenth centuries', unpublished DPhil thesis, University of Oxford (1999), pp. 208–61.

97 The background to the establishment of the Repository is set out in Ray Desmond, *The India Museum, 1801–1879* (1982), pp. 4–14. The following quotations are from pp. 10 and 6 respectively.

well as books and manuscripts, and thus from the very beginning a considerable variety of materials and objects was brought under his guardianship in the Library and Museum. The collections were established by the gathering together of printed books and 'articles of curiosity' hitherto dispersed throughout East India House and the London warehouses,[98] and in 1805 the Company's charts, drawings, and maps were also placed under Wilkins's supervision. Thereafter the Company received collections of miscellaneous items from overseas servants on a regular basis. The materials in the Library were used first and foremost to support the administrative work of the Company but they were also loaned out to orientalists and scholars, and the Repository itself proved to be a popular attraction, drawing 'immense crowds of visitors of all classes' so that in 1817 the opening hours had to be strictly regulated.[99] By the end of the 1820s, the Museum was considered to be 'inferior to none in the display of oriental rarities', and observers were equally impressed by the Library. It was reported that 'Every book known to have been published in any language whatever, relative to the history, laws, or jurisprudence of Asia is to be found here, besides an unparalleled collection of manuscripts in all oriental languages, and among them Tippoo Saib's copy of the Koran.'[100] Even fierce critics of the Company later agreed that the Library was indeed the 'most valuable oriental collection in the world', even though they bemoaned the fact that it remained underused because 'the Company does not wish for visitors'.[101]

During the late eighteenth century the East India Company added a number of new information-handling systems to its long-established commercial bureaucracy, and a much greater degree of organisational coherence was brought to the written communication exchanged between Britain and Asia. News and information flowed in, around, and out of East India House in increasingly well-regulated and reliable flows, and attempts were made to utilise and exploit the great variety of data contained in despatches, memoranda, and proceedings sent home from the East. The aim was to facilitate closer control of the overseas servants and better administration of the Company's affairs, but it was also hoped

---

98 Minutes of the Committee for superintending the Library, 2 December 1801, MS Eur. F.303, vol. 35 (no pagination).
99 Ibid., 16 July 1817.
100 Thomas H. Shepherd and James Elmes, *London and its environs in the nineteenth century . . .* (1829), p. 44.
101 *East India Magazine*, vol. XXI (1841), p. 221.

that the gathering of information would lead to a better knowledge and understanding of India.

Some contemporaries expressed a healthy scepticism about the Company's accumulation of great piles of documents, and not everyone applauded the way in which the directors encouraged the commitment of everything to paper. During the early 1830s Thomas Courtenay, the former Secretary to the Board of Control, certainly believed that the length of the despatches and proceedings hindered administrative efficiency and good government. He took the view that 'a great portion of the voluminous proceedings consists of general disquisitions and observations on general principles, sometimes extremely obvious and almost trifling, which cannot in any way tend to inform the authorities to whom such dispatches are addressed'.[102] Thomas Munro, the Governor of Madras, had earlier reported that it was only when he had inspected the Company's records in London that he fully realised that 'they contained such a mass of useless trash'. He believed that a distorted, anglicised, picture of India was being presented to those in London because 'Every man writes as much as he can, and quotes Montesquieu, and Hume, and Adam Smith, and speaks as if we were living in a country [India] where people were free and governed themselves.'[103] Others doubted whether the Company's directors and officials actually knew much at all about the lands they were endeavouring to govern. Hence in 1814 the stockholder Peter Moore told the General Court that the Company had 'undoubtedly the power of *strength*, but they had not the best power, the power of *knowledge*'.[104] The Company, he thought, 'have so little knowledge, that they hardly know the number of Empires which are subject to their sway!' This was of course an exaggeration but twenty years later Sir John Malcolm warned that many of the problems of empire lay beyond the understanding of the directors because they were always obliged to construct a view that was based solely upon the written word. He told the Company's stockholders that 'having seen much of India, he could safely declare that the records of the Company afforded but a faint picture of the difficulties which attended the proper government of India'.[105]

The comments of Malcolm, Munro, and others raise the all-important question of what was actually achieved by the Company's relentless and

---

102 *Alexander's East India Magazine*, vol. III (1832), p. 448.
103 Quoted in T. H. Beaglehole, *Thomas Munro and the development of administrative policy in Madras, 1792–1818: the origins of the 'Munro system'* (Cambridge, 1966), p. 131.
104 *Debate at the East India House . . . 18th March 1814* (1814), pp. 52–3.
105 *Debates at the General Court of Proprietors of East India stock . . .* (1833), p. 12.

often indiscriminate collection of news and information in London. As Malcolm suggested, the directors were certainly deluding themselves if they ever thought that they possessed a full understanding of the Company's affairs in India and elsewhere, but that was not their primary aim when they set about the task of gathering and ordering information. Rather, by seeking to establish control over all forms of written communication they were endeavouring to demonstrate to their employees, to politicians, and to public onlookers that they were able to control the empire itself. In other words, the increasingly well-regulated paper empire they created inside East India House acted as a surrogate for the territorial empire that had been established on the subcontinent, and they hoped that the order they imposed upon the former could be projected on to the latter through the application of high standards of accuracy and attention to detail.

The importance of the bureaucratic order and efficiency brought to East India House cannot be underestimated at a time when serious questions were being asked about the Company's fitness to govern India. Indeed, the Company developed a great sense of corporate pride in its record keeping and communication systems, and many came to believe that they were unrivalled in terms of their sophistication and efficiency. This was certainly true of the stockholder Humphrey Howorth who declared in 1814 that 'So wonderfully exact was their system; so accurately methodical was the whole series of their details; so extremely perfect was their arrangement; that through all the immense extent of their civil, military, financial, revenue, and commercial establishments, both at home and abroad, they could refer to any one paper, which might be called for, at a minute's notice.'[106] This was fanciful,[107] but publicly expressed views such as these helped to encourage the belief that the Company's affairs had become better ordered and thus the overseas empire was now better administered at home and abroad. At the same time, the directors' insistence that their overseas servants record and report every single local action and event supported the notion that the Company's bureaucratic system formed the very bedrock of an efficient and enlightened colonial administration that paid due attention to the happiness, protection, and well-being of the people of India. By the time the Company's communication systems had fully matured during the 1820s and 1830s, the directors

---

106 *Debate at the East India House . . . 18th March 1814* (1814), p. 19.
107 In fact, large collections of important paper lay unused at East India House and were only consulted by chance. See, for example, Beaglehole, *Thomas Munro*, pp. 94–5.

were able to congratulate themselves on the fact that their correspondence with India was 'conducted with a comprehensiveness and in a detail quite unexampled', and they observed that the 'minutest proceeding of the local governments' was placed on record.[108] Indeed, when John Stuart Mill later looked back on almost thirty years of Company service, he considered that one of the great virtues and strengths of the Indian government was that it had been 'carried on in writing'.[109] For Mill, as for many of his predecessors at East India House, the pen was as mighty as the sword in the making of the Company's Indian empire.

---

108 Directors to the Board of Control, 27 August 1829, Frederick Madden with David Fieldhouse (eds.), *Select documents on the constitutional history of the British Empire and Commonwealth*, vol. III, *Imperial reconstruction, 1763–1840: the evolution of alternative systems of colonial government* (Westport, Conn., 1987), p. 244.
109 Examination in the House of Lords, 21 June 1852, *Collected works of John Stuart Mill*, vol. XXX; John M. Robson, Martin Moir, Zawahir Moir (eds.), *Writings on India* (Toronto, 1990), p. 33.

CHAPTER 7

Methods: the government of empire

By the beginning of the nineteenth century the collection and organisation of information had brought a much-admired sense of order and purpose to the domestic affairs of the East India Company, but the Company was also acquiring a reputation for general administrative sophistication and excellence. Friends of the Company praised the hard work and dedication of the directors and home servants, and the management of East Indian affairs suggested to some that the Company should serve as a model for other British institutions. This began to convince onlookers that the Company was able to govern its empire not only in the interests of Britain, but also to the benefit of the Indian population. As a result, in 1813 Lord Castlereagh was able to use words that could scarcely have been whispered forty years earlier when he described the Company's Indian government as 'founded on theory so wise, and brought to such practical perfection, that he did not believe the history of the world could exhibit its equal'. Nothing, he thought, 'could be more ably and more efficiently managed than the affairs of the East India House'.[1]

Castlereagh might well have been motivated by a desire to flatter the directors in return for political concessions, but his public declaration of faith in the Company was broadly representative of a remarkable trans-formation that occurred in attitudes towards the administration of East Indian affairs during the half-century or so after 1756. Once widely pilloried for misrule, corruption, and oppression in India, the Company was now held up as a paragon of imperial administrative virtue, and at the heart of this change was a widely held view that the Company was now being much better run by its directors and senior managers in London. This prompted one commentator to suggest that there had been a 'revolution of the public sentiment' towards the Company's Indian

---

1 Speech of 22 March 1813, T. C. Hansard, *The parliamentary debates from the year 1803 to the present time*, vol. XXIII (1813), col. 229.

administration based upon a belief that those in East India House were now able to exert greater control over their overseas servants than had hitherto been the case.[2] He and many others pointed to a much better management of the Company's overseas affairs, and it is with this in mind that this chapter seeks to examine the methods adopted by the directors as they endeavoured to come to terms with the acquisition of an empire in India.

Of course, as the directors often acknowledged, the realities of time and distance were such that they could seldom do much to determine the course of events in India. Those in London could no more prevent the Bengal Council building an expensive road during the 1780s than they could later rein in the territorial ambitions of Governor-General Richard Wellesley,[3] and, as had been the case throughout the Company's history, actions were always determined by men of influence 'on the spot'. It would be quite wrong to suggest, however, that the directors were simply helpless bystanders in the development of the Indian empire. Throughout the period they were entirely consistent in their efforts to control their overseas employees, and they endeavoured to ensure that those in India worked to high standards of behaviour within clearly defined general policy guidelines. Their successes were never dramatic, but over time they did achieve incremental improvements to the Company's administration. This was eventually sufficient to persuade many in Britain that the empire was being held in safe and responsible hands, and mid-nineteenth-century Whig writers such as John Kaye were later able to proclaim that the Company's institutional development since 1756 had been a triumph for the forces of progress and civilisation.[4]

THE MAKING OF AN IMPERIAL BUREAUCRACY

The directors were often condemned as being ineffectual and pusillanimous managers of East Indian affairs, but it should not be thought that they

---

2 Anon., *Observations on the territorial rights and commercial privileges of the East India Company, with a view to the renewal of the Company's charter; in a letter to a Member of Parliament* (1813), p. 4. Changes in public attitudes towards the Company are traced in J. R. Osborn, 'India, Parliament and the press under George III: a study of English attitudes towards the East India Company and empire in the late eighteenth and early nineteenth centuries', unpublished DPhil thesis, University of Oxford (1999).

3 The directors declared angrily that they were 'astonished' when they learned of the building of the road, but since the project was nearing completion they could do little other than complain loudly and lay down spending limits for annual repairs. See *FWIHC*, vol. IX, pp. 70–1.

4 John W. Kaye, *The administration of the East India Company: a history of Indian progress* (1853), p. 134.

were incapable of exerting any influence on the development of the Company after 1756. They were not oblivious to the fact that the acquisition of a territorial empire required a response from them, and they did not concede all initiative to ministers and Parliament. They certainly did have to bow to some of the strong external reformist pressures that were discussed in chapter 3, but they were not feeble victims of circumstances who were unable to shape the Company's destiny in any way, shape, or form. They played an important part in the Company's reinvention of itself as an imperial agency, and this should not really have been a matter of any great surprise to contemporaries because the Company had already proven itself well capable of adapting to changing external situations. Resilient and resourceful, it had recast itself on several occasions, both in terms of the nature and direction of its overseas activities and also in the way that it was constituted at home.[5] As a result, the Company possessed an established and largely successful track record of accommodating change alongside continuity, and this remained the case after 1756. The process of transformation was largely haphazard and unplanned but over time it found expression in the changing external fabric of East India House, and, most importantly, in the creation of an imperial bureaucracy located at the very heart of the Company in London.

By the end of the period, an extended and redecorated East India House was described as a 'vast edifice', and it offered architectural expression to the values and virtues that were held to have underpinned the Company's commercial and imperial expansion.[6] Few observers would have been inclined to suggest, however, that internal administrative or decision-making processes had been altered to any similarly great degree. Indeed, the Company continued to adhere to organisational arrangements and practices that had been first established and developed with the conduct

---

5 For a discussion of this theme see H. V. Bowen, '"No longer mere traders": continuities and change in the metropolitan development of the East India Company, 1600–1834', in H. V. Bowen, Margarette Lincoln, and Nigel Rigby (eds.), *The worlds of the East India Company* (Woodbridge, 2002), pp. 19–32.

6 Thomas H. Shepherd and James Elmes, *London and its environs in the nineteenth century*, 2 vols. (1829), vol. I, p. 43. For a description of East India House in the early nineteenth century see C. Northcote Parkinson, *Trade in the eastern seas, 1793–1813* (Cambridge, 1937), pp. 1–28. Much information on the development of the Company's headquarters is to be found in Sir William Foster, *The East India House: its history and associations* (1924), and idem, *John Company* (1926). For a recent study of the Leadenhall Street site and the buildings acquired by the Company see Vanessa Harding and Priscilla Metcalf, *Lloyd's at home* (1986), pp. 50–69, 123–30. The artwork, decorations, and furnishings of East India House are described in Mildred Archer, 'The East India Company and British art', *Apollo* (1965), 402–6 and John Hardy, *India Office furniture* (1982), pp. 5–8.

of trade in mind. This brought an extraordinary degree of permanence and continuity to the management of the Company's affairs and, although personnel came and went, the 'system' itself endured with little by way of fundamental modification or reform. If a director or clerk of the 1680s had been reincarnated 100 years later he would have found much that would have been familiar to him in East India House, and only on a close reading of the Company's books and ledgers would the full consequences of the transformation from trader to sovereign have become apparent.

A casual inspection of the Company's domestic administrative arrangements might indeed suggest that the transformation of overseas fortunes that occurred during the 1760s did remarkably little to disturb the committees and administrative departments. Figure 7.1 offers an organisational chart of the Company, based upon a description of the management structure written by a senior official in 1785.[7] In general, offices or departments were answerable to a particular subcommittee of the Court of Directors, with a link being provided by the Clerk to the Committee who served as the head of the subordinate administrative unit.[8] In most cases, this was a straightforward relationship with, for example, the Accountant's Office serving the Committee of Accounts, and only a few departments, such as the warehouses, found themselves linked with two or more committees. Most of the departments continued to exist through to 1834, although important additions were made when a Military Department was created in 1809 to conduct routine military communication with India, and a China Department took on responsibility for correspondence with Canton in 1814.

During the mid-1780s, an increasing volume of Company business did, however, lead to the system being adjusted to new circumstances, and the committees of the Court of Directors were arranged into three 'classes'.[9]

---

7 In 1785 the Company Secretary, Thomas Morton, compiled a detailed analysis of the home establishment in response to a request for information about how the Company organised its home affairs from the newly established Board of Control. The information eventually provided by Morton was based upon returns made by all the departmental heads, and it included job descriptions, details of salaries, and the number of employees. See Thomas Morton to Charles William Boughton Rouse, 28 April 1785, H/362, pp. 5–77. This is the only surviving eighteenth-century description of each administrative unit, and it allows a detailed reconstruction to be made of the Company's inner workings. Unless otherwise stated, the following analysis is based upon this source.

8 For a modern description of the committees and departments see Martin Moir, *A general guide to the India Office Records* (1996), pp. 26–38.

9 For the background see 'The Chairman's hints for the future arrangements of the committees' (9 April 1785), D/120. The outgoing Chairman, Nathaniel Smith, who advocated the creation of four classes of committee, probably wrote this paper. For details of the background to the changes see also Philips, *East India Company*, pp. 44–5.

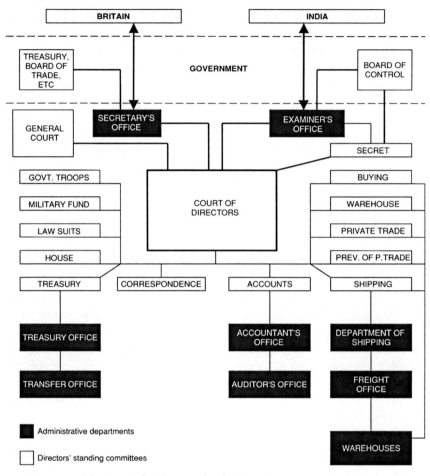

Figure 7.1. The East India Company's administrative structure in Britain, 1785.
Source: see note 7, p. 185.

The first class – 'Correspondence' – contained the Committees of Correspondence, Law Suits, Military Fund, and Treasury; the second class – 'Warehouse' – contained the Committees of Warehouse, Accounts, Buying, and House; and the third class – 'Shipping' – included the Committees of Shipping, Government Troops and Stores, Private Trade, and Preventing the Growth of Private Trade. In addition, a three-man Secret Committee was created by Pitt's India Act. This body liaised directly with the Board of Control on sensitive matters related to war, peace, and diplomacy, and it provided a channel through which the government could send secret despatches to India.[10] Hitherto, a small 'Committee of Secrecy' had undertaken such tasks only in wartime, although a Secret Committee (sometimes confused with the later committee of that name) had long organised sailing instructions and protection for Company ships.[11] Later, between 1803 and 1812, a Secret Committee of Treasury conducted transactions such as the purchase of bullion, while between 1815 and 1833 a Secret Commercial Committee handled trading matters of a sensitive nature. However, these two secret subcommittees operated within the areas of responsibility of existing committees, and their creation did not effect any alteration in the overall distribution of business. Indeed, there were only a couple of occasions when changes were made to the main committee structure, first in 1813 when the ending of the Company's India trade monopoly made redundant the Committee for Preventing the Growth of Private Trade; and second in 1815 when administrative logic dictated the merger of the Committees of Warehouse and Buying.[12] The other committees functioned through to 1833, thereby ensuring that most of them enjoyed a single unbroken existence stretching back to the very first days of the United Company in 1709. This ensured that the Company's domestic structure continued to have the appearance of a commercial company rather than an imperial agency, and, as their names imply, few of the standing committees were routinely involved in the conduct of Company affairs in India. Most committees remained preoccupied with the supervision of the Company's commercial and financial activities in Britain.[13]

10 24 Geo. III, c.25, xvi.

11 The existence of these two committees was ignored by some historians, and perhaps understandably confused by others, during the early years of the twentieth century. Matters were only clarified when C. H. Philips described in detail the evolution and role of the committee(s). See C. H. Philips, 'The Secret Committee of the East India Company', *Bulletin of the School of Oriental Studies*, 10 (1940–2), pp. 299–316, 699–716. Philips was correct to emphasise the wartime importance of the Committee of Secrecy before 1784, but it cannot be said that it had 'emerged as the cabinet council of the Company' long before that date (ibid., 299). If any such body existed, then it was the Committee of Correspondence (for which, see below, p. 191).

12 Several minor committees were also brought into existence to take on very specific managerial tasks. This practice began in 1771 when a small standing body of directors was established to supervise the pension fund established by Lord Clive, and similar committees were later set up to manage the Company's Library (1801), the East India College (1804), and the Military Seminary (1809). In addition, temporary committees of directors were set up from time to time to undertake inquiries into different aspects of the Company's affairs.

13 The functions of the directors' committees are described in 'Statement of business allotted to the several classes of committee of the Court of Directors' (no date, but probably 1785–6), H/67, pp. 69–81. For details of the little-changed duties of each committee in 1813 see *Proceedings of the Select Committee appointed by the General Court of Proprietors, on the 6th October to consider and report upon the expediency of augmenting the allowances to the directors for their attendance upon the business of the Company* (1814).

The essentially unaltering nature of the Company's domestic organisational arrangements would seem to suggest that the directors did very little to come to terms with changed circumstances in India after 1756. Contemporaries certainly thought so and, long after the Company had embarked upon the process of expansion in Bengal, it remained vulnerable to the accusation that it was entirely ill suited to the formidable task of governing territory and people. As a writer in the *Edinburgh Review* put it in 1810, 'Among all the visionary and extravagant systems of policy that have been suggested, no one has been absurd enough to maintain that the most advisable way of governing a mighty empire was by committing it to the care of a body of merchants residing at a distance of many thousands of miles.'[14] Four decades earlier Clive had asked 'Can the laws and charters which are calculated for the guidance of a limited company of merchants be adequate for the government of such a vast Empire?',[15] and he was often answered emphatically in the negative. In the words of one of many critics, 'A body of merchants, originally constituted for the management of commerce, and not for the government of an empire, continued without any system of rules, without the aid of precedent, without the light of experience . . .'[16] Consequently, much was made of the fact that in Britain the Company continued to be organised as a commercial institution, and it was often asserted that misrule in India was a direct and inevitable consequence of the fact that the empire was being governed by an entirely inappropriate body in Britain.

There is no denying many of these charges. The cautious and pragmatic approach to administration that was so characteristic of the eighteenth century ensured that the Company's offices and departments remained largely undisturbed by events and transformations in India. It would be quite wrong, however, to suggest that the directors were entirely resistant to administrative change or that they failed to consider how best they could manage their overseas possessions. As was seen in the last chapter, they made some effort to regulate and reorder communication between Britain and Asia, and they acted on the belief that the problems of empire required detailed attention from specialists freed from the need to supervise the Company's commercial and maritime activities. Thus,

---

14 Ainslie Thomas Embree, *Charles Grant and British rule in India* (1962), p. 262. The author was probably James Mill (see n. 1).

15 H/211, p. 8.

16 Anon., *The present state of the English East India Company's affairs comprehending the accounts delivered in to the Treasury which were laid before the Committee of Secrecy* (1772), p. i.

although the formal committee and departmental structure remained almost untouched by the effects of events in India, a closer examination of the organisational chart reveals that by 1785 significant alterations had already been made to the lines of communication and decision-making existing inside and outside East India House. Most notably, the establishment of the Board of Control had recently facilitated ministerial contributions to the administration of British India, but within the Company itself an important move had been made some years earlier towards the establishment of a small bureaucracy dedicated to the government of the Indian empire. This office was staffed by men whose primary function was to translate the general policy guidelines of the directors into detailed instructions for those charged with responsibility for the Company's affairs in India. This important process began in earnest in 1769 with the appointment of an Examiner of Indian Correspondence.

In November 1769 the directors observed that the volume of correspondence with India had greatly increased, and 'the consultations and registers of their proceedings are become extremely voluminous and enlarged in number by means of the extension of the Company's trade and possessions'. Requiring a 'better arrangement and a more strict inspection' of this material than was possible under the present system, they sought an 'able person' to 'inspect, examine, and make up the necessary references to and observations on the important branches of the Indian correspondence'. Samuel Wilks, who had been engaged in 'public business', was deemed to fit the bill, and he was appointed to work under the supervision of the Secretary.[17] In January 1770 his son Thomas was appointed as assistant examiner,[18] and two other sons, Samuel and William, were later found positions in the new office. In May 1770 the directors noted a further great increase in the Company's correspondence, and declaring that it required 'the closest application for keeping up the same' they appointed the Auditor, George Oldmixon, as 'Compiler and Writer of the Company's foreign Correspondence with their settlements in the East Indies'.[19] Subsequent reorganisations saw the formal separation of the Examiner's Office from that of the Secretary in 1776, but in 1782 the post of Compiler was abolished. As a result, the Examiner's Office began to act as the sole bureaucratic mechanism through which formal written communication passed between India House and the

17 D/26, pp. 33–4; B/85, p. 284. 18 D/26, p. 125.
19 Ibid., pp. 189–90 (30 May 1770).

Company's overseas Presidencies. A small team of clerks prepared reports on particular subjects and gathered 'collections' of information for use by the directors and the head of office,[20] but at this point the Examiner was alone responsible for drafting the letters that carried the signatures of the directors. After 1784 he almost single-handedly prepared the drafts of the regular despatches that were sent to the Board of Control for approval and amendment prior to despatch to India, and he also served as Secretary to the Secret Committee which meant that he acted as the conduit for all confidential communications sent to India by the Committee on behalf of the Board of Control.[21] As such, the voice of the Examiner became the voice of the Company as it was heard in India.

When Samuel Johnson became Acting Examiner in 1782, he was frustrated by the fact that there was 'no regular mode' for conducting business in the office, but his plans for reform were obstructed by the uncooperative Wilks brothers whose own hopes for advancement had been dashed by his appointment.[22] Nevertheless, when Johnson became Examiner on a permanent basis in 1785 he arranged the office in line with the structure of the Company's overseas operations, so that one clerk now took responsibility for materials relating to each of the three Indian Presidencies. Communication with Canton and the Company's other overseas outposts, together with correspondence on trade and maritime affairs, continued to be dealt with elsewhere in East India House, illustrating that an internal separation of imperial and commercial business was being established. The scheme of organisation and division of labour within the Examiner's Office continued until 1804 when, as a result the considerable pressures imposed upon Johnson by the number and length of the despatches being prepared for India, subject departments were established under the supervision of two assistants, who were each given

---

20 For a brief outline of the Examiner's Office in 1785 see H/362, p. 17. For an example of one of the lengthy reports of the late 1770s produced by the Examiner's Office see 'Narrative of the conduct of the Governor-General and Council respecting the war with the Marattas commenced by the Presidency of Bengal' (L/P&S/19, box 48).

21 For the drafting of secret despatches see Philips, *East India Company*, p. 11.

22 Johnson to the directors, 25 May 1786, E/1/78, ff. 432–3. For the deep hostility that existed between Johnson and the Wilks brothers see also the memorials sent to the directors on 24 May by Thomas (ibid., ff. 412–14) and Samuel and William (ibid., f. 422). The poisonous atmosphere in the Examiner's office at the time was such that it later prompted an intervention from Mrs Johnson who wrote to the clerk William Cabell reminding him of her husband's 'mild, liberal and gentlemanly treatment' in contrast to that of Wilks senior who 'had been so great a tyrant over you; that he not only made you a slave to him day and night' but also, with his sons, had acted with the 'utmost insolence and brutality' (ibid., ff. 435–7 (28 August 1786)).

responsibility for 'public' and 'revenue and judicial' affairs respectively.[23] Johnson continued to deal with political matters, but military subjects were referred elsewhere in East India House, first to the Auditor's Office and then from 1809 to the newly established Military Secretary. Although overall responsibility for the drafting of despatches remained with Johnson, some paragraphs were now prepared by his assistants, Jeremiah Hill and Robert Hudson, and it was from this point that the Examiner's Office began to contain a small group of men whose drafting work was distinguished from the routine copying and collecting tasks undertaken by ordinary clerks.

In theory, Johnson's drafts were based upon decisions and instructions emanating from the Committee of Correspondence, but in practice he was granted considerable freedom to frame paragraphs as he saw fit. Johnson later indicated this to a committee of stockholders when he explained that 'it is possible that, on some particular and important points, I may receive directions from the chairs; but that seldom happens [and] I generally originate, and the drafts of the replies are submitted to the Chairs, Committee, and Court'.[24] Johnson might well have been inflating the importance of his role in policy-making, because the Assistant Secretary James Cobb reported that, while on matters of 'mere routine' officials prepared despatches, 'upon points of importance, the chairs, and sometimes other directors, generally suggest the leading ideas for the formation of the dispatch'.[25] Striking a balance between these two different views was the assistant examiner Robert Hudson who indicated that 'it is not unfrequent that the directors frame paragraphs themselves, though the general practice . . . is for the Examiner to prepare them in the first instance, and when so prepared they are submitted first to the Chairs, then to the Committee of Correspondence, and lastly to the Court, for such alterations and amendments as shall be deemed fit in the various stages'.[26] Whichever of these three statements is the most accurate (and the differences between them are of emphasis rather than substance), it is

---

23 The remainder of this section is based upon the definitive account of the development of the Examiner's Office in the early nineteenth century in Martin Moir, 'The emergence of an administrative elite in East India House (1804–1858)', *India Office Library and Records. Report for the year 1977* (1979), pp. 25–42. For further detail and a description of how despatches were drafted see Martin Moir, 'The Examiner's Office and the drafting of East India Company dispatches', in K. Ballhatchet and J. Harrison (eds.), *East India Company studies: papers presented to Professor Sir Cyril Philips* (Hong Kong, 1986), pp. 123–52. See also Philips, *East India Company*, pp. 16–22.
24 *Proceedings of the Select Committee*, p. 47.
25 Ibid., p. 28.   26 Ibid., pp. 64–5.

clear that the Examiner and his staff played an increasingly important role in helping to articulate the views of the Company as they were expressed, first to the Board of Control and then to senior servants in India.[27]

The reorganisation of the Examiner's Office in 1804 saw the creation in East India House of the group of men described by Martin Moir as an 'administrative élite'. The definition of this élite was then quite significantly sharpened when, in a notable break with tradition, individuals with specialist knowledge of India were recruited from outside East India House. The first external appointments were made in 1809 when, under some pressure from the Board of Control, which was frustrated by the slow rate at which despatches were prepared, the Committee of Correspondence affirmed its belief that communication with India needed to be 'conducted with expedition, intelligence and ability'.[28] Unable to transfer men of 'matured knowledge and talents' from within the Company, the directors resolved to look elsewhere for two new assistant secretaries, and they did so in the face of considerable opposition from stockholders who felt that long-established promotion practices were being abandoned. As a result, the Oriental scholar and former Bengal servant Nathaniel Brassey Halhed, author of *A code of Gentoo laws* (1776) and *A grammar of the Bengal Language* (1778), was appointed to the Examiner's Office, together with William McCulloch, who had distinguished himself with a well-regarded series of articles published in the *Morning Chronicle*.[29] At the same time, the former Bengal army officer James Salmond was appointed as Military Secretary.

The appointments of 1809 paved the way for the external recruitment of other talented men into the Examiner's Office a decade later: historian James Mill who had recently completed his *History of British India*; Edward Strachey who had extensive experience of Bengal; and the poet Thomas Love Peacock who was required to take a special aptitude test by writing a paper on Indian revenue. These men entered a working environment in which the preparation of despatches had usually been based upon the statement of general principles and the use of precedent, but there proved to be plenty of scope for them to give expression to their personal

---

27 For the preparation of despatches in 1832, as described by the Company's Secretary Peter Auber see *PP* (1831–2), 735-1, vol. IX, pp. 7–8.

28 Quoted in Moir, 'Administrative elite', p. 28. For the detailed proposals of Robert Dundas, President of the Board, to tackle the arrears of correspondence that had built up, see his letter to the Chairs, 10 July 1809, L/P&S/19, box 13, 'Letterbook of Robert Dundas, 1807–11', pp. 136–40.

29 For a study of the unorthodox Halhed see Rosane Rocher, *Orientalism, poetry and the millennium: the checkered life of Nathaniel Brassey Hallbed, 1751–1830* (Delhi, 1983).

convictions about how the Company might influence the future development of Indian society. Thus the utilitarian views of James Mill were felt in the formulation of revenue policy between 1819 and 1830,[30] and, although they were perhaps not driven by the same degree of philosophical conviction as Mill, some of his colleagues also believed that they were in a position to shape the lives of millions of the Company's Indian subjects.[31] This was not entirely fanciful because, as we have seen, although the Board of Control had some input into the framing of despatches, most of the content originated in East India House, thus ensuring that the influence of the Chief Examiner and his assistants was strongly exerted within the whole process through which policy for British India was developed and expressed in London. Indeed, prior to his departure for Calcutta in 1828, Lord William Bentinck reportedly went as far as to tell James Mill that 'I am going to British India, but I shall not be Governor-General. It is you that will be Governor-General.'[32] As has been pointed out, this famous remark can be interpreted in a number of different ways,[33] but at the very least it indicates the extent of the influence thought to be exerted by some of those who occupied the Examiner's Office.

Relations between Mill, Peacock, and Strachey were not always easy, especially when they fell out over matters of pay and seniority, but they brought a knowledge and perspective to their duties well beyond that of their colleagues who had spent their entire working lives inside East India House. Nevertheless, the Chairman of the Company, James Pattison, had still been moved to declare in 1819 that 'a stranger was never introduced into that House without the deepest regret', and there continued to be some resistance to the appointment of individuals from outside the Company. Naturally, ordinary clerks in the Examiner's Office resented the fact that long service no longer automatically qualified them for promotion but, as Pattison observed, many in the Company were now prepared to concede that 'Talent and ability could not, like fruit trees, be placed into a hot house and forced into premature perfection'.[34] The logic of this situation was acknowledged in 1825 when the Examiner's Office

---

30 Eric Stokes, *The English utilitarians and India* (Oxford, 1959), pp. 87–9.
31 See above, p. 146.
32 This has been quoted in many works, including John Rosselli, *Lord William Bentinck: the making of a liberal imperialist, 1774–1839* (1974), p. 84.
33 Ibid., pp. 85–6.
34 James Pattison, General Court speech of 24 March 1819, as reported in *Asiatic Journal and Monthly Register*, vol. VII (1819), p. 516.

was formally divided between the senior officers who worked in the Correspondence Department, and those who performed basic clerical tasks. As Moir has observed, the directors had 'firmly come out in favour of a more flexible meritocratic approach to the choice of Examiners and their Assistants'.[35] This meant that, although other departments within the Company continued to operate a promotion system based upon seniority, advancement in the Examiner's Office was henceforth to be based upon talent. That said, the fast-tracking of the junior clerk John Stuart Mill into the Correspondence Department in 1825 was testimony to the fact that family influence was still important to those who wished to move swiftly up the hierarchies of different offices. Mill was undoubtedly a young man of unusual abilities but his entry to, and subsequent progress within, the Department was almost indecently rapid as a result of the influence exerted by his father, James. Yet, even though old habits of patronage and nepotism died hard inside the Examiner's Office, the Company's use of specialist administrative expertise was becoming widely admired.

PRINCIPLES AND POLICY

The establishment and development of the Examiner's Office offered the directors a more effective means of translating their wishes into the lengthy and detailed despatches that were sent to India. They were forced to concede, however, that as far as general policy was concerned the best that they could hope realistically to achieve was the creation of a broadly defined framework of guidelines in which their overseas servants were expected to operate. As the Secret Committee of directors confessed quite candidly to the Earl of Egremont in January 1762, it was often entirely futile for them to issue specific instructions because 'As the Company must be totally ignorant of the present situation of their affairs in India, general or conditional orders can only be given.'[36] The directors then had to trust their servants to act in the best interests of the Company, while allowing them some degree of discretion to depart from their guidelines as and when circumstances determined this to be necessary. Thus in 1795 the directors declared that although they did not ever wish their servants to 'depart from the general line of policy that has been drawn for your guidance', they were prepared to offer *ex post facto* approval to deviations

---

35 Moir, 'Adminstrative élite', p. 36.
36 Secret Committee to Egremont, 14 January 1762, reprinted in Nicholas P. Cushner (ed.), *Documents illustrating the British conquest of Manilla, 1762–3* (1971), p. 16.

when it appeared that actions were reasonable and proper in the light of changing local circumstances.[37] When, however, departures from the line were not deemed to be acceptable, as in 1825 when the Bengal Council sanctioned the retrospective payment of allowances to the Company's marine pilots, the directors expressed their displeasure in no uncertain terms and told their servants that they should not have 'deviated in so marked a manner from the general principle by which we have repeatedly enjoined you to regulate your conduct'.[38]

When the Company first began to acquire its empire, the directors took the view that the general principles required for the government of territory and people were very different from those that had long applied to the conduct of long-distance trade. But since they had little knowledge of local conditions, no precedents to guide them, and no administrative blueprint to apply to their empire, they were able to offer very little by way of firm advice to their servants in India. This became evident when the directors received news of the grant of the *diwani* in 1766 – 'the first view of affairs so totally new to us' – and they responded by delegating responsibility for administrative 'regulations' and 'plans for a peaceable possession of our acquisitions' to those in Bengal.[39] Those in Calcutta were told that 'We trust entirely to the continuance of your zealous endeavours to bring the great work to perfection', and thus, in addition to the reform and the rooting out of corruption with which he had been charged, Clive was asked to establish a general political and administrative settlement in Bengal in order to consolidate recent gains. This he did, and by preserving the existing forms of local government he established what became known as the 'dual system' of government in which primary responsibility for administration and revenue collection remained in Indian hands subject to general supervision from Company officials. Preoccupied by political events in Parliament and East India House, the directors placed great faith in the abilities of Clive, the architect of their success, and he was urged to remain in Bengal for a further year in order to complete his task.[40] Those in London thus had little direct input into

---

37 Directors to Bengal, 5 June 1795, *FWIHC*, vol. XVII, p. 81. On this occasion the directors were approving Company involvement in a dispute between the Rajah of Assam and the Rajah of Deringh even though they had previously declared a policy of avoiding all interference in conflicts between 'country powers'.

38 Directors to Bengal, 9 March 1825, 9 March 1825, E/714, p. 198.

39 Directors to Bengal, 17 May 1766, *FWIHC*, vol. IV, p. 182.

40 For a good summary outline of Clive's actions during his second governorship of Bengal see V. T. Harlow, *The founding of the second British empire, 1763–93*, 2 vols. (1952 and 1964), vol. II, pp. 20–40.

the initial process of empire building, and Clive's settlement was whole-heartedly endorsed, subject to some minor amendments. The directors simply echoed Clive's belief that the 'ancient' forms of the Bengal government should be preserved, with the 'dignity' of the Nawab upheld; and they declared that the Company should exert only the lightest of touches on local administration and the collection of revenue.[41]

Subsequent generations of directors no doubt regretted that the Court of 1766 had conceded so much administrative and political initiative to a senior figure in India, but it was not long before those in London were able more firmly to imprint their own attitudes and outlook upon the Company's overseas empire. They were able to do so for two reasons. Firstly, in 1767 they received news that Clive was returning home in order to recover from depressive illness; and, secondly, it became evident that the settlement of 1765–6 was not having the desired effect, particularly in terms of the amount of revenue being collected. As a result, the directors were obliged to formulate guidelines for those in India who were charged with responsibility for the administration, defence, and economic development of an extended territorial empire. As they did this, the directors began to articulate the fundamental beliefs and attitudes that were to shape the form taken by the Company's empire over the next seventy years or so.

For the most part, despatches sent to India always contained detailed instructions formulated in response to events and proceedings previously reported by the Company's overseas servants, and thus letters from London were littered with approval, criticism, or outright condemnation of actions that had already been taken in Asia. From 1767 onwards, however, the directors' thoughts on how the empire should be governed were also represented in despatches in the form of general principles of conduct established with a view to guiding the future actions of senior officers in India. Accordingly, in May 1768 the directors informed those in Madras that 'The quick succession of important events in Indian wars puts it out of our powers to direct your measures; we can only give you the outline of that system which we judge most conducive to give harmony and tranquillity to our possessions.'[42] While the local context in which this 'system' was applied changed considerably over time, the governing principles used to define it during the late 1760s remained

---

41 For details of the political and administrative settlement established by Clive and endorsed by the directors see Bowen, *Revenue and reform*, pp. 7–10.
42 Extract of letter to Madras, 13 November 1768, BL, Add. MS, 38397, f. 141.

broadly the same in the decades that followed. The principles reflected the fact that the directors always held a narrowly circumscribed view of how the Company should act in India. As befitting men from mercantile and maritime backgrounds, the directors of the 1760s and 1770s remained resolutely non-doctrinaire in their outlook and attitudes, and they applied to the government of empire the basic lessons that they had absorbed from the successful management of long-distance trade. In an institution that always proclaimed the virtues of continuity and precedent, this left a powerful legacy to be inherited by later generations of directors. Thus, even during the 1820s and 1830s, when the influence of those pressing for the Company to engage more actively in the reform of India was being exerted inside and outside East India House, the core governing principles of the directors continued to be characterised by a cautious pragmatism first established during the late 1760s.

Between 1767 and 1769 the directors established basic ground rules for those who were administering the overseas empire, and they developed a corporate code of acceptable behaviour. In doing this, the directors looked back to the corruption, extortion, and misrule that had accompanied territorial expansion between 1757 and 1765, but they also looked forward to the creation of an efficient, moderate, rational, and well-ordered regime. The Company's servants in Calcutta were urged to practise economy and retrenchment; consolidate recent advances; keep a close eye on European and Indian rivals; impose strict discipline upon junior servants; avoid further wars of conquest or a 'march on Delhi'; and ensure that the local population was in no way 'oppressed' by the Company's efforts to increase trade and the collection of revenue. Uniting all of these aims was the directors' desire to secure the 'permanency' of their territorial possessions, and they endlessly repeated the view that prosperity for the Company and the people who now lived under its rule could only be forthcoming once recent gains were made secure. Establishing these general guidelines in November 1767, the directors declared that 'If these rules are strictly adhered to, we shall flatter ourselves our power and advantages in Bengal will obtain that permanency we have so long laboured at.'[43] They also acknowledged that Bengal formed only part of a wider Indian empire, and therefore the same basic principles were to be applied to Bombay and Madras. The directors deemed it to be of the utmost importance that those in the different Presidencies did not pursue

---

43 Directors to Bengal, 20 November 1767, *FWIHC*, vol. XIV, p. 15.

independent courses of action that might damage the greater whole, and thus an important final theme running through the despatches from London was that the Company's territories belonged to a 'common concern'.[44] Although the directors often wavered in their commitment to Bombay in the years that followed, they always stressed the need for the three Presidencies to offer financial and military aid to one another.

Having established a general policy for the sound management of the Company's overseas possessions, the directors' 'rules' of governance quickly coalesced around a number of key terms that were to be repeated in despatch after despatch in the decades that followed. Words such as 'simplicity', 'oeconomy', 'uniformity', 'frugality', 'regularity', and 'permanency' were all borrowed from the Company's commercial lexicon and used time and again to enunciate the key principles that the directors hoped would guide the day-to-day actions of overseas servants. Taken together, these words underpinned a general system of 'economy', incorporating both financial retrenchment and administrative efficiency, and this meant that the directors had in effect anticipated many of the axioms used by those who were to promote reform of the British state from the 1780s onwards.[45] Ironically, in view of the Company's general antipathy towards innovation of any sort, this placed the directors close to the leading edge of those in Britain who were promoting administrative reform and it can be argued that, consciously or otherwise, they were in fact seeking to apply prevailing metropolitan ideals of governance within the imperial arena. As has recently been pointed out, this ensured that although the form taken by the Company state in India was shaped by local circumstances to a considerable degree, some of its key aspects were 'derived from contemporary statecraft in England'.[46] The directors were the main agents in this process and their despatches provided a relentless

---

44 Directors to Bengal, 15 February 1765, ibid., vol. IV, p. 85. For similar sentiments see ibid., vol. V, 183 (17 March 1769).

45 For the central importance of 'economy' in late eighteenth-century reform see John Torrance, 'Social class and bureaucratic innovation: the commissioners for examining the public accounts, 1780–1787', *Past and Present*, 78 (1978), pp. 56–81. See also Philip Harling, *The waning of 'old corruption'. The politics of economical reform in Britain, 1779–1846* (Oxford, 1996).

46 Sudipta Sen, 'Liberal government and illiberal trade: the political economy of "responsible government" in early British India', in Kathleen Wilson (ed.), *A new imperial history: culture, identity, and modernity in Britain and the empire, 1660–1840* (Cambridge, 2004), pp. 136–54 (quotation on p. 136). For another study which emphasises that the core characteristics of the Company's regime were those of the British state, but which also stresses that 'this core was hedged around with institutions and ideologies of a different stamp', see C. A. Bayly, 'The British military-fiscal state and indigenous resistance. India 1750–1820', in Lawrence Stone (ed.), *An imperial state at war. Britain from 1689 to 1815* (1994), pp. 322–54 (quotation on p. 333).

message to senior overseas servants about the principles upon which the Company's regime was to be based. In turn, that message was relayed from Calcutta, Bombay, and Madras to those working in all of the subordinate branches of the Company.

There was an obvious danger that repeated use of key words and phrases would eventually render them hollow and meaningless. There was, however, a need for regular reminders of guiding principles to be issued from London because the directors were sometimes guilty of sending mixed messages to India which could encourage the belief among servants that they had been empowered to act in a manner that was contrary to earlier statements of general policy. During the 1760s and 1770s, for example, the directors routinely professed their desire to secure the happiness and prosperity of the Indian people who lived under their protection, but when dwindling levels of revenue income became evident in London despatches from East India House soon became punctuated with passages authorising servants to use robust methods and force if they deemed it necessary for the collection of taxes. In effect, this gave Company servants the freedom to act as they wished, but if such instructions ever pricked the consciences of the directors they were always able to distance themselves from charges of condoning unrestrained violence by insisting, as in April 1786, that the 'coercion' of the local populations by Company servants should not involve 'every species of cruelty' as had been the case under previous Indian regimes.[47]

A strong tension always existed between the Company's stated desire to offer protection and dignity to the population under its control and the need for revenue collection to be maximised, and much the same could be said of the directors' promotion of 'free trade' within the Company's territories, a policy that coexisted during the 1770s and 1780s alongside strident demands from London that ever more competitively priced textiles be secured for export to Britain. Thus much depended upon how local Company officials interpreted an order such as that sent to Bengal in 1785, instructing that textile purchases be made 'on the most frugal terms possible'.[48] For no matter how much any form of 'oppression' was always frowned upon by the directors, commercial instructions of this type sent to Bengal and Madras served only to legitimise the aggressive actions of Company servants and their agents whose severe regulation of the textile trade led to very harsh effects being felt by

47 *FWIHC*, vol. X, p. 128.
48 Ibid., vol. X, p. 112.

weavers. In particular, wages were reduced among the Company's weavers, and this served to cause very high rates of mortality when famine prompted sharp increases in food prices.[49]

For all the professed moderation and responsibility of the Company's regime, these examples illustrate that there were always occasions when the directors were prepared to sanction harsh measures, and this ensured that a ruthless streak of authoritarianism always coexisted alongside a governing ideology that in many ways was liberal in tone.[50] Indeed, on occasions the recasting or abandonment of a governing principle could arise from the need to drive forward the growth of trade and revenue. This was very much the case during the early 1770s when the directors sanctioned a new revenue policy that went much further than the one originally implemented by Clive. A decline in revenue collections during the late 1760s suggested to the directors that loose supervision of local Indian officials was not best serving the Company's economic interests, and thus in August 1771 they famously declared their determination 'to stand forth as duan, and by the agency of the Company's servants to take upon ourselves the entire care and management of the revenues'.[51] In fact, this served only to endorse a more interventionist form of revenue administration that had already been pursued by those in Bengal and, apart from ordering the sacking of senior Indian revenue officials, the directors once more conceded the reformist initiative to those in Calcutta by conspicuously failing to offer any instructions or guidance as to how any new revenue policy might be implemented. Company servants led by Warren Hastings were left to find their own way further into the realms of revenue collection, government, and the administration of justice. As the directors themselves later conceded, the reason for this was that 'So much depends on local knowledge that it is impossible for us to give any specific direction upon the subject.'[52] This ensured that the locus of revenue and administrative reform was always to be found in Calcutta rather than

---

49 Rajat Datta, *Society, economy and the market: commercialisation in rural Bengal c.1760–1800* (Delhi, 2000), pp. 294–305. See also Hameeda Hossain, *The Company weavers in Bengal: the East India Company and the organization of textile production in Bengal, 1750–1813* (Delhi, 1988), pp. 78, 111–12; Arvind Sinha, *The politics of trade: Anglo-French commerce of the Coromandel coast 1763–1793* (New Delhi, 2002), pp. 158–63.

50 For a perceptive treatment of this important theme see Sudipta Sen, 'Liberal government and illiberal trade'.

51 Directors to Bengal, 28 August 1771, *FWIHC*, vol. VI, p. 123.

52 Directors to Bengal, 15 January 1783, ibid., vol. IX, p. 92.

London, but it also meant that the effects of Company rule were to be far more keenly felt than had ever been intended or desired by the directors.[53]

By the mid-1780s the directors were endeavouring to seize back some control over revenue policy. In 1786 they declared to the Bengal Council their 'positive direction that no essential change of system be ever made' without reference to East India House, and they instructed that outline plans of action should always be submitted so that 'we may be enabled to exercise our judgment upon the comparative advantages, and send you our definitive orders'.[54] They were prompted into action by Pitt's India Act and concerns about rising costs, but they were also expressing their frustration that local experimentation and innovation within the revenue system had 'created a cloud of intricacy and confusion which almost defeated controul'. They therefore encouraged the Bengal Council to revert to first principles by developing a policy that was 'simple in its principle and uniform in its operation', and they expressed their desire 'to adopt some permanent system, compatible with the nature of our Government, the actual situation of the Company, and the ease of the inhabitants'. The directors were once more setting out 'such rules and principles as may in our opinion best conduce [*sic*] to the establishment of general system', although as was so often the case they did not advance much further and engage themselves in the making of the detailed and far-reaching revenue reforms that found expression in Cornwallis's famous Permanent Settlement of 1793.[55] Henry Dundas was inclined to suggest somewhat cynically that this was because discussion of a complex matter such as revenue policy was beyond the capacity of most members of the Court,[56] but their attitude can also be seen to reflect a long-held belief that once general principles had been established in London

---

53 For the development of the Company's revenue administration between 1765 and 1785 see P. J. Marshall, *Bengal: the British bridgehead. Eastern India, 1740–1828*, The New Cambridge History of India, vol. II. 2 (Cambridge, 1987), pp. 116–22. The effect of Company rule upon the territory under its control has long been a matter for heated debate among historians. For a recent trenchant discussion which emphasises change rather than continuity see Rajat Kanta Ray, 'Indian society and the establishment of British supremacy, 1765–1818', *OHBE*, vol. II: P. J. Marshall (ed.), *The eighteenth century*, pp. 513–16.

54 Unless otherwise indicated, quotations in the following paragraph are taken from Directors to Bengal, 12 April 1786, *FWIHC*, vol. X, pp. 122–3.

55 There has been considerable debate about the genesis of the Permanent Settlement, and in particular about the nature of the influences that shaped the views of Governor-General Cornwallis. Whatever the case, it is clear that the Settlement was formulated in Bengal and not London. Indeed, the directors were initially reluctant to sanction the settlement, and they only accepted it when Pitt and Dundas made their views known (Embree, *Charles Grant*, pp. 113–17). For the Permanent Settlement and discussion of its effects see Marshall, *Bengal*, pp. 122–7, 144–50.

56 Embree, *Charles Grant*, p. 116.

detailed reform in India should be developed and implemented by those *in situ* who possessed up-to-date local knowledge.

It was only at the beginning of the nineteenth century that the directors managed to exert a more direct form of influence upon the implementation of revenue policy, as shortcomings slowly became evident in the widely revered Permanent Settlement. They intervened to approve a form of settlement with peasant farmers (*ryots*) adopted in parts of the Madras Presidency that was quite unlike the settlement with landowners (*zamindari*) that had formed the basis of Cornwallis's system in Bengal. Between 1808 and 1813 they were fully briefed on the subject in London by Thomas Munro, the revenue settlement officer of Madras, and, prompted by the Board of Control, they were eventually prepared to reverse Governor-General Wellesley's earlier decision to extend the Bengal settlement to Madras and elsewhere.[57] Even in this case, however, the directors were following a lead given to them by one who was well-versed in the practical difficulties associated with the collection of revenue and, although listening to and then acting upon expert advice on unfamiliar subjects might be considered good managerial practice, it again illustrates the extent to which the details of revenue policy and other important matters continued to be shaped primarily by inputs from local officials in India rather than by the implementation of any specific instructions issued in London.

Successive changes of attitude towards revenue collection demonstrate that not all of the general policies outlined in London were set in stone, and when the Company's economic well-being was threatened the directors were always prepared to modify or abandon previously held positions. Over the period as a whole, however, the directors remained remarkably consistent in their formulation of the Company's core governing principles, and as a result the despatches of the 1820s contained very strong echoes of those that had been written sixty years earlier. The need for economy, simplicity, and uniformity in the Company's overseas administration continued to be writ large in the letters sent to India, and this helped to ensure that by the 1830s the Company was moving along with gathering currents of reform which laid great emphasis on the need for

---

57 For full details of the combination of circumstances that saw those in London move towards acceptance of the *ryotwari* system see T. H. Beaglehole, *Thomas Munro and the development of administrative policy in Madras, 1792–1818: the origins of the 'Munro system'* (Cambridge, 1966), pp. 87–101. Long-run changes in revenue policy are set out in B. B. Misra, *The central administration of the East India Company, 1773–1834* (Manchester, 1959), pp. 108–211.

efficient institutions of government.[58] Repeated drives for retrenchment, which culminated in the period 1828–33, mirrored the moves towards 'cheap government' that were being implemented by ministers in Britain, and a desire for rational and well-ordered administration struck some of the same notes sounded by utilitarians and others who saw the efficiency of bureaucratic systems as the key to securing 'good government' for as many people as possible.[59] As a result, in 1833 a reform-minded individual such as Sir John Malcolm, the former Governor of Bombay, applauded the application of 'political economy' to the Indian empire, which he saw as being achieved through the Company's 'development and fixing of general principles [of government]'.[60] Malcolm was indeed correct to identify this as a characteristic of the Company's governing methods but, as he would have known from his own experience, this was not a recent development.

Yet, for all the consistency of principle embodied in the despatches sent to India, a slow underlying change is discernible in the Company's metropolitan attitude towards the effect of British rule upon Indian society. Whereas it had once been commonplace for the directors to write, as in 1782, that a primary aim was 'to secure to the natives, under the immediate government of the Company, the undisturbed exercise of their religion and customs',[61] by the 1820s they were advocating administrative actions that were intended to 'improve' Indian society. The well-being of the Indian population was now to be achieved through education and religious reform, not by the old policy of non-intervention. As the Company's Secretary, Peter Auber, put it in 1829, 'The welfare of India – the happiness of its immense population and the blessings of British rule are the leading principles which must be kept in view and any system which shall militate against the extension of them must be amended or abolished.'[62]

There were a number of reasons for this considerable shift in emphasis, which historians see as helping to promote the emergence of anglicising

---

58 For a discussion of the interplay of bureaucratic developments in Britain and India at this time which stresses the lead taken by the former see E. T. Stokes, 'Bureaucracy and ideology: Britain and India in the nineteenth century', *Transactions of the Royal Historical Society*, fifth series, 30 (1980), pp. 131–56.

59 For the coexistence of retrenchment and reform after 1815, and the effect that this had on the British state, see Harling, *The waning of 'old corruption'*, pp. 11–13, 136–227.

60 Speech of 15 April 1833, *Debates at the General Court of Proprietors of East India stock on 15th, 16th, 18th, 19th, 22nd, 23rd, 25th, April 1833 . . .* (1833), p. 13.

61 *FWIHC*, vol. IX, p. 62.

62 Auber to Lord William Bentinck, 11 April 1829, *Bentinck correspondence*, vol. I, p. 186.

attitudes among Company servants in India that were very different from those of an 'orientalist' type that had been much in evidence during the days of Clive and Hastings. In a purely pragmatic sense, the Company's supremacy was more or less secure following the defeat of the Marathas in 1818, and this meant that more attention could be paid to non-military matters. At the same time, evangelicals and other reformers in Britain who adopted an increasingly hostile attitude towards Hinduism had generated political pressures inside East India House and Parliament to ensure that the Company took fuller advantage of its position to promote change and improvement in India. Most obviously, this had manifested itself in the Charter Act of 1813, which not only allowed Christian missionaries into British India but also obliged the Company to spend one lakh of rupees a year on education.[63] The reformers hoped that the security and happiness of Indians were to be achieved not by leaving them to their traditional ways, as had long been Company practice, but by introducing them to the benefits of western civilisation.

Many at East India House long continued to be uneasy about interfering too deeply in Indian society, and hence there was always considerable opposition to any scheme promoting the colonisation of India, but the influence of evangelicals such as Charles Grant, Edward Parry, and William Astell was much in evidence when education and religious matters were discussed in the Court of Directors. As a result, although there was often heated debate about the reform of Indian society, the directors were nevertheless prepared to sign off despatches that carried a striking new tone in some of their paragraphs. As was written in 1825, for example, 'There is nothing, we have informed you, which we regard as of greater importance than the diffusion of the English language, and of European Arts and Sciences among the natives.'[64] Nothing could have been further from the sentiments expressed during the 1760s, when the directors repeatedly warned against any substantial Company interference in local Indian society. If only slowly, the directors absorbed prevailing general ideas about the nature and purpose of imperial government and, although they were always deeply suspicious of radical thought and experimentation, they were increasingly inclined to believe that the Company's power and influence could be used to anglicise, civilise, and

---

63 For evangelicals, missionaries, and the East India Company see Andrew Porter, *Religion versus empire? British Protestant missionaries and overseas expansion, 1700–1914* (Manchester, 2004), pp. 68–75, 99–103.
64 Directors to Bengal, 9 March 1825, E/4/714, pp. 167–8.

educate the Indian population under their control. As pragmatic as ever, the directors acknowledged first and foremost that this would bring immediate practical benefits to the Company, but they began also to articulate the belief that in the longer term Company policy could serve to improve and reshape Indian society.[65]

COMMAND, CONTROL, AND REFORM

It was, of course, one matter for the directors to formulate general principles and rules of conduct in London, but quite another to ensure that their wishes and instructions were acted upon in India. Indeed, the inability of the directors to control events in India was no more clearly exposed than by their sustained failure to prevent further territorial expansion after 1765. Wars and conquests were routinely denounced as being dangerous and ruinously expensive, and those in India were continually reminded of the need to consolidate existing possessions rather than strive after new ones. All in London were agreed that unrestrained expansion threatened the Company's very existence, yet in practice very little could be done to control those in India who were determined to embark upon ambitious military campaigns. As the Bengal ship owner Joseph Price remarked in characteristically colourful terms, 'Whilst the managers at home say that trade is their only object, their military servants abroad pant after conquests.'[66]

Price exaggerated, and it would be wrong to suggest a straightforward division of outlook between expansionists in India and consolidators in Britain, but tensions were always created between Calcutta and London when those on the spot proclaimed that they were adopting an aggressive external policy as the best means of protecting the Company's interests.[67] This was especially the case after 1784 when a clause in Pitt's India Act had declared that 'schemes of conquest and extension of dominion in India are measures repugnant to the wish, the honour, and the policy of this nation', and decreed that all wars other than those of self-defence could be

---

65 Ibid, pp. 167–74. On this occasion the directors were discussing the 'Hindoo College' established in Calcutta in 1816.

66 Captain Joseph Price, *Five letters from a free merchant in Bengal to Warren Hastings esq. . . .* (1777, reprinted 1783), p. 88.

67 Moreover, as the leading historian of the Company's eighteenth-century army has noted, 'there was a genuine and long-standing difference of perspective between the directors in Europe and their servants in the East over the degree of interventionist politics and the use of force required to promote viable trade'. G. J. Bryant, 'The military imperative in early British expansion in India, 1750–1815', *Indo-British Review: A Journal of History*, 21 (1993), p. 19.

fought only after approval had been granted by the directors and Board of Control.[68] As was demonstrated by Richard Wellesley's bold strategy of conquest after 1798, however, the clause was a dead letter and nothing of immediate effect could be done by the directors when Company instructions were simply ignored, especially when the Governor-General was being encouraged privately in an aggressive policy by the President of the Board of Control Henry Dundas who, as War Minister, saw the annexation of territory as a means of establishing the long-term security of British India.[69] Instead, the directors had to mount a long and bitter political campaign to force Wellesley's return to Britain in 1805, the essence of their case being that he had created a 'new species of government and of power' in India, which took the form of a 'government of discretion' that had 'widely departed from the principles of foreign policy, and from the subjection and obedience to the authority at home enjoined by the law'.[70] Even then, however, any sense of triumph among the directors was more than offset by their knowledge that Wellesley's actions had generated a mountain of additional debt for an already hard-pressed Company. In their minds, the outcome simply confirmed what they had always argued: the price of further territorial expansion was so great as to be not worth paying.

The directors' inability to restrain Wellesley's actions provides the most graphic example of the ineffectiveness of Company rule from London. Wellesley, however, cannot be considered to have been a typical Company servant. He was an enormously single-minded Governor-General who was reluctant to acknowledge the authority of the directors over him, and who also developed a vision of empire that was fundamentally different from most of those in London. Other influential Governors-General such as Lord Cornwallis (1786–93 and 1805), Sir John Shore (1793–8), and Lord William Bentinck (1828–35) were rather more inclined to listen to the noises emanating from Leadenhall Street, and during their terms of office the Company's administration in India generally moved more in step with the wishes of the directors and the Board of Control. Ultimately, a great deal depended on the personality, qualities, and ambitions of those supervising the Company's affairs in India for as Sir

---

68 24 Geo. III, c.25, xxxiv.
69 Philips, *East India Company*, pp. 100–4.
70 The Court of Directors to the Board of Control, 6 November 1805, printed in Marshall, *Problems of empire*, p. 143. For the ferocious debate over Wellesley's expansionist policies and his methods of government see Embree, *Charles Grant*, pp. 205–30. For the events leading to Wellesley's return to London see Philips, *East India Company*, pp. 130–44.

John Macpherson had put it in 1783 the 'real security of India' was founded 'upon Britain's choice of men who are to rule these possessions and not in a thirtieth degree upon the wisdom of those regulations which King, Parliament, and Company may lay down'.[71] Thus, when the directors lost all confidence in a Governor-General, as was the case with Lord Amherst between 1823 and 1826, the Company's sense of unity of purpose in Britain and India was thrown into jeopardy.[72]

It would be wrong to suggest, however, that it was the men not measures that were the only determining factors in the development of the Company's overseas empire. The Company in London had to deal with men other than senior figures in India, and the directors were much exercised by the need to find methods through which they could control and regulate those in the middling and low-ranking stations on the Company's payroll. The need for them to do this arose primarily from the fact that the Company's servants in India had long been engaged in the vigorous and largely unrestrained pursuit of private trade and enterprise.[73] Their illicit actions had always posed a considerable challenge to the authority of the directors, but the scope of the problem was broadened greatly by events in the decade after Plassey when servants were able to take advantage of the Company's growing military and political ascendancy in Bengal in order to diversify and intensify their activities. It proved to be even more difficult to control servants as they moved beyond commerce into political administration and revenue collection, which bred new forms of abuse including, most notoriously, the taking of large sums of money as 'presents' from Indians.[74] Emboldened by the opportunities presented by the expansionist process, servants in India were aggressive in their pursuit of private fortunes and far less inclined than ever before to adhere to any new regulations. They simply ignored explicit instructions and, as a result, some directors believed that their control over the servants had almost entirely broken down during the upheavals of the 1750s and 1760s. The Chairman Thomas Rous complained somewhat wearily in the House of Commons in April 1767 that 'We have never

---

71 Quoted in Holden Furber, *Henry Dundas, First Viscount Melville, 1742–1811: political manager of Scotland, statesman, administrator of British India* (London, 1931), p. 34.

72 For the difficulties of Amherst during the Burmese war and the accompanying political turmoil within the Company and government see Philips, *East India Company*, pp. 254–60.

73 Marshall, *East Indian fortunes*, pp. 159–62. See also Ian Bruce Watson, *Foundations for empire: English private trade in India, 1659–1760* (New Delhi, 1980), ch. 3.

74 Marshall, *East Indian fortunes*, pp. 160–79. Marshall estimates that presents amounting to around £2.5 million were distributed in Bengal between 1757 and 1773.

had our orders complied with – not a quarter, nor a fifth, or a sixth for
these ten years past',[75] and a parliamentary inquiry later took the view that
the instructions of the directors had become 'habitually despised' by those
in India.[76]

Yet, contrary to the view often taken by their critics, the directors did
not meekly accept the continued erosion of their authority over their
overseas servants. Instead, they developed a number of strategies designed
to ensure compliance with orders and the long-term creation of a civil
service that would act responsibly on behalf of both the Company and the
nation.[77] Throughout the period, senior overseas servants were always
referred to by the directors as 'our loving friends' or our 'affectionate
friends', but, in case this warm familiarity bred any contempt or compla-
cency in India, those in London also often used robust and direct
language to keep individuals in their place and on their toes. Servants
were regularly reminded of where they stood in relation to their superiors
in London, and the first general response to any acts of defiance was
usually a restatement of the power and authority held by the directors.
Thus, in 1784 a strongly worded letter from Warren Hastings brought the
response that he was 'bound to yield to their decrees' and it was his 'duty'
to obey the directors.[78] More routinely, servants were reminded of their
individual and collective responsibilities, and the directors often demonstrated the great length of the corporate memory by referring to trivial
uncompleted business from previous decades.[79]

When reminders or instructions fell upon deaf ears, as was often the
case, the directors censured the behaviour and actions of their servants.
These censures ranged from mild rebukes, through expressions of 'much
disapprobation', to the 'severest tokens of displeasure'. The directors
declared great surprise and astonishment at actions variously described
as being 'extraordinary', 'unwarrantable', or 'unworthy'. Servants were
accused of paying little attention to the Company's affairs or of displaying
the utmost contempt for the directors' authority. Such comments left

75 BL, Add. MS 18469, f. 68.
76 Quoted in Frederick Madden with David Fieldhouse (eds.), *Select documents on the constitutional
    history of the British Empire and Commonwealth*, vol. III, *Imperial reconstruction, 1763–1840: the
    evolution of alternative systems of colonial government* (Westport, Conn., 1987), pp. 178–9.
77 For the corruption of the period and initial Company responses see Bowen, *Revenue and reform*,
    pp. 85–8.
78 Directors to Bengal, 21 January 1784, *FWIHC*, vol. IX, p. 143. Hastings had been critical of the
    directors' resolutions relating to his handling of relations with Raja Chait Singh.
79 See e.g. ibid, vol. IX, p. 19.

overseas servants in no doubt about the view taken in London, but their effects on the ground were limited, as the directors themselves were forced to confess in 1769 when they wrote that 'We are tired of censuring such flagrant instances of disobedience to our express orders.'[80] As a result, when they anticipated that servants might not comply with their instructions they resorted to the use of ever more emphatic orders, as in January 1783 when the Bengal Council was told that 'lest a pretence should be sought after for evading such directions, we shall here repeat our orders, with the most positive injunctions, that you comply therewith in every particular'.[81]

The very fact that constant reminders had to be issued suggests that those in India often showed scant regard to their superiors. Distance bred the belief that instructions from London were an unwelcome intrusion into local affairs. As a result, the directors sought practical ways of demonstrating their authority over their distant servants. Attempts to exercise control from London often took the form of specific campaigns to root out corruption, and from time to time the directors chose relentlessly to pursue matters relating to unacceptable practices that were damaging to the Company's interests. The purpose of such action was not simply to stem financial losses but also to remind servants that their behaviour was not beyond close scrutiny from their employers. The directors chose the ground for their campaigns very carefully, tacitly acknowledging that they often did not possess the information or expertise that was necessary to pursue cases into areas where their own lack of local knowledge invited procrastination and delay from suspected malefactors. They focused on any potential accounting fraud that might be evident in books returned to London and thus during the late 1780s private profiteering from bullock contracts was singled out for particularly close attention, as was the illicit disposal of Company stationery and marine stores in Bengal.[82]

The directors were prepared to give a free rein to trusted senior figures such as Cornwallis whose expert knowledge and reasoned arguments encouraged the development of a particular line of policy,[83] but in general they were not inclined to encourage any form of innovation or

---

80 Directors to Bengal, 17 March 1769, ibid., vol. V, p. 185.
81 Ibid., vol. IX, p. 97. The directors were endeavouring to prevent non-covenanted servants being offered employment in India.
82 Ibid., vol. X, pp. 189–94, 258, 325–6.
83 For an explicit statement of this see Directors to Bengal, 27 March 1787, ibid., vol. X, p. 206.

independent action, and they always adhered to the view that the role of Company servants was to enact policy only after it had been approved by the home administration. Thus, they were often furious when even small-scale initiatives were introduced at local level without any prior notice or statement of intent. Hence, to give just one example, when the Bengal Council reported in 1824 that it had provided a house for the newly appointed Bishop Heber of Calcutta it was told that 'the practice of anticipating our orders is one which is liable to substantial objection, and ought never to be resorted to, but in cases of emergency'.[84] Similar words had been written many times before and, as with numerous other similar episodes, they revealed the weakness of the directors when presented with a *fait accompli*. Bishop Heber remained in his house, but on other occasions it was possible for the directors to overturn particularly objectionable decisions taken at local level. In 1782, for example, they annulled a grant that had been made to establish a monopoly trade with Assam, declaring that the action of the Bengal Council 'was so repugnant to every principle of commerce, so detrimential [sic] to the revenue and so prejudicial to the interests of the natives and others, who ought to be allowed a free and uncontrouled trade over India'.[85] They believed that such a policy could unsettle local affairs, but they also feared that if it was unchecked it would concede far too much power to the servants in India.

The directors always had to acknowledge that their scope for intervention in India was limited because without real sanctions or penalties even their harshest threats carried little weight with those servants who were determined to ignore instructions or act in a manner that was harmful to the Company's interests. Dismissal or legal action against miscreants was always a theoretical possibility but the directors were all too aware that they were usually unable to secure the intended outcome. Dismissed servants were often able to secure reinstatement through a majority vote in the General Court, and it proved costly and difficult to sue individuals for breach of their employment contract.[86] Indeed, as contemporaries and historians have pointed out, it is doubtful whether the directors really

---

84 Despatch to Bengal, 23 February 1825, E/4/714, p. 75.
85 *FWIHC*, vol. IX, p. 54.
86 For the failure or unwillingness of the directors to rid themselves of guilty servants see Holden Furber, *John Company at work: a study of European expansion in India in the late eighteenth century* (Cambridge, Mass., 1951), pp. 332–8. Individuals signed a covenant specifying terms and conditions and a bond, the latter of which was countersigned by two sureties who undertook to repay the Company if the contract was breached. The directors rarely sued for breach of contract.

possessed the resolve necessary to pursue miscreants to the bitter end, and thus in Furber's words their actions can be seen as little more than 'pious gestures in nearly every case'.[87] Certainly Laurence Sulivan anticipated this judgement when he wrote that 'I do not assert that the directors have not felt and pointed out to their servants abroad most of the evils complained of, denouncing vengeance upon proof of guilt; but the detection of mal-practice or misconduct has in general issued in the admission of some flimsy vindication or in threats never carried into execution.'[88]

The directors might have sometimes lacked the stomach for battle with their employees, but they did look beyond the narrow enforcement of the Company's terms and conditions set out in the covenants signed by their employees. Consequently, when serious matters arose individuals were reminded that the authority of the directors carried with it the weight of English law and could not simply be ignored or dismissed as being irrelevant. This practice can be traced to 1766 when an opinion of the Attorney and Solicitor General was used by the Company in an attempt to bring to trial in Calcutta some of the senior officers in Bengal who had ignored instructions prohibiting the acceptance of 'presents' from the Nawab.[89] Although the action was beset with legal and political difficulties, it nevertheless encouraged the directors to seek ministerial support for parliamentary measures designed to strengthen their control over the Company's internal affairs in Asia. From the time of the first parliamentary inquiry of 1767 onwards, therefore, the directors often actively sought legislation designed specifically to regulate the behaviour of Company servants and British subjects in India. Individual Acts of Parliament sought to address particular problems, while major statutes such as the Regulating Act or the India Act contained clauses intended to prohibit illegal practices such as the acceptance of presents by officials or the conduct of private trade by those engaged in revenue collection.[90] This greatly assisted the directors in their campaigns against miscreants, and statutes were often invoked in despatches in order to remind individuals or councils that they had to adhere to the laws of Parliament as well as to the instructions issued from Leadenhall Street. Thus in 1782 the directors wrote of an Act intended to prevent Company servants lending money to

---

87 Furber, *John Company at work*, p. 331.
88 Quoted in Ibid., p. 332.
89 Bowen, *Revenue and reform*, pp. 85–7.
90 See, for example, 13 Geo. III, c.63, xxiii and xxvii; 24 Geo. III, c.25, xlv and lii.

foreign East India companies, 'We hope that the legislative prohibition (independent of punishment) will be sufficient to stop the mischief.'[91] And in March 1786 the Bengal Council was told in no uncertain terms that its recent appointment of servants without the prior approval of the directors was a flagrant breach of the terms of the Regulating Act and thus deemed to be unlawful.[92]

Although the directors enjoyed occasional victories in their attempts to regulate the Company's affairs in India, they were realistic enough to acknowledge that any short-term success was always likely to be tempered by the emergence of new forms of abuse or by the continued pursuit of local initiatives by ambitious men on the spot. Either of these might threaten the Company's wider interests, and thus instead of simply reacting to events through *ex post facto* inquiries and punitive actions, the directors sought to recast their relationship with those in India and reform the civil service. Most radical were the attempts made during the late 1760s and early 1770s to send out 'supervisory commissions' from Britain to ensure that instructions were acted upon. Such a scheme was first developed in 1769 when the near loss of Madras to Haidar Ali was attributed to the 'manifest disobedience' of the Company's orders.[93] In response, three commissioners were appointed to superintend and control all of the Company's settlements 'as if we the Court of Directors were ourselves present upon the spot'.[94] Unfortunately, the commissioners perished when the frigate carrying them to India was lost between the Cape and Calcutta, and a subsequent attempt to establish a new supervisory commission foundered in acrimonious circumstances in late 1772 amidst disagreements over the appointments, the cost of the commission, and the vexed question of whether the Royal Navy's commander in the Indian Ocean should be given a 'voice' in the deliberations of the commissioners.[95]

Under the terms of the Regulating Act of 1773, the newly established office of Governor-General was intended to act as a 'superintending power' over all of the Company's Indian settlements,[96] and this meant

---

91 *FWIHC*, vol. IX, p. 21.   92 *FWIHC*, vol. X, pp. 61–2.   93 B/85, p. 64.

94 *FWIHC*, vol. V, p. 216.

95 Bowen, *Revenue and reform*, pp. 133–4, 136–9, 148–50. In April 1772 the Prime Minister, Lord North, had suggested that he favoured granting new supervisors some degree of power to act as 'commissioners of state' in India (BL, Eg. MS, 240, pp. 246–8).

96 Lord North took the lead in the development of this measure (see Bowen, *Revenue and reform*, pp. 166–7).

that the directors did not again seek to establish supervisory commissions as a means of controlling their overseas servants.[97] Instead, they endeavoured to promote the reform of the Company's civil service in the hope that a body of men could be created in India whose outlook and attitude were more similar to their own. Although the pace and direction of administrative reform in India were always driven by leading figures in Calcutta such as Hastings and Cornwallis, this should not obscure the fact that the directors themselves routinely preached the need for higher standards of professional and responsible behaviour from the Company's servants. Attempts had been made from the late 1760s to improve the behaviour, manners, and morals of Company servants, and the introduction of very detailed codes of conduct focused attention on junior staff in the hope that extravagance and luxury would be replaced by frugal and sober lifestyles.[98] As those in Bengal were told in 1769, the directors believed that 'European simplicity is much more likely to engage the respect of the natives than an imitation of their manners',[99] and they repeatedly warned against the dangers of Company servants becoming 'Indianised'.

In many ways this was wishful thinking, but time and again the directors returned to the subject of the need for European simplicity and order because, as we have seen, they believed that the proper place of their servants was within a 'system of subordination and economy' and their attempts at reform consistently sought to achieve this.[100] An unswerving commitment to financial retrenchment meant that the directors were always deeply concerned about rising salaries, but they were prepared to sanction substantial increases in the emoluments of Company servants in India, as recommended by Hastings and Cornwallis.[101] They did so in the hope that this would help to create a more professional and well-ordered civil service whose members were not preoccupied with the pursuit of private profit, and as a result the average official earnings in the Bengal civil service rose from less £150 a year before 1757 to £2,261

---

97 They did, however, occasionally appoint special commissioners to implement specific policies, as was the case with Thomas Munro who was charged with the revision of the Madras judicial system between 1814 and 1818 (Beaglehole, *Thomas Munro*, pp. 102–20).

98 Bowen, *Revenue and reform*, p. 87.

99 *FWIHC*, vol. V, p. 189.

100 Directors to Bengal, 12 April, 1786, ibid., vol. X, p. 122.

101 For the rise of official earnings under Hastings see Marshall, *East Indian fortunes*, pp. 182–9. On the question of salaries and other matters Cornwallis was greatly influenced by Charles Grant who was then serving in Bengal. See Embree, *Charles Grant*, pp. 100–1.

a year in 1783.[102] By 1825 civil servants in Bengal who were not members of the Council earned, on average, just under £2,600 a year.[103]

The directors also became more inclined to cultivate the development of men who were capable of coming to terms with the Company's new responsibilities. During the 1770s Hastings had already begun to urge the use of administrative specialists who possessed more than the basic skills of the merchant,[104] and the directors themselves came to acknowledge that a lack of formal training remained a significant problem. As they observed in 1782, without any instruction servants tended to 'contract habits of idleness, conceive a contempt for many material parts of their duty, and when they advance in situation find themselves ignorant of the Company's concerns'.[105] Consequently, attempts were made to introduce rudimentary training and a system of promotion based upon merit as well as seniority. Thus in July 1785 the directors told the Bengal Council that 'in order that our junior servants may be properly trained to a knowledge of our affairs in the several departments we direct that they may distributed in the several public offices, and that the diligence and ability they may manifest therein be considered as the only road to appointments of greater consequence and emolument'.[106]

The need for proper education became a recurring theme during the late eighteenth century because there were obvious limitations to any system based on 'training by doing', and it became evident to the directors that a more formal method of instruction was required. This was recognised by others in the Company, and although the directors protested loudly against the enormous cost of the College of Fort William established in Calcutta by Richard Wellesley in 1800, the Governor-General's initiative in fact represented no more than the institutional manifestation of sentiments they themselves had been expressing since the 1760s. Indeed, during the mid-1790s the directors had been discussing the need for overseas servants to be trained in an establishment in Britain and, spurred into action by Wellesley, they responded by limiting his 'University of the East' to the teaching of Indian languages and instruction in the workings of the Company's local bureaucracies.

---

102 Marshall, *East Indian fortunes*, pp. 180, 182.
103 Calculated from details in *PP*, 1832, 735-1, pp. 758–65.
104 See, for example, his letter to Lord North, 2 April 1775, G. R. Gleig (ed.), *Memoirs of the life of the Right Hon. Warren Hastings, first Governor-General of Bengal*, 3 vols. (1841), vol. I, p. 539.
105 *FWIHC*, vol. IX, p. 79.
106 Ibid., p. 232.

Guided and prompted by the evangelical Charles Grant, the directors then created a college in Britain where 'principles of every kind were to be formed' and 'minds cultivated' through the study of European history, literature, natural philosophy, religion, and science, as well as more practical subjects such as accountancy, law, mathematics, and, notably, political economy, which was taught until 1834 by Thomas Malthus.[107] There was some place for Indian languages and Oriental studies in this ambitious and wide-ranging curriculum, but the overall aim was to provide a better stock of 'European acquirements' in order to create not just 'good servants' but also 'good subjects, and enlightened patriots' who would carry to India a 'reverence and love for The Religions, The Constitution, and Laws of their own country'. As has been noted, these ideas were to shape British attitudes towards India for years to come,[108] but in the short term it was hoped that the East India College would produce men who were better equipped to meet the practical administrative challenges of governing people and territory. As the College's prospectus put it in 1806, the Company servants had hitherto acted 'in the capacity of factors and merchants', but they were now required 'to administer, throughout their respective districts, an extensive system of finance; and to fill the important offices of Magistrates, Ambassadors, and Provincial Governors'.[109] These were widely acknowledged to be onerous responsibilities requiring a wide range of personal abilities, and thus when the East India College first opened its doors at Hertford Castle in February 1806 it was hoped that future civil servants would travel to India with rather more than private fortunes on their minds.

The establishment of the East India College was a very public expression of the directors' commitment to reform, improvement, and good government, and in the propaganda wars leading up to the renewal of the Company's charter in 1813 it helped to convince people that the Company was now fit to govern an empire. The establishment of the College also suggested to onlookers that the directors were beginning more effectively to shape the general attitudes of the Company's overseas servants by

---

107 For the *raison d'être* for the establishment of the College see 'Report of the Committee appointed to enquire into the plan for forming an establishment at home for the education of young men intended for the Company's civil service in India, 26 October 1804', printed in Anthony Farrington, *The records of the East India College Haileybury and other institutions* (1976), pp. 14–21. The following quotations are taken from this report. For the background to, and development of, the East India College see ibid., pp. 3–10.

108 Ibid., p. 7.

109 *A preliminary view of the establishment of the East India Company's establishment in Hertfordshire for the education of young persons appointed to the civil service in India* (1806).

inculcating them with prevailing metropolitan ideas of administrative order, efficiency, and purpose. Certainly better training and education, together with the payment of larger salaries, served to convert some to the view that the Company had managed to create a new breed of overseas servant whose standards and conduct were very different from those practised by the freebooters and adventurers of earlier years. It was claimed that the directors 'by a wise policy, in awarding a most ample provision to their public functionaries, have removed the temptation to offence, and have secured the fidelity of those in trust, by raising, in every well-constituted mind in their service, so general an abhorrence of abuse, as to render the practice of it dangerous, and consequently rare'.[110] This judgement may be taken with a large pinch of salt, but it does stand as testimony to the increasingly widespread belief that the directors had managed to curb the worst excesses of those serving the Company in India.

Historians must be wary of endorsing contemporary claims that the Company's government of India was rapidly transformed for the better from the 1780s onwards. Men such as Charles Grant who made bold assertions of improvement were themselves the architects of reform, and they were far from objective when they submitted reports to directors, ministers, and others.[111] During the 1820s a rather different view was put forward by some of the senior officials in India who encountered serious deficiencies in the civil administration and judicial systems, and they were especially critical of the poor quality of the Company's junior civil servants. Sir Charles Metcalfe was ferocious in his condemnation of the practical training offered to the new servants who arrived in Calcutta from Britain, and he argued that the College of Fort William did little other than promote idleness and extravagance; while Lord William Bentinck took the view that the payment of large salaries to Company servants had only encouraged them to borrow large amounts of money and pile up huge debts.[112] To reform-minded men such as these, the Company's Indian administration of the 1820s had not yet undergone a permanent and deep-rooted transformation for the better but, having said that, even sceptical onlookers were prepared to concede that Company rule was no longer characterised by the gross excesses and abuses that had been evident

---

110 Anon., *Observations on the territorial rights*, p. 4.
111 See, for example, Embree, *Charles Grant*, p. 178.
112 See Metcalfe's minutes on the College of Fort William, 28 December 1828, printed in *Bentinck correspondence*, vol. I, pp. 124–7, and Bentinck to John Loch, 12 August 1828, ibid., p. 62.

during the 1760s. This suggested to some that things could have been good deal worse for the people of India, particularly if consideration was given to alternative forms of British imperial rule. In 1829 it was reported that Sir Charles Forbes, who had long experience of Bombay, had 'remarked that it was a matter of congratulation to the natives of India that they were under the Company's government rather than the King's',[113] and Joseph Hume made the same point four years later. He told the Company's stockholders that as well as serving the Company in India he had visited many colonies of the Crown, 'and the result of his experience was that, bad as the government [of India] was when he was there, it was infinitely superior to the state of government of the Crown'.[114]

It had once been routine to condemn Company misrule in general and the failings of the directors in particular, but there was a growing willingness to concede that those at East India House were doing their best to tackle the near-impossible task of supervising far-distant territories and employees. And as some observers pointed out, few could take issue with the contents of the orders and instructions sent to India. One reform-minded Member of Parliament wrote during the early 1780s that although the directors had not always been wholly competent it could not be denied that 'upon a fair review of their dispatches for sixty years back, that they have generally given their orders with precision and dignity; that they have distinguished between good and bad servants; and they have reprobated oppressive acts and wanton usurpations'. Indeed, he suggested that the imperial record of the Company was rather better than that of those who governed the nation's affairs, and he pointed out that 'when our western dominion [in North America] was crumbling away under the management of ministers, conquests were made over our national enemies, and India has at least been preserved under that of the Company'.[115] At the very end of its days, over seventy years later, the Company itself made exactly the same point in a petition to the House of Lords, when it emphasised that its 'civil and military servants originally acquired for this country its magnificent empire in the East . . . at the same period when a succession of administrations under the control of Parliament

---

113 *Review of the arguments and allegations which have been offered to Parliament against the renewal of the East India Company's charter* (1829), p. 37.
114 *Debates at the General Court of Proprietors* (1833), p. 139.
115 'A Member of Parliament', *Review of the question concerning the government of the British possessions in India* (?1783), pp. 15, 21.

were losing to the Crown of Great Britain another great Empire on the opposite side of the Atlantic'.[116] Exhibiting a strong degree of corporate pride and self-confidence that did not appear to have been unduly shaken by the recent Indian Uprising of 1857, the directors pointed to the fact that, unlike ministers, they and their predecessors had achieved their primary aim, which had been to secure the 'permanency' of the Company's overseas possessions.

---

116 Quoted in Alan Ryan, 'Utilitarianism and bureaucracy: the views of J. S. Mill', in Gillian Sutherland (ed.), *Studies in the growth of nineteenth-century government* (1972), p. 49.

CHAPTER 8

Methods: the management of trade

During the late eighteenth century the directors of the East India Company were obliged to devote ever greater amounts of time and attention to the problems of empire, but they could ill-afford to neglect their supervision of the Company's commercial affairs. It was very much a case of business as usual and commodities were procured, cargoes assembled, and ships despatched in time-honoured fashion. The management of the Company's trade was, however, far from unaffected by the acquisition of empire because events in Bengal during the 1760s caused the whole nature and purpose of the East India trade to be altered as an attempt was made to secure the transfer of 'tribute' from India to Britain. In 1765, as a parliamentary committee later put it, 'a very great revolution took place in commerce as well as dominion' and a 'new way of supplying the market of Europe, by means of British power and influence was invented'.[1] This commercial 'revolution' – the ploughing of revenue surplus into enlarged investment in commodities for shipment to Britain – was far from successful, however, and when the Company was plunged into a series of deep financial crises during the 1770s and 1780s the directors were held to have squandered a glorious opportunity to strengthen the nation's wealth and prosperity. At the same time, they were blamed for a failure to expand exports and there was a growing clamour of opposition to the Company from the supporters of free trade who believed that private merchants were better equipped to exploit markets in Asia. The charge sheet against the directors thus grew to be a lengthy one. Their methods were seen to be ineffective and they were widely condemned for a lack of vision, knowledge, commercial acumen, and, above all, entrepreneurial spirit. Their

---

1 *Ninth report of the select committee, appointed to take into consideration the state of the administration of justice in the provinces of Bengal, Bahar, and Orissa* (1783), reprinted in Paul Langford (general ed.), *The writings and speeches of Edmund Burke*, vol. V: P. J. Marshall (ed.), *India: Madras and Bengal* (Oxford, 1981), p. 223.

collective failings were held to represent all that was wrong with obsolete monopoly practices, and consequently it seems hardly surprising that, against a political background in which free-trade doctrines were gathering strength, the Company lost its India trade monopoly in 1813 and then twenty years later was deprived of its China trade privileges.

As with contemporaries, historians have often been harsh in their assessment of the East India Company's late eighteenth-century commercial performance, and especially sharp criticism has been levelled at the directors for a supposed failure to pay much attention to the export of British raw materials and manufactures to Asia. Furber, for example, referred to the 'farcical nature' of the Company's role as an exporter, with the export of metals to India only being undertaken as a 'gesture'; while Parkinson portrayed the Company as a somewhat unwilling exporter that only shipped out woollens and metals to Asia because it was obliged to do so by Parliament.[2] More recently, a detailed study by Om Prakash of European trade with India before 1800 makes no mention at all of the Company's late eighteenth-century commodity exports, and the implication to be drawn from this is that such exports were of little importance in the overall scheme of things.[3] It is certainly true that East Indiamen did sometimes sail to the east in ballast, and the Company often encountered great difficulty when trying to sell its woollens and metals in Asia, but it would be quite wrong to conclude that the directors were only interested in stimulating the growth of imports into Britain.

A negative view of the Company's export trade needs to be reconciled with detailed studies indicating that, on the whole, the Company's business activity was managed in an efficient and careful manner. For the period before 1760, Chaudhuri has reconstructed a sophisticated and well-regulated commercial system, and Mui and Mui have presented a very favourable assessment of the Company's conduct of its tea trade after 1784.[4] These works establish that the methods of the directors and officials in London were careful, thorough, and well planned, and it is thus necessary to explore whether this assessment can be applied to all branches

2 Holden Furber, *John Company at work: a study of European expansion in India in the late eighteenth century* (Cambridge, Mass., 1951), p. 285; C. N. Parkinson, *Trade in the Eastern seas, 1793–1813* (Cambridge, 1937), p. 75.

3 Om Prakash, *European commercial enterprise in pre-colonial India*, The New Cambridge History of India, vol. II. 5 (Cambridge, 1988).

4 K. N. Chaudhuri, *The trading world of Asia and the English East India Company, 1660–1760* (Cambridge, 1978). Hoh-cheung Mui and Lorna H. Mui, *The management of monopoly. A study of the East India Company's conduct of its tea trade, 1784–1833* (Vancouver, 1984).

of the Company's trading activity for the years after 1756. In addressing this important question, there can certainly be no denying that serious strategic mistakes were made by the directors, especially before 1785, but they did not leave many stones unturned in their efforts to expand the Company's trade, and the outcome of their efforts can be seen in the long-run growth of imports *and* exports that occurred before the effects of the loss of monopoly were eventually felt during the 1820s. The very fact that this growth was achieved in the face of immense difficulties arising from repeated disruptions to trade caused by war suggests that the directors were not perhaps the hapless incompetents often ridiculed by private merchants and manufacturers.

It must be stressed that this chapter does not aim to provide a comprehensive analysis of the development of the East India trade after 1756. Such an examination would require a book-length study of interrelated activities in India and China, and several distinguished works have already explored different aspects of the Company's overseas commercial activities.[5] Instead, the focus here is very much on the directors in London and how they sought to address the considerable challenge that was posed to their management of the Company's trade by the acquisition of an empire in India. Thus, the opening section of the chapter considers the extent to which the directors' pursuit of an inappropriate and misguided strategy after 1765 caused the domestic commercial and financial misfortunes that befell the Company during the 1770s and 1780s. The section then examines the ways in which the directors eventually absorbed the harsh lesson that the acquisition of territorial revenues in Bengal did not translate easily into the realisation of commercial profit in London. In the second section, closer attention is paid to the import trade with a view to establishing how the directors' policies served to alter the distribution profile of the goods shipped into Britain. A third section evaluates the

---

5 The main features are detailed in Marshall, *Problems of empire*, pp. 78–101. There are many studies of the Company's trade during this period, but, in addition to those noted above, the following remain indispensable to students of the subject and have, by and large, stood the test of time: V. T. Harlow, *The founding of the second British empire 1763–93*, 2 vols. (1952 and 1964); Michael Greenberg, *British trade and the opening of China, 1800–1842* (Cambridge, 1951); Amales Tripathi, *Trade and finance in the Bengal Presidency 1793–1833* (second edition, Calcutta, 1979); H. R. C. Wright, *East Indian economic problems in the age of Cornwallis and Raffles* (1961). Much light is thrown on British commercial activity at Canton in H. B. Morse, *Chronicles of the East India Company trading to China, 1635–1834*, 5 vols. (1926–9); and Earl H. Pritchard, 'Private trade between England and China in the eighteenth century (1680–1833)', *Journal of the Economic and Social History of the Orient*, I (1958), pp. 111–37, 222–55.

charge that the directors lacked a spirit of commercial enterprise and were unwilling or reluctant to dedicate themselves to an expansion of British exports to Asia. A final section then examines how the directors responded to the Company's loss of its Indian trade monopoly in 1813.

REVENUE, BULLION, AND THE SWING TO CHINA

There can be little doubt that the directors committed a number of serious errors during the late 1760s when they abandoned many of the commercial strategies that had generated steady profits for the Company during the previous half-century or so. After the signing of the Peace of Paris in 1763, the Company had made determined efforts to restore its commercial investment and activities to the levels of the early 1750s, but this promised only a slow recovery to a position that had been badly damaged by the Seven Years War. It was thus hardly surprising that the directors responded with undisguised delight in April 1766 when they were presented with news of the acquisition of the *diwani*. Like many modern-day lottery winners, they proclaimed that a windfall would not alter them, but new and unexpected riches soon profoundly changed their outlook and economic behaviour. The commercial actions and calculations of the directors had long been characterised by an innate sense of caution and conservatism, together with a strong commitment to orthodox accounting principles, and this meant that they had always adhered to carefully considered investment strategies. Now, however, they embarked on an ill-advised dash for growth, in which they sought to take immediate advantage of the Company's military success in Bengal by utilising local revenue surpluses for increased levels of investment in Indian and Chinese goods for export to Britain.

Although the directors were not easily taken in by reports that the acquisition of the *diwani* would realise untold riches, a review of reports from Bengal did nevertheless suggest to them in November 1766 'the probability of their having such a flow of cash there as will render it necessary to open every channel for its centering here'.[6] They urged their servants in Bengal to invest much more heavily in cotton piece goods and raw silk, with the importation of the latter described as being of 'national benefit and the consumption more unlimited than that of manufactured

6 IOR, D/24 (18 November 1766).

goods'.[7] The directors framed their commercial instructions accordingly,[8] and it was ordered that resources should be diverted from Calcutta to the Company's other Indian Presidencies, and to Canton via Madras.

The reason for the enhanced importance of the Canton trade was spelled out to those in India when they were told that 'for bringing home through that channel, as large a proportion of the produce of our Bengal revenues as can be done, we wish to have the cargoes of the China ships as valuable as possible'.[9] In order to underline the point, the authorities in Calcutta were later told that trade with China had become a 'national concern wherein the revenue is very materially interested'.[10] Consequently, the directors ordered that considerable resources be ploughed into the trade between India and China. In May 1767 the Madras Council shipped to Canton 24 lakhs of current rupees (c.£300,000) that had been consigned to them from Calcutta, and six months later they were told that a similar sum should be exported the following season.[11] Such a policy certainly gave the Company's supercargoes greater funds with which to purchase tea and silk, but this was achieved at considerable cost in India. As early as May 1767, the Madras Council was complaining to the supercargoes that 'The Coast and Bengal have long laboured under great inconveniences from the continual drains which have been made from both, for the China investment', and they expressed the forlorn hope that the increased balances calculated to be accumulating at Canton might preclude the need for any further exports of silver.[12]

The immediate effect of the acquisition of the territorial revenues upon the conduct of the Company's trade was felt in several other ways, most notably in the composition of cargoes despatched from Britain to India and China.[13] As is well known, the Company's long-standing efforts to

---

7 Directors to Bengal, 16 March 1768, *FWIHC*, vol. V, pp. 80–1. For the directors' schemes to increase the production of raw silk in Bengal see Bowen, *Revenue and reform*, pp. 106–7.

8 The detailed instructions and commercial policy guidelines first established in response to the acquisition of the revenues sent are set out in the lengthy despatch sent to Bengal on 21 November 1766, *FWIHC*, vol. IV, pp. 196–219.

9 Directors to Bengal, 21 November 1766, ibid., vol. IV, p. 207.

10 Ibid. vol. V, p. 136 (11 November 1768).

11 R/10/6, p. 9; In May 1766 the directors had ordered that 40 lakhs of rupees be sent from Bengal to Madras, from where the silver was to be divided equally among the Company and country ships destined for Canton in the next season (Directors to Madras, 17 May 1766, E/4/863, p. 383).

12 R/10/6, p.9. As early as 30 September 1765 Clive had noted the importance of encouraging the trade of other European companies with Bengal so that they could supply bullion to replace that being shipped to Canton by the British Company (*FWIHC*, vol. IV, p. 338).

13 For a number of strategies designed to reduce the amount of unused specie held in the Company's Indian treasuries see D/24 (16 October, 6, 7, 18 November, and 30 December 1766).

find overseas markets for wool textiles and metals had met with only
partial success, and this had always dictated that export cargoes contained
large amounts of silver bullion to balance the trade between Britain and
Asia. The value of this bullion had been considerable, and the 'treasure'
worth £6,492,473 shipped out during the 1750s had accounted for almost
two-thirds of the Company exports.[14] This practice had long been denounced by critics who condemned the East India trade as a 'losing' trade
that simply exchanged the nation's precious metals for luxury items of
dubious worth, and because the directors were sensitive to such criticism
they endeavoured whenever possible to reduce exports of bullion. As the
directors reported to John Pownall, the Secretary to the Lords of Trade, in
1763, they strove to 'send out as large proportions of the produce of Great
Britain in preference to bullion and gold as they possibly can'.[15] Consequently, even before the acquisition of the *diwani* the directors had cut
back their exports of bullion and, although some consignments were sent
to China during the early 1760s, silver was not despatched to India. No
bullion was shipped to anywhere in Asia in 1766 and 1767, but consignments to the value of between £152,055 and £294,300 a year were sent to
Canton between 1768 and 1771 in order to fund the tea trade. Thereafter,
the only shipment of bullion to China from London before 1785 was a
small amount sent in 1776, despite the fact that a growing scarcity of
specie in India obliged the Company to rely increasingly heavily upon
private 'country' traders for the supply of liquid funds to the supercargoes
at Canton.[16] Very little silver was sent to India after 1757, and none at all
was despatched to Bengal. Indeed, between 1757 and 1785, far more
bullion was sent to the Company's factory at Benkulen (Sumatra) than
to the whole of India (see figure 8.1).[17]

The directors' sharp reduction of bullion exports represented the
abandonment of a practice that had long defined the conduct of British

---

14 Calculated from Chaudhuri, *Trading world of Asia*, p. 507. Between 1700 and 1757 treasure
    always represented more than 65 per cent of the value of export cargoes, and often more than 80
    per cent (ibid., p. 512).
15 E/1/211, p. 432.
16 P. J. Marshall, *East Indian fortunes: the British in Bengal in the eighteenth century* (Oxford, 1976),
    pp. 97–9. The Company's failure to send bullion to China from Britain between 1773 and 1785 is
    sometimes attributed to the difficulty of obtaining silver in wartime, but in fact the directors'
    aim during those years was to supply Canton from India.
17 The figures are computed from details of consignments of silver in the Company's Commerce
    Journals (L/AG/1/6, vols. 14–29). Details of bullion exports to each of the Indian Presidencies
    were presented to Parliament in 1813 but they contain some notable errors and omissions (*PP*,
    1812–13, vol. VIII, p. 401).

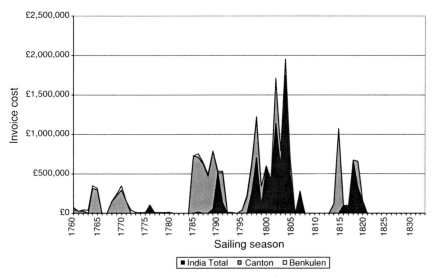

Figure 8.1. East India Company exports of silver, 1760–1833.
Source: L/AG/14/6, vols. 14–29.

trade with the East Indies. Yet although the directors were decisive in this particular action, they were deeply uncertain about how best to achieve their overall aim of remitting wealth to Britain. Consistency and clarity of purpose had previously defined commercial policy, but dangerously mixed messages were now sent to the Company's servants in India. The most graphic illustration of this came when the directors ignored warnings about the drain of specie from Bengal and in January 1768 ordered that silver worth £500,000 be shipped to London because it was proving impossible to invest it in goods for export. Those in Calcutta were told that 'as specie laying dead in your Treasury is equally locked up from circulation as if brought home we do not see how the country can be injured by it'.[18] Only a year later, however, the acute shortage of currency in Bengal obliged the directors to address a serious problem of their own making by instructing those in Calcutta to buy the 'great quantities' of silver imported by other European companies so that the China trade could be properly funded.[19] This sharp change of direction serves as an example of how commercial policy could now alter quite dramatically

18 *FWIHC*, vol. XIV, pp. 17, 18.
19 Ibid, vol. V, p. 174.

from one year to the next, and it also highlights the tensions that existed within the Company's commercial system as the directors sought to adapt their trade to the primary purpose of revenue transfer. Early concerns about these policies were voiced by well-informed observers such Harry Verelst who replaced Clive as Governor of Bengal in 1767 and was then confronted with the damaging local economic effects of decisions arising from the directors' all-consuming preoccupation with revenue transfer.[20]

It is evident that the directors' immediate post-1765 commercial strategy was underpinned by a belief that a large revenue surplus could be used to prime the pump of Company trade. Yet it soon became clear that Clive and others had exaggerated the size of the revenues, and it also proved impossible to sustain increased levels of collection. Against a darkening background of recession in Bengal and the great famine of 1769–70, the Company's revenue receipts began to fall steadily from an early peak of £3,954,079 in 1766/7.[21] In overall terms, the total net income derived from the Bengal revenues between 1766 and 1781 amounted to almost £38 million, with just under £5 million being collected elsewhere in India,[22] but these sums were well short of what had been anticipated during the mid-1760s. More importantly, wartime necessity had dictated use of the revenues to defray rising civil and military costs, and thus a calculation produced by the director Francis Baring suggested that between 1766 and 1778 less than one-fifth of the Company's total income from territorial revenue had been applied to investment in goods for export to Britain.[23]

Baring offered a statistical indication of how difficult it was for the Company to sustain any growth of its trade by using financial inputs derived from surplus revenues. Conflict with Indian powers and European rivals had served to upset the calculations, and as a widely circulated

20 For Verelst's calculations on the shortage of specie in Bengal see ibid., vol. V, pp. 549–50. Unsurprisingly, the effects of Company policy upon the Bengal economy have received considerable attention from scholars. For very different interpretations of the extent and effects of Company bullion imports see, for example, Rajat Datta, *Society, economy and the market: commercialization in rural Bengal c.1760–1800* (New Delhi, 2000) and Irfan Habib, 'The eighteenth century in Indian economic history', in P. J. Marshall (ed.), *The eighteenth century in Indian history. Evolution or revolution?* (New Delhi, 2003), pp. 100–19.

21 Figures produced in March 1784 by John Annis, Auditor of Indian Accounts, in 'Report from the select committee appointed to examine the reports of the directors of the East India Company', H/343, p. 117.

22 Ibid., p. 127.

23 H/338, p. 1. Baring arrived at the figure of £6,945,447 by deducting the value of the 'supply' (i.e. exports from Britain plus bills of exchange issued in India) from the total amount of the Company's investment in goods in India. He calculated that in two years, 1766 and 1771, imports were 'deficient'.

printed paper prepared on behalf of the General Court noted in 1783, 'The war in India has for some years past not only exhausted the whole revenue in India, which used to supply the investment for India and China . . . but has also been a very heavy burden upon the Company's trade.'[24] The authorities in India had been left with no choice other than to raise loans and issue a large number of bills of exchange in order to fund the purchase of goods for export,[25] but heavy losses of shipping between 1780 and 1783 then badly disrupted the flow of commodities to Britain.[26] This underlines how fragile the Company's trade and revenue operations could be during times of war, yet hopes were still entertained that a substantial revenue surplus could be generated following the return of peace. In 1783 the General Court expressed the belief that the Company's peacetime civil and military expenses would amount to no more than £3.1 million, a figure that would be comfortably offset by non-commercial income in India of over £5 million.[27]

Such thoughts became orthodox in Company and government circles, and the directors made optimistic assessments about the extent to which revenue income might be increased in the absence of 'all the calamities and obstructions occasioned by the war'.[28] Consequently, hopes were entertained that a significant revenue surplus could still be remitted to Britain through the Company's trade, and as late as 1802–3 the directors and the new President of the Board, Lord Castlereagh, still believed that a quarter of the Company's £4 million investment in Indian and Chinese goods might be funded from surplus revenues.[29] Again, however, this was wishful thinking, occasioned by news of momentary return to peace in the middle of Wellesley's wars, and over the next decade an overall deficit was usually recorded for the combined Indian Presidencies.[30]

24 *State of affairs of the East India Company in England on 19 November 1783 and according to the latest advices from overseas* (1783), H/340, p. 10.
25 The Committee of Secrecy had endorsed this action in August 1781 in response to 'truly disagreeable and alarming' news about the war which threatened a 'stoppage of the Company's investment' (L/P&S/1, vol. 5, part 3, p. 23).
26 Fifteen vessels were lost during this period.
27 *State of affairs*, p. 9.
28 *Report of the Court of Directors in obedience to an order of the House of Commons* (23 January 1784), p. 15.
29 For a paper of 1793 see H/399, pp. 186–91, and for the calculations of 1802–3 see H/500, pp. 104–5, 187; Directors to Bengal, 1 June 1803, *Third report from the select committee on the affairs of the East India Company* (1811), *PP*, 1810–11 (250), vol. XII, p. 411. When Dundas presented his last East India budget in June 1801 he also believed that a 'full million' from the surplus could still be applied to the investment in goods (L/AG/11/1, vol. 1, p. 1010).
30 *Second report from the select committee* (1810), pp. 78–9.

While optimistic noises continued to be made about the possibilities of transferring tribute from India to Britain, harder-headed assessments of the Company's performance since 1765 painted a gloomy picture, which suggested that the directors were failing in their duty to the stockholders and the nation at large. Critics delighted in pointing out that the steady profits of the early eighteenth century had disappeared and doubts were raised about whether the territorial revenues represented any form of economic prize at all.[31] A common refrain of the early 1780s was that East Indian commercial affairs were not now founded upon proper mercantile principles, and a parliamentary committee of inquiry led by Edmund Burke was emphatic in its declaration of 1783 that 'the principles and oeconomy of the Company's trade have been . . . completely corrupted by turning it into a vehicle for tribute'.[32] As Thomas Pownall put it, the 'first origin' of the Company's financial difficulties or 'evil' was that it had forsaken the traditional role of the merchant.[33] The directors had made the funding of the Company's trade almost entirely dependent on the Bengal revenues, and when those revenues failed to deliver the expected returns the Company's remodelled commercial and financial system moved steadily towards the point of collapse.

Under growing pressure from their critics, the directors gradually returned to the use of more conventional commercial strategies. In particular, they acted in close partnership with Pitt's government to stimulate the growth of the tea trade. As part of a co-ordinated strategy, a sharp reduction in tea duties was implemented in 1784, together with a reduction in price, thereby temporarily defeating smugglers who had been shipping in large quantities of cheap, duty-free tea from the Continent. At the same time, attempts were made to generate the substantial additional funds that were necessary for larger purchases of tea at Canton, and the directors and ministers developed a range of commercial schemes in the East Asia and Pacific region.[34] Much closer attention was paid to trade between India and China, although the directors would not go so far as to

---

31 'An old proprietor', manuscript 'Reflections on the Company's trade, possessions and present state of commerce in the East Indies, with some hints relative to a reform thereof' (1784), H/211, p. 120.

32 *Ninth report of the select committee*, in Marshall (ed.), *Writings and speeches of Burke*, vol. V, p. 241.

33 Thomas Pownall, *The right, interest, and duty of government, as concerned in the affairs of the East Indies* . . . (revised edition 1781), p. 3.

34 Alan Frost, *The global reach of empire. Britain's maritime expansion in the Indian and Pacific oceans, 1764–1815* (Melbourne, 2003), chs. 6 and 7; Harlow, *Founding of the second British Empire*, vol. II, chs. 8 and 9.

sanction Company involvement in trafficking opium because this was prohibited by the Chinese authorities. They had already made the famously disingenuous declaration that 'it is beneath the Company to be engaged in such a clandestine trade',[35] but they did now encourage those in Calcutta to explore alternative ways of ensuring the supply of Bengal opium to the China market, through private trade conducted via Indonesia.[36] The directors acknowledged, however, that the currently weak state of the Bengal economy meant that it could contribute little to the China investment, and thus in 1786 they sanctioned the export of a small amount of bullion to Bombay in order to fund the purchase of 500 tons of cotton for shipment to Canton on the Company's account.[37] This decision marked the beginning of a sustained attempt to enlarge the Company's trade between western India and China, and it helped to ensure the survival of the hitherto rather vulnerable and neglected Bombay Presidency.[38]

The shipment of a consignment of silver to Bombay in 1786 marked the resumption of exports of bullion to India and more was to follow. In 1791 Governor-General Cornwallis was told that £514,227 of silver sent to Madras during the previous season had been part of an attempt to 'strengthen your treasury by every means in our power',[39] and large sums were sent in the years that followed (see figure 8.1). In 1805, for example, 'the great scarcity of funds' in India was such that the directors decided to send shipments of £400,000 silver to Bengal.[40] In total, almost £3.9 million was sent to Bengal between 1800 and 1806, but although such consignments of silver to India were essentially emergency actions

---

35 *FWIHC*, vol. IX, p. 61.

36 Ibid., vol. X, pp. 208–9. For the trade in opium see Wright, *East Indian economic problems*, pp. 106–65 and Richard Connors, 'Opium and imperial expansion: the East India Company in eighteenth-century Asia', in Stephen Taylor, Richard Connors, and Clyve Jones (eds.), *Hanoverian Britain and empire. Essays in memory of Philip Lawson* (Woodbridge, 1998), pp. 248–66.

37 Minutes of Secret Committee, 1 June 1786, L/P&S/1/9, ff. 143–4. For a detailed plan which suggested that the Company should take complete control of the 'country trade' between Western India and China see H/340, pp. 359–67.

38 For the background to the decision, and the important part played by Henry Dundas, see Pamela Nightingale, *Trade and empire in western India, 1784–1806* (Cambridge, 1970), pp. 47–55.

39 *FWIHC*, vol. XI, p. 174.

40 Minutes of Secret Committee of Treasury, 8 May and 18 September 1805, L/AG/9/5, vol. 1 (no pagination). Some bullion sent to India for commercial purposes was also appropriated by the authorities to shore up the Company's military finances, as happened between 1802 and 1804 (Minutes of 26 January 1808, ibid.).

intended to relieve wartime pressures, occasional shipments were made as part of attempts to increase the export of Indian cotton to China.[41]

The directors also believed, however, that the direct export of silver to China would provide them with the most effective means of procuring the greatly increased quantities of tea that were required for the home market. It was thought that the arrival of large amounts of bullion at Canton would 'impress the Chinese with a confidence in the stability of the Company, and their capacity to fulfil commercial engagements of such magnitude'.[42] As a result, consignments of silver amounting to £3,257,783 were sent to China between 1785 and 1789, and the directors encouraged the private export of silver to Canton where it could be loaned to the Company in return for bills of exchange.[43] Not all of this silver reached its intended destination because some of it was appropriated by the authorities in India to be used in the Company's war against Tipu Sultan,[44] but by 1793 the directors were able to declare that the 'treasury in China was so abundant as to have rendered the export of bullion for commercial purposes, during the last season, totally unnecessary'.[45] Even so, bullion was again used to provide a large injection of funds for the China trade in the years 1795–1800, 1802–6, and 1814–16, and this meant that between 1760 and 1833 just over half of all the Company exports of silver were directed to Canton (table 8.1).[46]

The resumption of bullion shipments to Asia during the late 1780s meant that the Company's trade reverted to a form that was similar to that which had existed during the first half of the century, but an important difference lay in the fact that much more attention was now paid to the export of commodities from Britain than had been the case during the 1760s and 1770s. In part this occurred because the directors needed to provide funds for the purchase of tea, and thus between 1785 and 1790 there were sharp increases in the volume and value of broadcloth, serge or long ells, and copper sent to Asia. At the same time, however, pressures exerted by ministers, via the Board of Trade, and those who were advocates of a

---

41 Directors to Bombay, 22 August 1804, Commercial letters, 4, p. 266, MSA. A further £1.36 million was despatched to Bengal between 1816 and 1820 as part of a strategy to relieve the Company's debt in India (see the Directors to Bengal, 7 January 1820, E/4/698, p. 15).

42 H/400, p. 245.

43 L/AG/10/2, vol. 2, p. 68.

44 Bengal to Directors, 31 July 1790, *FWIHC*, vol. XI, p. 335. The Council had empowered the authorities at Madras to remove £70,000 silver from the ships en route to Canton.

45 H/400, p. 244.

46 Some of the bullion that accumulated in the Canton treasury was, however, despatched to India in order to relieve wartime financial pressures. Consequently, between 1792 and 1809, £1,310,318 was sent from China to India (*Third report* (1811), p. 394).

Table 8.1. *East India Company exports of silver, 1760–1833*

Destination	Invoice cost (£)	% of total
Bengal	5,338,267	29.2
Madras	1,155,836	6.3
Bombay	1,766,167	9.7
'India'	264,910	1.4
Canton	9,204,439	50.3
Benkulen	559,562	3.1
Total	18,289,181	100

Note: Totals have been calculated from details of individual ships' cargoes. In addition, £50,000 silver was sent to St Helena in 1819, and some small quantities of gold were sent to India. Not all of the silver arrived at the intended destination stated in the Commerce Journals (see, for example, note 45), and some was lost to shipwreck and capture by the enemy. The entry under 'India' relates to consignments made in four ships in season 1797. In the event, all of these ships sailed in season 1798 to Madras and Bombay, but it is not clear where the silver was eventually unloaded.
Source: L/AG/1/6, vols. 14–29.

more open trade with India, prompted the directors to review their export activity. As such, this marked the beginning of a long-run process in which the directors were obliged to come to terms with increasing levels of domestic competition in the East India trade, and they responded by adopting a commercial strategy that paid much closer attention to the commodities they despatched to India and China.

The new strategy of the directors emerged in response to several proposals made by one of their number, David Scott, who had gathered valuable experience as a partner in a Bombay Agency House. Scott was a close ally of Henry Dundas who acted as a champion of private trade and endeavoured to open the East India trade in the belief that much greater benefit could be brought to British merchants and manufacturers. Yet he also found it found politically expedient to suggest ways in which the Company might expand its own export trade in the face of stiff competition from foreigners and illicit traders.[47] Scott, it was said by Dundas, was aiming to make the directors 'act in a very new character, I mean to make them think now and then as merchants, in place of viewing themselves only in the light of sovereigns and great generals'.[48] Consideration

47 For a detailed discussion of the plans of Scott and the pressure applied on the Company by the ministry see Harlow, *Founding of the second British empire*, vol. II, pp. 499–526.
48 Quoted in Jean Sutton, *Lords of the east. The East India Company and its ships (1600–1874)* (second edition, 2002), p. 33.

of his proposals occupied a great deal of time between 1787 and 1790, and although the directors baulked at some of the more radical ideas they agreed that it was essential that 'a quantity of European goods etc sufficient for the consumption of India are exported by the Company or by individuals authorized for that purpose'.[49] Consequently, while they conceded that some surplus tonnage should be offered to individuals, they also sought to provide a 'sufficiency' of goods for India and China. It was acknowledged that the export of woollens to India could not be increased, so an 'augmentation' was not thought possible, but it was believed that shipments of copper to Asia could be doubled, with most of that metal being directed to India where there was believed to be a large market. At the same time, an increased volume of long ells were to be sent to Canton, and a renewed attempt was to be made to find markets there for worsted 'stuffs' and tin.

Not all of the directors endorsed this strategy,[50] but the 1790s began with a reinvigorated export trade. Commodity exports had already increased between 1785 and 1790, and following the partial adoption of Scott's proposals they were boosted again between 1790 and 1792 (see figure 8.2). There was a threefold increase in consignments of long ells, and worsted stuffs and tin were both exported in significant quantities for the first time. As a result, when the government ordered the directors to prepare a series of reports on the Company's export trade in 1791, they responded with a cautiously optimistic assessment of future prospects, especially with regard to the trade with China.[51] The export of British commodities to Canton, in particular, was not as limited as some historians have suggested, and it played an important role in supporting the Company's purchase of a greater volume of Chinese goods for shipment to London.[52] Even so, it was later shown that the amount of woollens and metals sent to Canton was considerably in excess of that actually requested by the supercargoes, and between 1794 and 1809 there were regular

---

49 Report from a special committee of directors, 22 July 1789, H/404, p. 290.
50 See, for example, the dissent of Francis Baring entered on the minutes of the Court of Directors in August 1790 (B/111, p. 386). Baring was opposed to increasing the export of copper and tin because he believed it would only add to the Company's financial difficulties.
51 Between 1791 and 1793 a select committee of directors produced five reports on different aspects of the Company's trade. Manuscript and printed copies of these important reports are to be found in H/400 and H/401.
52 This point is made by Ward who correctly criticises the view that the expansion of the Company's China trade was wholly dependent upon the sale of Indian cotton and opium at Canton, J. R. Ward, 'The industrial revolution and British imperialism, 1750–1850', *Ec. Hist. Rev.*, 47 (1994), pp. 55–7.

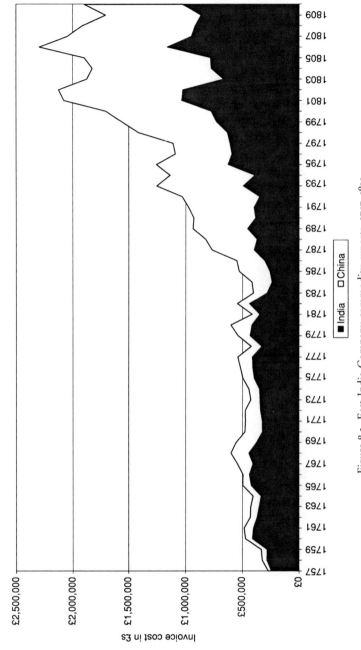

Figure 8.2. East India Company commodity exports, 1757–1810.
Source: PP, 1812–13, vol. VIII, p. 402.

complaints that the Chinese market was being heavily overstocked from London.[53] The supercargoes often struggled to sell all of the Company's goods, and they were obliged to use a 'truck' system to dispose of woollens in exchange for tea. Nevertheless, a renewed belief that the Company was capable of sustaining an expanding export trade enabled the directors to face with some confidence the challenges that were made to them as their monopoly privileges came under heavy political fire from 1790 onwards. Even though great difficulties were caused by war in Europe and Asia, the value of goods sent to India and China reached new peaks during the first decade of the nineteenth century.

That the late eighteenth-century expansion of the Company's export trade was based upon China was in part reflected by the fact that between 1785 and 1810 cargoes despatched to Canton accounted for 53.6 per cent of the invoice value of all commodities sent to Asia. This was in marked contrast with the 1750s when less than 11 per cent of all commodity exports had been directed to China.[54] The growth of the China trade was most evident, however, in a much increased volume of imports from Asia, caused primarily by the shipment of greater amounts of tea from Canton. In turn, sales of tea in London greatly boosted the overall level of income that the Company derived from its imports, as can be seen in figure 8.3. This altered the entire geographical profile of the Company trade, and during the first decade of the nineteenth century China was elevated to a position of primary importance, with goods from Canton accounting for 67 per cent of all sale income earned in London between 1803 and 1808.[55] This underlines the extent to which the directors had been successful in their post-1785 efforts to increase the volume of trade with China, and by doing this they had made Canton the linchpin of the Indian remittance system. As a result, in 1812 a parliamentary committee was able to claim without fear of contradiction that in commercial terms China was now the 'most important branch of the Company's concerns'.[56]

IMPORTS: SALES AND RETURNS

Judged solely in terms of the cargoes passing between Britain and Asia, the directors' efforts to expand the Company's trade can be seen to have met with some success, and this helped to enhance the position of 'East

53 *Fourth report from the select committee* (1812), pp. 463–7.
54 *PP*, 1812–13, vol. VIII, p. 402.
55 *First report from the select committee* (1808), pp. 60–1.
56 *Fourth report from the select committee* (1812), p. 418.

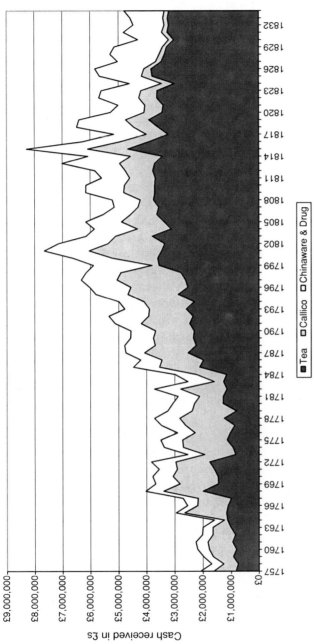

Figure 8.3. East India Company sale income, 1757–1833.

Source: L/AG/1/5, vols. 17–34.

Note: Company sale income was recorded in three separate ledgers. As its name suggests, the 'Tea ledger' contained details of all tea sales. The 'Callico ledger' recorded sales of all Indian cotton textiles, but it also detailed income from the sale of wrought silks as well as nankeens and Canton cloths imported from China. The 'Chinaware and Drug ledger', which by the early nineteenth century was known simply as the 'Drug ledger', noted sales of a wide variety of commodities. These included drugs, peppers, and spices, but over time the range broadened significantly to include bulk items such as raw silk, saltpetre, indigo, sugar, rice, and cotton. The ledgers themselves have not survived, but figures derived from them were abstracted and then recorded in the Cash Journals and thus it is possible to calculate total Company income from the sale of commodities in London.

India' within British overseas trade as a whole, but this was ultimately of little benefit to the Company unless the sale of goods in London could be increased in order to generate an ever greater flow of cash into the treasury at East India House. There was no point in importing commodities into Britain if nobody wished to buy them, and therefore considerable attention had to be paid to domestic demand. As had always been the case, therefore, the directors relayed very detailed commercial instructions to their servants in India and China in the hope that they would purchase goods of sufficient quantity and appropriate quality.

Much depended upon the commercial acumen and methods adopted by the Company's representatives in Asia, but the directors sought to leave as little as possible to chance by very precisely defining the goods they wished to bring to the market in London. As in previous years, they regularly assessed the Company's sales figures, calculated rates of profitability on different commodities, gathered feedback from buyers, and kept a very close eye on the activities of their continental rivals by employing agents to gather commercial intelligence in the major European port cities. All this information was processed in the committees of Buying and Shipping and then translated into lengthy despatches containing indents with very detailed commodity specifications.[57] For textiles, the directors defined the number, weight, length, width, colour, and pattern of cloths they required; while for tea they prescribed the type and qualities of the varieties they wished to receive. They adhered to this practice throughout the period, and provided those in Asia with details of sales, prices, and samples of goods sold by the European East India Companies.

Continuing close attention to detail, together with the fact that the directors had long experience of gauging the quantity of goods required for the home market, might suggest that the Company was well-placed to translate its imports into sales. This proved not to be the case, however, as commercial judgements became clouded in the years immediately following the acquisition of the *diwani*. As with so much else, the directors set aside their long-established calculations and they paid surprisingly little attention to the need to boost sales. They appear to have believed that an increase would occur naturally and were no doubt reassured when there was a sharp growth in sales at the Company's half-yearly auctions, as is evident in figure 8.3. In the financial year 1767/8 the Company's cash journal recorded sale income of £4,034,411, over twice

57 See, for example, *FWIHC*, vol. X, pp. 96–112, 340–52.

the amount recorded five years earlier. Some of this increase can be attributed to the return of peace in 1763, however, and the growth of sale income could not be maintained. Consequently, in the sixteen years to 1783/4 the cash received from sales of goods averaged £3,092,725 a year.

A number of factors help to explain the Company's failure to convert a greatly expanded volume of imports into sustained growth of sale income. First and foremost, the Company was only one of a number of East India companies endeavouring to exploit demand for Asian goods in Europe and elsewhere. The Company was not alone in seeking to meet the growing demands of consumers and as far as the tea trade was concerned, the Company conceded important competitive advantages to rivals at home as well as on the Continent. Most importantly, perhaps, the Company's commercial costs were high because of the freight rates paid to those who owned East Indiamen and, as Ralph Davis remarked, the structural organisation of the Company's trade was such that 'It seems to be true that in this trade as in no other, freight rates failed to decline under the technical improvements in ships.'[58] Moreover, as far as the tea trade was concerned, duties reached an astonishing 119 per cent *ad valorem* by 1784, and this made the Company and its associated tea dealers vulnerable to substantial price undercutting from smugglers who imported cheap duty-free tea from Europe, as well as from those on board Company ships who 'ran' ashore substantial amounts of tea during the final stage of return voyages from China.[59] Indeed, when the Company's Accountant-General, William Richardson, prepared an assessment of the tea trade in 1785 he estimated that, on average, 7.5 million lb of tea a year had been smuggled into Britain and its dependencies between 1772 and 1780. By some considerable margin, this exceeded the total amount of tea delivered from the Company's warehouses for both home consumption and re-export.[60] By 1772 the amount of tea in the warehouses had already reached 17.75 million lb and, with a potential sale value of over £2 million, this represented almost two-thirds of all the Company's unsold goods.[61] Finally, as is well known, sales of tea for re-export did not offer much by way of compensation for poor performance in the domestic

---

58 Ralph Davis, *The rise of the English shipping industry in the seventeenth and eighteenth centuries* (second impression, Newton Abbot, 1972), p. 265. Tabulated details of freight rates before 1773 are to be found on p. 263.

59 H. V. Bowen, '"So alarming an evil": smuggling, pilfering and the English East India Company, 1750–1810', *International Journal of Maritime History*, 14 (2002), pp. 1–31.

60 L/AG/18/2, vol. 1, p. 11.

61 Bowen, *Revenue and reform*, p. 122.

market, and the Company suffered especially badly when the North American market for tea was first reduced, and then closed, during the political ferment in the colonies that preceded the American War of Independence.[62]

Other branches of the Company's import trade did not suffer such acute difficulties, but nevertheless some problems were encountered as attempts were made to boost sales and ensure that the right balance was struck between supply and demand. Advances were made in the imports of Indian and Chinese finished and raw silk in the face of competition from Italy, but efforts to increase the shipment of calicoes and muslins from India always met with stiff resistance from domestic textile manufacturers. The Company always strenuously denied that its sales of textiles were 'prejudicial to the improvement and extension of the manufactures of Great Britain',[63] and figures produced in 1788 suggested that 85 per cent of all calicoes and 60 per cent of all muslins it imported into Britain were subsequently re-exported. This enabled the Company to advance the claim that the 'home manufacture has increased to an immense extent; whilst the internal consumption of Indian calicoes and muslins has been reduced almost to nothing'.[64] The Company's dependence upon textiles sales for re-export was increased, but trading conditions experienced in Atlantic markets during the American War of Independence did not allow for easy growth and expansion.

In particular, the American war dealt a blow to the sale of East India goods to merchants who operated in the West Africa and slave trade. After 1763 the directors had made a considerable effort to increase the Company's share of what they perceived to be a large and expanding market, and the indents sent to India contained detailed lists of goods required for the Africa trade.[65] The success of this strategy was such that by the end of the 1760s it was said to be 'well known' that over half of British exports to West Africa consisted of Indian goods such as cotton textiles, pepper, and

---

62 For full details and calculation of the cost to the Company see ibid., pp. 121–5. See also B. W. Labaree, *The Boston tea party* (Oxford, 1964).

63 Manuscript copy of 'Fifth Report of the Company's Select Committee appointed by the Court of Directors to take into consideration the export trade from Great Britain and Ireland' (1793), H/400, p. 442. The fifth report was devoted to the cotton trade.

64 Ibid., p. 449.

65 Directors to Bengal, 15 February 1765, *FWIHC*, vol. IV, p. 92; 'List of articles to be provided for the Africa trade' (15 February 1765), Public Department, despatches from England, vol. 68, p. 113, TNSA; Public Department, enclosures to despatches, vol. 3, 'List of goods to be procured at Bombay for the ships going out, 1754–86', MSA. For the Company's long-standing interest in the West Africa trade see Joseph E. Inikori, *Africans and the Industrial Revolution in England. A study in international trade and economic development* (Cambridge, 2002), pp. 430–1, 516–19.

saltpetre.[66] In particular, although sales of Indian textiles were beginning to be threatened by imitations manufactured in Britain,[67] the value of East India cotton goods re-exported to West Africa quadrupled, from £39,477 in 1762 to £166,103 a decade later.[68] The return of war to the Atlantic nipped this growth in the bud, and between 1776 and 1782 the value of the cotton re-exports to West Africa averaged only £56,482 a year. Indian cottons still represented around two-thirds of the foreign products exported from England to West Africa, but the disruption caused by war was untimely for the hard-pressed Company.

As had always been the case, the issue of quality control remained closely bound up with the sale of Company commodities, and the directors acknowledged that there was little point in increasing the volume of imports if goods were then found to be so poor that they could not be sold to discerning buyers. Servants in India routinely proclaimed that they gave 'unwearied attention' to the procurement of textiles for export to Britain,[69] but they were repeatedly taken to task by the directors for sending poor quality cloths to London, and for putting their own commercial interests before those of the Company.[70] The problem of 'rubbish teas' also emerged during the mid-1750s,[71] and because greatly increased amounts of tea were purchased after 1765 the inspection of chests became much more difficult. As a result there were striking examples of very poor quality tea finding their way on to the Company's ships. By the 1780s the inspection of teas had become a burning issue and the directors reacted angrily to the discovery of large quantities of inferior leaves in their London warehouses. Time and again, poor-quality teas, dyed teas, or chests packed with rubbish were sent back to Canton for replacement by the Hong merchants from whom the supercargoes had bought the tea in the first place.[72] There followed

---

66 'Proposals offered to the consideration of the Honourable the East India Company' (n.d., late 1760s), L/P&S/19, box 48. Analysis of commercial data for the mid-1780s suggests that this estimate was correct (Ralph Davis, *The industrial revolution and British overseas trade* (Leicester, 1979), p. 102). For the importance of Indian goods traded in West Africa by British merchants during the 1750s and 1760s see David Hancock, *Citizens of the world: London merchants and the integration of the British Atlantic community* (Cambridge, 1995), pp. 190–1, 200–1.

67 Inikori, *Africans*, p. 440.

68 Ibid, p. 444.

69 *FWIHC*, vol. V, p. 389.

70 *FWIHC*, passim.

71 Morse, *Chronicles*, vol. V, pp. 24–5.

72 Directors to Canton, 12 May 1780, R/10/Misc., vol. 1, p. 255. For further examples see ibid., pp. 261, 275, 310. Nankeen cloth was also affected, and in 1785 directors returned nine chests that had been packed with wood (ibid., p. 282).

a steady stream of instructions related to the packing and stowage of tea, and although the appointment of an inspector of teas at Canton in 1790 served to reduce the problem, the securing of a steady supply of good-quality tea remained a cause for concern.

The directors' inability to ensure the supply of good quality products from Asia served only to exacerbate their failure to sustain commodity profit rates at the levels enjoyed before the acquisition of the *diwani*. Reductions in the sale price of tea were necessary to make it competitive in the marketplace, and a variety of rising charges drove down profit margins, especially during the uncertainties following the outbreak of war with America in 1775. Detailed calculations produced by the Accountant-General William Richardson in 1780 pointed to sharp reductions in overall levels of trading profit, from 57 per cent on all goods sold between 1761 and 1765 to only 9 per cent between 1776 and 1779.[73] Although sales of China goods still generated a return of above 16 per cent throughout the 1770s, and goods from Madras and Benkulen always sold at a profit, Richardson calculated losses on the sale of imports from Bengal and Bombay. This was not of much significance as far as the small volume of goods from Bombay was concerned, but the large consignments from Bengal met with annual losses from 1776 onwards.[74]

Evidence suggests that the reason for losses on Bengal goods lay primarily in a failure to return any profit on imports of raw silk, the cultivation of which had been strenuously promoted by the directors since 1766.[75] As a result, imports of raw silk from Bengal were temporarily suspended by the directors until the authorities in Calcutta could guarantee a supply of good-quality silk that was cheaper than that produced in Italy.[76] This was eventually achieved and imports of raw silk later increased markedly, but the problems experienced with this commodity during the mid-1780s demonstrate many of the failures embodied in a commercial strategy designed with the primary purpose of transferring surplus revenue to Britain. As the former Chairman Nathaniel Smith noted when summarising the Company's parlous commercial position in

---

73 L/AG/18/2, vol. 1, p. 8.

74 Ibid., vol. 1, pp. 18–23.

75 Losses on raw silk sales grew from £3,367 in 1775 to £146,609 in 1778, H/449, p. 22.

76 Directors to Bengal, 16 March 1784, *FWIHC*, vol. IX, p. 158. For the directors' instructions of the following year detailing how those in Bengal should resume the trade in raw silk see ibid., vol. IX, pp. 192–6. For a very positive assessment of the Company's contribution to the long-term development of the raw silk and raw cotton industries in Bengal see Tripathi, *Trade and finance*, p. 210.

1781, since the acquisition of the *diwani* the Company had 'reduced the natural advantages arising from the profits of the trade'. He came to the inescapable conclusion that because the Company had 'imported much larger quantities of goods than the regular demand required', the markets had become overstocked with the result that many articles had been sold at below their cost price.[77] Hence, when the directors and ministers reappraised the Company's commercial strategy during the mid-1780s they devoted considerable attention to the sale of East India goods, with tea being identified as offering the best hope of salvation.

The implementation of Pitt's Commutation Act of 1784, with its reduction of Crown duties on tea from 119 per cent to 12½ per cent *ad valorem*, was intended to increase the consumption of 'legal' tea on which duties were paid in Britain, but in order to achieve this the Company was forced into a series of complex commercial manoeuvres in order to help the minister eliminate the threat to sales and revenue posed by smugglers. In order to guarantee a steady flow of cheap tea on to the market, the Company was obliged to hold at least year's supply of tea in reserve at all times, and the conduct of its sales was regulated, but in an immediate effort to wrest the advantage from well-organised smugglers, the Company was authorised to buy back tea from dealers who had earlier purchased it at prices inflated by the higher rate of duty. Then, in an attempt to engross the entire supply of tea from the Continent, the Company was given the financial assistance necessary to enable it systematically to purchase on the open market in Europe, and throughout 1785 and 1786 substantial consignments of tea were bought on behalf of the Company in Amsterdam, Ostend, Lisbon, Gothenburg, and L'Orient.[78]

These concerted actions enabled the Company to offer a large quantity of tea at low prices even before the arrival of new supplies from Canton, and there was a dramatic growth of sales. In 1784 just under 10 million lb of tea had been sold, but the amount increased sharply to almost 15 million lb the following year, and sales topped 20 million lb for the first time in 1795.[79] The rate of growth then slowed as wartime financial

---

77 Nathaniel Smith, *Remarks on the East India Company's balances in England from their trade and revenues . . .* (1781), p. 2.

78 These purchases and payments are detailed in L/AG/1/6, vol. 19, pp. 26, 43, 44, 53. In total, over 25 million lb of tea was purchased on behalf of the Company in Europe. For the introduction and implementation of the Commutation Act see H.-c. and L. H. Mui, 'William Pitt and the enforcement of the Commutation Act, 1784–1788', *Eng. Hist. Rev.*, 76 (1961), pp. 447–65; H.-c. and L. H. Mui, 'The Commutation and the tea trade in Britain, 1784–1793', *Ec. Hist. Rev.*, 16 (1963), pp. 234–53.

79 *PP*, 1812–13, vol. VIII, p. 233.

pressures led to the restoration of higher rates of duty, but between 1798 and 1812 annual sales averaged almost 24 million lb, and steady increases continued until 1833, thereby demonstrating the directors' ability to organise an adequate supply from Canton.[80] As early as 1788 one former director was moved to suggest that tea had already become the 'food of the whole people of Great Britain'[81] and the strength of such demand helped to treble income from tea sales from just over £1 million in 1784 to well above £3 million a year during the first decade of the nineteenth century. Moreover, increasing levels of sales of better-quality tea helped to ensure that government revenue did not suffer too greatly in the long run, and pre-1784 levels of revenue income were restored by 1794 before they then rose sharply as progressively higher rates of duty were charged during the wars against France.

Tea was the Company's great commercial success story after 1785 but it did not completely dominate the import trade, and in some years it did not generate more than half of all sale income. The directors entertained hopes of increasing sales of other commodities and they believed, for example, that an adjustment of duties would serve to make London the great 'mart of Indian drugs'.[82] As a result, a constant dialogue on duties was kept up between East India House and the Treasury, although the spectacular success that had been achieved with tea was not repeated with other commodities, and the sales income recorded in the calico and drugs ledgers moved unpredictably from year to year. There were a number of reasons for this, but the strength of domestic competition certainly began to have an adverse affect on sales of textiles, both for home consumption and re-export. Textile manufacturers reacted with great hostility when the Company improved the quality of the printed goods it imported from Bengal and, rather than provoking a 'parliamentary contest' with the cotton interest, the directors agreed in 1783 not to put any such cloths on sale for seven years 'excepting such as may be imported of the manufacture of the coast of Malabar, not exceeding 2,000 pieces a year'.[83]

80 Mui and Mui, *Management of monopoly*, ch. 5
81 Thomas Bates Rous, *An explanation of the mistaken principle on which the Commutation Act was founded* . . . (1788), p. 4. Rous believed that Pitt's Act would have a deeply damaging effect on the Company's trade, the nation's revenue, and the diet of working people. For estimates of the consumption of tea and other imported groceries see Carole Shammas, *The pre-industrial consumer in England and America* (Oxford, 1990), pp. 136–7, 142–8.
82 *FWIHC*, vol. X, p. 113.
83 Directors to Madras, 24 Sept. 1783, despatches from England, vol. 87, pp. 42–3, TNSA. For the long running 'contest' between British and Indian cottons see Wright, *East Indian economic problems*, pp. 192–223.

This did little to appease the manufacturers, however, and between 1788 and 1793 they agitated aggressively for further regulation of Company imports.

The directors also had much to fear from the technical advances which caused Asian commodities to be substituted by home-produced goods in the domestic market. Improvements in the production of porcelain resulted in the Company's abandonment of Chinaware imports by 1813, but much more threatening were developments in the textile industry. In 1782 the directors sent to Calcutta samples of a cheap new form of muslin manufactured in Manchester, and they declared that unless Bengali producers responded effectively to this competition 'we shall find them most powerful rivals where those articles are vended'.[84] This problem certainly affected the sale of Company textiles destined for re-export from Britain, and it has been said that 'Manchester manufacturers . . . achieved remarkable success in their competition with Indian cottons in Western Africa.'[85] The export of East India cottons to that region continued to grow, albeit erratically, during the late eighteenth century, but the Company struggled to make any profit on its sales of textiles to West Africa merchants, and from 1806 English cottons managed to secure a decisive victory.[86] At the same time, the resumption of war in Europe in 1803 had a considerable effect on sales of Indian cottons for re-export to the Continent, and there was a precipitous fall in income from the sale of piece goods, from over £2.5 million in 1800–1 to £1.1 million in 1809–10.[87] Even before then, however, the Company was finding it difficult to sell its Indian textiles in London, and between 1785 and 1805 the Secret Committee found it necessary to sanction off-the-record payments of £229,793 to agents who were charged with keeping up the price of the piece goods sold at the East India House auctions.[88]

Mindful of the problems it was encountering with sales of traditional East Indian goods, the directors displayed some willingness to import new types of commodity into Britain. They were encouraged in this action by

84 *FWIHC*, vol. IX, p. 113.

85 Inikori, *Africans*, p. 446.

86 Ibid., pp. 444, 447, 516. For the Company's problems in selling textiles to West Africa merchants, and its subsequent cutting back of purchases in Bombay, see Directors to Bombay, 5 March 1801, Commercial Dept., letters from the directors, vol. 4, p. 6, MSA.

87 *Fourth report from the select committee*, pp. 492–3.

88 The agents were Thomas Brown, Charles Rogers, Edward Wheelhouse, and John Whitfield, who were contracted to act against combinations of buyers and undertook to ensure that sales were made at prices 10 per cent above those listed in the catalogue. For detailed papers relating to this price-fixing operation see L/P&S/19, box 7.

those who believed that India could generate supplies of groceries and raw materials of benefit to domestic manufacturers.[89] Notable in this respect was the naturalist and President of the Royal Society, Joseph Banks, who wrote extensively to the directors on the need to seek out supplies of products that could be obtained much more cheaply in India than in other parts of the world. Thus in 1788 Banks proposed that the Company consider cultivating tea in India, and he also suggested that it develop production of 'coffee, chocolate, vanilla, cochineal, cotton, and even sugar'. Acknowledging that these goods were already produced in abundance in the West Indies and the Americas, he argued that whenever a 'rivalship' was established it was 'evident every article now received from the West may on the account of the comparative cheapness of labor be furnished cheaper from the East, notwithstanding the difference of freight'.[90]

Others lobbied the authorities in London from India itself, and in 1780 the private indigo merchant John Prinsep wrote to Lord North from Calcutta, outlining his intention of introducing indigo, sugar, and tobacco into Britain from South Asia. He did so in the belief that a 'richer tribute may by such means be drawn from Bengal than is furnished by the present almost worn out system of investing it in manufactures which are every day falling in estimation at home since European industry has adopted such variety of imitation and improvement upon the fabricks of the East'.[91] The directors might have been sceptical about such claims but they did not reject these proposals out of hand and, although they were always wary of antagonising the West India interest, they sanctioned domestic experiments with a range of new products during the last two decades of the century. These were not always successful, and the early sales of samples of Indian indigo were a notable failure,[92] but the establishment of botanical gardens in Calcutta, Madras, and Bombay enabled the directors to assert in 1792 that they 'have made experiments with almost every article which India affords or which could be procured from the more eastern countries'.[93]

89 On this point see Ward, 'The industrial revolution and British imperialism', pp. 49–50.
90 Memorial to the Deputy Chairman, 27 December 1788, MS Eur. D993, ff. 1–3.
91 John Prinsep to Lord North, 25 January 1780, MS Eur. D624/1.
92 Directors to Bengal, 28 March 1788, *FWIHC*, vol. X, 352–4. For the directors' earlier instructions about the procurement and shipment of indigo see ibid, pp. 196–7. In the long run, imports of indigo into Britain increased markedly, from 154,291 lb in 1785 to 4,447,947 lb in 1812, and the latter figure represented over 90 per cent of all British indigo imports (*Reports from committees*, vol. X, part II (1831–2), p. 640).
93 H/400, pp. 319, 317.

Table 8.2. *The sale of Company goods, 1809/10 (£s)*

Teas	3,410,753
Bengal piece goods	333,768
Coast and Surat piece goods	769,870
Raw silk	555,531
Nankeens	133,472
Pepper	50,476
Saltpetre	223,794
Spices	153,824
Drugs, sugar, indigo etc.	357,787
Total	5,989,275

Source: Fourth report of the select committee on the affairs of the East India Company (1812), p. 493.

The harsh reality was that trials and experimentation in India did not translate easily into extensive sales of new commodities in London. Thus in the years immediately prior to the loss of the Indian monopoly, products such as sugar and indigo accounted for only a very small percentage of the Company's sale of goods. Instead, these commodities loomed large in the officially sanctioned private trade conducted between India and Britain.[94] As can be seen in table 8.2, tea very much dominated the Company's import trade, and one effect of this was that between 1793 and 1810 the Company made a profit of almost £22 million on its China goods, while the profit on India goods over the same period was put at only £5.2 million. Moreover, annual profits on China sales had risen, more or less steadily, to a peak of £1,344,233 in 1810, whereas losses on Indian goods were calculated for both 1807 and 1808.[95] This shortcoming in the import trade from India was exposed at a particularly inopportune moment, just as Parliament was preparing to consider the renewal of the charter and Indian monopoly, and the statistical evidence

---

94 Between 1793 and 1810 sales of 'Drugs, sugar, indigo etc.' accounted for £20,191,183 or 60 per cent of all the private trade goods sold at the Company's auctions (*Fourth report from the select committee*, pp. 492–3).

95 Ibid., pp. 494–5. Contemporary calculations of the Company's overall commercial profits often contained considerable margins of error because there was no agreement on the actual size of the Company's trading capital. See, for example, 'Memorandum as to what may be termed the commercial capital of the E. I. Company on the amount actually employed by them in trade', H/500, pp. 171–3. For a detailed discussion of profit which argues that the Company did not take advantage of its monopoly position to extort high prices from tea buyers in London see Mui and Mui, *Management of monopoly*, ch. 3.

of commercial failing greatly weakened the directors' case that trade with the subcontinent should remain in their hands.

EXPORTS: ENTERPRISE AND INNOVATION

By the beginning of the nineteenth century many people outside the East India Company would have accepted that the directors had succeeded in their aim of making the China trade a 'national concern', but few were prepared to defend the Company's record as an exporter. Instead, critics concentrated on the Company's failure to create a greater 'vent' for British manufacture, and they portrayed the directors as men whose methods or 'system' for conducting business curbed enterprise and innovation.[96] Such claims became ever more strident during successive debates about the renewal of the Company's charter, and it was increasingly asserted that private merchants alone possessed the vigour and skills necessary for the full exploitation of Indian markets.

Substance to these claims was given by the fact that although the overall value of the commodities exported to India and China increased over time, the Company was unable to dispose of a large proportion of the cargoes shipped to Asia. The full extent of the problem had been revealed for the first time in 1773 when, in response to a ministerial proposal that the Company send manufactures worth £387,000 to India each year, the directors pointed out that woollen cloth valued at over £400,000 was already lying unsold in the warehouses of the three Presidencies.[97] This allowed some to argue, without any fear of contradiction, that 'The Company long exported for some years past, too many goods for their Indian markets', prompting the suggestion of the very obvious solution that 'a diminution therefore of £150,000 per annum in the article of exports may be justified on general principles of commerce, as well as notions of economy'.[98] The weight of the Company problems by 1773 was such that the directors could not ignore this advice, and their immediate response was to embark upon a policy of short-term commercial

---

96 See, for example, William Playfair, *Strictures on the Asiatic establishments of Great Britain . . .* (1799).

97 B/89, pp. 224–5. A Company account of 18 November 1772 submitted to the ministry estimated that the value of goods for sale in the Company's Indian warehouses stood at £303,451 (*The present state of the East India Company's affairs, comprehending the accounts delivered in by the Court of Directors to the Treasury . . . drawn up by Mr Hoole, Auditor of Indian accounts and others . . .* (1773), p. 25).

98 *The present state of the East India Company's affairs*, p. 30.

retrenchment which saw sharp reductions in the number of ships des-patched to the East as well as the value of goods purchased for export.

To some degree, the Company's failure to generate better sales of its exported goods can be attributed to the strength of competition from European companies and also Britons who were engaged in private trading activity. Freight-free 'privilege' trade allowances enabled the offi-cers on board Indiamen to export 'luxuries' and 'necessaries' to India and China, but they were also granted permission to export some bulk items such as iron, steel, lead, and, occasionally, copper. These commodities were in the main purchased by Europeans, but increasingly they also began to find their way into Indian markets. More significant, however, was unlicensed trade or smuggling in bulk commodities which at times greatly tested the patience of the directors. This was a particularly acute problem during the mid-1760s when well-organised groups used elaborate arrangements to overcome Company restrictions on the export of certain commodities. Thus in 1765 reports to the directors provided information on large consignments of cloth, iron, steel, lead, and firearms that had been transferred to several different East Indiamen in the Channel, as well as off Tenerife, Madeira, and the Cape Verde islands.[99] At the same time, the clandestine trade, which involved the shipment of domestic manufac-tures to Asia in British-owned foreign vessels, was growing to such an extent that by the late 1780s it was estimated that the volume of such trade far exceeded that of the Company itself.[100] These problems remained throughout the period, and the Company could never be said to have held the major share of the trade between Britain and Asia.

Even so, the root of the Company's problems lay in the uncomfortable fact that European goods, and especially woollen cloth, were not in great demand in India or China. By the 1780s, estimates of the profitability on exports to the three Indian Presidencies suggested an overall loss of £4,652 a year on the Company's sale of woollens and metals in India.[101] The situation was much the same in China, and in 1788 a review of a century of Company trade with Canton made by a former director suggested that the export of British woollens and manufactures 'has been done at a considerable loss'.[102] Statistics supported this claim, although the deficit was perhaps not as large as many thought. A net loss of £82,519 was

99 See, for example, Directors to Madras, 17 May 1766, E/4/863, pp. 385, 399.
100 H/399, p. 1; L/Mar/1, vol. 26, p. 305.
101 H/449, pp. 3–6.
102 Rous, *Explanation of the mistaken*, p. 5.

reported on the export of woollens between 1781/2 and 1791/2, and a net loss of £108,401 was recorded on metals during the same decade.[103] This prompted one observer to draw the conclusion that the state of the Company's trade with Asia was such that 'the iron ballasts which went annually out in their India and China ships had exceeded in tonnage the merchandize exported by them to either of these countries'.[104]

Yet, a review of the evidence suggests that the Company's failure to conduct its export trade more effectively was not caused by any lack of effort or imagination on the part of the directors. As had always been the case, they periodically undertook strategic reviews of their commercial activities with the aim of identifying the 'most effectual measures for extending the trade of the Company',[105] and arising from this process were attempts to open up new markets to British manufactures. This happened throughout the period, and right across the Asia-Pacific region. Thus, to take just two examples, during the early 1770s encouragement was given to efforts to discover whether trade with Nepal offered a possible outlet for sales of cloth and European goods in Lhassa, Tibet, and Western China;[106] while in 1811 the directors responded swiftly to the conquest of Java by arranging the shipment of 500 tons of manufactures to Batavia.[107]

The directors also gathered the commercial intelligence that was deemed necessary to ensure that the goods exported to Asia were appropriate to the needs of consumers. They requested detailed reports on the tastes and habits of local populations and, as far as cloth was concerned, they responded by sending out consignments of goods that conformed as closely as possible to favoured styles, qualities, and colours.[108] Sales feedback was gathered from the overseas servants, and this vital information was fed into the decisions that underpinned the annual process of tender, contract, and supply. Domestic manufacturers were required to adhere to very exact commodity specifications, and those who could not meet the considerable challenge of adapting their products to the needs of the Asian market were not granted orders.

---

103 H/449, pp. 9–11.

104 H/399, p. 146.

105 For the commercial review of 1768 see the minutes of meetings held by a joint committee of Correspondence and Treasury, H/771, pp. 115–22.

106 *FWIHC*, vols. V and VI, passim. For the development of early British contact with Tibet see A. Lamb, *British India and Tibet, 1766–1810* (second edition, 1986), ch. 1.

107 B/154, pp. 935–6 (31 December 1811).

108 For this type of activity in the early part of the century see Chaudhuri, *Trading world of Asia*, pp. 220–7.

Extensive trials of new products were sanctioned by the directors in the hope that they might create demand. This had always been done on a regular basis, and the methods of testing were well established. Unlabelled batches of samples produced by different manufacturers were sent out to Asia to be put up for sale, and the Company's servants were requested to make detailed notes on the responses of local buyers. Entirely typical was the experiment conducted with a small consignment of tabbinets or coarse silk sent to Calcutta in April 1786. At the same time, the directors despatched samples of textiles made in Halifax, Manchester, and Norwich, and the authorities at Calcutta were asked to assess whether these could be sold 'without interfering with or proving injurious to the interest of the native manufacturers whom we conceive ourselves likewise bound to protect to the utmost of our power'.[109] While the directors were uneasy about encouraging the export of cotton manufactures to India, their willingness to experiment certainly brought rewards for some textile manufacturers who were prepared to adapt and innovate. The makers of worsted 'stuffs' in Norwich benefited greatly from their switch from superfine to single woollen camlets made light by boiling in water, and this enabled them to overcome Dutch competition for sales at Canton, a victory that greatly assisted the city's ailing textile industry.[110]

Experiments also took place with different types of metals. Quality trials had long been conducted with bar iron and copper, and the servants had been ordered to report back on the preferences of buyers, blacksmiths, and metalworkers.[111] Alongside these continued trials, the directors arranged for the testing of consignments of brass, imitation Japan copper, and ironmongery.[112] Then in 1812, they sent to Bombay a bundle of the 'best bar steel which has been manufactured in Sheffield from the best Swedish ore', together with some 'grain tin' which they believed to be 'essential to the art of dying'.[113] As with textiles, the directors encouraged British producers to adapt metals to the demands of Asian

---

109 Directors to Bengal, 12 April 1786, *FWIHC*, vol. X, p. 93. For further consignments of Manchester goods made in 1788 see ibid., p. 340. In 1802 the directors sent to Bombay two 'bales of cloth made waterproof by different persons' with instructions that they be tested to see if they were 'likely to succeed in resisting the wet in India' (Commercial letters, vol. 4, p. 249, MSA).

110 See 'Description of and remarks upon the goods manufactured at Norwich' (1786), Public department, enclosures, vol. 22, pp. 3–4, MSA; H/400, p.239; Trevor Fawcett, 'Argonauts and commercial travellers: the foreign marketing of Norwich stuffs in the later eighteenth century', *Textile History*, 16 (1985), pp. 172, 175.

111 See, for example, *FWIHC*, vol. I, p. 721.

112 Directors to Madras, 4 July 1777, 2 December 1781; despatches from England, vol. 81, p. 46; vol. 84, p. 111, TNSA.

113 Commercial letters, vol. 7, pp. 48, 116–17, MSA.

markets, and in certain cases this acted as a spur to innovation. Hence, when the Company attempted to introduce a new metallic currency to Bengal during the 1780s, its first action was to procure samples of the coins currently in circulation with a view to establishing the weight and quality of the alloy.[114] Consignments of copper were sent by the Company to Matthew Boulton's works in Soho, Birmingham. Boulton, who had inspected minting operations in France and drew on the expertise of French engineers, then designed and built several coining presses driven by a steam engine. According to James Watt, 'Much ingenuity, time, and great expense were required to perfect the application of the steam engine to coining', and Boulton was eventually able to fulfil the large orders for copper coin that had been made to him by the Company and government.[115]

Boulton offers a striking example of a manufacturer responding effectively to the needs of the Asian market, although there is no escaping the fact that in the long run the Company's product-testing regime met with mixed success, especially at Canton. During his famous embassy to Peking in 1793 Lord Macartney was unable to encourage the sale of textiles, and twenty years later a Commons committee commended the Company's for its 'promotion of national interests' in China but then went on to note that the limitations of the Chinese market were such that 'different trials made for the introduction on new articles [such] as Scotch and Irish linens, and the coarser kind of woollens have failed of success'.[116]

If some defence can be made of the directors' commercial methods, there is still a need to explain their failure to expand the Company's export trade beyond the extent actually achieved. First, the directors adhered doggedly to the belief that the Company's interests were best served by the export of bulk goods, and no attempt was made to diversify cargoes beyond woollens and metals. The directors were never prepared to trade in the groceries or commodities such as furniture and glassware that figured prominently in the private trade conducted by the officers of East Indiamen. They conceded that a 'great number of trifling articles are exported which are beneficial both to the public and to the individuals' who exported them but they continued to express a long-held belief that they would be 'productive of embarrassment and loss if attempted by the

---

114 Directors to Bengal, 31 July 1787, *FWIHC*, vol. X, p. 289.
115 'Memoir of Boulton by [James] Watt, 1809', in H.W. Dickinson, *Matthew Boulton* (1936), pp. 205–6.
116 *Fourth report from the select committee* (1812), p. 421. For details of the extensive trials undertaken with British manufactures in China between 1793 and 1810 see ibid., pp. 467–79.

Company'.[117] The directors might well be commended for allowing this trade in 'trifling articles' to flourish within the monopoly under their control, and this certainly enabled a good number of domestic merchants and manufacturers to participate in the East India trade even though they did not have direct dealings with the Company itself. Yet, by adopting a strategy that was intended to encourage their maritime officers to devote their best efforts to serving the Company, the directors were denying themselves participation in a lucrative segment of the trade that passed between Britain and Asia. Indeed, this trade had become so considerable by the 1790s that an informed observer such as Francis Russell believed that it was almost as valuable as the Company's own export trade.[118] This limited the Company's own prospects of expanding British trade in Asia and it conceded a growth area to others, thus serving only to strengthen the arguments of those who believed that private trade offered the best means of deepening British penetration of Indian and Chinese markets.

Secondly, the Company was saddled with high shipping costs even though a bitter decades-long struggle between old and new shipping interests eventually led to reform which opened up fairer competition between those who wished to hire ships to the Company. Unfortunately, the successive victories won by reformers such as John Fiott between 1796 and 1803 occurred at a time of war which meant that any potential gains to the Company from lower freight rates were reduced by the need to pay ship owners extraordinary charges to cover the greatly increased cost of insurance.[119]

Finally, the directors suffered from the fact that, ultimately, they relied upon their overseas servants to promote the Company's commercial interests. These servants, and especially those in India, were regularly reminded that they had free rein to implement any reasonable measures designed to 'increase the vend of manufactures to as great an extent as possible'.[120] Equally regularly, however, the servants had to be taken to task for their failure to follow the most basic commercial instructions or act with any degree of initiative. Hence, a letter sent from London to Bombay in November 1807 released the pent-up frustration of the directors in the bitter complaint that

---

117 H/404, p. 295.
118 F.R. [Francis Russell], *A short history of the East India Company* (1793), p. 28.
119 Sutton, *Lords of the east*, pp. 29–36. On this important issue see also Philips, *East India Company*, pp. 80–117 and Tripathi, *Trade and finance*, pp. 66–70.
120 Directors to Bengal, 21 November 1764, *FWIHC*, vol. IV, p. 65.

We have long and frequently urged upon you the duty and importance of endeavouring to extend in India the sale of the manufactures and produce of this country . . . We cannot suppose that our frequent injunctions have been overlooked by you, but we nevertheless judge it expedient to repeat our orders, and have therefore now urgently to desire that it may be made matter of strict and particular enquiry under your government whether the vent of British articles already known there can be increased or other British articles not yet known can be introduced.[121]

As even some of the Company's sternest critics acknowledged, the directors were unable to ensure that their employees in Asia complied with orders and instructions. As one put it, the directors had 'formed excellent plans relative to increasing the exports etc', but they were unable to follow them up 'by practice'.[122] This was a reflection of the fact that, as with other areas of Company policy, the directors were unable to translate wishes into action in India. They were prisoners of a situation in which indifference or the pursuit of private interest by the 'men on the spot' determined the outcome of the Company's commercial strategies carefully worked out in London. The directors' inability to expand further the export of British manufactures should not be seen as a failure of intent, and the charge that they were indifferent to the trade is both harsh and unfair.

THE END OF MONOPOLY

Of the many commercial challenges faced by the directors, none was greater than that posed by the erosion of the Company's exclusive trading privileges. As successive breaches were made in the monopoly, greater commercial concessions were granted to the Company's own maritime officers as well as to private traders in India and Britain. In 1788 the directors established a new private trade (rather confusingly also described as a 'privilege trade'), which permitted individuals to ship commodities at a freight of £31 16s. a ton whenever the Company itself could not obtain full cargoes of goods; and the Charter Act of 1793 stipulated that the Company should make 3,000 tons of shipping a year available to private individuals for the purpose of exchanging manufactured goods for raw materials, at £5 per ton outward and £15 per ton homeward. In the event,

---

121 Commercial Department, Letters from the directors, 6 November 1807, vol. 5 (no pagination), MSA.
122 H/399, p. 32.

this did little to stimulate private exports in Company ships, but the effect on imports was considerable, and there was a marked increase in the value of private goods sold at East India House, from £774,030 in 1788/9 to £2,965,194 in 1812/13.[123] As noted earlier, the directors responded to this situation by expanding their own import and export trades during the 1790s but, although they met with some success, they continued to be protected from the full force of competition by the existence of what Henry Dundas described as a 'regulated monopoly'.[124] Within this new organisational framework, the Company still possessed several important advantages over private traders, the most notable of which were that all British trade with Asia had to be conducted on Company ships, even though some of them were now 'India-built', and dealings in key commodities such as piece goods continued to be restricted. It was thus not until the Company lost its Indian trade monopoly in 1813 that the directors had fully to come to terms with the commercial threat posed by British merchants and traders operating with more or less open access to the markets of the subcontinent.

The response of the directors to the new trading world created by the Charter Act was immediate because they were obliged to separate the Company's commercial activities from those of a territorial and political nature. This meant that the different strands of Company finance had to be untangled, and clearer systems of accounting had to be established to ensure that, for the first time, remittances were applied properly to the appropriate commercial and political charges in London.[125] The directors also acknowledged that, in a new era of open competition, the trade with India had to be organised on conventional business lines and, as those in Bengal were told in February 1814, this meant that the commercial department was 'henceforward to stand entirely upon its own basis, insulated from all consideration of political or public events'.[126] With the directors required to meet specific financial obligations of a 'political' nature in London, as defined by the Charter Act, it was essential that the Company's trade was able to generate a profit of more than £1 million a year, and accordingly funds amounting to £3.5 million were earmarked to provide 'regular commercial means in India and China'.[127]

---

123 Calculated from L/AG/1/5, vols. 22 and 28.
124 For Dundas's definition of this regulated monopoly see Tripathi, *Trade and finance*, p. 26.
125 For the new accounting arrangements see the plan, as amended and approved by the Board of Control, placed at the beginning of L/AG/13/1, vol. 1. The plan lists those accounts deemed to be 'territorial and political' in nature.
126 E/4/768, p. 160.   127 E/4/769, pp. 207–34.

As part of their revised strategy, the directors declared in February 1814 that they were still 'fully as desirous of facilitating the consumption of the manufactures of Great Britain in India and China', but they warned that this 'national object should no longer expose us to absolute loss'.[128] Consequently, they began to abandon those parts of the trade that were unprofitable, and almost at once there was a sharp reduction in the export of woollens to India. None were sent to Bengal in 1813/14 and, although exports of cloth to that Presidency were resumed in the following year, hardly any woollens were despatched to Madras between 1815 and 1820.[129] Since the export of copper to India still offered the prospect of some success, large quantities were sent to Calcutta and Bombay, and a renewed attempt was made to find a market for British manufactures and other commodities. Consignments of cotton manufactures were sent to India, along with parcels of 'spelter' or zinc, and the directors were now prepared to sanction the despatch of 'petty merchandise', such as cutlery and tools.[130] Even so, against a background of falling sale prices for Company goods, these were essentially futile gestures that could not delay the inevitable. The trade with Madras was all-but abandoned and, despite one final general export drive to India between 1819 and 1821 when increased quantities of goods were sent out in small 'chartered ships' hired at very low freight rates,[131] the strength of unfettered private competition could not be resisted. The Company continued to export stores for civil, military, and marine use in India, but no consignments of commercial goods were sent to the subcontinent after 1826, even though the directors continued to encourage their servants to seek out new markets for British goods in the Punjab and elsewhere.[132]

It is noteworthy that the private merchants who had long boasted of their commercial skills were themselves incapable of expanding the export of the metal and woollen commodities long traded by the Company. Instead, they achieved considerable growth of Britain's export trade with India through a vigorous promotion of cotton manufactures, twist, and yarn. Cotton goods worth only £107,306 had been sent India in 1812, but by 1829 there had been a seventeenfold increase in their export value to

128 Commercial letters, vol. 8, p. 36, MSA.
129 L/AG/1/6, vols. 25 and 26, passim.
130 Ibid., vols. 26 and 27, passim. For the samples of hardware sent to Bombay in December 1814 see MSA, Commercial letters, vol. 8, pp. 343–4.
131 Directors to Bengal, 25 February 1820, E/4/698, pp. 473–6.
132 See, for example, the instructions of February 1830 relating to an attempt to open up trade with the Punjab, Commercial letters, vol. 18, pp. 5–10, MSA.

£1,894,602.[133] Allied to more modest growth in the trade in other non-traditional items, this surge in consignments of cotton helped to double the total invoice value of British exports despatched to India between 1812 and 1829.

The advance of domestically produced cotton textiles certainly helped private merchants capture by far the largest share of the British export trade to India after 1813, but new domestic production processes also helped to deliver a knock-out blow to the Company's importation of manufactured goods from India. With the build up of 'a large unsaleable stock in our warehouses in London', the directors abandoned the trade in piece goods from Western India in 1820.[134] Three years later, a further fall in demand for piece goods was caused by 'the improved state of machinery in Europe and the protection which different nations in Europe and the United States are giving to their own manufactures', and the directors observed that the result of this was that 'many industrious people in different parts of India are thence thrown out of employment and reduced to distress'.[135] The directors were undoubtedly concerned about the well-being of those who lived under the Company's administration but, characteristically, they also noted that the ongoing collapse of their textile trade would cause the financial resources of the Indian government to be significantly weakened. By way of a response, they proposed the abolition of all internal trade duties in India, but they had already conceded that the 'successful rivalry of British goods' had undermined the competitive position of Bengal textiles in domestic markets to such an extent that it was necessary to downgrade the long-established Patna factory from chief to subordinate station.[136] In many ways, this action symbolised the end of the Company's 200-year trade in Indian cotton textiles, and until the cessation of Company commercial activity in 1833 the directors concentrated their attention on indigo, raw silk, and other raw materials.[137]

The rapid demise of the Company's trade with India encouraged the belief among private merchants in Britain that the China trade was also ripe for exploitation, and as a result the directors soon found it increasingly

---

133 For comparative figures on exports from Britain to Asia (except China) between 1812 and 1829 see *Reports from committees*, vol. X, II (1831–2), p. 625.
134 Commercial letters, vol. 12, p. 99, MSA.
135 E/4/709, pp. 104–5.
136 E/4/708, pp. 593–4.
137 For a detailed study of the effects of this, and the general economic circumstances surrounding the end of the Company's India trade, see K. N. Chaudhuri, 'India's foreign trade and the cessation of the East India Company's trading activities, 1828–40', *Ec. Hist. Rev.*, 19 (1966), pp. 345–63.

difficult to maintain exports of commodities to Canton at pre-1813 levels. The value of goods sent to China fell by almost a third between 1812 and 1815, although the level of annual exports then stabilised at between £500,000 and £750,000. This was a far cry from the situation during the 1790s and, despite continued experimentation with a wide range of new products,[138] the directors were unable to restore the Company's earlier position.

Private merchants were especially adept at finding ways to break the Company's monopoly and this enabled them to capture a growing share of the Chinese market for British manufactures. Indeed, by the 1820s domestic manufacturers were able to consign commodities to China in a number of different ways without having to sell them to the Company. As in the earlier clandestine trade with India, some consignments went out via Europe and thus Richard Shaw, a major manufacturer of camlets in Norwich, despatched cloth to Germany from where it was sent on to Canton. Shaw, who was a major supplier to the Company, also dealt heavily with American private traders to Canton and he estimated that he supplied them with nine-tenths of their camlet requirements between 1821 and 1828. Indeed, Shaw, who boasted that he produced the finest camlets ever made, admitted that he preferred dealing with the Americans because they were far less likely to reject his cloths than the Company.[139] British manufactures also found their way to Canton via W. and J. Brown & Co. of Liverpool who acted as agents for American merchants. Between November 1821 and July 1829 this one firm sent to Canton consignments of mainly British manufactures valued at £805,527. The firm's goods were usually cleared for Batavia, and William Brown freely confessed that this was for the purposes of 'concealment'.[140] All those engaged in exporting British manufactures to China on behalf of Americans were firmly of the opinion that they purchased commodities of similar quality at a cheaper price than did the Company whose tender system made it vulnerable to combinations of suppliers. As result, it was widely believed that the Company was losing steadily on its export trade, and thus it was argued

138 Cotton wool valued at £93,401 was sent to Canton in 1820/1 and several consignments of furs were despatched between 1823 and 1826 (L/AG/1/6, vol. 26).
139 *Report from the Select Committee of the House of Lords appointed to enquire into the present state of the affairs of the East India Company . . .* (1830), pp. 819–33.
140 Ibid., pp. 748–50. Others engaged in this illicit trade declared that their goods were destined for Singapore. See also the evidence of Joshua Bates, an American merchant in London and a partner in Baring Brothers, who purchased British manufactures for export to China by his countrymen; and details of Charles Everitt's purchases on American account for the China markets, 1818–28 (ibid., pp. 653–60, 666–9).

that it was only by removing the Company's remaining commercial privileges that the American trade could be destroyed, thereby enabling the carrying of British goods to be restored to British-owned ships.

The Company was better able to protect its import trade from China because of the regulated nature of its sales in London, and, together with the sharp decline of the trade in Indian piece goods, this served further to strengthen the position of tea within the Company's import commodity profile. In the last years of the Company's trade, income from tea sales accounted for between 65 and 70 per cent of all commodity sale income in London (see figure 8.3); and most of the rest was generated by sales of raw materials. The ongoing success of the tea trade could not disguise the fact, however, that there was a considerable fall in annual sale income from the record peak of over £8 million achieved in 1815, and by the early 1830s it stood at less than £5 million.

This worsening situation made it difficult for the Company to meet its obligations in London, and increasingly the directors had to resort to the import of bullion from China and India. A small amount of silver from China, originally intended for shipment to Madras, had first arrived in London on the Company's account in 1810, but thereafter the transfer of bullion from Asia occurred on a semi-regular basis.[141] The scale of this transfer from India, derived from cash balances and surplus revenues allocated to the 'territorial finance' account, was at times considerable. In 1823, for example, when the directors were struggling to meet the demand for payments on bills of exchange drawn to facilitate private loans to the Company in India, they ordered that an 'extraordinary remittance' of £2 million be made from India, and they expressed the hope that as much as possible should be sent in gold because it is 'a considerably more favourable remittance than silver'. The directors were confident that this emergency action would cause 'no inconvenience' to the Company's finances in India, but they revealed more than a hint of anxiety about circumstances in London when they told the authorities in Calcutta that a failure to comply with these remittance instructions would cause 'considerable financial embarrassment' at East India House.[142] These fears were realised in 1828 when a failure to receive any bullion from India forced the directors to dispose of a much-prized '*nest egg*'. They sold £1 million of the government securities owned by the Company so that they could meet the domestic demands for payment that were

141 For full details see the invoices, manifests, and related correspondence in L/AG/17/2, vols. 1–7.
142 Directors to Bengal, 4 June 1823, E/4/709, pp. 14–24.

being made upon them.[143] In general, the directors were now being driven to short-circuit the system of remitting funds through commerce, and they sought to achieve this by ordering the direct transfer of chests of bullion. Some, such as the financier Nathan Rothschild, later declared that this was the best way of transferring tribute to Britain,[144] but others simply recognised that the Company's financial wheels could no longer turn at all in London without such lubrication from Asia. This was acknowledged by the Chairman William Astell in 1830 when he wrote on the subject of bullion shipments from India: 'I hardly know how we could get on without them.'[145]

Between 1814 and 1833, the directors of the East India Company struggled to manage a declining and diminishing trade. They endeavoured in vain to apply long-standing methods and practices to a world of open competition, but they were unable, until it was far too late, to free themselves from internal organisational constraints and high costs that combined to make the Company's commodities uncompetitive in both Asia and Britain. All too often, important changes were made from a position of weakness rather than strength. In that sense, they succumbed rather meekly to what seems like an almost inevitable failure to sustain the Company's active commercial life much beyond the loss of the Indian monopoly in 1813. The directors were somewhat unfortunate, however, that the loss of the Indian monopoly occurred when it did, because the opening up of the Company's trade coincided with the end of war in Europe, which restored more stable commercial conditions and released pent-up demand; and the loss of monopoly just predated the 'take-off' of exports of cheap British cotton goods to India. If the Company's Indian trading privileges had stayed intact for a few more years, the directors might just have been able to establish a hold on the export of cottons to Asia, and in turn this could have prevented the Company sliding towards the complete commercial destruction that was confirmed by the Charter Act of 1833.

The whole point and purpose of the Company's trade between 1765 and 1833 was to provide a means of transferring wealth from India to Britain, and the directors adapted their commercial methods accordingly. They

---

143 J. G. Ravenshaw to Bentinck, 3 March 1828, *Bentinck correspondence*, vol. I, p. 15.
144 Asiya Siddiqi (ed.), *Trade and finance in colonial India, 1750–1860* (Delhi, 1995), p. 20. Rothschild himself had benefited greatly from the Company's transfer of bullion from Asia because he purchased large consignments in 1822/3 and then again during the late 1820s and early 1830s.
145 Astell to Bentinck, 3 June 1830, *Bentinck correspondence*, vol. I, p. 451.

were not without their successes in this endeavour, but the flow of tribute was never established in anything like the volume that was first anticipated during the 1760s. There was certainly a great increase in the movement of commodities between Britain and Asia between 1765 and 1813, but a failure to put the revenues properly 'in train' was fully exposed when the Company lost its Indian trade monopoly. A well-regulated tea trade continued to provide a channel through which funds could be remitted from India, but the directors had to resort somewhat desperately to the transfer of large amounts of bullion from Asia in order to meet the increasingly heavy empire-related charges made upon the Company in London. This was deeply ironic in view of the extent to which the Company had exported silver to Asia in the decades before it acquired its territories in India.

CHAPTER 9

Influences: the Company and the British economy

This study has concentrated primarily upon the internal changes that occurred to the East India Company in Britain as a result of the transition from trade to empire in Asia, and examinations have been undertaken of what happened inside East India House. But, as was established in the last chapter, the Company's relationships with domestic merchants and manufacturers ensured that it always had links with the wider British economy, and this raises the question of how the late eighteenth-century expansion of trade and empire affected the Company's interactions with the world beyond Leadenhall Street. Certainly, many of those who were sympathetic towards the Company believed that the material benefits of expansion were widely felt in Britain, and they were able to argue that financial rewards filtered through to many different sections of society. This was made clear in 1813 by Thomas Plummer who argued 'without pressing this calculation to an extreme' that a 'large portion of the community are directly or indirectly interested, by themselves or their connections, in the prosperity of the East India Company, especially in the metropolis'. He identified nine groups of people who drew benefit from the Company, ranging from the stockholders through to those who were dealers in India and China goods, and he concluded that 'When all these classes of people are taken into consideration, and we reflect for a moment how widely their connections are diffused, it may surely be said, with fairness, that scarcely any part of the British community is distinct from some personal or collateral interest in the welfare of the East India Company.'[1]

---

1 Thomas William Plummer, *A letter to the Right Honourable the Earl of Buckinghamshire, President of the Board of Controul, on the renewal of the East India Company's charter* (1813), pp. xxx–xxxi. Plummer, who had wide-ranging economic interests, had been MP for Yarmouth between 1806 and 1807.

Plummer exaggerated, but he was correct to suggest that an ever-widening circle of people in Britain had been brought into economic contact with the Company since 1756. The size and scale of the Company's operations at home and abroad had changed dramatically, and as a result there was a considerable increase in the number of investors and employees who gained income from the Company's military and commercial expansion in Asia. At the same time, the merchants, contractors, and ship owners who supplied the Company in Britain derived considerable benefit from the growth of trade and empire, and the knock-on effects were felt by manufacturers, shipbuilders, shopkeepers, artisans, farmers, and labourers in different parts of the country. Over time, this meant that an ever greater number of points of contact were established between Britons and the Indian empire or East India trade, and the lives of thousands of individuals in London and the provinces became tied to the process of expansion in Asia. Company wages, salaries, dividends, and interest payments, together with a variety of private profits, all contributed to the making of East Indian fortunes, great and small, and the capital accumulated by individuals was deployed in different forms of economic activity. People from all over Britain became participants in the process of commercial and imperial expansion whether or not they actually went abroad, and their material stake in overseas activity ensured that a commitment to trade and empire was always well to the fore when public expression was given to attitudes and identities.[2]

It is impossible to measure the full effects of the financial flows that were carried along the arteries of trade and empire that extended from East India House into the British economy, but this chapter does nevertheless seek to explore some of the ways in which the economic consequences of the Company's overseas expansion were felt in Britain. The chapter begins by considering the opportunities for employment created by the Company's acquisition of an empire in South Asia. The second section endeavours to estimate the Company's domestic expenditure on goods and services, before attempting to quantify some of the incomes and profits that were generated from Company-related activity in Britain. The final section then identifies some of the ways in which Company

---

2 Linda Colley, *Britons: forging the nation, 1707–1837* (New Haven, Conn., 1992), pp. 55–100; Kathleen Wilson, *The sense of the people: politics, culture, and imperialism in England, 1715–1785* (Cambridge, 1995), pp. 158–65, and passim.

fortunes were channelled into investment in different parts of the British economy.

EXPANSION, EMPLOYMENT, AND OPPORTUNITY

Commercial and imperial expansion after 1756 served greatly to increase employment opportunities in every branch of the Company's service and, understandably, the attention of historians has been directed towards India, where from small beginnings there was a steady increase in the size of the British communities established in each of the three Presidencies. By 1830 the Company employed 895 civil servants and 745 medical officers in India,[3] and the 'European' element of the Company's Indian army had reached 36,409 men within an overall establishment of 223,476.[4] In sum, therefore, it can be estimated that around 40,000 men were on the Company's payroll in India during the early 1830s, and, under the terms of Charter Act of 1813, there were 20,000 regular troops on the subcontinent who were paid for by the Company.[5]

In addition, there were also men and women who arrived as private individuals in India, with or without the permission of the directors, and in each of the Presidencies there were merchants, seamen, shopkeepers, tavern-keepers, teachers, lawyers, and so on. The Company, which was always resolutely opposed to the colonisation of the subcontinent, was of the view that there were 1,501 non-Company British residents in India in 1815, and it took great pride in the fact that the number had only risen to 2,016 in 1828.[6] All things considered, however, it seems reasonable to suggest that by the end of the period there were perhaps 5,000 British males in India who were not on the Company's payroll.[7] If this number is added to those on the official Company and regular army establishments, it can be estimated that there were perhaps 65,000 British men serving or residing in India during the early 1830s, and the addition of women and

---

3 L/F/10, vols. 14 (Bengal, 522 civil servants), 115 (Madras, 212), 139 (Bombay, 161); D. G. Crawford, *A history of the Indian medical service 1600–1813*, 2 vols. (1914), vol. I, pp. 213, 215.
4 *Reports from the select committee on the affairs of the East India Company* (1831–2), vol. V. p. 195.
5 Ibid., vol. V, p. xv.
6 Ibid., vol. IV, p. 27. For summary details of the 1,253 licences granted by the directors between 1814 and 1831 see ibid., vol. IV, pp. 268–9. In addition, the Board of Control issued seventy-one licences to those who had been refused by the Company (ibid., vol. IV, pp. 270–1).
7 The number of non-official British has been put at 2,150 (Raymond K. Renford, *The non-official British in India to 1920* (Delhi, 1987), p. 15), but this only takes licensed males into account. For Bengal alone, the *East India register and directory* of 1830 listed 1,710 private 'European' males, the majority of whom appear to have been British.

children might then serve to increase the total number of Britons to around 70,000 or 75,000.[8]

The causes and effects of the increasing numbers of Britons in India have been analysed in some detail by P. J. Marshall and others who have traced the emergence and development of Anglo-Indian societies in the main Presidency towns.[9] Marshall has also examined the economic activities of those men who hoped to earn a personal fortune in Bengal, especially during the 1750s and 1760s when many in Britain were attracted by the prospect of securing fabulous riches of the type acquired by Robert Clive and his fellow 'nabobs'.[10] However, the close attention devoted to the British in India has tended to obscure the fact that for much of the period the Britons who lived or served in South Asia were outnumbered by the combined total of those who were employed by the Company in Britain, served on board its ships, or provided it with domestic goods and services. In various ways, and to varying degrees, these people all derived sustained financial benefit from the Company's overseas expansion, as did the members of private metropolitan interest groups whose investments and entrepreneurial activities sustained the Company's commercial and maritime operations.

In London the size of the Company's workforce grew remorselessly during the late-eighteenth century. As noted in chapter 5, an increasing volume of administrative work contributed to a rise in the number of full-time 'regular officers' on the home establishment.[11] At the same time, the post-1785 expansion of the Company's tea trade resulted in the building of a large integrated complex of new tea warehouses at Cutler Street, just north of Leadenhall Street, between 1792 and 1800,[12] and this required more men to be employed to ensure that goods were correctly organised

---

8 For other calculations of the British population of India during the nineteenth century, and the difficulties in making accurate estimates, see P. J. Marshall, 'British immigration into India in the nineteenth century', in P. C. Emmer and M. Mörner (eds.), *European expansion and migration. Essays on the intercontinental migration from Africa, Asia, and Europe* (New York, 1992), p. 139.

9 P. J. Marshall, 'The white town of Calcutta under the rule of the East India Company', *Modern Asian Studies*, 34 (2000), pp. 307–31; Holden Furber, 'Madras in 1787', in Charles Seymour (ed.), *Essays in modern English history in honor of Wilbur Cortez Abbott* (Cambridge, Mass., 1941), pp. 255–69; Holden Furber, *Bombay presidency in the mid-eighteenth century* (New York, 1965).

10 P. J. Marshall, *East Indian fortunes: the British in Bengal in the eighteenth century* (Oxford, 1976).

11 See above, p. 139.

12 This building programme had a considerable impact upon the locality, and contemporaries were impressed with not only the size and scale of the buildings but also with the sense of order and cleanliness that was brought to a hitherto dirty and densely populated neighbourhood. See Penelope Hunting, *Cutler's gardens* (1984), pp. 59–67. For a map of 1806 indicating the location of all of the Company's London properties see H/763, pp. 7–8. For the Company's London

and stored. In 1785 the Company employed a total staff of 1,541 in the capital, and this included 1,393 labourers, porters, watchmen, warders, and commodores who were distributed across the various warehouses and paid on a daily basis.[13] Over the next twenty-five years the size of the labouring force grew rapidly, and by 1813 it had reached 2,700 men. This contributed to a doubling in the overall size of the workforce, which meant that in 1813 there were 3,090 people on the Company's domestic payroll.[14] The rate of growth slowed thereafter, but in 1828 the Company employed just fewer than 4,000 people before a campaign of retrenchment cut back the numbers to 3,490 in 1830.[15] In spite of this late reduction, it is fair to say that throughout the period the Company was one of the largest employers of labour in London.

The Company also provided regular employment for labourers and artisans in London who were not on the payroll but nevertheless routinely participated in the commercial and maritime activities that underpinned the East India trade. Tradesmen provided the goods and services that enabled East India House and the warehouses to function properly; a whole host of merchants, retailers, and manufacturers supplied an infinite variety of stores, equipment, and general merchandise that was sent out to sustain the Company's operations in India and China; a considerable number of dyers, dressers, pressers, and packers prepared the woollen cloth exported by the Company to Asia; an extended chain of lumpers, boatmen, carriers, cart men, and porters handled cargo as it was moved to and from the Company's ships; and in private dockyards on the River Thames a large workforce built, serviced, and repaired the Company's fleet of East Indiamen.

The sum total of these people cannot be established with any degree of accuracy, but by the beginning of the nineteenth century it was routinely asserted that 30,000 people in London were employed in commercial and industrial establishments that were connected to the Company.[16] Indeed,

properties see Margaret Makepeace, 'Sources for London history at the India Office Library and Records', *London Topographical Record*, 26 (1990), pp. 153–76, and 'The East India Company London warehouses', *Journal of the Families in British India Society*, 12 (2004), pp. 1–10.

13 Figures calculated from H/362, pp. 51–65. At this stage the daily pay for these workers ranged from 2s. 6d. for commodores to 1s. 6d. for some of the watchmen.

14 *Proceedings of the Select Committee appointed by the General Court of Proprietors on the 6th October 1813 . . .* (1814), p. 119. Annual figures for the number of labourers appointed are to be found at ibid., p. 155.

15 *PP* (1831–2), 735–1, vol. IX, p. 15.

16 See, for example, the speeches of Alderman Atkins of 5 January 1813, and Mr Impey of 22 January 1813, in the General Court, as reported in *Debates at the East India House, during the negociation for a renewal of the Company's charter . . .* (1813) vol. I, pp. 40, 133.

in 1813 a resolution of the General Court went as far as to claim that the destruction of the Company would mean that 'nearly forty thousand persons, directly employed by the Company, with many others indirectly concerned in its prosperity, would be brought to a state of absolute beggary'.[17] Of course, such an estimate should be treated with caution since it was made by stockholders who were attempting to defend the Company's monopoly privileges, but when Francis Russell, Solicitor to the Board of Control, offered an informed and balanced assessment of the Company and its trade he declared that 'The number of families in London and its environs whose whole support is dependent on the Company's trade is great beyond conception.' He concluded that 'It would be almost impossible to enumerate the tradesmen, artificers, and others, who, by the means of this regular, and as it were, fixed trade, earn and obtain honest livelihoods in building, rigging, and careening of ships, and furnishing guns, anchors, timber, iron, cordage, and various other sorts of implements and tackle used therein.'[18]

Beyond London, the Company generated employment in the regions and localities from whence it derived the manufactures and raw materials that were exported to Asia for sale or for use by its servants. Between 1756 and 1834 the Company itself spent over £70 million on commodities for export (See table 9.1).

Annual commodity expenditure rose from an average of £440,536 during the 1760s to £1,890,546 during the first decade of the nineteenth century, and this helped to sustain demand for wool textiles, metals, and military equipment produced in the provinces. It is difficult to establish exactly how much benefit was felt by manufacturers, farmers, artisans, and labourers at local level because a good proportion of the sums paid out by the Company remained in the pockets of London-based middlemen such as the powerful cloth factors of Blackwell Hall. Local areas did, however, undoubtedly feel the pinch when Company orders were not forthcoming for any reason, and commentators were often swift to point to the importance of the East India trade in keeping up levels of employment during periods of economic depression. Hence, in 1829 when the Company cut back its quarterly order from 40,000 to 28,000 pieces of serge or long ells because of difficulties it was experiencing with the Hong merchants in Canton, the *Hampshire Telegraph* feared that this would 'be

---

17 Ibid., vol. I, p. 337.
18 F. R. [Francis Russell], *A short history of the East India Company . . .* (1793), pp. 39–40.

Table 9.1. *Company expenditure on commodities for export, 1756–1834*

	Invoice cost in £s	% of total
Broadcloth	18,069,733	25.6
Long ells	21,427,715	30.4
Worsted stuffs	5,080,915	7.2
Copper	9,366,519	13.3
Iron	1,715,202	2.4
Lead	2,449,476	3.5
Tin	1,505,096	2.1
General merchandise	10,890,624	15.5
Total	70,505,280	100.0

Note: The figures for broadcloth, long ells, and worsted stuffs include payments made for dyeing and packing as well as the cloth itself.
Source: Figures calculated from payments to merchants and manufacturers recorded in L/AG/1/1, vols. 20–32.

the cause of considerable difficulty and distress among the labouring class of manufactures in the west [of England]'.[19]

The importance of the Company has been acknowledged by historians of particular trades and industries who have established that from the 1760s through to the 1820s its orders helped to extend the lives of the hard-pressed textile industries of Gloucestershire, Devon, and Norwich, and that it offered much-needed relief to the struggling tin industry of Cornwall.[20] Rather more positively, the East India trade also supported the development of the copper mining and smelting industries. By the 1780s, exports to Asia represented between one-sixth and one-quarter of total national output of copper, and in 1789/90 the Company accounted for almost two-thirds of Cornish copper sales.[21] With Company ships gradually being coppered during the last two decades of the century, the

19 As reported in *The Times*, 16 January 1829.
20 J. de L. Mann, *The cloth industry in the west of England from 1640 to 1880* (Oxford, 1971), pp. 37–62, 157; W. G. Hoskins, *Industry, trade and people in Exeter, 1688–1800* (Exeter, 1968), p. 86; T. Fawcett, 'Argonauts and commercial travellers: the foreign marketing of Norwich stuffs in the later eighteenth century', *Textile History*, 16 (1985), pp. 172, 175; John James, *History of the worsted manufacture in England, from the earliest times . . .* (1867), pp. 308–10. J. Rowe, *Cornwall in the age of the industrial revolution* (St Austell, 1993), pp. 170–85.
21 J. R. Harris, *The copper king: a biography of Thomas Williams of Llanidan* (Liverpool, 1964), p. 11; Henry Hamilton, *The English brass and copper industries to 1800* (second edition, 1967), p. 196. Full details of the Company's relationships with copper mining and smelting companies are to be found in Harris, *Copper King*, passim. During the 1790s exports to Asia accounted for 60 per cent of total exports of 'brass and plated goods' and 35 per cent of total wrought copper exports, *Report of the Committee [of the House of Commons] appointed to enquire into the state of the copper mines and copper trade of this kingdom (7 May 1799)*, Appendix 33, pp. 166–9.

expansion of the East India trade bore directly on the growth of the mines of Cornwall and Anglesey, as well as the smelting establishments located in the Swansea and Neath valleys and elsewhere. Finally, beneficial 'spin-off' effects from Company orders were also felt in the localities. An increasing volume of commodities needed to be carried by land, sea, and canal to the Company's cargo assembly points at London and Graves-end, which benefited local transport industries;[22] and manufacturers generated orders of their own for raw materials, as happened, for example, with Richard Shaw of Norwich. Shaw was one of the main suppliers of woollen camlets to the Company during the 1820s, and he procured most of his wool from farmers in Leicestershire and Lincolnshire.[23]

What all of this amounted to in terms of offering employment to people in the regions of Britain awaits detailed study, but in some instances the Company's local influences could be considerable. During the late 1790s the Cornish copper mine owner John Vivian was reported to have declared that the ending of copper exports to Asia would mean that 'England will not long to have to boast of her mines and metallic manufactures', while the leading figure in the industry, Thomas Williams, predicted in such an event the 'mines of Anglesea, as well as those of Cornwall', must be involved in the general ruin'.[24] A few years later the woollen manufacturers of Cornwall, Devon, and Somerset claimed that half of the long ells they produced for export was destined for Chinese markets, and they suggested that this annually consumed wool from 800,000 sheep and generated employment for 16,000 labourers.[25] Of course, whether local populations would have derived any greater benefit from an 'open' or free trade with Asia trade is a matter for debate, and the issue was fiercely discussed prior to the passage of the Charter Act of 1813.

---

22 At the same time, Company orders played some part in causing the movement of raw materials from their place of origin to different points of manufacture. See, for example, the growth in the number of Anglesey ships that accompanied the late eighteenth-century expansion of copper-mining operations on the island (Aled Eames, *Ships and seamen of Anglesey, 1558–1918*, republished edition (1981), pp. 184–92).

23 *Report of the Select Committee of the House of Lords appointed to enquire into the present state of the East India Company* . . . (1830), p. 832.

24 *A short abstract of the evidence given before the Committee of the House of Commons, appointed in April 1799 to enquire into the state of the copper mines and copper trade in this kingdom* (1800), p. 41. These comments were made in response to a move to prohibit exports intended to prevent the loss of stocks required by brass and copper manufacturers in Birmingham and elsewhere. Vivian estimated that the Cornish copper mines employed 5–6,000 men and 4–5,000 women and children. He reported that 10,000–12,000 tons of shipping was required to carry ore to South Wales and to return with coal to be used in the Cornish mines (ibid., p. 22).

25 *Journal of the House of Commons*, vol. XLVII (1812), pp. 490–1 (petition of 29 June).

The Company's Chairman Jacob Bosanquet was able to claim in 1798, however, that through the Company's export trade 'several of the largest counties in England are relieved to a very great extent by the liberal conduct of the Company, in looking more to the general state of the mother country than its more immediate profit'.[26] It was indeed sometimes the case that the Company ordered goods even though they could not be sold abroad, and it is possible to find occasions, such as in 1820, when cloth purchases were made with the deliberate intention of reducing distress experienced by the labouring poor in different parts of the country.[27]

It can thus be suggested that in terms of employment the domestic influence exerted by the Company was rather greater than has been acknowledged by historians of the British economy, and beyond London several thousands of livelihoods were very heavily, if not wholly, dependent upon the annual orders for commodities issued from East India House. This was especially the case before the overall volume of Company exports began to diminish during the 1820s, and it must be remembered that the private trade conducted between Britain and Asia on Company ships also generated substantial orders for an even wider circle of domestic merchants and manufacturers, from those who brewed ale through to the makers of watches, clocks, jewellery, musical instruments, and 'sing-songs' sent to Canton.[28]

Just as the Company's overseas expansion generated employment in Britain, so too it created more openings for men to serve as commanders, officers, and seamen on board the ships that plied the trade routes between London, India, and China. The late eighteenth-century growth in the volume of goods imported from the East required the Company to hire more ships, and from the 1780s it also began to use larger vessels in the tea trade with China. These ships only ever represented a small

26 Bosanquet to Pitt, 14 April 1798, H/61, p. 189.
27 Directors to Bombay, 9 May 1820, Commercial Department, vol. 12, pp. 95–6, 100, MSA. On this occasion the directors were offering relief to the manufacturers of long ells in the West Country, and to weavers in the north of England. They ordered 12,000 cloths from the former and goods costing £10,000 from the latter.
28 Exports of ale to Asia passed mainly through the privilege trade and increased from 1,480 barrels in 1750 to 9,000 barrels in 1800. See Peter Mathias, *The brewing industry in England, 1750–1800* (Cambridge, 1959), pp. 189–90. For the private trade in musical instruments see Ian Woodfield, *Music of the Raj: a social and economic history of music in late eighteenth-century Anglo-Indian society* (Oxford, 2000), pp. 15–48. For the manufacturing of 'sing-songs' etc. for the privilege trade see Roger Smith, 'James Cox (c.1723–1800): a revised biography', *Burlington Magazine*, 142 (2000), pp. 353–61.

proportion of the overall tonnage employed in foreign trade – 6 per cent in 1792[29] – but the crews of the East Indiamen were always much larger than those on other merchant vessels. Standard 499-ton Company ships of the 1760s had a company size of 100 men, but the later 800- to 1,200-ton ships carried up to 130 men.[30] As a result, the Company's maritime establishment grew apace, and by 1800 it accounted for around a fifth of the 105,000 seamen employed on British-owned merchant ships.[31]

During the 1760s the directors despatched, on average, twenty-five ships a year, each between 499 and 650 tons, and thus the annual fleet sent to Asia would have had a notional strength of 2,500 officers and men. By the first decade of the nineteenth century, the directors were sending out fifty-one ships a year, and between them these larger vessels should in theory have had over 6,500 men on board.[32] Of course, the reality was rather different. Vessels did not always have a full crew, especially during times of war when men were often pressed out of Indiamen by the navy, and a variable proportion of the men on board would not have been Britons, especially on return voyages when deserters had to be replaced by Indian lascar and Chinese seamen. Bearing these factors in mind, when all of the officers and seamen are taken into account – that is those who at any one time were outward, homeward, abroad, or between sailings in Britain – a conservative estimate might suggest that the number of men in the Company's maritime service rose from around 8–10,000 during the 1760s to somewhere in the region of 20–25,000 during the 1800s when the fleet of East Indiamen was at its largest. Although the number of Britons would have fluctuated according to the ebb and flow of war and peace, it seems reasonable to surmise that, on average, perhaps two-thirds of these men originated from the British Isles.[33]

---

29 Joseph E. Inikori, *Africans and the Industrial Revolution in England. A study in international trade and economic development* (Cambridge, 2002), p. 280.

30 For the size and composition of the ships' companies see Jean Sutton, *Lords of the east. The East India Company and its ships (1600–1874)* (second edition, 2000), pp. 76–86.

31 Inikori, *Africans*, p. 274.

32 The calculation of the annual number of sailings is based on voyage information in Anthony Farrington, *Catalogue of East India Company ships' journals and logs 1600–1834* (1999), pp. 743–5, 752–5.

33 In line with the Navigation Acts, the Company's regulations stipulated that three-quarters of all crews should be Englishmen. However, practical necessity dictated that this rule often had to be relaxed or ignored and, following several modifications, the government in 1823 eventually permitted the Company to employ only four Englishmen for every hundred tons of a ship's burthen (Sutton, *Lords of the east*, p. 86).

Men of ambition were not drawn to serve on Company vessels by the meagre monthly wages on offer.[34] Instead, they were attracted by the lure of adventure and, in particular, by the prospect of profiting from the legal 'privilege' trade or associated smuggling activities. The private trade licensed by the Company was indeed a great privilege, and freight-free cargo allowances ranged from fifty-six tons for a commander to a few cubic feet for a skilled tradesman. It was primarily for this reason that qualified officers were prepared to pay large sums of money for commands, which, over time, had become a form of property that could be bought and sold. Men blessed with sharp business acumen could take advantage of the private trading opportunities that this system presented to them, and during the late eighteenth century it was often suggested that a commander who enjoyed good fortune might earn himself a profit of up to £10,000 on a single voyage to Asia. Such estimates were not fanciful. Spurred on by the prospect of rich pickings, officers endeavoured to make a personal fortune as quickly as possible and, as one commander was told, the basic aim was to 'make hay while the sun shines, and settle at home'.[35]

There were of course considerable risks involved. If they did not fall victim to the sea, there were always plenty of commercial hazards and by no means all commanders and officers were in possession of good commercial skills. Moreover, although some men were elevated from the crew to serve as officers, most ordinary Company sailors eked out a pitiful existence below decks with little real hope of improvement in their material or financial circumstances.[36] Those who did become officers and were fortunate to survive were able to have long careers, however, and thus by the time George Simpson died in 1802 at the age of sixty-eight he had completed eighteen voyages to the East, six of them as commander; while William Hay made seventeen voyages between 1786 and 1826, nine of them in command.[37] It was said that for men such as these a voyage to the East 'is become to you a walk as to Epsom or Tunbridge to a citizen of London; once season'd to the climate there is little to fear'.[38] Regular voyages between Britain and Asia enabled them and their

---

34 Throughout the Company's history, the commanders of East Indiamen were paid a nominal £10 a month, and the basic wage rates of others remained unaltered between 1746 and 1813 (ibid., pp. 65, 142).

35 The Earl Marischal to William Fullerton Elphinstone, 20 November 1768, MS Eur. F89/131.

36 For details of the wages and value of the effects belonging to deceased seamen who served on board the *Hector* in 1769 see L/MAR/B486S.

37 For outline details of their careers see Anthony Farrington, *A biographical index of East India Company maritime service officers 1600–1834* (1999), pp. 364, 718.

38 The Earl Marischal to William Fullerton Elphinstone, 28 June 1768, MS Eur. F89/131.

associates to build up extended networks of commercial activities that spanned half the globe, and this placed them in an ideal position to exploit the commercial opportunities that opened up as a result of the Company's expansion.[39]

In every sphere of the Company's operations, then, the interrelated expansion of trade and empire in Asia served to provide employment for an ever greater number of individuals. In 1815 the political economist Patrick Colquhoun calculated that the Company offered direct employment to 48,315 British subjects,[40] but it can be suggested that in 1800 over 90,000 Britons were dependent in one way or another upon the Company for their livelihoods at home, abroad, or on the oceans. This admittedly very rough calculation errs on the side of caution, and it does not include the 20,000 or so Crown troops serving in India who were paid for by the Company. The calculation summarised in table 9.2 also takes some contemporary estimates at face value, and assumptions are made about those who provided services or produced goods for the Company.[41] The distribution of numbers between overseas, maritime service, and Britain was to change when the directors began to scale back the Company's commercial and maritime operations following the loss of the India trade monopoly in 1813, but at the peak of its influence around 1800 it would seem that the Company offered more employment to Britons at home and on the seas than it did in Asia. Of course, many of these people earned only very modest amounts of money but nevertheless their personal fortunes were tied in one way or another to those of the East India Company.

The increase of employment opportunities within the Company attracted individuals from across all parts of British society. During the second half of the eighteenth century, the Company's Indian civil service lost its hitherto close, almost exclusive, connection with London's merchant classes, and it gradually became the preserve of well-connected

---

39 For a case study of such activity undertaken by the Lennox family of Campsie in Stirlingshire see B. R. Tomlinson, 'From Campsie to Kedgeree: Scottish enterprise, Asian trade and the Company Raj', *Modern Asian Studies*, 36 (2002), pp. 769–91.

40 Patrick Colquhoun, *Treatise on the wealth, power, and resources of the British Empire* (1815), appendix, p. 45. Colquhoun believed that there were 2,146 men in the 'civil service' in Britain and 1,056 in India. He estimated the maritime service at 25,000 (but wrongly assumed that these were all Britons) and put British officers, NCOs, and soldiers in the Company's army at 20,000.

41 Most notably, it assumes that the labour of those included in the calculation was directed only towards serving the needs of the Company. The size of the Company's military and civil presence in India in 1800 is calculated from *Reports from the Select Committee on the affairs of the East India Company* (1831–2), vol. V, p. 195; L/F/10, vols. 6, 113, 139.

Table 9.2. *The East India Company and the employment of Britons in 1800*

1. *Overseas*		
a. Civil and Medical servants	1,000	
b. Company troops	20,000	21,000
2. *Maritime service*	15,000	15,000
3. *Britain*		
a. Home establishment	2,500	
b. Private individuals providing goods and services in:		
i. London	30,000	
ii. The provinces	25,000	57,500
Total		93,500

gentlemen.[42] The Company's army and marine service still offered opportunities for advancement to individuals who were from humble backgrounds, however, and it was by no means impossible for men from the
English provinces, Ireland, Scotland, and Wales to climb the rungs of
different Company hierarchies. Thus, to take just one example, John Lloyd
from Llanwrtyd in Breconshire first served as surgeon's mate on the *Anson*
in 1766, but he then rose steadily up the list of ships' officers and eventually
became Commander of the *Manship* in 1790. During most stages of his
progress he was able to advance his personal fortune through private trade,
and as a result he became prominent in the economic and political life of
Brecknock following his retirement from Company service in 1796.[43]

Scots were especially adept at infiltrating different branches of the
Company's service. This has been well documented in recent years, so
suffice it to say that the patronage networks that were extended from
Whitehall and Leadenhall Street to Scotland from the 1720s onwards
facilitated an increasing flow of well-educated, well-connected men from
north of the border to Asia via London.[44] As a result, Scots became

42 Marshall, *East Indian fortunes*, pp. 11–17; Suresh Chandra Ghosh, *The British in Bengal. A study
   of the British society and life in the late eighteenth century* (second edition, New Delhi, 1998), pp.
   30–2.
43 Ken Jones, 'John Lloyd (1748–1818): an adventurous Welshman', Part I, *Brycheiniog*, 33 (2001),
   pp. 59–92; Part II, 34 (2002), pp. 67–118.
44 For a detailed study see George Kirk McGilvary, 'East India patronage and the political
   management of Scotland, 1720–1774', unpublished PhD thesis, Open University (1989). See also
   J. G. Parker, 'The directors of the East India Company, 1754–1790', unpublished PhD thesis,
   University of Edinburgh (1977).

strongly represented within the Company's civil, military, and medical service in India.[45] Far less attention has been paid by historians to the Company's maritime service, but it can be calculated that even here Scots represented 28 per cent of those who were first appointed to command of an East Indiaman between 1777 and 1813, and for whom there is a known place of birth or baptism.[46] Twenty Scots were appointed to a command for the first time during the 1780s, thirty-six during the 1790s, and forty-eight during the 1800s. In part, this advance was facilitated by Scottish former commanders such as Robert Preston, who became a powerful managing owner of East Indiamen and then favoured Scots when he appointed commanders and officers. Scots commanded twenty-nine of the forty-five voyages undertaken by Preston's ships, and in turn Scottish commanders were often believed to be instrumental in the recruitment of officers and crew members from north of the border. As a result, in some sailing seasons the Scottish presence in the Company's outward-bound fleets must have been formidable. This was certainly the case in 1805 when twenty (or 42.5 per cent) of the forty-seven ships despatched to Asia were under Scottish command. And, as noted earlier, the British presence in Asia and the East India trade did not end with the East India Company. Half of the regular army regiments sent to India between 1754 and 1784 were raised in Scotland,[47] and this tradition continued thereafter. As private sectors began to flourish in Bombay, Calcutta, and Madras, Scots were also well to the fore in the establishment of agency houses.[48]

It is clear that Scots became well represented in most branches of the Company established beyond the shores of Britain. By comparison, men from Ireland and Wales were rather less visible, although the Company's

---

45 For estimates see John Riddy, 'Warren Hastings: Scotland's benefactor?', in Geoffrey Carnall and Colin Nicholson (eds.), *The impeachment of Warren Hastings. Papers from a bicentenary commemoration* (Edinburgh, 1989), pp. 50–7. See also G. J. Bryant, 'Scots in India in the eighteenth century', *Scottish History Review*, 64 (1985), pp. 22–41; David Arnold, *Science, technology, and medicine in colonial India*, The New Cambridge History of India, vol. III. 5 (Cambridge, 2000), p. 60. For a recent study placing the Scottish presence in India within a broader imperial context, and explaining why Scots were so successful in securing East India appointments, see T. M. Devine, *Scotland's empire 1600–1815* (2003), esp. ch. 11. A detailed study of the Scottish and Irish presence in the East India Company is currently being prepared by Andrew Mackillop. This will revise downwards some of Riddy's high estimates of the Scottish presence in the Company in India. I have gained much from my conversations with Dr Mackillop.

46 The following figures are based upon analysis of biographical data contained in Farrington, *Biographical index* (1999).

47 Bryant, 'Scots in India', pp. 23–4.

48 B. R. Tomlinson, 'The "empire of enterprise": Scottish business networks in Asian trade, 1793–1810', *KIU Journal of Economics and Business Studies*, 8 (2001), pp. 67–83.

army contained a large and rapidly growing body of Irishmen. During the Seven Years War, Irish recruits accounted for 17 per cent of those sent to India to bolster the Company's land forces, and after 1800 Irish recruits usually represented more than half of the men despatched to the East.[49] Members of Irish gentry families were also to be found in significant numbers in the officer corps, and some such as the Wellesley brothers were able to secure the most senior commands. This is not to say, of course, that individuals or families of Irish origin could not achieve a considerable degree of personal success in other fields of East Indian endeavour.[50] For example, Sir Robert Wigram, born in Wexford in 1744, was a surgeon in the Company's maritime service before he became one of the most powerful builders and owners of East India shipping.[51] Some Welshmen were also able to use the Company's expansion to advance themselves, and thus Thomas Parry, born in Welshpool, Montgomeryshire, in 1768, drifted in and out of Company service as he gradually became established as one of the leading figures in the world of trade, shipping, and marine insurance at Madras.[52] But men such as Wigram and Parry usually had to find their way without much support from their fellow countrymen, and they were often unable to take advantage of extended kinship networks in the manner of the Scots.

Although the presence of large numbers of Scots in India and elsewhere was clearly of considerable importance to the development of British overseas activity, Scotsmen should not be regarded as having effected a takeover of the East India Company during the second half of the eighteenth century. Scots did indeed become disproportionately represented in several different branches of the Company, but Englishmen and Irishmen (in the case of the army) were often to be found in a majority. This is often overlooked when analysis is focused narrowly on the Scots, and the English ascendancy was especially marked at East India House

---

49 On the growing Irish presence in the Company's army during this period see Thomas Bartlett, 'The Irish soldier in India, 1750–1947', in Michael Holmes and Denis Holmes (eds.), *Ireland and India: connections, comparisons, contrasts* (Dublin, 1997), pp. 13–18. For details of Welshmen in the Company's army see *Index of Welshmen in the East India Company army compiled by the Welsh family history societies in London* (1997). Although there are 3,223 entries for the period 1753–1860 some names are noted more than once, which makes it impossible to arrive at an accurate total for the number of Welshmen who served in India.

50 For a study of the several members of the Irish branch of the Popham family who found their way into Company service see Frederick W. Popham, *A west country family: the Pophams from 1150* (Sevenoaks, 1976), ch. 13.

51 See below, pp. 293–4.

52 For a detailed study of Parry see N. S. Ramaswami and S. Muthiah, *Parrys 200: a saga of resilience* (New Delhi, 1988), pp. 17–54.

and the warehouses where employment was based primarily upon recruitment in and around London.[53] Moreover, as far as the provision of men for the Company's maritime or overseas service is concerned, very little attention has been paid to any patronage connections that might have existed between East India House and the provinces of England, and not much is known about the extent to which the Company drew regularly from pools of labour in English counties such as Devon or Dorset.[54] No detailed group analysis has yet been undertaken of the Englishmen who were in Company service, but their numbers are enough to suggest that by drawing on recruits from England as well as the Celtic provinces the Company was creating workforces that were as diverse and cosmopolitan as Britain itself. During the second half of the eighteenth century the Company was still formally the 'United Company of Merchants of England trading to the East Indies', and it was commonly referred to as the 'English East India Company', but in terms of its personnel it was well on its way to becoming truly a British East India Company.

COMPANY EXPENDITURE

It is well known that the establishment of a territorial empire in India created large fortunes for some Company servants, with plunder, prize money, 'presents', and the profits of private trade all contributing to wealth that was remitted by individuals to Britain. Corruption, extortion, and abuse of office ensured that when the pagoda tree was shaken in Bengal during the 1750s and 1760s some men were able to acquire fabulous riches, although comparatively few Company servants were either lucky enough, or lived long enough, to be able retire to Britain with a substantial fortune. For every Robert Clive or Sir Thomas Rumbold there were many failures, and those who did return home as conspicuously wealthy men often had to endure deep hostility from critics in

---

53 This is evident from the great majority of the addresses of those who acted as sureties for the bonds of the clerical staff and elders or senior labourers employed at East India House and the warehouses. See Z/o/1/6, Bond book of officers of the home establishment, 1788–1860. A detailed study of the Company's warehouse labourers is currently being prepared by Margaret Makepeace.

54 There is a paucity of studies exploring connections between the Company and different English regions. See, however, James H. Thomas, 'The East India Company and the Isle of Wight, 1700–1840', *The Local Historian*, 30 (2000), pp. 4–22; James H. Thomas, *Portsmouth and the East India Company, 1700–1815* (Lampeter, 1999); Arthur C. Wardle, 'The East India Company: some local associations', *Transactions of the Historic Society of Lancashire and Cheshire*, 99 (1949), pp. 63–78.

metropolitan society who denounced the money, manners, and morals of the 'nabobs'.[55] Rather less is known about the East Indian fortunes that were made elsewhere in India, or indeed in Bengal after 1784, although it is fair to say that while they might still sometimes have been substantial they were not acquired as rapidly as those during the first phase of Company expansion. They certainly did not attract the same amount of attention from contemporaries, despite the fact that suspicions about 'nabobs' lingered on into the nineteenth century.

It is important to stress, however, that East Indian fortunes were not only earned by individuals who served in India. The Company's expansion in Asia generated income and profit for a large number of people in Britain itself: those who were connected directly to the Company, and also private individuals who benefited from the growth of the East Indian trade. Thus, for example, Asian goods imported into Britain were distributed further and wider during the late eighteenth century by a process that operated independently of the Company. A nationwide network of private dealers, merchants, and retailers purchased goods at the Company's sales and then directed the transportation and distribution of those commodities to outlets in provincial towns, cities, and villages. As is made clear by the historians of the tea trade, control over the distribution of tea lay with the main London dealers and not with the Company, and it was they who shaped the development of the market, organised re-exports, and, as a result, reaped substantial personal rewards.[56] And they were not the only ones who derived benefit from the import trade, because spin-off effects were felt elsewhere within the domestic economy. As Francis Russell put it, dealers in East India goods gained 'advantages' from

profits on the re-sales, by carriage and agency; and the Port of London being thus made the chief depot for the supply of Europe, and of many parts of Africa and America, of the merchandise of the East, is necessarily resorted to by foreign merchants for its purchases, who, at the same time, buy various commodities of our own manufacture, which would probably not otherwise have been called for, by all which the national prosperity is promoted.[57]

The Company itself exerted a number of increasingly strong influences within the domestic economy through expenditure that was translated

---

55 Philip Lawson and Jim Phillips, '"Our execrable banditti": perceptions of nabobs in mid-eighteenth century Britain', *Albion*, 16 (1984), pp. 225–41.
56 Hoh-cheung Mui and Lorna H. Mui, *The management of monopoly. A study of the East India Company's conduct of its tea trade, 1784–1833* (Vancouver, 1984), pp. 12–22.
57 Russell, *Short history*, p. 31.

into incomes and profits for thousands of individuals. The Company paid salaries, gratuities, and pensions to its staff and their dependants; it distributed stock dividends and interest on bonds and loans; it hired ships; it bought commodities and military equipment for export; and it purchased a great variety of the goods and services that were necessary to ensure the routine functioning of its commercial, administrative, and military operations. In total, between 1756 and 1834 the Company made cash payments in Britain amounting to almost £667 million, at an average of just over £8.5 million a year. To put the last figure into some sort of comparative perspective, the Company's yearly outgoings usually stood at between one-quarter and one-fifth of the figure attributed to annual government expenditure.[58] This helps to establish an order of magnitude for Company expenditure, but it does have to be remembered that not all of the payments that passed through the Company's books were generated by its own commercial and imperial activities.

Just over 13 per cent (£87,631,839) of domestic expenditure was accounted for by payments made on bills and certificates drawn upon the Company by individuals in India and China. Individuals were granted these bills in return for cash paid into the Company's treasuries at Bombay, Calcutta, Madras, and Canton and they used them a means of remitting their private fortunes to Britain from India.[59] In addition, from the mid-1780s onwards, the Company issued 'India debt' bills to its creditors in India as a means of transferring some of its local rupee debt payments to London.[60] There were several other ways by which Company servants and others could transfer wealth from Asia to Britain, notably by investing in an expanding private trade, but the Company's bills were

---

58 The figures for government expenditure are taken from B. R. Mitchell with the collaboration of Phyllis Deane, *Abstract of British historical statistics* (Cambridge, 1962), pp. 390, 396.

59 For a full discussion of the use of bills and other ways of remitting fortunes see Marshall, *East Indian fortunes*, pp. 214–56. As Marshall points out, after 1769 individuals in India were able to remit their fortunes home via Canton, where the Company desperately needed cash to expand its tea trade, and this is reflected in growth in the number of 'China bills'. In his discussion of Bengal remittances, Marshall has provided details of the value of bills drawn in India and China, but the rather different figures offered here are based upon the cash payments on bills eventually made by the Company in London. Obviously there was often a considerable delay between an individual drawing a bill in India and presenting it for payment at East India House. In theory, bills should have been paid within a year of being presented, but this seldom happened in practice.

60 For details of the initial organisation of this scheme see the directors' letter to Bengal, 15 September 1785, *FWIHC*, vol. IX, pp. 240–3. As the Company's Accountant-General later pointed out, it was not always possible to distinguish between 'debt' bills and those issued in India for 'general purposes' (*Third report of the Select Committee on East India Company affairs*, *PP*, 1810–11 (250), vol. XII, p. 384).

always safe and secure, even though the rate of exchange was not competitive, the number of bills was often restricted by statute, and payments were sometimes delayed by four or five years during periods of financial crisis. Accordingly, the Company's payments mechanism facilitated the transfer to Britain of a large proportion of the fortunes generated by private activity in Asia.[61] As can be seen from the peaks evident in figure 9.1, bills of exchange were issued in especially large amounts in India whenever the Company's servants needed to raise funds locally for war but, overall, there was a significant upward trend in the volume of payments on bills cashed in London. In 1756/7 payments on bills were just over £120,000; in the peak year of 1812/13 such payments amounted to over £4 million. Table 9.3 allocates total payments to the Company bills drawn overseas between 1756 and 1834, although it must be borne in mind that small amounts were also paid out on bills drawn at Benkulen, St Helena, and elsewhere.

By 1828 the Company was said to be cashing 6,000–7,000 bills of exchange every year, but it was also paying out around 3,500 dividends and making 12,000–13,000 miscellaneous payments.[62] As these figures suggest, the Company was thus not only facilitating the transfer of private capital from Asia to Britain but it was also generating funds for distribution into the metropolitan economy. The extent of this distribution had increased greatly over time. As can be seen in figure 9.2, the Company's aggregate cash expenditure in Britain (including payments on bills) more than doubled during the initial phase of expansion, from under £2.5 million a year during the mid-1750s to over £5 million during the late 1780s. Heavy military expenditure and the rapid growth of the export trade then further doubled annual cash payments in Britain, with over £10 million being paid out from East India House for the first time in 1797/8. Wartime expenditure peaked at almost £19 million in 1812/13, before annual payments settled at £11–15 million a year between 1815 and 1829. The winding down of the Company's trading operations saw payments fall below £10 million for the first time in over thirty years in 1832–3, although strong surges in outgoings then occurred in 1833/4 and 1836/7 as the ending of commercial activity obliged the Company to repay

---

61 As is evident from Marshall's overall estimate of the money sent to Britain from Bengal between 1707 and 1784 (*East Indian fortunes*, p. 255).

62 These estimates were made by the Deputy Chairman, John Loch (letter to the Governor and Deputy Governor of the Bank of England, 14 August 1828, E/1/264, no. 2136). Loch thought that a thousand of the vouchers issued for the payment of dividends went to a group of thirty bankers.

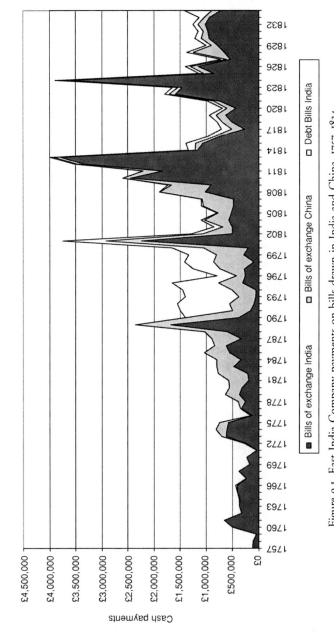

Figure 9.1. East India Company payments on bills drawn in India and China, 1757–1834.
Source: L/AG/1/1, vols. 20–31.

Table 9.3. *Total payments on bills from India and China, 1756–1834*

Type of payment	Total payments	% of total
Bills of exchange on Bengal	£31,623,870	36.1
Bills of exchange on Madras	£13,158,583	15.0
Bills of exchange on Bombay	£9,890,788	11.3
Bills of exchange on Canton	£19,999,755	22.8
Interest on bills of exchange	£1,203,542	1.4
India debt bills (1791–1809)	£8,802,794	10.0
Carnatic Debt bills (1809–34)	£2,952,057	3.4
Total	£87,631,389	100

Source: L/AG/1/1, vols. 20–32.

long-term loans and make compensation payments to some of its former servants.

Underlying the growth of annual Company expenditure were increases in the outgoings recorded in most of the account headings in the Company's general ledgers. Adjustments to the names of accounts, and occasional alterations to the allocation of expenditure, make it difficult to be precise about changes to payments over time. Nevertheless, in table 9.4 regular outgoings have been collected at thirty-year intervals, for 1759/60, 1789/90, and 1819/20, all of which were years when the effects of current or very recent wars were being felt. They have then been grouped under seven main headings to present a moving picture of expenditure.

These figures have to be treated with some degree of caution because, as was the case with freight payments to ship owners in 1759/60, the Company sometimes deferred expenditure when it was experiencing cash-flow problems. Nevertheless, the expansion of the Company's trade is fully reflected in the regular outgoings noted under headings three to six. The marked reduction of freight payments between 1789/90 and 1819/20 arises from a reform of the shipping system as well as a contraction in the size of the Company's fleet after the loss of the Indian monopoly in 1813. Especially noteworthy, however, is the considerable growth of outgoings on salaries and pensions. At the beginning of the period, the Company paid salaries and wages to its clerical and labouring staff in London and it made a small number of discretionary payments to others. Over time, though, as noted in chapter 5, a greater range of payments began to be made to former employees, the sick and wounded, widows and their dependants. By 1793 the Company was also underwriting the

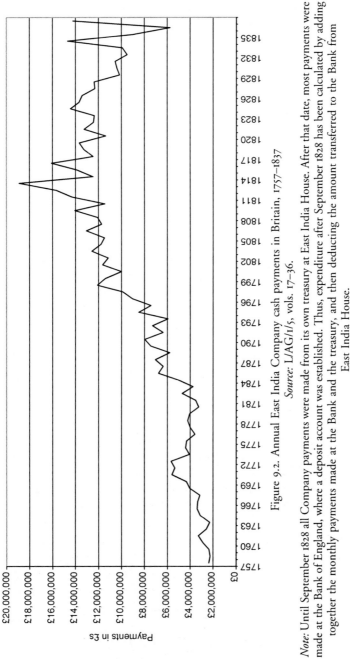

Figure 9.2. Annual East India Company cash payments in Britain, 1757–1837
Source: I/AG/1/5, vols. 17–36.

Note: Until September 1828 all Company payments were made from its own treasury at East India House. After that date, most payments were made at the Bank of England, where a deposit account was established. Thus, expenditure after September 1828 has been calculated by adding together the monthly payments made at the Bank and the treasury, and then deducting the amount transferred to the Bank from East India House.

Table 9.4. *Allocations of regular East India Company cash payments in Britain, 1759/60, 1789/90, 1819/20*

	1759/60	1789/90	1819/20
1. Salaries, gratuities, pensions	17,320	62,898	692,387
2. Stock dividends and bond interest	294,141	479,619	780,592
3. Commodities and bullion for export	485,331	1,603,677	2,548,530
4. Freight and transport of troop payments to ship owners	138,818	1,241,350	775,374
5. Goods and services	39,875	165,958	144,928
6. Customs and duty payments to government	516,410	993,497	3,189,296
7. Bills drawn on India and China	515,506	1,598,002	694,198

Source: L/AG/1/1, vols. 20, 26, 31.

salaries of the staff at the Board of Control at an annual cost of £16,000; while from 1796 considerable expenditure was devoted to pay for military officers on furlough, and pensions were paid to those who had retired from the army. In 1819/20 payments to such officers amounted to £257,152, and this served greatly to increase the numbers of those who were in some way dependent upon the Company in Britain.

As far as the trade with Asia was concerned, the Company's domestic expenditure was channelled in the first instance into the pockets of a relatively small number of merchants, manufacturers, and shipbuilders. Although the Company ostensibly operated a system of tender, the influence of private interest groups at East India House was such that in practice, year after year, the directors returned to the same suppliers of commodities and shipping.[63] This meant that large sums of money were paid to firms who operated in small cartels over long periods of time. Hence, for example, during the 1760s the Blackwell Hall factor Nicholas Pearse was paid between £19,000 and £25,000 a year for supplying broadcloth to the Company. His firm Nicholas Pearse & Sons was still being paid £40,000 a year three decades later; while at the beginning of the 1820s six suppliers with the name of Pearse were selling long ells to the Company.[64] It was the same with suppliers of metals, and from the 1780s though to the 1820s, the Company procured much of its lead from

63 H. V. Bowen, 'Sinews of trade and empire: the supply of commodity exports to the East India Company during the late eighteenth century', *Ec. Hist. Rev.*, 55 (2002), pp. 466–86.
64 L/AG/1/1, vol. 21, pp. 225–31; vol. 27, p. 116; L/AG/13/1/1, p. 521.

Walker, Maltby & Co., which was the London branch of the Walkers lead partnership of Newcastle-upon-Tyne.[65] Unfortunately, the absence of private papers and accounts makes it impossible to calculate exactly how much profit suppliers like Pearse and Walkers made from their transactions with the Company. The very fact that they enjoyed long and cosy relationships with the directors does suggest that it was well worth their while to remain strongly connected with the East India trade for, as Francis Russell put it, 'Those with whom the Company have dealings are certain of liberal treatment and punctual payment.'[66] As a result, they stoutly resisted competition from other companies.

Firmer evidence of profitability is available, however, for some of those who hired ships to the Company. Considerable capital was necessary to build East Indiamen, which were much larger than other merchant ships and had a cost per ton that was substantially more expensive.[67] Thus in 1780 the owners Charles Foulis and Robert Preston paid £10,239 to John Perry & Co. for the purchase of the 765-ton ship *Pigot*; in 1791 the 1,206-ton *Woodford* cost Preston £14,753 from the same yard; while in 1797 wartime increases had pushed up the price of the hull of the 1,456-ton *Coutts* to £24,784 when Preston bought it from Randall Brent & Sons.[68] As has been pointed out, the fact that Company ships had to be replaced after four (later six) voyages to Asia provided shipbuilders on the River Thames with 'conspicuously profitable employment'.[69]

---

65 Bowen, 'Sinews of trade and empire', pp. 481–2.

66 Russell, *Short history*, p. 39.

67 In 1781 the cost of a hull for an 800-ton Indiaman was £14 14s. 0d. per ton, whereas the price of London-built hulls for other merchant ships was between £8 8s. 0d. and £9 9s. 0d. per ton. By the end of the century the price of a hull of an Indiaman reached nearly £22 per ton. See R. Craig, 'Capital formation in shipping', in J. J. P. Higgins and Sidney Pollard (eds.), *Aspects of capital investment in Great Britain 1750–1850: a preliminary survey* (1971), p. 143.

68 Details from the unnumbered papers of Sir Robert Preston in GD1/453/1, NAS. For outline construction agreements struck between John Perry & Co. and the managing owners of several East Indiamen see the contract book at SPB/27, NMM. For an example of the detailed construction specifications of an East Indiaman see the articles of agreement between the shipbuilder Francis Barnard and the merchant William Hamilton who was the managing owner of a 674-ton vessel (the *Preston*) to be built for the Company's service in 1798 (SCS/2, NMM). Between 1763 and 1825 the shipyards of the Barnard family built sixty-two Indiamen for thirty-six different managing owners. See John E. Barnard, *Building Britain's wooden walls: the Barnard dynasty, c.1697–1851* (Oswestry, 1997), pp. 100–1. For details of the building of East Indiamen see Sutton, *Lords of the east*, pp. 37–52.

69 Craig, 'Capital formation', p. 140. Most East Indiamen were indeed built in dockyards at Blackwall and Deptford, although some were constructed at outlying yards in places such as Bristol, Buckler's Hard, Harwich, Hull, Itchenor, Liverpool, Rochester, and South Shields.

In order to meet the substantial costs of purchasing an East Indiaman, managing owners sought funds from small syndicates of investors who usually purchased sixteenth or thirty-second shares in the venture. These part-owners realised profits when the total cost of construction, fitting, repair, insurance, and other expenses was deducted from the freight and demurrage payments made by the Company in return for its cargoes being shipped to Asia and back. The proceeds were then divided on a voyage-by-voyage basis between the investors according to their share of the initial investment.

The papers of Robert Preston, a prominent managing owner of the 1780s and 1790s, reveal much about the costs and profits of this type of enterprise, and they show that, despite the obvious risks involved, the high freight rates paid by the Company meant that the returns to investors could be considerable. Thus, after Nicholas Carter, a London butcher, invested £600 in a thirty-second share in the *Hillsborough* in 1781 he received dividend payments amounting to £2,390 spread over six voyages from 1784 to 1798, which represented a return of almost 20 per cent a year on his original outlay.[70] John Walker, a ships' chandler of Wapping, did less well but still earned 14 per cent a year from his investment in the *William Pitt.* He invested £630 in a thirty-second share in 1786, and then received £2,085 in dividend payments from six voyages over a sixteen-year period. Preston's investors were, on the whole, successful but others were less fortunate and it was reported that when the *Addington* was wrecked on the Isle of Wight in December 1798 David Hunter lost an anticipated return of £400 a year for twelve years because he had not insured his sixteenth-share in the ship.[71] Even so, many were attracted by the prospects of rich pickings from investment in Company shipping and some individuals built up large holdings spread across many vessels. In 1810 Sir Robert Wigram had £88,048 invested in seventeen ships in the Company's service.[72] Few were able to operate on this scale, and most investors seem to have held a small number of shares. Unfortunately, it is not yet possible to be precise about the total number of shareholders who were part-owners of East Indiamen although, if we take the cost of a vessel to

---

70 GD1/453/1, NAS. In 1792 it was believed that ship owners earned 18 per cent a year on their capital outlay, although it was usual for 12 per cent to be reinvested in the stock (Inikori, *Africans,* p. 276). Such reinvestment of profits did not happen with the owners of East Indiamen, although occasional calls for additional funds were made by managing owners.

71 *The diary of Joseph Farington,* vol. III: Kenneth Garlick and Angus Macintyre (eds.), *September 1796–December 1798* (New Haven, 1979), p. 1121.

72 Figure calculated from shares listed in Wigram's journal, WIG/2, p. 1, NMM.

have been between £12,000 and £15,000 during the 1780s, we can estimate that the 100 or so shipping 'bottoms' then taken up at any one time by the Company represented a total capital investment of around £1.5 million.[73]

Major export suppliers and ship owners received large annual payments from the Company over long periods of time, but war drove up domestic expenditure, and the Company's construction of a large military machine in India also required regular supply from Britain. This was reflected in increasingly heavy outlay on iron guns, small arms, gunpowder, shot, shells, uniforms, shoes, tents, and equipment. There are numerous examples of the way in which this brought benefit to firms in the metropolis, but one will suffice in order to illustrate the point.

The effect of the Company's change of status in India, and the increasing size of its army, was most clearly evident in its export of small arms. On only three occasions before 1765 had the annual bill for small arms been above £10,000, but subsequently there was a great increase in expenditure on such weapons. Payments of over £60,000 were made in both 1767 and 1769, and an annual outlay of between £20,000 and £50,000 on small arms became commonplace. Unsurprisingly, sustained periods of warfare led to much heavier expenditure, and thus in both 1810 and 1811 payments exceeded £125,000, while the Burma war saw outgoings top £130,000 in both 1826 and 1827.[74] In order to facilitate the regular supply of weapons of a standard pattern, the Company was by 1775 dividing its orders between a small group of approved London gun makers who manufactured or purchased the component parts and then 'set up' the Company's small arms and muskets in their workshops. Some setters-up supplied the Company for decades, and several received total career payments of over £100,000.[75] Prior to 1807 these men (and women) passed some orders on to those who produced barrels, locks, bayonets, and ramrods in the Midlands, but after that date the Company itself began to procure parts directly from source and it dealt regularly

73 In 1786 the managing owner Thomas Newte estimated that almost £2 million was invested in East India shipping. See his paper presented to Henry Dundas, Melville Papers, MS 1066, f. 5, NLS. Holden Furber suggested that in 1750 the number of investors in sixty Company ships 'must have exceeded 800' (*Rival empires of trade in the Orient, 1600–1800* (1976), p. 363, n. 35), and he estimated that between 1700 and 1750 the gross amount invested in East Indiamen at any one time had been between £480,000 and £640,000 (ibid., p. 363, n. 39).

74 D. F. Harding, *Small arms of the East India Company 1600–1856*, 4 vols. (1997), I: *Procurement and design*, pp. 361–2. This book provides an exhaustive study of the supply of small arms to the Company.

75 For a full list and details of almost 100 'setters-up' of the period 1771–1856 see ibid., vol. I, pp. 293–304.

with groups of specialist manufacturers in Birmingham, Wednesbury, and Darlaston in Staffordshire, thus illustrating once more how the economic effects of expansion in Asia were felt in the British provinces.[76]

As the Company expanded and changed, the directors also spent heavily on the non-military items that were necessary to sustain commercial and territorial expansion. Thus under the export heading of 'general merchandise' was an infinite variety of items intended for use by the Company's servants in India, China, and elsewhere. This included everything from marine stores to pens, ink, paper, union flags, bunting, speaking trumpets, and a surprisingly large number of rupture trusses. The great variety of these types of purchases is evident in the details of Company expenditure undertaken during the typical month of June 1787, as set out in table 9.5.

Items such as these were procured from tradesmen, retailers, and merchants in London on a regular or semi-regular basis, with individual payments often amounting to no more than £10 or £20. Some single purchases were, however, often on a grander scale, as was the case when an organ for the newly completed St Mary's Church in Madras was bought for £633 16s. 0d. from Robert and William Graham in March 1788. Capital-intensive projects in India required much heavier expenditure again, and thus the positive effects were felt by manufacturers in Britain when the Company decided to build a new mint at Calcutta during the early 1820s. In the year to July 1823 the machinery destined for the mint led to payments of £33,428 being made to Boulton, Watt & Co., £29,152 to G. & J. Rennie, and £12,313 to H. Maudslay.[77] Later, £49,189 was divided between the manufacturers who supplied equipment for a new mint at Bombay.[78] During the 1820s, technological advances were also reflected in purchases of coal for shipment to St Helena, where it was used to fuel engines, while a cast iron bridge and steam engine were purchased for use by the Nawab of Awadh.[79]

Closer to home, the Company's expanding presence in London required an increased annual outlay of goods and services of one type or

76 Ibid., vol. I, pp. 44–6. For a full list of those who supplied musket parts to the Company after 1807 see pp. 305–23. See also De Witt Bailey and Douglas A. Nie, *English gunmakers. The Birmingham and provincial gun trade in the 18th and 19th century* (1978).

77 L/AG/1/5, vol. 31, pp. 407, 454, 468, 580.

78 L/AG/1/1, vol. 31, p. 344. These sums included the salaries of mechanics that accompanied the equipment to India, and the Company also had to hire three ships specifically for the task of carrying out the machinery (E/4, vol. 708, pp. 908, 1029).

79 Ibid., L/AG/1/1, vol. 31, pp. 99, 335, 378 (coal), 343 (bridge and engine).

Table 9.5. *Company expenditure on general merchandise for export, June 1787*

Commodity	Tradesman	Invoice price (£sd)
Pitch and tar	Nathaniel Taylor	203-16-00
Drums	Robert Horne	27-06-00
Musket flints	William Levett	26-10-00
A clock, etc.	Ainsworth Thwaites	130-02-00
Tinware	David Fossick & Sons	118-11-11
Anchors	Harrisons, Gordons & Stanley	365-09-00
Printers' colours etc.	William Quamill	176-18-00
Pewter	Joseph Spackman	306-01-00
Leather	William Newman & Sons	8-02-08
Gilt buttons etc.	Christopher Corrall	46-17-00
Cart wheels	William Wilson	831-16-00
Soldiers' clothes	Nicholas Pearse & Sons	760-19-00
Scales and weights	William How	566-03-00
Ironmongers' ware	Jukes, Coulson & Co.	2566-16-03
Linseed oil etc.	Thomas Day	1051-14-00
Hats	Melchier Henry Wagner	694-00-00
Surgeons' instruments	Rice Price	581-06-00
Steel	Isaiah Millington	4,041-05-00
Ironmongers' ware	Isaiah Millington	1,322-14-01
Ironmongery	Goodchild, Slater & Co.	1,028-16-00
Dr James's powder	Francis Newbery	9-06-05
Small arms	William Debenham	270-00-00
Rupture trusses	Margaret Richardson	40-19-00
Compasses etc.	Anna Scatcliffe	45-02-06

Source: L/AG/1/5, vol. 22, pp. 195–6.

another, and routine expenditure was supplemented by spending on particular projects. The great Company building boom of the late eighteenth and early nineteenth centuries resulted in heavy outgoings on construction as well as on the purchase of houses to be demolished. As a result, the Company spent £694,036 on 'buildings' in the fifteen years after 1796, at an average annual cost of £46,269.[80] This generated contracts for a firm such as Sarah Poynder & Son, which was paid £1,590 for plumbing work in 1799/1800 and £2,080 the following year.[81] Buildings always had to be maintained and serviced, and the extended property empire that came into being after 1800 ensured that there was always regular expenditure on work carried out by tradesmen at East India House and in the warehouses and other Company establishments. This meant

---

80 Calculated from L/AG/1/1, vols. 28, 29, and 30.   81 Ibid., vol. 28, p. 204.

that in the twenty years after 1814 payments of tradesmen's bills for repairs, coals, candles, and expenses at East India House averaged £21,526 a year, while similar expenditure on the warehouses averaged £31,807 a year.[82]

The Company's commercial activities also generated a demand for the transport services that were necessary to ensure the safe transit of goods from ship to shore to warehouse and back. Thus, early in the period there was expenditure on carriage, cartage, and porterage as well as the hire of the boats and hoys that transported imported goods from East Indiamen anchored in Blackwall Reach to the crowded Legal Quays alongside the Pool of London, from where they were then taken to the warehouses. Inevitably, much of this outlay was of a seasonal nature, but the late eighteenth-century growth of the Company's trade saw an increase in such expenditure. The type of payments recorded as 'Charges on Merchandise' were extended during the 1790s, but even before then there had been a marked growth in outlay, from £27,175 in 1756/7 to £133,644 in 1789/90.[83] The later restructuring of the Company's cargo-handling operations that accompanied the opening of the East India Docks in 1806 resulted in an adjustment of accounts, and some of the Company's charges were now allocated to the annual payments that were made to the East India Dock Company. Yet in 1819/20 £3,776 was still being spent on hoys, and £7,546 went on hiring the armed caravans that were now needed to carry goods along Commercial Road to the warehouses in the City.[84] In the broader scheme of Company expenditure in Britain such payments were modest, but they were very necessary to ensure that the commercial cogs of the Company continued to turn and, as has been stressed throughout this section, they provided income for some of those employed in the metropolitan workforce. Whether he was conscious of it or not, the livelihood of a man such as William Jury, who was paid £3 16s. 2d. to carry woollens from the Cloth Warehouse to the Bengal Warehouse in 1832,[85] was ultimately dependent upon the Company's overseas expansion.

COMPANY FORTUNES

The question of how, and to what extent, the private fortunes generated by those in Company service were spent or invested in Britain has rarely

82 Ibid., vol. 31. 83 Ibid., vols. 20, 26. 84 Ibid., vol. 31.
85 L/AG/1/5, vol. 34, p. 372.

been explored in any great depth, although it used to be commonly asserted that the plundering of Bengal helped to prime the pump of the Industrial Revolution. However, the detailed work of P. J. Marshall has helped to explode this myth, and although Marshall thought that remittances from Bengal to individuals in Britain were 'certainly impressive', averaging over £500,000 between 1757 and 1784, he made two important qualifying points. First, this sum was a very small proportion of annual national income as a whole and, second, there is little evidence that much of it was ever invested in industry or transport.[86]

During the period of easy fortune-making, which lasted between 1757 and the mid-1770s, the nabobs who returned to Britain in the possession of large wealth mainly used their money to purchase country estates and houses around London and in the provinces. As a result, colonies of former Company servants were established in counties such as Berkshire and Surrey.[87] Scots who were seeking to assimilate themselves into the London elite played their part in this process, but some East Indian wealth was also channelled north of the border where it was used to save some families from ruin, and in counties such as Roxburghshire it provided funds for investment in landed property and agricultural improvement.[88] At the same time, many East Indians sought to generate income from investment in the funds or lending on mortgage. As Marshall puts it, neither the sons of merchants nor the sons of existing landowners 'regarded their fortunes as capital for further venturing in trade or manufacturing in Britain'. Consequently, 'after Indian service, most men hoped for ease and relaxation, not for a strenuous new career'.[89] This appears to have remained the case in later years although, as morals and outlooks changed, some East Indian fortunes began to find their way into philanthropic and educational activity. Thus, in 1807 Alexander Gray of the Bengal Medical Service left £30,000 to the City of Elgin for the establishment of a hospital; and the Company surgeon Thomas Phillips retired in 1817 with a 'competent fortune', a large part of which he then spent on charitable donations, the distribution

86 Marshall, *East Indian fortunes*, p. 256.
87 For details of some, but by no means all, nabob country seats see James M. Holzman, *The nabobs in England. A study of the returned Anglo-Indian, 1760–1785* (New York, 1926), pp. 123–30.
88 Bryant, 'Scots in India', pp. 35–40.
89 Marshall, *East Indian fortunes*, p. 215. For the size of fortunes and the uses to which they were put see ibid., pp. 214–56.

of books, scholarships for Welsh students, and the eventual establishment of the Welsh Collegiate Institution at Llandovery in Camarthenshire.[90]

Research at local level might yet unearth examples of nabob investment in industrial and commercial enterprise,[91] but Marshall's broad conclusions will remain unchallenged. Nevertheless, it must be remembered that the group of people that Marshall was analysing – the British in Bengal – formed only a small segment of the wider Company community. Little attention has been devoted to the very much larger number of people whose fortunes were generated from Company-related activity in Britain and on the high seas. They represented a much wider spectrum of society than the nabobs and former Company servants, and the effects of their direct engagement with domestic trade and industry were felt across many parts of Britain.

East India stock and bonds formed an important part of the broad investment portfolios that were held by gentlemanly capitalists, but, as was noted in chapter 4, the stock also helped to support small investors such as widows and spinsters who were seeking a steady income. In total, the annual dividend and interest income derived from East India stock and bonds was quite substantial and, to put it into perspective, at a time when annual private remittances to Britain were around £500,000, the Company's average yearly payments to its stock- and bondholders amounted to £333,659.[92] Later, as the size of the Company's stock was expanded and the dividend was fixed at 10½ per cent, these annual outgoings rose considerably, so that between 1814 and 1834 payments on stock dividends and bond interest averaged £788,253 a year.[93] Some of this was utilised by merchants and others as part of their attempts to maximise the use of idle funds, although income derived from this source cannot be considered to have contributed greatly to direct investment in metropolitan trade and industry.

It does seem reasonable to assume, however, that part of the profits of the merchants and manufacturers who supplied the Company would have

90 D. G. Crawford, *Roll of the Indian medical service, 1615–1930* (1930), p. 35; D. T. W. Price, 'Thomas Phillips of Brunswick Square', in William Marx (ed.), *The founders' library University of Wales, Lampeter. Bibliographical and contextual studies. Essays in memory of Robin Rider. Trivium*, vol. 29/30 (Lampeter, 1997), pp. 169–76.

91 For a recent case study which suggests that Richard Griffith, who served as acting Company accountant at Patna during the 1770s, invested most of his fortune (unsuccessfully) in the Grand Canal Company of Ireland see J. R. Owen, 'A nabob at Holyhead: Richard Griffith, Post Office packet agent, 1815–1820', *Maritime Wales*, 25 (2004), pp. 27–33.

92 Calculated from L/AG/1/1, vols. 20–24.

93 Calculated from ibid., vol. 31.

been ploughed back into firms. The evidence to support such a claim is admittedly sketchy, but Company orders certainly appear to have assisted the long-term survival and development of firms such as Boulton & Co., Carron Company, and Crawshay & Co., the Merthyr ironmasters. Rather stronger is evidence illustrating that individuals in the Company's maritime service garnered profits from private trading activity and were then able to put some of their accumulated funds to work in domestic trade and industry when they retired from the sea.

Of course, like those in the Indian civil service, some commanders of East Indiamen sought little more than a fashionable country seat and a comfortable lifestyle in retirement based upon investment in land and the funds. Thus, when Alexander Macleod, originally from the Isle of Harris, retired from the Company's maritime service with a 'noble fortune' during the 1770s he decided to live in 'ease and splendour'. Accordingly, he purchased Theobalds Park, near Cheshunt in Hertfordshire, where he kept a 'truly hospitable house'.[94] Nearby, at Wormleybury Manor, lived his brother-in-law Sir Abraham Hume whose family had long moved in the world of Company shipping.[95] Hume retained some interest in the ownership of East Indiamen but, as directed by his father's will, most of the funds he inherited in 1772 were ploughed into estate development in Lincolnshire, Norfolk, Essex, and, primarily, Hertfordshire where he became a noted gardener, collector of minerals, precious stones, paintings, and exotic imported plants.[96] Like many of their contemporaries, Macleod and the Hume family used maritime service and investment as a means of establishing themselves in landed society. They were not always readily accepted, and Macleod's coarse sea manners and habits were a matter for ridicule, but their efforts to carve out a respectable position for themselves saw their East Indian fortunes being channelled into land, property, and the funds.

Others were more inclined to use the Company's maritime service as a stepping-stone to busy second careers in the world of domestic trade

---

94 Alan Valentine, *The British establishment 1760–84: an eighteenth-century biographical dictionary* (1970), p. 572. Macleod had commanded the *Marlborough* during Clive's expedition to recapture Calcutta in 1756.

95 For the East Indian and other commercial activities of Alexander Hume and the first baronet Sir Abraham Hume, see Parker, 'Directors', p. 408, n. 3.

96 For the estate papers, marriage settlements, and wills of Sir Abraham Hume senior and junior which throw light on this family transition from sea to land see D/Ewb E3, F3, F11, Hertfordshire Record Office. Hume's career as a collector of plants is discussed in Kate Harwood, 'A Hertfordshire garden in the eighteenth century: Sir Abraham Hume of Wormleybury, plant collector', *Herts Past and Present*, third series, 2 (2003), pp. 12–16.

and industry. In part, this was because the size of their fortunes was often modest in comparison with the wealthiest nabobs, but it would also seem that they held a different view of how money should be made and spent. Unsurprisingly, a good number of these former maritime servants invested in East India shipping, and on their retirement from the Company men such as Donald Cameron, John Durand, Charles Foulis, William Fraser, Jeffrey Jackson, Thomas Newte, Robert Preston, Charles Raymond, and William Webber moved easily from command into ship ownership, and some, notably Foulis, Raymond, and John Williams, advanced into banking and insurance.[97] As noted earlier, they formed a powerful private interest bloc within the Company, but they also created tight-knit social groups reinforced by marriage, and many of them lived in close proximity to one another in and around Ilford, Walthamstow, and Woodford in Essex.[98] Several of them died as very wealthy men, notably Raymond who was said to be worth £200,000 at the time of his death in 1788.

Some commanders used profits made in the privilege trade as a form of start-up capital for other forms of enterprise, and they supplemented their interest in shipping by investing in a wide range of other commercial and industrial projects. Thus, although the young William Elphinstone (1740–1834) had no resources of his own at his disposal when he began his career in Company service, he engaged in private trading activities with funds initially provided by the Earl Marischal, and this enabled him to restore his family's flagging financial fortunes. By the time he retired from command of the *Triton* in the mid-1770s he was in a position to establish a shipping firm to carry the iron of Carron Company, and he later embarked on a long career as a director and influential Chairman of the East India Company.[99] By the beginning of 1792 he calculated his net worth to be £36,984, and he was in possession of a varied investment portfolio. Some of his resources were still tied up in private trade with Asia through loans made to men who had served under his command, and some were committed to the funds and personal advances. But he was

97 Foulis ended his days in 1783 as a director of the Sun Fire Office. Raymond and Williams were co-founders of Deacon's Bank in 1771. Later partners in the bank included other prominent managing owners of Indiamen Robert Williams and William Moffat. See Kenneth Holden, *William Deacon's 1771–1970* (Manchester, 1970), pp. 1–16.

98 I am indebted to Georgina Green for supplying me with much detailed information on the large number of ship owners who lived in this part of Essex.

99 For outline details of Elphinstone's Company service and career as a director see McGilvary, 'East India patronage', pp. 260–5 and Parker 'Directors', pp. 114–17. At the time of his marriage in 1774 Elphinstone assumed the name Fullerton-Elphinstone.

also involved in a wide range of merchant and manufacturing enterprise, mainly in Scotland. Among other investments, he held £1,000 shares in each of Carron Company, the Cumbernauld Road project, the Glasgow Tan Work Company, the Greenock Bone Work Company, and the Glasgow Glasswork Company. Thereafter, Elphinstone consolidated his investments by concentrating on the funds but his activities before 1795 provide a good example of how profits generated in private trade could contribute to the development of provincial British industrial activity.[100]

In a similar fashion, private trade played a crucial part in the establishment of one of the largest business fortunes of the day. Elphinstone's near-contemporary Robert Wigram arrived in London from Ireland in the early 1760s with only £200 to his name but, having qualified as a surgeon, he put his funds to good effect while serving on Company voyages to Bengal, Benkulen, and Canton between 1764 and 1772.[101] He later recalled that at this stage of his career 'my accumulations were but small', but when ill-health and failing eyesight caused him to retire from the Company's maritime service he was worth £3,000 and, being in possession of a 'perfect knowledge of the trade of India and China', he was able to carve out a position for himself as a leading importer of drugs destined for European markets. In order to facilitate this, he continued to participate in the privilege trade in partnership with Commanders such as William Hambly of the *Lord North*,[102] and this ultimately enabled him to turn 'my small capital to very great advantage'. In 1788 Wigram ventured into East India ship owning for the first time, and as he extended his shipping interests during the late eighteenth century he was elevated to a position of pre-eminence in the Port of London. He also diversified his activities, enabling him later to claim that 'I was a general merchant over the whole world, a brewer, shipbuilder, India husband, and a great promoter of Huddart's patent for cables etc.'

Wigram was created a baronet in 1805, and contemporaries represented his career as a miracle story of rags to riches.[103] There were good grounds

100 Details of Elphinstone's financial activities from MS Eur. F89/40, 'Stocks and bills of William Elphinstone c.1778–1799'. On 1 August 1795 Elphinstone calculated his net worth to be £41,042; in October 1797 he put it at £43,142.

101 Unless otherwise stated, the following paragraph is based upon R. G. Thorne, *The History of Parliament. The House of Commons 1790–1820*, 5 vols. (1986), vol. V, pp. 554–6, and Henry Green and Robert Wigram, *Chronicles of Blackwall Yard Part 1* (1881), pp. 50–5.

102 For details of Hambly's 'Adventure to China in Compy Robt Wigram' see MS Eur. C425 (no pagination). This refers to Hambly's voyage to Benkulen and Canton as Commander of the *Lord North* in 1781.

103 See, for example, *Farington diary*, vol. X: Kathryn Cave (ed.), *July 1809–December 1810* (New Haven, 1982), p. 3701.

for this and, even though the size of his fortune was often exaggerated, his net assets stood at £369,703 in 1810. In addition to his investments in East India shipping, he owned the Blackwall shipyard valued at £40,250, and held £11,988 in the East India Dock Company, of which he was Chairman.[104] In addition, he had committed £50,000 to the brewers Meux, Reid & Co. of Liquor Pond Street and £17,000 to the rope manufacturers Huddart & Co. of Limehouse, and these ventures, together with investments in the funds and insurance companies, generated an income of £7,647 in the financial year 1811–12.[105] When Wigram calculated his worth ten years later the figure stood at £320,747, distributed between shipping concerns (£10,385), stocks and funds (£108,274), land (£35,498), co-partnerships (£93,400), loans to his thirteen sons (£61,080), and goods and effects including Walthamstow House, Essex (£12,110).[106] As with Elphinstone, Wigram's early small-scale private participation in the expanding East India trade had provided him with the means of establishing himself in business, and the profits he generated were successfully redeployed in substantial commercial activity.

Striking success and a rise to public prominence mean that the experiences of Elphinstone and Wigram cannot be considered to have been typical, but other less well-known figures followed similar paths and were able to generate funds that allowed them to participate in a wide range of commercial, industrial, and financial endeavours. Naturally, some remained close to the world of maritime enterprise, and thus when Robert Hudson retired as Commander of the East Indiaman *Houghton* 1796, he took the natural step of becoming an owner of Company shipping. At the same time, however, he also invested in five whaling vessels destined for the Southern Ocean and in the ship *Unicorn* that was heading for the north-west coast of America. He lost money on the whaling vessels, and the *Unicorn* was captured by the French in 1804, but these setbacks were more than offset by the return on his investment in Company ships, so that following his death his personal estate was valued at £77,806 in 1818.[107] Others turned away from the sea and chose to invest in enterprises in the provinces. In mid-Wales, the former commander John Lloyd, who was noted earlier, bought the estate of Abercynrig for £12,500, but he also

---

104 WIG/2, p. 1, NMM.   105 WIG/1, p. 35, NMM.
106 Ibid., p. 146. For a copy of Wigram's forty-six-page will of 1825 detailing the distribution of his assets to his wife and eighteen surviving children, see ibid., WIG/3/12, NMM.
107 See MS Eur. E257, vols. 1–12, passim. The valuation of his estate is to be found on a loose paper in vol. 3.

invested in local industry and infrastructure. He became one of the four shareholders of the Brecon Boat Company, which monopolised trade on the local canal and owned a coal mine. In addition, Lloyd himself owned a fulling mill and he became a founder investor in the local tramway.[108] As the case of Lloyd well illustrates, Company fortunes could have a significant bearing on local economic activity.

Historians have often tended to focus their attention on internal factors in order to explain growth and development of Britain's economy during the eighteenth and early nineteenth centuries. Over the last decade or so, however, attention has turned back once more on to the importance of overseas trade, and, as noted in the introduction, detailed analyses have been made of British economic interactions with the Atlantic economy. It cannot be claimed that the growth of commerce with Asia had a similar impact on the development of the British economy – not least because the value and volume of the Atlantic trade were of a very different scale and order – but this chapter has suggested that the expansion of trade and empire in Asia did generate rather stronger domestic economic impulses than have hitherto been recognised by historians.

Much work still remains to be done on Britain's economic interactions with Asia, and especially on the vigorous private trade with India and China that coexisted with commerce of the East India Company, but it seems abundantly clear that a wide range of individuals were drawn into the Company's economic orbit during the late eighteenth century. Both directly and indirectly, these people derived opportunity, income, and profit from the Company, and their earnings found their way into a variety of different forms of economic activity in London and several provinces. It might not have been until after the Company lost its Indian commercial monopoly that British manufacturers felt the full force of Asian demand for cheap cotton textiles and other commodities, but it would be wrong to assume that until then the East Indian trade and empire bore only lightly on the development of the British economy. As this chapter has shown, during the late eighteenth and early nineteenth centuries the funds that flowed out of East India House added to the commercial, financial, and industrial strength of the metropolis, and the private fortunes generated by those connected to the Company became increasingly tightly woven into the economic fabric of imperial Britain.

---

108 I am indebted to Ken Jones for this information.

Afterword

The East India Company Charter Bill of 1833 prompted very little debate or controversy in Parliament or the Company.[1] In part this was because the political nation had been preoccupied with the Reform Act of 1832; in part it was because people had tired of East Indian affairs; and in part it was because the Company had long been set on course to lose its remaining commercial privileges. Indeed, many within the Company regarded the loss of the China monopoly as inevitable,[2] and between 1830 and 1833 the stockholders preoccupied themselves with ensuring that they would continue to receive an annual dividend of 10½ per cent charged on the Indian revenues. Unlike in 1792–3 or 1812–13, there was little discussion of the profitability of the Company's trade or the contribution made by the Company to the well-being of Britain's economy or state finances, and there was widespread agreement that the Company's commercial days were over. As Thomas Babington Macaulay, the Secretary of the Board of Control who framed the settlement of 1833 with the Company, said of the opening of the trade with China, 'On that subject all public men of all public parties seem agreed.'[3] He was correct and, when the Company's stockholders learned that their future dividends were to be guaranteed, they meekly accepted the settlement agreed between the directors and government. Taking a narrow view of their own interests, they acquiesced in the ending of 230 years of Company trade with Asia, and the belief that they had secured a very good deal was reflected in a buoyant stock price. In 1834 the Company's last trading voyages attracted little public attention, and instead the cessation of commercial activity was marked by the systematic selling of warehouse

---

1 For full details see Philips, *East India Company*, pp. 276–98.
2 See, for example, J. G. Ravenshaw to Bentinck, 7 December 1833, *Bentinck correspondence*, vol. II, p. 1152.
3 Speech of 10 July 1833 reported in *Hansard's parliamentary debates*, third series, vol. XIX (1833), col. 504. See also *The Times*, 15 June 1833.

establishments and the payment of pensions and compensation to labourers, ships' commanders, and clerical staff.

There was also widespread agreement that the government of India should remain in the hands of the Company. Many people were convinced that the Company now exercised good, responsible, economical rule that bestowed considerable benefits upon the people of India, and this enraged enemies of the directors such as James Silk Buckingham, the former editor of the *Calcutta Journal*, who led the campaign to end the monopoly. He declared in July 1833 that

The idea of consigning over to a joint-stock association, composed of such heterogenous materials as the East India Company, the political administration of an empire peopled with a hundred millions of souls was so preposterous that if it were now for the first time to be proposed it would be deemed not merely an absurdity, but an insult to the meanest understanding in the realm.

He went on to suggest that

The ground on which this monstrous proposition was maintained was that the East India Company had given such proofs of their capacity for business, and talent for government, that it was difficult to say in which they most excelled, and that in consequence of their excellent system of rule, India had progressively advanced in happiness and prosperity, with such a rapidity as made it dangerous to change that system, or hazard its destruction by placing it in other hands.[4]

Macaulay, who had been a stern critic of the directors but later moderated his views, certainly accepted most of the 'monstrous proposition', and he adopted the position that there was no guarantee that anybody else could govern India better than the Company. As he put it, 'But of all the substitutes for the Company which have hitherto been suggested, not one has proved to be better than the Company, and most of them could, I think, easily be worse.' He conceded that the Company's government was far from perfect, but much was at risk in India and he declared 'I will not discard them [the Company] in the mere rage of experiment.'[5] Consequently, the Company's administrative responsibilities were extended for twenty years, subject to some alteration. The directors were to have little scope for independent action, which caused both of the Chairs to resign in October 1833, but the routine operation of the system of governance for India continued in much the same way that it had since 1784. For, as Peter Auber put it, many people still took the

4 *Hansard's parliamentary debates*, vol. XIX, cols. 479–80.
5 Ibid., col. 523.

view that 'the Company as the originating intermediate and independent body between the government is and must continue to be a valuable instrument in the administration of the affairs of India'.[6]

When weighing up the future of the East India Company during the early 1830s, most contemporaries believed that the Company was still fit to govern an empire but it should no longer engage in commercial activity. Such an attitude bore strong testimony to the Company's powers of institutional reinvention, and it represented a remarkable transformation of fortunes from the days of the 1760s and 1770s when the Company was widely condemned for misrule in India. The Company had once presided over a vast empire of business, but it entered its final decades devoted exclusively to the business of empire.

6 Auber to Bentinck, 24 July 1833, *Bentinck correspondence*, vol. II, p. 1089.

Index

Printed in the United Kingdom
by Lightning Source UK Ltd.
133976UK00002B/133-138/P